# PAGES FROM THE PAST

## Essays on Saskatchewan History

## Edited by D.H.Bocking

Western Producer Prairie Books, Saskatoon, Saskatchewan

# PAGES
## FROM THE
# PAST

Jacket design by Warren Clark

Printed and bound in Canada
by Modern Press
Saskatoon, Saskatchewan

Western Producer Prairie Books publications are produced and manufactured
in the middle of western Canada by a unique publishing venture owned by a
group of prairie farmers who are members of Saskatchewan Wheat Pool. Our
first book in 1954 was a reprint of a serial originally carried in *The Western
Producer*, a weekly newspaper serving western Canadian farmers since 1923.
We continue the tradition of providing enjoyable and informative reading for
all Canadians.

---

Canadian Cataloguing in Publication Data
Articles reprinted from Saskatchewan history.
Includes index.
ISBN 0-88833-013-8

   1. Saskatchewan — History — Addresses,
essays, lectures. I. Bocking, D. H., 1925-
II. Saskatchewan. Archives Board. III.
Saskatchewan history.
FC3511.7.P33     971.24     C79-091091-8
F1071.5.P33

# Contents

# Preface

In 1977 the Saskatchewan Archives Board decided to republish a selection of articles from the magazine *Saskatchewan History* in book form. This decision was made because some issues were no longer available outside of libraries or in microfilm copies, and it was desirable that some previously published material be made more accessible. The first issue of the magazine appeared in January, 1948, and it has been published three times a year ever since. In a way, the publication of an historical magazine was an unusual undertaking for an archival institution whose primary responsibility is the preservation of historical documents. In September, 1947, the Saskatchewan Archives Board was of the opinion that it should help to meet the need for published material on the history of Saskatchewan, a need which developed, according to Dr. Hilda Neatby, because the people of Saskatchewan "after much poetic concentration on the future, are suddenly realizing that they have a past, and that the past is important too."

In 1947 the board was fortunate in securing the services of the late Dr. Hilda Neatby, professor of history at the University of Saskatchewan, as the first editor of *Saskatchewan History*. In her foreword to the first issue, Dr. Neatby pointed out that the magazine was designed to give information and encouragement — "information about what some are doing, and encouragement to them and others to do much more." The magazine, she wrote, would publish articles by "the pioneer who tells not what he has read, but what he has lived" and by writers and students of the history of the province. The magazine would, of course, also publish book reviews and information about other publications on provincial history and related subjects.

To date there have been four editors of *Saskatchewan History,* all of whom, with the exception of Dr. Neatby, have held the post while employees of the Saskatchewan Archives Board. Dr. Neatby, with the title of editor-in-chief, held the post for the first five issues of the

vi

magazine. In the autumn of 1949 Dr. L. H. Thomas took over first as acting editor-in-chief and then, in the autumn of 1951, as editor, a post he retained until the winter edition of 1958. During the period when Dr. Neatby and Dr. Thomas served as editors, the magazine was establishing not only a publication format but an organizational structure as well. Initially there was an editorial committee to assist the editor-in-chief. By the autumn issue of 1951 the committee had been replaced by an advisory board and the editor-in-chief became an editor. The advisory board remained part of the organizational structure until 1972. The first members of the editorial committee, in addition to Dr. Neatby, were Alex R. Cameron and L. H. Thomas. Dr. Evelyn Eager took over as editor with the spring edition of 1958, retaining the post until the spring edition of 1960. The writer became acting editor in the autumn of 1960 and editor in 1962.

It is interesting to note the development of the first few numbers of the magazine. The inaugural issue, for example, contained an article under the heading "Documents," and the publication of documents became a familiar feature of the magazine. The heading was later changed to "Archival Studies" and then to "Documents of Western History." The first documents, edited by L. H. Thomas, were a number of letters dealing with the problem of finding water on the Canadian plains. Subsequent "Archival Studies" in early issues included "The Lieutenant-Governor's Proclamations and Minutes," information on "Early Territorial Hospitals," "The Reports of the Board of Education,"and "Governor Laird's Thanksgiving Day Address." The publication of "Documents of Western History" has made unique historical records available to the readers of the magazine. "Newspaper Scrapbook," a feature which was added in later editions, presented excerpts from early newspapers.

The first issue also contained a "Teachers' Section," an item which was included in only a few issues of the magazine. Its purpose was to make the magazine useful to school teachers by providing articles based directly on some item in the course of studies. "Before the Railways" by E. Kreutzweizer was the first article in this series. As might be expected, the article dealt with the rigors of travel experienced by the settler in reaching his new home. Other articles included in the series were "Railway and Settlement," "An Indian Description of the Making of a Buffalo Pound," and "Indian Treaties and the Settlement of the North-West."

In fulfillment of the promise made in the foreword, the first issue of *Saskatchewan History* included an article under the heading "Pioneer Stories." This particular account was based on a narrative written by James Clinkskill, a pioneer merchant and politician, about his experiences in 1882 while travelling from Winnipeg to Battleford, where he first established himself in business. Pioneer stories under the revised heading of "Recollections and Reminiscences" became a familiar feature of the magazine. Often these contained otherwise unobtainable material which added to our knowledge and understanding of the history of the West. They were, after all, accounts written by people who, as Dr. Neatby noted, had lived the experiences and not just read about them.

Original articles based on new research have been another important component of *Saskatchewan History*. The early issues of the magazine included a number of articles on the origin of place names and a few articles on historic sites. But perhaps the most interesting of the early series of articles were reviews of journals kept by early travellers on the prairies, men such as Dr. Cheadle, Philip Turnor, Daniel Harmon, the Earl of Southesk, Henry Kelsey, Paul Kane, and others.

In choosing material for this volume no attempt has been made to cover all aspects of the history of this province or to give any particular interpretation to our history. The articles have not been organized in any specific pattern. A selection inevitably means that not all articles can be used, and unfortunately much good material has had to be left out. Articles that have already been republished in other collections have not been used, and only a few articles based on reminiscences or documents have been included. Most of the articles chosen are on non-political aspects of our history because this is an area not well represented in the published literature.

*Saskatchewan History* has never paid for articles, and consequently editors have not been in a position to commission articles in the usual sense of that word, although, of course, they have always sought out suitable material. The number and kind of articles available has varied over the years, and in the final analysis the magazine reflects the research interests of its contributors. These interests have covered a wide range of historical subjects which has meant that there has been a variety of articles to choose from in making the selection for this book.

The fur trade which brought the first Europeans into the prairie region was entirely dependent on contact between the fur trader and the native Indian population. Contact with white men brought profound changes in the way of life of the Indian people, but as long as the buffalo remained a source of food, the native peoples were able to maintain their independence. R. S. Allen's article on Big Bear, which is the first article in this collection, tells the story of that Indian chief's attempt to maintain his own and his peoples' independence from the white man after the buffalo were gone. Big Bear's refusal to take treaty and settle down on a reserve and the later tragedy of Frog Lake marked his attempt to maintain the old ways. It is a moving and tragic story told with understanding and compassion.

Even before the problem of Big Bear and his people had been resolved, the government at Ottawa developed programs intended to bring settlers to the prairies to develop the new agricultural frontier. The offer of more-or-less free homesteads had not produced the results hoped for, so the government turned to private enterprise to help bring in settlers. New regulations provided for the sale of land at reduced prices to colonization companies who, in return for the land they received, were required to locate settlers on lands in the colonization tract. A. N. Lalonde, in his article "Colonization Companies in the 1880's," examines the program and the causes of its failure.

A factor which contributed to the failure of the colonization companies and to the virtual end, for a time, of immigration into the area was the rebellion of 1885. Much has been written about the causes and events of the rebellion, but relatively little attention has been paid to what happened immediately afterwards. Jean Larmour's article, "Edgar Dewdney and the Aftermath of the Rebellion," carefully examines the policies and programs instituted by the government in an effort to restore normal conditions to the area and to encourage a renewed flow of immigrants.

"The Bell Farm," by E. C. Morgan, is the story of a large farming enterprise, a portent of future trends in Saskatchewan agriculture. Located near Indian Head it was started in 1882 and survived the rebellion, but for a variety of reasons failed in the 1890's. While the Bell farm was not a business success, it did attract attention to the area and proved that the prairie soil could be productive.

The York Colony, founded by a colonization company in 1882, grew slowly. In "Yorkton During the Territorial Period, 1882-1905," Jane McCracken concludes that the settlement was undertaken because of federal government policies. Its survival was assured by the development of a branch railway, and its expansion was due to the arrival of eastern European immigrants who came as a result of government initiatives. The settlement and early development of Yorkton clearly show the close relationship between government, private enterprise, and the settler in the development of the West.

Through his book *Utopia* published in 1516, Sir Thomas More gave a name to the concept of ideal states, an idea which has been explored by many writers since his time. Utopias are usually associated with an economically self-sufficient, idealistic, agricultural community. An attempt was made to establish just such a community in the Qu'Appelle Valley in 1895. The colony, known as the Harmony Industrial Association, had a short life and was dissolved by mutual agreement in 1900. According to Gilbert Johnson's article on the colony, it failed for a number of reasons including the enthusiasm of some of its members who wanted to "push communal living beyond the limits envisaged by its founders." While this attempt failed, it was the forerunner of other co-operative programs in Saskatchewan.

Group settlements of immigrants united by religion or nationality were common in the early days. The Patagonia Welsh were one of the many national groups who came to settle on the prairies. They were unusual in that they did not come directly to Canada from their ancestral homes but from another agricultural frontier, the pampas of the southern Argentine, Patagonia, where a Welsh colony had been established in 1865. Lewis H. Thomas, in his article "From the Pampas to the Prairies," tells the story of these people, pointing out that while they "became part of the western Canadian mosaic . . . they made their chief contribution to the nation as successful farmers and builders of a community, cherishing the values of their nationality in family traditions and outlook, and not in the form of exclusive and intransigent assertions of national identity."

In the 1950's, before tape recorders were readily available, the Saskatchewan Archives Board attempted to gather information about pioneer life by circulating a series of questionnaires to early settlers. These are preserved in the archives and provide a valuable source of material on what it was like to be a pioneer. They have been used, as it was intended they should be, for articles, a number of which have been published in *Saskatchewan History*. Two are included in this collection. The first, written by Edith Rowles-Simpson and entitled "Bannock, Beans, and Bacon," deals with the diet of the pioneers, while the other, by Christine MacDonald, on "Pioneer Church Life in Saskatchewan," discusses the spiritual hunger of the pioneers which often came second in importance only to food.

It was financial considerations which led to demands for the establishment of provinces in the North-West Territories. As Evelyn Eager notes in her article on "The Constitution of Saskatchewan," the first official expression of the need for provincial rights came in 1900 and was followed by a series of requests until the granting of provincial status in 1905. The constitution for Saskatchewan followed the accepted traditions and practices of parliamentary government and was in part predetermined by the provisions of the British North America Act. Some of the other provisions proved to be controversial and gave rise to considerable debate. The constitution provided the framework for the government of the province and has been added to over the years by legislative enactments.

Local government has been of great importance in the development of the West. In the early years co-operation was essential to survival and necessary to the development and maintenance of essential services in communities. A later period of urban growth in the province is examined in the article by R. Rees which discusses the real-estate boom of 1910 to 1913 in Saskatoon. The boom in Saskatoon was promoted by an expectation of growth and development which, as Rees notes, seems to have characterized the western world in the period just before the First World War. The Saskatoon story was repeated with variations in other communities, and when the collapse came, individuals and communities suffered considerable financial difficulties.

In the early years of the province, a significant debate on the principles of public owership took place over the elevator issue. The government was able to withstand the demand for public owership of grain elevators, an outcome which was an important achievement for the Saskatchewan co-operative movement. In his article "The Elevator Issue, The Organized Farmers, and the Government," D. S. Spafford examines the interaction between government and farmers on the issue of government ownership.

Peopled as the province was by representatives of many ethnic groups, it is perhaps not surprising that there has been controversy in Saskatchewan over racial and religious issues. Raymond Huel, in his article "The French-Canadians and the Language Question," examines one such dispute. In its initial phase it saw an intemperate public debate between the Premier and his pastor and in a later stage the resignation of a cabinet minister. French language rights were linked with the separate-school issue and with the relationship between Protestants and Catholics. The French-Canadians emerged from the 1918 controversy with their rights relatively intact, though Saskatchewan had not seen the end of this kind of dispute.

During and following the First World War, many farmers were unhappy with the old-line political parties and sought alternative courses for political action through the formation of new farmers' parties. In Saskatchewan the new party, the Progressives, won all but one of the seats in the federal election of 1921 but failed in a 1925 bid to dislodge the provincial Liberal party which had been in power since 1905. In his article "C. A. Dunning and the Challenge of the Progressives, 1922-1925," J. William Brennan examines the reasons for this failure and concludes it was due in large part to the effective leadership and administration of C. A. Dunning.

The strength of the Progressive movement had declined after 1925 and some Progressive supporters, who were active in the United Farmers of Canada (Saskatchewan Section), wanted the new organization to take political action. In 1932 the United Farmers and the Independent Labor Party formed the Farmer-Labor Party, which, after the 1934 election, changed its name to the Co-operative Commonwealth Federation. George Hoffman's article on the origins of the Farmer-Labor Party examines the thesis that it was radical and socialist in its origin but became more moderate after the 1930's because of the political realities of the time. While recognizing that the party was a good deal more radical than other major parties, the evidence "suggests that the policies and leaders of the Farmer-Labor party from the earliest point were not as radical nor as socialist as is commonly believed."

The optimism that characterized the pioneer years died in the depression of the "dirty thirties." It was an era in the history of the province which colored the thoughts and actions of a generation or more. In the poignant reminiscence "The Year We Moved," the late Mrs. A. W. Bailey tells the story of how her family made the decision to abandon a dust-bowl farm in southern Saskatchewan for more fertile bush land in the north. As Mrs. Bailey faced the new pioneer challenge, she recalls, "optimism was what we needed. Optimism like our forefathers had when they had done the same kind of thing. It was kind of exciting once we got going."

The depression for many city residents meant unemployment and the necessity of having to go on relief. In the decade of the thirties, the number on relief in the cities increased dramatically, placing a heavy burden on city governments. Alma Newman, in her article "Relief Administration in Saskatoon During the Depression," describes how one city coped with the difficult problem of providing adequate relief for its unemployed.

From Big Bear to the depression is a long and winding trail to follow, but the journey proves how colorful and interesting Saskatchewan's history is. It is hoped that this selection of articles will convey to the readers some understanding of the background of the province and that it will prove a useful source for the study of our history.

In closing I want to acknowledge the assistance I received from a number of persons who took the time to review the articles from the first thirty years of *Saskatchewan History* and to offer suggestions as to which articles ought to be reprinted in this collection. The final selection is, however, my responsibility. It is hoped the selection will be useful and of interest to students, teachers, and the general reader. I would like to express my thanks to the Saskatchewan Archives Board for asking me to edit this volume for them. The members of the board are Hon. H. Rolfes, chairman; Dr. N. Ward, vice-chairman; Dr. B. Zagorin; and Miss C. MacDonald. Finally I would like to thank Mr. I. E. Wilson, the provincial archivist, for his support and encouragement.

D. H. BOCKING

# 1    Big Bear

*by R. S. Allen*

MISTO-HA-A-MUSQUA (more commonly known in the white world as Big Bear) was born about 1825 near Fort Carlton in one of the many Plains Cree villages scattered along the North Saskatchewan River. His early years are unrecorded, but unquestionably he was reared in the teachings and skills of plains Indian life. Big Bear's people, the *Nai-ah-yah-og* (or Plains Cree) were initially quite removed from the prairie in both culture and geography. When first recorded in the *Jesuit Relations* in 1640, the Cree inhabited the forests between Hudson Bay and Lake Superior, where they were wandering hunters and gatherers of wild rice.[1] They soon became parasitic on the white trader for clothing, tools, metal implements, guns, and later, horses.*

As a result of this culture contact, Cree life rapidly changed from the fringe of a Stone Age culture to a complex tribal society.[2] With the acquisition of the gun, for example, they were able to dispossess their neighbors to the west, and by 1750 a number of Cree bands had ventured westward to the plains, where they discovered the resources of the bison. The tribe became particularly adept at driving the bison over designated jump sites,[3] and an American buffalo expert, William T. Hornaday, harshly commented that the Cree also impounded the buffalo and "slaughtered hundreds with the most fiendish glee . . . leaving all but the very choisest of meat to putrify."[4]

By 1800, with the introduction of the horse, Indian life was drastically transformed, and the Plains Cree had emerged as a typical equestrian plains tribe, dependent on the buffalo and horse nomadism. In custom and outlook they became very different from those Cree who still dwelled in the forest, although both groups were of the same Northern Algonkian linquistic stock. For the Plains Cree, life became modified and enriched. Their effective exploitation of the buffalo, residence in skin-covered tepees, use of the horse for the hunt and

---

*This article originally appeared in *Saskatchewan History* for winter, 1972.

transportation, their peculiar style of decorative and pictographic art, sign language, glorification of warfare, thirst dance (sun dance among most plains tribes), and their less conspicuous features of religion and supernaturalism all combined to provide outstanding features of their culture which was uniquely confined to the plains and not similarly combined elsewhere.[5]

The development and influence of Plains Cree life was retarded by smallpox epidemics in 1781-1782 and to a lesser extent in 1838. Diamond Jenness, in *Indians of Canada,* also states that wars and disease between 1838 and 1858 further reduced their numbers from 4,000 to less than 1,000.[6] Nonetheless the startling alteration of Cree culture from a forest people to a plains society in less than 100 years is remarkable, and their later demoralization and destitution was indeed a human tragedy.

Throughout the 1860's the Indians of the Canadian plains continued their nomadic existence of buffalo hunting and trading at the Hudson's Bay Company posts. The Cree and Blackfoot conducted a formal, almost ritualistic style of warfare, which was often broken to allow both sides to hunt and to continue unhindered their profitable trade with the white man. Peace was established for this purpose in 1863 so that both groups could trade at Fort Pitt, and a further cessation was arranged in the winter of 1864-1865 so that the Blackfoot could follow the buffalo north and hunt. Another truce was negotiated in the Peace Hills on the Battle River in 1867 because both the Cree and Blackfoot wished to hunt buffalo, and the Blackfoot were particularly anxious to trade that season at Edmonton. The buffalo were clearly the plains Indians' cattle, and all bands understood and respected the importance of this animal resource. The Indian was always a conscientious economist of the food supply, and although he killed to provide for the wants of his camp, he made positive efforts to control and maintain the numbers in the various buffalo herds.[7]

This exciting cultural and historical Cree background exerted a profound influence on the thinking of Big Bear. Prior to the 1860's he wintered with his family at Jackfish Lake, just north of Battleford, and traded at Fort Carlton. But in 1865, as a headman of a small, yet permanent band of about twelve lodges, he shifted to the Fort Pitt region. Here he became recognized as a leader of considerable ability and stature, and a man uncompromisingly wedded to the old way of life. By white standards Big Bear was a non-progressive, a traditionalist whose philosophy of life was directly opposed to the policy of the Canadian government which "was designed to lead the Indian people by degrees to mingle with the white race in the ordinary avocations of life."[8] The apprehensions of this Cree leader regarding the inexorable advance of civilization, with all its destructive qualities for plains Indian life, were accentuated by a surprising and ruthless invasion of American whites

2

*Big Bear in captivity, 1885*

from the south. For the Indians of the Canadian plains, a new dawn of civilization was to break upon them.

In the late 1860's a host of whiskey traders, many of them ex-soldiers from the American Civil War, poured into the Canadian plains from Montana, lusting for a quick profit through illicit trade with the Indians.

These Americans quickly usurped the trading monopoly of the Hudson's Bay Company, who had abandoned the use of liquor in trade since 1860. Indeed, the company had made great strides in attempting to preserve the Indian's sense of traditional values through a policy of justice and integrity. But the company could not compete against "whoop-up bug juice" — a mixture containing a quart of whiskey, a pound of chewing tobacco, a handful of red pepper, a bottle of Jamaica ginger, and a quart of molasses, all diluted with water, heated to make it true firewater, and then sold by the mugful.

The whole current of trade in the Canadian West had changed. In 1870 the Blackfoot, and some Cree bands, refused to appear at the Hudson Bay's Company posts, preferring to trade with the Americans instead. As early as 1871 Lieutenant William Butler wrote that "the Saskatchewan is without law, order or security for life or property . . .;"[9] and Colonel Robertson Ross reported in 1872 that "the demoralization of the Indians and injury resulting to the country from this illicit traffic are very great."[10] Orgies and killings became common, and drunken brawls frequently broke out between Blackfoot and Cree at the various trading posts. Whiskey was openly sold to the Indians at Fort Edmonton, as Americans showed a complete disdain for the sovereignty of the Canadian West. They told indignant Hudson's Bay Company employees and other officials that since there was no force in the country to prevent them, "they would do just as they pleased."[11]

The centre of American trading activity was Fort Whoop-Up in the Cypress Hills of southern Alberta. In addition, the whiskey men established themselves as such colorful stations as Robber's Roost, Whiskey Gap, and Slide-Out. It was indeed the "wild west." An oft-quoted but probably apocryphal letter said to have been written from Whoop-Up country in 1873 contained the following news:

Dear Friend:
My partner Will Geary got to putting on airs and I shot him and he is dead — the potatoes are looking well —

Yours truly,
Snookum Jim.[12]

Such was life in Whoop-Up country.

The chaos and anarchy reached a zenith in May of 1873. While encamped in the Cypress Hills, Little Soldier's band of Canadian Assiniboine and a group of American traders began to drink themselves into oblivion. One of the traders accused the Indians of stealing a horse (the animal in question was apparently grazing on a nearby hill), and a fight ensued. The firepower of the whites soon drove the warriors from the camp, and later that evening, reinforced by a more plentiful supply of alcohol, the Americans rushed the near-defenseless village, violated a number of squaws, and murdered about thirty old men and women.[13] The traders returned to Montana and were hailed as heroes.

The Cypress Hills Massacre; the reports of Butler and Ross; the urgent solicitation of Alexander Morris, the Lieutenant-Governor of Manitoba and the North-West Territories; and the mounting cries of protest from Hudson's Bay Company officials and concerned Canadian settlers finally prompted Ottawa to establish a federal police force to supervise and maintain law and order in the Dominion's West. The arrival of the North-West Mounted Police in Whoop-Up country in the autumn of 1874 soon rid the area of the whiskey traders and of that sense of violence so characteristic of the American West. But the years of ruthless exploitation of the Canadian plains tribes by the whiskey traders had resulted in mental anxieties and severe sociological difficulties for the Indians. The reconciliation of the needs of a native society with the demands of the incipient beginnings of a modern civilization in the North-West became a problem of paramount importance. For the Canadian West, 1870 to 1885 was a period of transition. In 1870 the plains were covered with buffalo, and the Indian was the supreme monarch; by 1885 prosperous villages and towns stood were only a few years ago the Indian had pitched his skin tepee.[14] As a result of these circumstances the policy finally adopted by Canada in regard to the plains tribes was to acknowledge Indian title to the land and to negotiate formal surrenders of specific areas. The Indians concerned were to agree to cede all proprietory claims in the region defined by the treaty and, in return, would receive promises of a reserve of their choosing, financial annuities, and practical assistance to help them adapt to an agrarian economy.[15] Between 1871 and 1877, as part of the successful implementation of this policy, seven treaties were negotiated with the Cree, Blackfoot, Assiniboine, Saulteaux, and Ojibway living between the Lake of the Woods and the Rocky Mountains.

For the Plains Cree, Treaty Six, signed by most chiefs at Fort Carlton on August 23 and 28 and at Fort Pitt on September 9, 1876, was a death blow to the continuation of their traditional existence. By ceding 121,000 acres of land, and accepting reserves and the Queen's payment, the Cree, perhaps unwittingly, had guaranteed their future status as wards of the state. Nonetheless at Fort Carlton during the previous summer, Big Bear had made strenuous attempts to deter the chiefs from negotiating any treaty with the whites and, acting as spokesman for a large group of malcontent Indians, had told the government representatives, "We want none of the Queen's presents; when we set a fox trap we scatter pieces of meat all around, but when the fox gets into the trap we knock him on the head; we want no bait. . . ."[16] Unlike many of the other Cree band leaders, Big Bear was not prepared to hurriedly sign treaties which would mean the end of his people's independence, land, and

5

birthright. The treaty provisions provided the Indians with annuity payments, agricultural tools, livestock, a medicine chest, and of vital significance, aid and rations in the future event of "any pestilence" or "general famine."[17] Yet Big Bear remained stubbornly aloof and refused to sign. He hoped to arrange better terms with the Canadian government and preserve his race from complete subjugation.[18]

The stand of Big Bear at Fort Carlton earned him the respect and admiration of other "unco-operative" Indians. Reinforced by the bands of two other treaty holdouts, Little Pine and Lucky Man, Big Bear trekked south to the Cypress Hills to hunt and contemplate. Because the police were able to precede settlement in the Canadian West, they were able to maintain order, and aided by the Hudson's Bay Company, a sense of honesty and justice was established in managing Indian affairs. But at the same time, owing to the slow development of the Canadian West, those native bands who refused to sign treaties and select a reserve, because of the vast emptiness of the North-West, were able to continue unmolested their old nomadic habits of hunting buffalo and moving as the season or hunt demanded. The Canadian government made little or no attempt to curb the wanderings of these "independent" bands.

In the Cypress Hills Big Bear and his followers met kindred spirits such as Piapot's Cree, and Assiniboine and Saulteaux, in all over 2,000 restless Indians. A further and alarming increase of numbers occurred in December when Sitting Bull and 1,500 hostile Sioux, fresh from the Custer fight, ducked across the border into the sanctuary of Canada and took up residence at Wood Mountain, south-east of the hills. The five-year visit of the Sioux in Canada was surprisingly uneventful, but the addition of these American Indians drastically accentuated the problem of feeding the tribes, a situation caused by the unbelievable extermination of the buffalo.

Prior to the 1870's an acute depletion of the mighty buffalo herds was considered unthinkable by most people. Travellers noted with awe the vast numbers of these animals. Along the North Saskatchewan in 1848 Paul Kane was astonished to see the buffalo "covering the plains as far as the eye could reach, and so numerous were they that at times they impeded our progress, filling the air with dust almost to suffocation."[19] In September of 1857 Captain John Palliser found the plains black with buffalo between the South Saskatchewan and Fort Carlton.[20] Even as late as 1874 Cecil Denny of the North-West Mounted Police recorded "thousands upon thousands of buffalo, as far as the eye could see"[21] near the Cypress Hills; and at Buffalo Lake, Alberta in the winter of 1874-1875 Sam Steele of the Mounties also reported "vast numbers of buffalo."[22]

But the influx of American whiskey traders and hide hunters who encouraged Indians to hunt for trade goods and alcohol soon resulted in a damaging slaughter of the northern herd. In addition, the steady advance of civilization west and the sight of thousands of buffalo was too much for the white "sportsman" to resist. Killing for the sake of killing and for the excitement became increasingly popular with the migrants, travellers or tourists. Buffalo Bill was said to have shot 500 buffalo in one day "just for fun."[23] In 1873 sixteen white hide hunters boasted that during the summer they had killed 28,000 buffalo for sport and for robes.[24] By 1875 the firm of I. G. Baker and Company of Fort Benton, Montana was shipping 40,000 buffalo robes a year out of the Fort MacLeod and Calgary regions of southern Alberta.[25]

This serious slaughter of the Indian's principal source of food and the protestations of the band leaders and members of the Indian Department regarding the impending extinction of the buffalo failed to revive Ottawa to the urgency of the problem. Finally, in March of 1877 the Council of the North-West Territories took the initiative and passed a Buffalo Ordinance which declared a closed season on buffalo hunting from November 15 to August 14 each year. The legislation also prohibited the use of pounds or the running of buffalo over banks and the indiscriminate slaughter of the animals merely for tongues and robes.[26] Although this ordinance was the first attempt at conservation, it came too late and proved unsuccessful. By 1877 the Indians were starving, and the few remaining buffalo, contrary to the provisions of the ordinance, were quickly butchered to feed hungry families.

A further calamitous blow for the Indians of western Canada was the adoption by the United States of a systematic program of buffalo extermination. As early as 1867 the touring William Butler was told by American army officers along the North Platte in Nebraska to "Kill every buffalo you can; every buffalo dead is an Indian gone...."[27] Following the defeat of Custer and the flight of the Sioux into Canada, the United States decided to starve Sitting Bull into surrender. In 1879 a series of prairie fires were started at different points almost simultaneously by the Americans, and the country north of the boundary line was burnt from Wood Mountain on the east to the Rocky Mountains on the west and as far north as Qu'Appelle.[28] To ensure the destruction of the buffalo, over 5,000 American hunters and skinners were placed strategically in a cordon of camps from the Upper Missouri west to the Idaho dividing line, thus "rendering it impossible for scarcely a single bison to escape through the chain of sentinel camps to the Canadian North-West."[29]

The selfish actions of the Americans brought complete destitution to the plains tribes of the North-West and rendered the task of the North-West Mounted Police almost impossible. In Canada the Cree, Blackfoot, Assiniboine, Saulteaux, and Sioux were all starving. "Not even a rabbit track is to be seen anywhere,"[30] wrote the Hudson's Bay

7

Company factor from Fort Carlton. In a desperate search for food Canadian Indians crossed the border into the United States looking for the diminishing buffalo herds. Near Fort Assiniboine in Montana the Cree band of Chief Thunderchild was found in extreme destitution.

> The men were selling their guns and every other article of value to procure food, while the women were prostituting themselves to save their children from starvation. . . . The men were weak and emaciated from hunger, and the women and children sick and covered with rags and filth. The Prostitution of the squaws brought the foulest diseases into camp which they had no medical or other means of curing or checking and several deaths had already occurred from this course alone. . . .[31]

To help relieve the situation the Canadian government now did everything possible to coax or induce the Indians to settle on their reserves and to convince them that the days of the buffalo hunt were over. The police and government agents told band leaders that Indian survival depended on the adoption of new methods of livelihood, and they encouraged farming. In 1879 the annuity payments were made at Sounding Lake because many of the Indians wished to stay on the plains and hunt. Big Bear attended the Sounding Lake payments, but when he was refused better terms he remained obstinate and, with a sizable group of followers, again trekked south. However, Little Pine and Lucky Man, one of Big Bear's headmen, finally succumbed to starvation, and at Fort Walsh in July they signed their Adhesion to Treaty Six and received rations.[32]

The increasing defections of bands and chiefs left Big Bear as "the head and soul of our Canadian Plains Indians."[33] This Cree leader symbolized and embodied the last free spirit of the plains Indians. His band became a beacon for the disaffected and was joined by families from Fort Carlton, Fort Pitt, Sounding Lake, and many other areas. Big Bear spent the extremely cold winter of 1879-1880 near the Big Bend of the Milk River in Montana. He had often talked with Sitting Bull at Wood Mountain about the preservation of Indian life and the advance of the white man. But in the Milk River region he was in frequent consultation with Louis Riel, the Métis visionary and nationalist who was equally concerned with the maintenance of a Métis existence in the Saskatchewan.[34] These meetings with Sitting Bull and Louis Riel convinced Big Bear that the only effective method of negotiating with the white man was through a confederated union of all the tribes of the North-West. If the tribes could speak with one united voice, reasoned the Cree patriot, perhaps better concessions of land, money, and Indian welfare could be achieved.

Throughout 1880 and much of 1881 the rumors of buffalo in the Milk River region of Montana kept several Canadian Indian bands south of the great "Medicine Line." But Cecil Denny observed in the summer of 1881 that Plains Cree and Assiniboine who had been looking for buffalo along the Missouri River had returned to Fort Walsh in a starving and wretched condition.[35] By the winter of 1881-1882, 5,000 utterly destitute Canadian Indians were clustered around Fort Walsh begging for supplies, and another 4,000 were in American territory vainly searching for buffalo which were no longer there.[36] The bands began again to gather in the Cypress Hills in the summer of 1882, and this concentration of wild and fearless independent Indians with no desire to abandon the old adventuresome and nomadic existence, yet reduced to poverty and starvation, presented a surly and troublesome crowd for the meager forces of the North-West Mounted Police to control and ration.

Big Bear passed the summer and autumn of 1882 in the hills. Many of the other bands, although they had not selected a reserve, were nonetheless treaty Indians and thus eligible to collect the government rations. But Big Bear's band was entitled to nothing. Unable to face another bitter winter and concerned for the needs of his people, Big Bear trudged to Fort Walsh in December and reluctantly signed his Adhesion to Treaty Six.[37]

The capitulation of Big Bear was caused by starvation through the loss of the buffalo, the mainstay of plains Indian life. In 1870 the northern herd numbered in the millions, but the ruthless slaughter of these animals quickly reduced their size. By the autumn of 1883 one old buffalo bull was seen near Souris in western Manitoba. H. W. O. Boger saw the animal in daylight as it crossed his farm. It was trotting and went off north-west. This was the last seen in the region. It was reported in all the newspapers.[38] The Game Report for 1888 recorded six buffalo still in existence — two old bulls in the Wood Mountain district, and three cows and a bull between the Red Deer and Battle rivers.[39] From millions to this in less than two decades. The plains Indian did not stand a chance.

William Hornaday, the American buffalo expert, offered a conclusion.

> If ever a thoughtless people were punished for their reckless improvidence, the Indians and half-breeds of the North-West Territories are now paying [1887] the penalty for the wasteful slaughter of the buffalo a few short years ago. . . . One can scarcely repress the feeling of grim satisfaction that arises when we also read that many of the ex-slaughterers are almost starving for the millions of pounds of fat and juicy buffalo meat they wasted. . . . People who are so utterly senseless as to wantonly destroy their own sources of food, as the Indians have done, certainly deserve to starve.[40]

It is utterly incredible that a man of Hornaday's reputation and alleged knowledge could dimiss or ignore the American whiskey traders

*Big Bear's camp, Maple Creek, June 6, 1883*

and hide hunters who descended upon the Canadian West in the 1870's and encouraged, indeed conditioned, the Indians into acquiring hides for trade. Trade and sport among the whites resulted in thousands of buffalo being slaughtered, and although the Indian contributed to the extinction by killing for trade and for domestic needs, the ruthlessness of the commercial slaughter for hides, tongues, or sport far outweighed the Indian effort.[41]

With the disappearance of the buffalo forever and with his Adhesion to Treaty Six, Big Bear led his band to Maple Creek, Saskatchewan where they spent the summer of 1883, devouring government rations and steadily avoiding selecting a reserve. Finally, and only after Indian Commissioner Dewdney promised to provide the Cree leader with a cabin, two horses, a buckboard and harness, a chest of tea, fifty pounds of sugar, twenty-five pounds of tobacco, a shotgun and ammunition, and a suit of clothes, did Big Bear consent to move north and select a reserve.[42] At Fort Pitt in October the 358 members of his band received their annuity payments for that year.[43] But Indian Agent Thomas Quinn reported that "Big Bear does not want to take a reserve this winter," and as a result of this action and as directed, rations would be withheld.[44]

The vacillation of this Cree chief was understandable. He had lived through the demoralization by the whiskey traders and the extermination of the buffalo which had destroyed the last vestige of his traditional lifestyle and reduced his people to poverty and starvation. Then he witnessed the beginnings of white settlement and the initiation of an industrial civilization on the plains. He watched desperate and starving chiefs sign treaties, select isolated reserves, and unsuccessfully attempt to adapt to an agrarian economy. He had no desire to meekly submit to these conditions, and hoping to force better concessions from the government before his race became an insignificant minority on the plains, Big Bear remained stubbornly aloof and spent the winter of 1883-1884 at Fort Pitt.

But any hopes for Indian improvement were shattered as a result of the North-West tour of Lawrence Vankoughnet, the Deputy Minister of Indian Affairs, in 1883. After inspecting a number of reserves Vankoughnet was convinced that Indian expenditures should be reduced. Thus, and as part of a decline in the national economy, Indian expenses were cut for 1883, 1884, and 1885. The gross reduction in the amount spent upon Indian provisions, annuities, education, and farm instruction in 1884 alone, for example, was $111,649.[45] For the Indians the application of this policy only increased the distress and hardship which the tribes were experiencing. The government's policy of semi-starvation was unanimously condemned in the North-West. Indian Agent Rae at Fort Carlton reported that the Cree were "badly off," but the Assiniboine were "mere skeletons"[46] and the influential Cecil Denny, now an agent for the Blackfoot, was so infuriated that he tendered his resignation.

The frustration and mounting Indian resentment against the white man encouraged Big Bear in the spring of 1884 to travel to several reserves and plead for unity. In June all the disaffected Indians of the North Saskatchewan assembled at the Poundmaker reserve to discuss relations with the Canadian government and to make plans for a possible confederation. The excuse offered by the Indians for this large council was the holding of the annual thirst dance. The meeting was unfortunately disrupted owing to the arrival of the North-West Mounted Police who were called following the assault on Farm Instructor Craig by a young man of Lucky Man's band who was refused flour. In attempting to arrest the young brave, Superintendent Crozier and his detachment were surrounded and jostled by "intensely excited" Indians. Big Bear rushed forward shouting for peace, but his efforts failed to restore order.[47] With their prisoner the police column managed to reach the agency buildings, but only after throwing provisions of beef and flour to the howling Indians did the noise and angry clamor subside.[48]

The reaction of Big Bear at Poundmaker's clearly indicated that he did not want an Indian uprising. His talks with Sitting Bull and personal awareness forced him to realize that overt resistance to the white man would be entirely futile. Rather he hoped for a large Indian confederation which would be capable of achieving concessions by a potential threat rather than by actual hostilities.[49]

Following the Craig incident, Big Bear invited Crozier and Agent Rae to the reserve and expressed his regret for the incident. But at the same time the Cree chief made it clear that he had no thought of abandoning the idea of a united Indian council. Indeed, towards the end

Public Archives of Canada PA117818

*Annuity time, Fort Pitt, 1884. Big Bear is third from the left.*

of July, Big Bear and other chiefs visited Louis Riel at Duck Lake. The rhetoric of this Métis leader encouraged the chiefs to renew their efforts at achieving Indian unity. A large council was subsequently arranged at Fort Carlton and between July 31 and August 6, 1884 chiefs from all over the Saskatchewan voiced their complaints against the Canadian government. Big Bear delivered a scathing denunciation of the lack of good faith of the whites and urged united Indian action. He said in part:

> As I see that they are not going to be honest I am afraid to take a reserve. They have given me to choose between several small reserves but I feel sad to abandon the liberty of my own land when they come to me and offer me small plots to stay there and in return not to get half of what they have promised me. . . .[50]

The Duck Lake and Fort Carlton conferences, and his open defiance in resisting a reserve, enhanced the reputation of Big Bear and his band among the discontented Indians of the North-West. In the autumn he met again with Riel at Prince Albert and then returned to Fort Pitt where his followers, now inflated to 494, received annuity payments. He decided to winter at Frog Lake and Inspector Dickens reported in January that the band was "drawing logs and cutting wood" and would receive rations as a result of this work.[51] During the winter of 1884-1885 Big Bear finally consented to take a reserve in the spring, but he wanted all the Indians to have a reserve at Red Deer, "so that they could be together."[52]

The peaceful ambitions of this Cree chief had caused dissent in his band, and throughout the winter the influence and authority of Big Bear steadily diminished. His leadership was replaced by warlike agitators such as Wandering Spirit, Lone Man, Little Poplar, Four-Sky-Thunder, Miserable Man, and even his son Imasees, who were prepared to fight to accomplish a restitution of Indian grievances. The news from Duck Lake exhilarated this hostile faction and convinced them that hope remained, for on March 26, 1885 the Métis had defeated the establishment — the North-West Mounted Police. William B. Cameron, the Hudson's Bay Company clerk at Frog Lake, noticed that Big Bear's band and the neighboring Wood Cree were in council and making proposals of some kind. As he walked home he "had a premonition of evil days at hand and I felt uneasy and depressed."[53]

Among the Plains Cree, April (*Aiiki Picim*) was the month of the frog, and on the morning of April 2 the Indians at the Frog Lake settlement were unusually aggressive and demanded that Cameron give them supplies and ammunition. Big Bear, who had just returned from an extended hunting trip, appeared melancholy and spoke sadly and quietly to Cameron and Quinn before proceeding to the house of Mrs. Simpson for his favorite pea soup. About 10:15 A.M. after a considerable amount of moving about, orders, threats, and seeming indecision, Wandering Spirit, after a verbal confrontation with Quinn, shot the agent, and his act signalled the beginning of a massacre of all the whites in the settlement. Big Bear rushed out of Mrs. Simpson's house shouting, *"Tesqua!"* ("Stop!"), but the years of hardship, resentment, and smouldering hatred for the white man unleashed a Cree fury for blood which knew no restraint. Nine white men were murdered but Cameron was spared because he was a Hudson Bay's Company man — a friend of the Indian.[54]

Following the massacre the jubilant Cree returned to their camp with Cameron and two white women from the settlement and celebrated their victory by feasting, dancing, and slaughtering cattle from horseback, as reminiscent of past, glorious, buffalo days. Big Bear told the prisoners that he was "sorry" for what happened and had cried over it, but that he had many bad men in his band and had no control over them. He informed Cameron that he was not a bad Indian and not a noisy drunk but "used to sit quietly and sing."[55] Although he remained the nominal leader and his name brought fear to all white civilians who heard it during the course of the North-West Rebellion, the real direction of leadership had shifted to Wandering Spirit.

During the ten days following the news of the Frog Lake Massacre, the civil and military inhabitants of nearby Fort Pitt remained in constant fear of being attacked. Finally, on April 13, Big Bear and 250 warriors appeared before the fort and demanded surrender. The officer in charge, Inspector Dickens refused but acceded to their request for tea, tobacco, clothing, kettles, and a blanket for Big Bear who complained that "he was very cold."[56] W. J. McLean, the Hudson's Bay Company trader at the post, agreed to go and parley with the Cree. The Indians promised McLean that unless the civilians surrendered and the police left, they would attack the fort. Dickens was prepared to fight, but the twenty-eight civilians decided to accept the Indian offer and prevent further blood-shed. Big Bear implored the commandant by way of letter to evacuate Fort Pitt: "Try and get away before the afternoon as the younger men are all wild and hard to keep in hand."[57] Accordingly the police detachment quickly evacuated the post and floated down the North Saskatchewan to Battleford on a leaky scow. The civilians warily trudged to the camp of Big Bear and eventually spent two months in captivity. The Indians concluded by gleefully pillaging and burning the empty fort.

In spite of the successes at Duck Lake, Frog Lake, and Fort Pitt, a general uprising of the Indians of the Canadian plains failed to materialize. Although there were rumblings of discontent throughout the Saskatchewan, fear, potential danger, and even some minor thievery, only a few Cree bands actually left their reserves in open support of the Métis. Of vital significance was the maintenance of a pacifistic policy by Crowfoot and the Blackfoot Confederacy to the south. In addition, the speedy arrival of troops from the East via the nearly completed Canadian Pacific Railway aided in discouraging any spreading of rebellion. The early surrenders of Riel and Poundmaker on May 15 and May 26 of 1885 left only the isolated and now somewhat bewildered band of Big Bear with which to contend.

Since the Fort Pitt affair, Miserable Man and others, contrary to the wishes of Big Bear, had tried to link with Poundmaker, but the aggressive, eager, and war-like Plains Cree section had increasingly alienated their recent allies, the now sullen and apathetic Wood Cree who had never been too excited about the prospect of rebellion. Relations between the two bands had become so strained that they no longer camped together but in separate groups. The news of the capitulation of Riel and Poundmaker only heightened the animosity. In consequence, at Frenchman's Butte, twelve miles east of Fort Pitt, a thirst dance was arranged in order to restore unity of spirit and harmony between the Plains and Wood Cree. But the dance was interrupted by the column of Brigadier General "Tom" Strange which had marched from Calgary and then Edmonton in pursuit of the "rebel" Indians.

Although the Cree were surprised, they quickly took up a position in a line of recently constructed rifle-pits along the north bank of Red Deer Creek. Wandering Spirit demonstrated a reckless bravery by exposing himself to the fire of the whites, and his efforts inspired the Plains Cree who shouted "*Astom schmognus, asum pugumawa*" (Come on white man and fight).[58] Little Poplar induced the Wood Cree to support their brothers and they consented. The combined Cree force, although

14

suffering somewhat from the bursts of the artillery shells, checked the frontal assault of Strange. Fearful of "committing a Custer" the commander of this Alberta Field Force withdrew and allowed Big Bear to escape north.[59]

But the mounted scouts of Major Sam Steele were despatched in pursuit, and after a relentless chase through wooded and muskeg-riddled country a skirmish was fought near Loon Lake on June 4. Little Poplar and Lone Man were prominent in this engagement, and when the whites again retired the Indians continued their now aimless wanderings. After the Steele fight, the camp disintegrated, with Wandering Spirit and the Wood Cree continuing north in the direction of Cold Lake, and the plains band turning east. Wandering Spirit eventually capitulated later in June at Fort Pitt and Four-Sky-Thunder, Miserable Man, and others surrendered at Battleford. Big Bear led his youngest son, Horse Child, and a councillor unobserved to Fort Carlton where on July 2 the proud and stoic old chief gave himself up to Sergeant Smart of the North-West Mounted Police.[60]

The surrenders were followed by the trial of the principal Indian leaders for their part in the rebellion. They were not punished with vindictive severity. Members of Big Bear's band, for example, were deprived of their annuities for 1885 and 1886 and then merged with several other Cree bands, thus destroying the main nucleus of Indian agitation.[61] Wandering Spirit and Miserable Man were condemned to death by hanging for the murders at Frog Lake. Four-Sky-Thunder was given fourteen years (commuted to six) for burning the Roman Catholic church at Frog Lake. Lone Man was not caught until January of 1886, when he was recognized while walking the streets of Edmonton. He was sentenced to six years in the Manitoba penitentiary. Imasees, Little Poplar, Lucky Man, and other fugitives escaped to Montana. In 1886 Little Poplar was shot and killed; and in 1896, after negotiations with the United States, Imasees and Lucky Man were allowed to return to Canada and settle on their old reserves.

Big Bear was charged with treason-felony and sentenced to three years at Stony Mountain Penitentiary. While serving his term he capitulated completely to the white world by accepting baptism into the Roman Catholic Church. Spiritually crushed at the irretrievable loss of a traditional lifestyle of buffalo and freedom, and disillusioned because of his inability to achieve a united confederation for his people, the old chief lost the will to live. He was returned to the Little Pine reserve in 1887, but Agent Williams reported that although sick he "refused medical aid."[62] In the winter of 1887-1888 he died quietly. Like Pontiac, Joseph Brant, Tecumseh, Crowfoot, Poundmaker, and others, Big Bear was placed by Providence among the riches of the new world only to enjoy them for a season; he was merely to wait until others came.

# 2     Colonization Companies in the 1880's

*by A. N. Lalonde*

THE creation of colonization companies as an instrument to promote the settlement of the Canadian West has to be viewed within the framework of Canada's National Policy which V. C. Fowke defines as "the group of policies and instruments which were designed to transform British North American territories of the mid-nineteenth century into a political and economic unit."[1] Confederation was the first step in the creation of a political and economic unit stretching from coast to coast. The final stages of the National Policy reached fruition in 1878 when J. A. Macdonald promised higher tariffs to protect infant Canadian industry, a transcontinental railroad, and a vigorous immigration policy to foster the development of the new agricultural frontier, the Canadian West.*

In 1879, the newly-elected Conservative government instituted its new tariff policy. In 1880, the Canadian Pacific Railway contract was presented to Parliament. To promote immigration and settlement, the Conservative ministry borrowed from the former Liberal government[2] and, on December 23, 1881, passed regulations to provide for the creation of colonization companies.

These new regulations made provision for the sale of the odd-numbered sections situated twenty-four miles or more north of the Canadian Pacific Railway at $2 per acre to any business concern satisfying the government of its goodwill, capabilities, and sincere interest in promoting settlement in Manitoba and the North-West Territories. The purchasing party was required to locate two settlers upon each of the odd- and even-numbered sections of the colonization tract within five years, although the Crown maintained exclusive ownership of the even-numbered sections within the colony, which remained open for entry as homesteads and pre-emptions. In acknowledgement of the satisfactory fulfillment of its settlement duties, the company was to receive a rebate of

---

*This article originally appeared in *Saskatchewan History* for autumn, 1971.

$160 for every newly established bona fide settler found living within the colonization tract by an appointed government inspector.[3]

The government anticipated that the amount of profit earned by colonization companies would be proportionate to the number of settlers they could induce to locate on their respective tracts of land. If it earned the maximum rebate, a company could pay as little as one dollar per acre for the odd-numbered sections and could demand prices ranging from three to fifteen dollars per acre for these same lands once the colony's even-numbered sections were fully occupied.

By enacting such regulations, the government hoped to sell 10,000,000 acres of land to private corporations, recover $10,000,000 of the $25,000,000 it had pledged to grant to the Canadian Pacific Railway syndicate, and simultaneously secure the assistance of the business community to develop the new western Canadian frontier. The 100,000 settlers located on the vast plains of the North-West would, once they had straightened out their own finances, send money home to penniless relatives wishing to join them in the Canadian West.[4] From a small nucleus of population installed by gentlemen with capital, the North-West would expand. The western settlers would constitute a market for eastern Canada's industrial goods and produce sufficient wheat for export, thus ensuring a sound financial basis for the operation of the Canadian Pacific Railway.

Since massive immigration and the expansion of the agricultural frontier in Upper Canada from 1825 to 1855 had coincided with an era of prosperity, Canadians believed that the construction of the Canadian Pacific Railway would trigger a resumption of immigration and inaugurate a new era of prosperity. The recovery of the national economy in 1879 and the speculative fever which gripped Manitoba following ratification of the Canadian Pacific Railway contract inspired politicians, businessmen, philanthropic associations, religious congregations, and town councils to appeal for land in the North-West. Within a few months following the approval by the Privy Council of the Land Regulations dated December 23, 1881, the Minister of the Interior was swamped with approximately 260 applications for tracts of prairie land.[5]

The presence of twenty-four senators and elected representatives among the applicants illustrates the faith the government placed in the future of the Canadian West. These politicians, along with several prominent Canadian businessmen, obviously believed that the development of the Canadian West would inaugurate a new era of expansive prosperity and that investments in western real estate would provide substantial profits.

All applicants professed the noblest of intentions. One applicant insisted that his only motive was to curtail the mass exodus to Minnesota and the Dakotas of young Canadian men from the counties of Kent and Essex by creating a colony of 100,000 acres in the North-West Territories.[6] Messrs. Vahey and Wilkinson affixed to their letter of application a petition signed by sixty-four residents of Warwick and Middlesex who wished to settle in the Canadian West.[7]

Other applicants tried to exercise political pressure on the Conservative government to obtain land. Alexander Manning, proprietor of a huge construction firm, added in his letter of application, "Independent of any services we may have rendered in the past we think that our application ought to be granted, and we do not think it out of place to say that these services were of importance to the party at a time when it involved some sacrifice to render them and which we would be ready to repeat in case of need."[8] William Bain Scarth, one of the Prime Minister's friends, stressed in his application that he had spent substantial sums of money supporting Conservative candidates and that the government should afford him some compensation by casting a favorable eye on his request for land.[9]

In the first half of 1882, the Minister of the Interior allotted approximately 6,000,000 acres of land to 106 applicants. However, the boom in Manitoba real estate which prevailed in 1880 and 1881 came to an end in 1882. As a result, the confidence of several successful applicants was badly shaken and after careful consideration they opted out of the scheme. Others were unable to muster the necessary funds to pay their first instalment. Land recipients who were simply speculating refused to sign a contract when the government demonstrated its determination to fully enforce its regulations. Of the 106 successful applicants, only 27 paid their first instalment, consisting of one-fifth the total purchase price of two dollars per acre.

| COMPANY | AREA OF ODD-NUMBERED SECTIONS | FIRST INSTALMENT |
|---|---|---|
| A. Scott and T. Hay | 25,550 acres | $11,680.00 |
| Armstrong and Cook | 10,240 | 4,077.20 |
| C. F. Ferguson and Associates | 30,720 | 12,288.00 |
| Dominion Land Colonization Company | 115,151 | 45,250.00 |
| Dundee Land and Investment Company | 10,244 | 4,097.91 |
| Edmonton and Saskatchewan Land Company | 57,383 | 24,576.00 |
| Farmers' North-West Land | 58,095 | 24,760.25 |
| Fertile Belt Colonization Company | 61,422 | 24,853.70 |
| Fertile Belt Western Agricultural Company | 30,624 | 18,432.00 |
| H. D. Smith | 10,240 | 4,096.00 |
| H. W. C. Meyer | 10,240 | 4,096.00 |
| Montreal and Western Land Company | 30,751 | 12,300.76 |
| Morrow, Armytage, and Beattie | 10,240 | 4,090.00 |
| P. V. Valin | 32,900 | 13,107.00 |
| Patrick Purcell | 56,322 | 22,578.00 |

| | | |
|---|---|---|
| Primitive Methodist Colonization Company | 63,513 | 24,576.00 |
| Prince Albert Colonization Company | 42,240 | 20,480.00 |
| Qu'Appelle and Long Lake Colonization Company | 36,990 | 10,000.00 |
| Qu'Appelle Land Company | 61,221 | 24,760:25 |
| Saskatchewan Land and Homestead Company | 200,554 | 81,197.58 |
| Scottish Ontario and Manitoba Land Company | 28,712 | 11,543.40 |
| Shell River Colonization Company | 30,624 | 6,144.00 |
| Temperance Colonization Society | 213,760 | 84,000.00 |
| Touchwood-Qu'Appelle Land and Colonization Company | 63,981 | 24,576.00 |
| W. Sharples | 20,480 | 8,192.00 |
| W. Vahey and J. Wilkinson | 10,240 | 5,000.00 |
| York Farmers' Colonization Company | 61,220 | 24,576.00 |
| | 1,383,836 acres | $555,328.05 |

The contract between the government and the land companies was drafted by Senator David Lewis Macpherson, acting Minister of the Interior, in consultation with the Justice Department. The contract clearly elaborated the reciprocal rights and duties of both contracting parties. The government retained the power to withdraw from the agreement all lands found to extend into the twenty-four-mile railway-belt once surveys were completed; lands where coal, gold, silver, and lead might be discovered; and all unoccupied odd-numbered sections which a branch railway might traverse. The company could not evict or expropriate squatters who had settled on the lands prior to the signing of the agreement nor could it cut timber upon the lands forming the subject of the agreement except for bona fide building purposes or to provide sufficient firewood for the settlers. In addition to sponsoring settlement and locating two settlers on every odd- and even-numbered section involved in the scheme as stipulated in the Land Regulations, the company was required to pay the salary and travelling expenses of a government-appointed inspector who would visit each tract yearly to enumerate the number of bona fide settlers and to calculate the amount of rebate to which each company was entitled. Without remuneration and at its own expense, the company was compelled to act as an agent of the Department of the Interior and grant entries for homesteads and pre-emptions on the even-numbered sections within the tract, collect entry fees and all other charges, deposit this money in the nearest chartered bank to the credit of the Receiver-General of Canada, and keep a record of all entries, settlers, and money collected. In compensation for these services, the company was pledged a rebate of $160 on the purchase price of $2 per acre for every bona fide settler enumerated on its tract by the government-appointed inspector. The agreement bound both contracting parties for five years. Upon fulfillment of all duties stipulated

19

in the contract, the government promised to issue letters patent granting to the company full ownership of all odd-numbered sections within the tract.[10]

The involvement in this scheme of prominent politicians such as Thomas W. Gibbs, Senator John Boyd, Senator Thomas Ryan, Thomas McGreevy, Nathaniel Clarke Wallace, and several others clearly demonstrates that the government was confident its National Policy would inaugurate a phase of expansive prosperity. Hugh and Andrew Allan of the Allan Steamship Company; H. S. Howland, president of the Imperial Bank of Commerce; George Maclean Rose, president of the Toronto Board of Trade; John Ogilvie, a major stockholder in the milling firm of A. W. Ogilvie and Company; and several other prominent Canadian businessmen held similar views and regarded the government regulations as an opportunity to invest funds in this land of the future during its initial stages of development. A few Protestant churches, particularly the Methodist Church, seized upon this opportunity to extend their religious activities beyond the confines of eastern Canada.

When incorporated colonization companies placed their stock on the market, they offered to the public "easy terms" of purchase. In several instances by investing $10 a potential purchaser could subscribe to a share nominally valued at $100. As a result, a speculative fever gripped the East, particularly Ontario. *The Globe* reported that thousands of people ceased honest and productive work to pursue riches at auction rooms and stock exchanges.[11] When the Qu'Appelle and Long Lake Land and Colonization Company opened its books in Toronto, the rush for stock was so great that there were at least twenty applications for every share offered.[12] In the midst of this frenzied rush for stock, one major shareholder in the Temperance Colonization Society jubilantly exclaimed, "There's millions in it."[13]

To justify their *raison d'être* and fulfill the terms of their contract, several colonization companies organized advertising campaigns designed to foster an interest in the Canadian West. However, instead of duplicating the efforts of the Canadian Pacific Railway Company and the Canadian government's Department of Agriculture, which had distributed tons of literature depicting the wealth and abundant resources of the North-West Territories, colonization companies adopted a more personal approach. They offered every individual settler free town lots, free grain for seeding the first year, the rental of farm implements, and financial assistance in the form of loans. In 1882 alone, the Temperance Colonization Society issued over 35,000 circulars, while the Montreal and Western Land Company distributed over 60,000 folders, maps, and pamphlets in Canada, the United States, and the British Isles.[14] Every land company in its pamphlets and circulars eulogized the quality and fertility of the soil in its colony and presented attestations of contented pioneers. Overstatements and half-truths were integrated into these circulars as indicated by the following quotation:

> During the bustle of landing at Quebec I found a pamphlet thrust into my hand by a clerical looking fellow in seedy dress. This paper-backed volume professed to show the glorious future which awaited anyone who took up land near the South Saskatchewan under the aegis of the Temperance Colonization Company. There was even an illustration of Saskatoon, above the title of North-West City. Tall chimneys were emitting volumes of smoke, there were wharves stocked with merchandise; and huge steamers such as adorn the levees at New Orleans, were taking in cargo. Subsequently, I found Saskatoon to consist of six houses at intervals and a store.[15]

In addition to the distribution of pamphlets, colonization companies resorted to other ways and means of publicizing their lands and promoting the settlement of their colonies. Several companies dispatched representatives to Britain and continental Europe to deliver lectures, distribute literature, converse with prospective immigrants, and arrange for the transportation of all interested parties to the North-West Territories.[16] The Saskatchewan Land and Homestead Company and the Temperance Colonization Society, along with several other companies, repeatedly placed lengthy ads in *The Globe* and *The Mail* encouraging young Ontario farmers to move west.

To render their scheme more enticing and tempting, land company officials publicly pledged to build branch railways, adequate highways, bridges, lumber mills, grist mills, town halls, general supply stores, and hotels. Success, in their estimation, was imminent. They were convinced that their ambitious building programs would attract hundreds of settlers to their respective colonies, thereby converting their investments into astronomical profits in the immediate future.

Only three companies commenced operations in 1882. In the spring of 1883, ten additional land companies undertook the development and settlement of their respective tracts of land. The work they accomplished prompted the government-appointed inspector, Rufus Stephenson, to report, "In my opinion they [land companies] have on the whole done excellent colonizing work and been directly instrumental in adding largely to the development and settlement of the North-West and the promises for the future, in the same direction are exceedingly hopeful."[17] Although Stephenson praised the land companies' accomplishments, if they hoped to meet their five-year deadline, they should have located 1,800 colonists on their tracts of land; Stephenson, during his tour of inspection, counted only 653 settlers.

In 1884, six companies which had patiently waited until government crews had completed the survey of their lands followed in the footsteps of the other operating land corporations. However, the crop failure

21

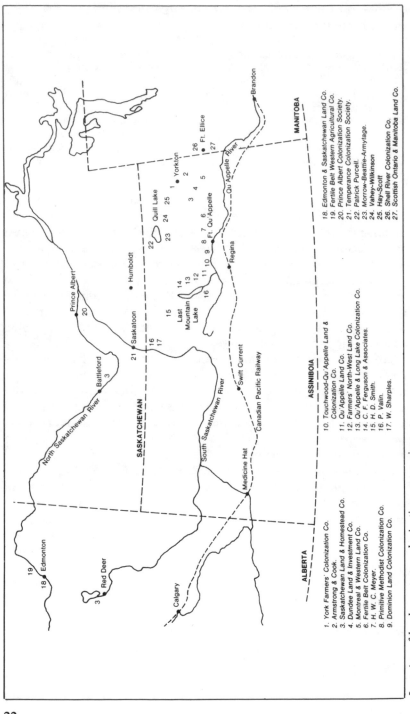

*Location of land grants to colonization companies.*

ALBERTA

1. York Farmers' Colonization Co.
2. Armstrong & Cook.
3. Saskatchewan Land & Homestead Co.
4. Dundee Land & Investment Co.
5. Montreal & Western Land Co.
6. Fertile Belt Colonization Co.
7. H. W. C. Meyer.
8. Primitive Methodist Colonization Co.
9. Dominion Land Colonization Co.

ASSINIBOIA

10. Touchwood-Qu'Appelle Land & Colonization Co.
11. Qu'Appelle Land Co.
12. Farmers' North-West Land Co.
13. Qu'Appelle & Long Lake Colonization Co.
14. C. F. Ferguson & Associates.
15. H. D. Smith.
16. P. Valin.
17. W. Sharples.

18. Edmonton & Saskatchewan Land Co.
19. Fertile Belt Western Agricultural Co.
20. Prince Albert Colonization Society.
21. Temperance Colonization Society.
22. Patrick Purcell.
23. Morrow–Beattie–Armytage.
24. Vahey–Wilkinson
25. Hay–Scott
26. Shell River Colonization Co.
27. Scottish Ontario & Manitoba Land Co.

throughout Manitoba and the North-West occasioned by an early frost in the fall of 1883 and the ensuing derogatory publicity rendered the recruitment of settlers increasingly difficult. Accordingly, land companies stressed consolidation of existing programs until the adverse climate of opinion had sufficiently subsided to permit resumption of immigration.

In the spring of 1885, the directors of the various colonization companies expected to finally receive returns on their investments. They had coped with the damaging publicity surrounding the crop failure of 1883 and now that hostility had waned, they anticipated a steady increase in settlement throughout the North-West Territories. The outbreak of the North-West Rebellion quashed the land-company directors' remaining hopes. As a result of the Métis uprising, immigration declined to a virtual standstill. From 1885 until the expiration of their five-year contract, colonization companies languished. The company directors admitted the futility of seeking to derive profits from this government-sponsored settlement and, instead of persevering till the end, requested that they be relieved of their contractual obligations.

Although immigration to the Canadian West increased modestly in 1886 following the completion of the Canadian Pacific Railway and the quashing of the North-West Rebellion by the Canadian militia, company directors resorted to lobbying and petitioning to pressure the government into accepting a satisfactory formula for the cancellation of their contracts instead of concentrating on the fulfillment of their settlement duties.

Beginning in 1884, company directors had requested that the government either alleviate their burdensome duties or cancel their respective contracts. The government refused to give serious consideration to the company directors' requests. The government refused to publicly admit the failure of its settlement scheme at this early date by liquidating colonization companies.

The outbreak of the North-West Rebellion and the crippling effects it had on immigration to the Canadian West compelled the government to recognize the plight of colonization companies. On July 5, 1885, David L. Macpherson, now Minister of the Interior, wrote to J. A. Macdonald:

> The collapse of the boom did much to defeat their efforts, and the outbreak of the Half-breeds and Indians completed that work. ... I think it is desirable to close the transactions with them, as otherwise they would drag on an unsuccessful existence, and be a constant source of trouble.[18]

Although the government was now prepared to negotiate with company directors, at least a year elapsed before a settlement satisfactory to both negotiating parties could be reached. In June, 1886, Thomas

White, Macpherson's successor as Minister of the Interior, proposed a compromise solution which was accepted by the Edmonton and Saskatchewan Land Company.

White, after an intensive study of all data available on colonization companies, had concluded that a reduction in the price of land from $2 to $1 per acre as requested by company directors would be too advantageous for those companies which had failed to undertake the development of their allotment. To protect the nation's interest and concurrently compensate part of the losses incurred by company directors who had endeavored to promote settlement, White proposed to allow colonization companies $160 for each bona fide settler and grant credit for expenses incurred in the fulfillment of their contractual obligations on the purchase of land at $2 per acre. Those companies which had remained idle merited no consideration and he suggested that they be allowed to purchase land at $2 per acre for the amount of their instalment.

In 1886 and 1887 twenty-six colonization companies negotiated the termination of their five-year contracts with the government. Only the Temperance Colonization Society remained in operation owing to the Minister of the Interior's reluctance to negotiate with the board of directors until it had succeeded in resolving the company's internal problems. The cancellation of the Temperance Colonization Society's contract with the government in 1891 marked the end of an experiment — the sale of lands by the Crown to private enterprise to promote the development of settlement in the North-West Territories.

The sale of public lands to private enterprises failed to provide the necessary funds to finance part of the cost of constructing the Canadian Pacific Railway[19] and failed to significantly advance the cause of settlement in the Canadian West. Although Thomas White had earlier stated that colonization companies had "been instrumental in inducing a very considerable proportion of the immigration which has taken place in the North-West,"[20] when conducting his last enumeration, the inspector of land companies had listed a total of only 1,080 entries or approximately 3,000 people on the basis of three persons per family. Admittedly, numerous homesteaders who had originally settled on company lands had abandoned their farms to settle on government lands in the vicinity of the Canadian Pacific Railway line, but, on the other hand, colonization companies had inherited a substantial number of squatters with their lands which offset their losses. Thus, colonization companies contributed approximately six to eight percent of the total growth of population in the North-West Territories between 1881 and 1891.[21]

Although the scheme failed to fulfill any of the purposes for which it was intended, the government absorbed the greater portion of the losses

24

incurred by colonization companies by offering a rebate of $160.00 for each individual entry and credit for all funds expended on the promotion of settlement. The government allotted scrip or patents on land valued at $1,159,182.32 to colonization companies as a final settlement of all accounts — $756,507.02 as a reimbursement of instalments paid by the companies to the Receiver-General of Canada and $402,675.30 as compensation for the losses incurred by the companies while attempting to fulfill their settlement duties. Thus the establishment of 1,080 heads of families within company colonies cost the government $402,675.30 or approximately $365.00 per entry. The generosity demonstrated by the government vis-à-vis land companies signified that a group of very prominent businessmen and government members had speculated at the expense of the Canadian public.

Beside the establishment of 1,080 heads of families, colonization companies provided the initial impetus for the birth of little communities such as Saskatoon, Yorkton, Crescent City, Kinbrae, Pheasant Forks, and several others. In 1886, Crescent City boasted a tailor shop, a privately owned hotel, a drugstore, a shoemaker shop, a tinsmith shop, and a grist mill. Saskatoon had a tinsmith shop, a large brick hotel, a dressmaker shop, a school, a Methodist church, a post office, a physician, a lawyer, a real-estate-and-insurance agency, and a detachment of Mounted Police.[22] Yorkton was the most populous company colony and its townsite was the most highly developed. However, it was the construction of branch railways through Yorkton and Saskatoon that ensured the eventual expansion and prosperity of these two communities during the immigration boom of the early 1900's. On the contrary, communities such as Crescent City, Kinbrae, Pheasant Forks, and others eventually disappeared owing to the distances separating them from major railway arteries.

The failure of colonization by private corporations in the Canadian West during the 1880's was occasioned by a variety of factors. The Conservative government leaders believed they could follow in the footsteps of American success in immigration by building a railway across the prairies and by offering prospective immigrants utopian homestead laws. These beliefs prompted the government to ride the tide of economic recovery, to disregard the importance of climatic conditions in the North-West, and to minimize the competition of its expanding neighbor to the south.

When the government and directors of land companies assumed that the construction of the Canadian Pacific Railway across the prairies would suffice to divert the steady influx of European immigrants from the American West to the Canadian West, they grossly underestimated the amount of arable soil available in the American Mid-West in the 1880's. European immigrants continued to flock into the American West, where countless railway lines stretched across the rolling plains, while only a trickle of immigrants ventured to the North-West Territories.

In addition to Canada's proximity to the United States, one of the most important causes of the North-West's slow rate of growth during the 1880's was the injurious publicity circulated by the British, American, and Canadian press. Newspapers carried editorials criticizing the railway monopoly, colonization companies, climatic conditions, and the quality of the soil. Leading the attack against the North-West Territories as a field of immigration was the Canadian nation's most prominent Liberal newspaper, *The Globe*. In an article published on March 29, 1884, the editor of *The Globe* wrote:

> The West with its cold snaps, cold and changeable winters, its summer cyclones and great heats certainly is inferior to Ontario in climate while the yield of nearly every grain and fruit is smaller there than here, the prices obtained there are smaller than here and land is nearly as dear in the most desirable localities while the best of lands in western Ontario are yet awaiting settlement and offering at $20 to $30 an acre while good lands in other districts of the province may be obtained for almost nothing. The advice Go West Young Man need not be given to young Ontario farmers.[23]

Similar observations were echoed in several Canadian, American, and British newspapers. *The London Standard*, for example, published an editorial stating that life was not safe in the North-West's capital, Regina, where the thermometer had registered temperatures of fifty-eight degrees below zero. The author of this article insisted that persons suffering from afflictions of the lungs or the heart would meet certain death if they emigrated to the Canadian West.[24] In addition to the derogatory reports published in newspapers, agents of American railway companies stationed in Great Britain circulated rumors of extensive losses of wheat crops in both Manitoba and the North-West Territories. As a result of this injurious publicity, only 886,000 immigrants chose Canada as their destination in the New World during the 1880's. However many immigrants used Canada solely as a port of entry into the New World. Although Canada attracted approximately 886,000 and the birthrate provided a natural increase of 686,000, its population increased by only 508,000 during the 1880's. Approximately 1,065,000 people emigrated from Canada to the United States, while only 40,000 people migrated to the North-West Territories during this decade.[25]

To further add to the misfortune of government officials, land-company agents, and C.P.R. representatives endeavoring to promote the development of a new frontier, the trade revival which had begun in 1879 faded away in the summer of 1883. Prices began to drop; the population's purchasing power declined rapidly; and manufacturers found a restricted market for their products. Western farmers saw the price of wheat drop in Montreal from $1.33 per bushel in 1881 to between $.80 and $.85 per bushel in 1883. In 1884, Manitoba farmers received only $.72 per bushel in Winnipeg for prime-quality wheat. Farmers suffered further distress when their wheat crops were damaged by an early frost in September, 1883. For wheat partially damaged by frosts, western farmers received only $.40 to $.60 per bushel.[26]

Western farmers suffered another severe blow in 1883, when the Macdonald ministry raised the duties on farm machinery from twenty-five to thirty-three percent.[27] The government's decision to protect eastern manufacturers against American competition imposed further hardship upon Manitoba and North-West farmers and aroused their anger. In March, 1884, the Manitoba and Northwest Farmers' Union met in Winnipeg and in the midst of heated discussions voted a resolution which asserted "that, until the grievances alleged by the Union had been remedied, further immigration to Manitoba and the Northwest should be discouraged."[28] The reform newspapers of eastern Canada, the American and the British press claimed that agitation was assuming gigantic proportions and alleged that the rebellious farmers were threatening to secede and join the United States. The Deputy Minister of the Interior acknowledged the harm done to the progress of settlement by the actions of the farmers' union and the ensuing injurious publicity when he wrote in his yearly report:

> There is very little reason to doubt that this decrease [in homestead entries] is largely owing to the unfortunate utterances of agitators. . . . These persons took advantage of the partial failure of the crop of 1883 to thrust themselves to the front, and gave expressions to views which were not entertained by those for whom they professed to speak, but which, nevertheless, worked much harm to the country.[29]

The turbulence occasioned by the militancy of the Manitoba and Northwest Farmers' Union had barely faded when the Métis of Saskatchewan rebelled against the federal government in March, 1885. The actual rebellion lasted less than two months. Nevertheless, the reports of Indian atrocities circulated by Canadian and foreign journalists and the "tall tales" related by some members of Canada's expeditionary force occasioned a substantial decline of immigration to the Canadian West. The number of entries for homesteads in Manitoba and the North-West diminished from 3,753 in 1884 to 1,858 in 1885.[30]

The number of settlers seeking a new home in the Canadian West increased slightly in 1886 as a result of the completion of the Canadian Pacific Railway but a devastating drought in the central region of the North-West Territories caused extreme hardships. As had been the case through the 1880's, many farmers abandoned their homesteads to seek refuge in a more hospitable climatic environment south of the forty-ninth parallel.

Under the prevailing conditions, land companies could not and did not play as successful a role in the promotion of settlement in the Canadian West as had been anticipated. To be successful, the settlement scheme devised by the government on December 23, 1881 necessitated a steady influx of immigrants. When only a handful of settlers ventured into the Canadian West, land companies were obliged to compete with government and Canadian Pacific Railway agents for the handful of settlers seeking productive land. Since choice homesteads situated in the vicinity of the railway were readily available for the minimal fee of ten dollars, land companies whose tracts lay a minimum of twenty-four miles north of the railway line were unable to recruit a sufficient number of settlers to fulfill the terms of their contract.

Although land-company directors expended time, money, and labor to attract settlers, their objectives were thwarted by the virulent attacks of Canada's Reform party press which accused the federal government of rewarding its political supporters, of creating a landed gentry in the Canadian West, and of establishing monopolies detrimental to the welfare of the Canadian populace. *The Globe* warned that colonization companies would likely retard rather than promote settlement. It called upon all Canadians to prevent "a mad government" from going on with its colonization scheme.[31] Furthermore, the Liberals vociferously denounced the government for placing prospective settlers at the mercy of land companies.

When colonization companies seriously undertook the development of their respective tracts of land in the spring of 1883, the speculative fever which had raged throughout Manitoba and parts of the North-West had petered out. The number of homestead entries in Manitoba and the North-West Territories declined from a high of 7,383 in 1882 to 6,063 in 1883.[32] Fewer people ventured west to search for a new home and land companies succeeded in locating only 650 settlers on their tracts of land.

The results achieved in 1883 were disheartening for shareholders who, in the midst of the speculative fever which had gripped Canada following the ratification of the Canadian Pacific Railway contract, had invested money in colonization companies in the hope of reaping lucrative profits. Instead of deriving a profit from their investment, stockholders were being forced to disburse more money for a scheme which now seemed less promising. When company directors threatened to cancel the shares of those who refused to pay their calls, internal dissension ensued.[33]

The government, which had anticipated that colonization companies would fulfill the same role as American branch-railway corporations in the promotion of settlement, lost faith in the system in the fall of 1883. The federal government had hoped that colonization companies would establish thriving communities north of the railway belt and that the existence of these towns would inspire eastern Canadian businessmen to build branch railways to link these company colonies with the Canadian Pacific Railway line. Corporations wishing to build a branch railway would receive 6,400 acres of land at one dollar per acre for every mile of track. The corporations which undertook the construction of branch railways under these conditions encountered serious financial difficulties and the construction of branch railways proceeded very slowly during the early 1880's. Similarly, land companies failed to measure up to the government's expectations and provide the necessary settlement to arouse the interest of businessmen who could build branch railways. Government officials gradually realized that land companies could never replace branch railways as agents of settlement and that those areas lying distant from the Canadian Pacific Railway line would be developed only after the construction of branch railways. As a result, the federal government relegated colonization companies to a secondary role in the area of settlement and looked to branch railways to develop the lands lying north of the railway belt. In 1884 and 1885, six railway companies were offered a free grant of 6,400 acres for every mile of rail.[34] Thus branch railways, which paid the same price for land as colonization companies had in the 1880's, received preferential treatment in 1884. Land company officials demanded the same privileges but were turned down. The federal government had lost faith in colonization companies and starting in 1884 turned to branch railways to promote the development of the land lying north of the Canadian Pacific Railway line.

To further aggravate the problems experienced by colonization companies, the even-numbered sections situated on both sides of the Canadian Pacific Railway, which had been withdrawn from homestead entry by the Order-in-Council of March 11, 1882, were opened for settlement on April 30, 1884. These lands, known as the "Mile Belt," amounting to approximately 4,000,000 acres and lying between Winnipeg in the east and the fourth meridian in the west, were made available under the terms respecting residence as stipulated in the Dominion Lands Act. Many company colonists cancelled their homestead entry to settle in the vicinity of the Canadian Pacific Railway lines. The manager of the York Farmers' Colonization Company lamented that forty-four settlers had left the Yorkton colony in 1884 alone owing to the opening of the Mile Belt.[35] The executive members of the Montreal and Western Land Company insisted that by opening the Mile Belt, the government was intentionally ruining colonization companies.[36]

The North-West Rebellion of 1885 brought settlement to a virtual

29

halt and inflicted a mortal blow upon the colonization companies' remaining hopes of survival. Several company directors admitted that further efforts on their part to promote the settlement of their lands would be futile and would result only in wasted time and money. The rebellion sealed the fate of the languishing colonization companies. Company directors suspended their operations and sought to negotiate a satisfactory cancellation of their contract.

The poorly conceived land companies developed without reference to economic reality. They could succeed only if the Canadian West experienced a very rapid increase in immigration. With the availability of substantial amounts of arable land in the United States and the sharp decline in the price of agricultural products, the development of the Canadian West stagnated. Macdonald dreamed of building the Canadian West while company directors entertained visions of securing astronomical profits. Their prognostics were based on hope rather than corroborative evidence. The failure of colonization companies contributed to the waning of the enthusiasm which had characterized the early 1880's and to the general discouragement and meagre progress of settlement which persisted into the next decade.

# 3  Edgar Dewdney and the Aftermath of the Rebellion

*by Jean Larmour*

THE rebellion of 1885 had disrupted the whole North-West and brought unrest and uneasiness to the settlers of the area. However, the rebellion had also brought commerce and ready cash into the area, alleviating for the time being many of the ills of the settlers. The restoration of peace and order, it was hoped, would bring much needed new settlers. Edgar Dewdney's task as Lieutenant-Governor of the North-West Territories was to restore confidence in the peace and progress of the territory. His task as Indian commissioner for the same area was to re-establish governmental authority over the Indians, to ensure that rebellion would not recur, and to resume the policy of agricultural development on the reserves. The leaders and participants in the rebellion had to be punished as a deterrent to any who would follow their course, and as a guarantee to the new and prospective settlers that such rebellion would not be tolerated. This process was to occupy some time since the underlying causes of discontent had not been removed, and rumors of new outbreaks persisted. The first step in this direction was the trial of those accused of responsibility for the uprising.*

The trial of Louis Riel began in Regina on July 20, sentence being passed on August 1, 1885. The jury found him guilty of high treason but recommended that mercy be extended to him. There was no mercy available, for Judge Richardson sentenced Riel to be hanged, a sentence which Dewdney approved. "Riel came out in his true light on making his final speech," Dewdney wrote to the Prime Minister. "He just showed that he was a consumate vilain [*sic*] — I hope sincerely that he will be hanged; he is too dangerous a man to have a chance of being loose on society."[1] Sir John replied, "The conviction of Riel is satisfactory."[2] Hayter Reed, the assistant Indian commissioner, whose position took

---

*This article is adapted from Chapter IX of the author's unpublished M.A. thesis, "Edgar Dewdney, Commissioner of Indian Affairs and Lieutenant-Governor of the North-West Territories, 1879-1888," University of Saskatchewan, Regina Campus, 1969. It originally appeared in *Saskatchewan History* for autumn, 1970.

Public Archives of Canada C1879

*The trial of Louis Riel*

him throughout the territory, agreed on the punishment of Riel. "I trust Riel will swing, for if he does not, it will have a great prejudicial effect on the minds of the Indians."[3]

After several reprieves to consider the question of his sanity, the law was allowed to take its course and Riel was hanged November 16, 1885. A rash of pamphlets and writings condemning the hanging appeared in the eastern press as well as in predominantly Métis areas in the Territories. The clerk of the territorial council, A. E. Forget, was alienated by this event. Dewdney said that he could no longer trust Forget after the hanging.[4] However, most of the settlers in the Territories, motivated by fear of Indian massacres, approved of Riel's death. It is likely that the territorial council was urged by Dewdney to pass a resolution approving of the hanging of Riel, for the preamble to the resolution mentioned meetings in different parts of the Dominion which had condemned the Dominion government. Only a dedicated Conservative would have worried about this aspect of the situation. The territorial interest in effective disposal of Riel was also apparent in the preamble to the resolution, passed December 12, 1885:

> Whereas the peace, progress and prosperity of these Territories would have been jeopardized and a feeling of insecurity would have existed among the settlers had the man . . . who had not shrunk from the terrible responsibilities of inciting the Half-Breeds and Indians to armed insurrection, been permitted to escape the just penalty of his misdeeds; . . . Therefore this Council desires to place on Record its

endorsement of the action of the Dominion Government in allowing the sentence of the Court to be carried into effect.[5]

Father André, spiritual adviser to Riel, applied to Dewdney for Riel's body after the hanging, but Dewdney insisted that the law must be observed and the body buried within the precincts of the jail.[6] Father André produced a will which Riel had made, appointing him executor of the estate. This was an order to which Dewdney felt that he must accede, but he was much afraid of the consequences. He reported that Orangemen had a scheme to take the body away, perhaps to mutilate it; others might take it to Quebec to stir up trouble there.[7] However, Pascal Bonneau, a strong Conservative and friend of Riel's who had been suggested as a guard for Riel's body, had told him "that after a few days he could take the body up, put it on the train and take it to St. Boniface, and no one know anything about it."[8] Secrecy was observed in the removal of Riel's remains and no trouble on this account developed in the Territories.

The trials of the other participants in the rebellion were conducted at Regina and Battleford, and extended into the autumn. Although Dewdney was in favor of the death penalty for Riel, he sought clemency for the remainder of the offenders. "It is my own most earnest desire to prevent the further effusion of blood if by any means possible," he wrote.[9] He felt that W. H. Jackson, Riel's secretary, was "crazy"[10] and should therefore be absolved of responsibility. Hon. A. Campbell, Minister of Justice, wrote to the prosecuting lawyers that the government would be satisfied if "thirty or forty leading half-breeds or white men and leading Indians" were found guilty.[11] In all there were forty-six half-breeds, eighty-one Indians, and two whites held for trial.[12] Forty-four of the Indians were convicted on various charges, mainly treason-felony,[13] eleven being condemned to be hanged, although three were reprieved; chiefs Big Bear and Poundmaker received three-year sentences which were reduced after one year; eighteen of the half-breeds were sentenced to terms varying from one to seven years; the two white men were discharged.[14]

Dewdney was worried about the sentencing of Poundmaker as he was the adopted son of Crowfoot, the powerful chief of the Blackfoot tribe. Crowfoot had written to Dewdney requesting that Poundmaker be pardoned.[15] Dewdney had also been informed that there would be trouble if Poundmaker were hanged.[16] He wired Macdonald to intervene in preventing the cutting of Poundmaker's hair, which was customary for convicts. He also assisted Poundmaker to wire Crowfoot "not to think anything of the trouble he was in."[17] In December, the territorial council passed a resolution recommending that the government reconsider the individual cases of the half-breeds and Indians on compassionate

*Edgar Dewdney*

grounds and where possible "extend the clemency of the crown to them."[18] In February, 1886, the Prince Albert *Times* reported that Ignace Poitras, Sr., Joseph Arcand, and Moise Parenteau had been pardoned.[19] No doubt this helped to dissipate some of the ill will and unrest among the Métis settlers.

Efforts to restore order on the affected reserves began soon after the surrender of the Indians. Macrae, an Indian agent, and Reed visited Poundmaker's camp to collect arms and plunder, and farming operations were undertaken. By the middle of June, corn, potatoes, and barley were being sown.[20] New farm instructors had been appointed by Reed under Dewdney's direction and every effort was made to return to normal. Reed accompanied the commander of the military forces, General Middleton, to Fort Pitt where he attempted to advance Dewdney's ideas

34

*Poundmaker*

as to the method of handling the Indians[21] and to re-establish order among them.[22]

That both Indians and settlers remained upset was evident in a letter from Father Lacombe about the Blackfoot Indians.[23] Dewdney, General Middleton, and Father Lacombe went to Blackfoot Crossing where they found the reports of trouble had no foundation.[24] The rumors of and the possibility of more trouble in the Territories prompted the government to introduce legislation forbidding arms and ammunition to all in the

35

territory, without a permit issued by the Lieutenant-Governor. This bill was passed July 16.[25]

For those tribes which had been involved in the rebellion fairly strict measures were taken. Their annuity payments were withheld to pay for the damage which they had done. Reed recommended that any future payments to those bands which had rebelled should be concessions, not treaty rights. Dewdney was in complete agreement with withholding annuity payments although he demurred on negating the treaties.[26] Later Dewdney reported that the policy of rewarding the faithful and depriving the rebels of their annuities had worked well. It kept alive the memory of the consequences of rebellion.[27] In 1888 the annuity payments to rebel Indians were partially re-established. A small percentage were paid in that year with the promise that more would be paid in the ensuing years, if they proved themselves worthy.[28]

Reed also recommended that the tribal system should be abolished where possible in the peaceful tribes, a policy which had been more or less approved prior to the rebellion, but for those tribes which had rebelled and broken the treaty, the chiefs and councillors should be abolished. Dewdney noted that he approved of this suggestion, but it was not found feasible as some type of organization was required. All the Indians were to be disarmed although the northern Indians who lived by the hunt should be furnished with shotguns. Dewdney's recommendation was that the disarming should be done by persuasion, not compulsion.

> If it is known by the Indians that we want to get their arms, they will be cached . . . but if they found we care little about it and they cannot get fixed ammunition they will sell their rifles.[29]

Reed further recommended that all rebel Indians should require passes to leave their reserves, that Big Bear's band should be scattered among the other bands, and that many of the Carlton bands, being uneconomic units, should be regrouped. Dewdney agreed that these recommendations should be carried out as far as possible. Reed noted several of the bands in Treaty Six which had held aloof from the rebellion and suggested that special recognition should be given to these bands. Dewdney agreed wholeheartedly with this suggestion. He sent a report to Macdonald in which he mentioned those who took a loyal part during the rebellion, recommending that they be rewarded.[30] The policy of insisting that the Indians work for their provisions had been adopted much earlier, but would be enforced as far as possible. However, Dewdney did not feel that the Indians could be brought under the Masters and Servants Act and made to give full value, as Reed recommended. The ponies and wagons of the Indians had been confiscated after the rebellion. Reed proposed to sell the horses, purchasing cattle in their stead. Dewdney agreed at first but later reconsidered, believing that the government had no right to dispose of the Indian property without their consent.[31]

The Indian commissioner's policy regarding the Indians who had been implicated in the rebellion was set forth in his report for that year:

> Any Indians who thought that they could subsist better by the chase than by tilling the soil have been given a fowling piece, with the injunction that they must support themselves. . . . As they fail in the future to gain their livelihood by their own methods they will have the proof of experience to convince them. . . . Firmness in withholding assistance should be exercised, until they ask to be taken into the reserves, when the extension to them of fair and liberal treatment will complete the settlement.[32]

The general policy "of liberal treatment during working times, and a refusal to issue food when unjustifiable laziness was shown" was adopted for all the Indian tribes not involved in the trouble.[33] Dewdney mentioned that this policy had been adopted prior to the rebellion with some of the bands and that in Moosomin's band, which had not joined the trouble, they had managed to save enough money to buy 100 sheep.[34] Reed reported at the end of August that most of the Indian bands at Battleford "bow to the inevitable and it would take very much indeed to get them to rise again," although the Stoneys were still a little unsettled.[35]

The Indians in the Edmonton area were still restless in August. Some of the rebel Indians had joined those at Bear Hills, keeping them in a state of agitation. Dewdney wrote Macdonald that he had "instructed Irvine to send fifty men there as soon as possible."[36] He also pressed Macdonald with the fact that "we must be very strict about the sale of ammunition."[37] The Peace Hills Indians in the same area were also unsettled.[38] Dewdney made a tour of the area during payments, promising the bands more working oxen.[39] He also invited the Bear Hills Indians to visit him in Regina. Father Scollen wrote that the Cree chiefs were much impressed and spoke of Dewdney's kind hospitality.[40] These methods brought a more settled atmosphere to the Edmonton district.

In Treaty Seven Dewdney strongly recommended that C. E. Denny, a former Indian agent, be reappointed as Indian agent for "he can do more with these Indians and find out what is going on better than any man I know."[41] Denny had been appointed special agent at Crowfoot's request during the rebellion. He retained this position during the following winter although he left the Indian Department the next year. He said that he had been promised the position of inspector for the next year, but that this had not materialized.[42]

Dewdney himself took the treaty money to Blackfoot Crossing at the end of September, stating that he anticipated that the late payment of treaty would reduce any tendency to roam.[43] There had been some unrest at Blackfoot Crossing caused by Herchmer taking brown-coated men onto the reserve instead of the accustomed red-coated police, but this misunderstanding had been cleared up.[44] Another cause of irritation was General Strange, who had led the military thrust against the rebellious Indians at Frog Lake and Loon Lake. He was a shareholder in one of the large cattle companies in the Calgary area. Dewdney advised the largest shareholder in the company to get rid of Strange, since he antagonized the Indians and was apt to cause trouble. Dewdney was afraid that Strange might cause trouble while the Governor-General was visiting the reserve.[45] No doubt this was possible, for Strange complained to Macdonald that Dewdney had "pooh poohed" the charges which Strange laid against the Indians, when Dewdney met him at Gleichen on the edge of the Blackfoot Reserve.[46]

William Pearce, Superintendent of Mines for the Dominion Lands Board; Lieutenant-Colonel J. F. Turnbull, commanding officer of the Cavalry School Corps, "A" Troop, in the rebellion; missionaries who had been in the Territories; and others wrote critically of Indian administration and advised on how the Indians should be treated. Although Dewdney relied heavily on the advice of Hayter Reed, who was in the field in constant contact with the Indians, and on that of the Indian agents, he objected to advice from other quarters, which he regarded as uninformed and unwarranted interference. However, he answered most of the criticism and advice with explanations of his policy to Macdonald.

To ensure that order was maintained after the suppression of the uprising, 300 of the militia remained in the West, while the police force was raised to its full strength of 1,000 men.[47] There were problems with the troops, however. J. M. Rae, agent at Battleford, complained that the troops would not aid him in carrying out his Indian work. He also stated that what "little was left in our houses by the Indians had been carried away by the troops, in fact they act towards us as if they were in the enemy's country and we were the enemy."[48] P. G. Laurie, editor of the newspaper at Battleford, complained that his house had been looted,[49] while others mentioned the looting of Indian reserves by the military.[50] Dewdney was conscious of the need for troops, but also of the problem they created.

> If it were not for the effect it might have of making the Indians and half-breeds very impudent . . . I would like to have seen them all sent home. They are unaccustomed to Indians and are more than likely to get us into trouble, if brought in contact with them.[51]

Although there were objections to the militia there were also demands for its assurance of protection. Father Lacombe was much distressed about the removal of the troops, especially before the Mounted

Police arrived. His letter expressing his unease was passed by Dewdney to Macdonald with the proposal that a strong force of Mounted Police be stationed near the Blackfoot Reserve.[52] The Prince Albert *Times* mentioned Indian unrest in that area. The editor felt that these rumors were not without foundation. "We think steps should be taken immediately to give us greater protection."[53]

Commissions were established to investigate causes of unrest in the Territories. The Half-Breed Commission, hurriedly appointed just prior to the outbreak of hostilities, held hearings throughout the Territories to ascertain the half-breed claim to land or scrip. It was hoped that this would reduce some of the cause of unrest. A Rebellion Losses Commission was established to compensate Métis and white settlers who suffered losses in the rebellion. On Dewdney's recommendation this commission included a western man — at first Lawrence Herchmer but later Thomas MacKay, a prominent Métis.[54] The hearings held by these bodies provided a legitimate outlet for the expression of grievances felt by both Métis and white and tended to mollify these settlers.

The interruption of regular commerce and of seeding operations caused by the rebellion and the confiscation of food, seed grain, and cattle by the military led to considerable hardship in the affected areas. As early as May 20, 1885 Dewdney telegraphed Macdonald that the settlers at Battleford were applying to him for clothing. He said that Agent Rae had already spent $600: "Am I authorized to do more for them?"[55] Rae wrote to Dewdney, on June 15, that the militia had taken all the Indian Department supplies. He also mentioned the plight of the settlers who had lost their cattle and horses.[56]

The government at Ottawa was not inclined to be overly generous in providing aid to the destitute. Macdonald suggested that there should be little need for relief at Prince Albert although Battleford and Frog Lake were a different question. The government did not want to have people starving, Macdonald wrote, but it would not "vote extravagant sums to meet prospective or speculative losses." He ordered Dewdney to "take hold of this subject with a good deal of vigour and with a view to prevent imposition on the Treasury."[57] Dewdney's suggestion was that the police, who knew the people, would be the best ones to assess the relief needed.[58] He added that the settlers were better able to support themselves now that they had their horses back.

Earlier, Dewdney had wired Macdonald about the desperate circumstances of the Métis at Batoche.[59] Macdonald telegraphed Dewdney on July 15 to arrange for those at Batoche "and report your course."[60] This was two weeks after Dewdney had wired concerning their destitution. Action had been taken, however, for Dewdney's reply the next day, was: "Need have no anxiety about Batoche at present. Lash just arrived states all who can freight can get employment and present needs

*Gabriel Dumont*

of destitute families are supplied."[61] The same day Macdonald reported in the House that the poor people of Batoche were not allowed to starve.[62]

In obedience to Macdonald's demand for economy Dewdney reported that although 460 had been given rations at Battleford, this number had been cut to 90.[63] This was decreased to eight or ten families in August.[64] Dewdney, on Macdonald's suggestion, requested permission to take over militia supplies at Edmonton, if they were not spoiled, for use by the Indian Department and for the destitute at Batoche.[65] This would provide relief at a lesser cost than if the food had to be imported. One could speculate that the specification that the supplies not be spoiled was added by Dewdney.

While much was being done to settle the populace, and to restore confidence in law and order, many of the Métis remained in a disturbed state, a possible fuse to further explosion. Gabriel Dumont and a number of the other leaders in the rebellion had escaped into Montana, whence came rumors and messengers of unrest. One half-breed had been reported as saying, "Last spring there was a rebellion but next spring there would be a war."[66] The half-breeds under Dumont would clear the white men out of their country. Dewdney wrote Macdonald early in November that Dumont, Dumas, Delorme, and a fourth half-breed had been north among the Indians the previous month. "Since then a number of men have been leaving their Reserves and going south not taking their families with them."[67] The Indians were reported to believe that any fight would be worse than the last. Dewdney recommended that the Mounted Police should have more men at MacLeod. He had spoken of this to Irvine, commissioner of the police, and had sent Cotton, one of the officers, to the Piegan reserve to obtain information.[68] A few days later he wrote that "the exodus of our Indians from a couple of the Reserves in the north was occasioned by the fear of being arrested.... We cannot find out where they are, but I feel sure they are south of the line."[69]

Dewdney enrolled James Anderson to go to Montana to the Indian and Métis settlements for the purpose of obtaining accurate information about the Canadian half-breeds and Indians.[70] At Billings, Montana, Anderson found no feeling about or interest in the late rebellion. However, he found Dumont and a large half-breed population at Lewiston, Montana.[71] Dumont stated that they all intended settling at Turtle Mountain. The half-breeds in that area considered the late rebellion a mistake, Anderson wrote. He was confident that Dumont wished no more disorder, but he warned that Dumas meant trouble.[72] At Benton the feeling was against the half-breed rebellion, with approval for the execution of Riel. Anderson stated that Dumas and Dumont had had to abandon an attempt to raise funds there.[73]

Anderson found that Little Poplar and his band, with some Assiniboine and Gros Ventre Indians, had been to Fort Belknap and the Crow reserve. However, the American government would drive them from the reserves.[74] There were no half-breeds at the Blackfoot agency and only a few at Sun River.[75] Anderson wrote that "should the half-breeds intend to give further trouble their base will be at the Turtle

Mountains."[76] He recommended that the government pardon those who were tools of Riel.

Following this recommendation Dewdney gave a written guarantee to O. E. Hughes, the member for the district of Lorne where the Métis unrest had centred, "that the half-breeds who had identified themselves with the late rebellion will not be prosecuted or interfered with by the government."[77] It was hoped that this would relieve the anxiety of the Métis and persuade those who were doubtful to remain farming or to return to their farms. There were still rumors of risings and unrest in the Territories at the end of December. Dewdney wrote to Macdonald, "It would be as well to accept the reports as constantly circulating of further trouble in the spring as having foundation and let it be known that the government . . . will not put up with any such nonsense — that if the present force is not considered sufficient to keep the peace then other steps must be taken."[78]

In January Dewdney sent McKay to Turtle Mountain to assess the situation. He visited a number of centres, finding that the word had gone out "to leave north as there would be a row in the spring."[79] He stayed in the area until February 24, when it was rumored that he was a spy, and his usefulness was ended. I. G. Baker and Company also forwarded any reports which they had on half-breed and Indian activities. They forwarded a letter to Dewdney from a resident of Lewiston, stating that Dumont received mail from Jackson, from Manitoba, and from the north.[80] There had been a half-breed meeting in January, in that area. Later six Cree Indians, well armed, appeared in Lewiston, looking for Dumont.[81]

On March 2, Dewdney suggested sending a "reliable man to Turtle Mountain to assure half-breeds they could return."[82] He added that there was an improving feeling towards the government among the half-breeds and Indians and he felt that such a move would increase this feeling.[83] Dewdney reported, March 30, "the messenger has today returned from Turtle Mountain. Those to whom we went are coming back. Others are anxious to return."[84] In the House of Commons Edward Blake asked "whether Mr. Dewdney has been authorized to inform the Indians . . . that no arrests will be made of any who took part in last year's troubles?"[85] Sir John denied that he had, but added that "to certain half-breeds in the vicinity of Turtle Mountain . . . who . . . were simply misguided . . . he has been authorized to say that if they will return and behave peacefully and loyally, they will not be disturbed."[86]

Dewdney feared that there had been so many rumors of Indian risings during the winter that settlers and no doubt would-be settlers were nervous, that "our chances of immigration" had been damaged, and he suggested a flying column of military men be sent through the territory to calm the fever of unease.[87] He had contacted General Middleton concerning this possibility, and he had recommended about 1,200 men to make up a flying column. Dewdney emphasized that it would be necessary to inform the Indians of the purpose of such an expedition even though the column would be advised to stay away from the reserves.[88] If such a column were to be sent, Dewdney asked to be informed in time to prepare the Indians. Neither the Edmonton *Bulletin* nor the Regina *Leader* made comment about the proposed expedition but the Prince Albert *Times* welcomed the arrival of a flying column.[89] On February 14, Sir John wired Dewdney, "Flying column will probably go west."[90] In reply Dewdney questioned the number of men being placed at 700 for he thought that a smaller number would suffice. Such a large force would "be a very expensive matter; does the present position of affairs warrant it?"[91]

On February 16, Dewdney issued a proclamation that the soldiers were coming, although not to harm the Indians or take their arms. There would be no arrests made of any who took part in last year's troubles, he said. The soldiers were to keep the peace, to stop horse stealing and whiskey smuggling.[92] Wilfrid Laurier questioned Macdonald about this proclamation, for he had said that only the Turtle Mountain Métis were to be exempted from arrest for their part in the rebellion.[93] Macdonald had denied knowledge of this proclamation, which denial now required an explanation: "While I stated that the proclamation was not authorized and was not seen by us, we knew Mr. Dewdney had represented, as others had, that it was of great consequence, if new troops were sent . . . that they would be sent in such a way as not to alarm the Indian tribes."[94]

Reed warned Dewdney that the prevailing opinion was against the formation of a flying column. Reed himself, however, felt that "no demonstrations which could be made by our soldiers would ever overawe the Indians. It would take a well disciplined and drilled regular."[95] By April 12 it had been decided not to send a flying column through the Territories. Robert Watson, member for Marquette, spoke in the House on this changeability. Dewdney had first announced that a column would be sent and then announced that it would not be sent. He felt that the effect of the announcement that no column would be sent would disturb the Indians even more.[96] When it was decided that no flying column would be sent, Dewdney requested that General Middleton's force be kept in the West until summer. By that time the Mounted Police under their new commissioner would be better organized and trained.[97]

The fear and unrest which had been generated in the Territories formed the basis of an indignant outburst in Dewdney's annual report as Commissioner of Indian Affairs, for 1886.

> Those unprincipled persons who, actuated by questionable motives, or by those undoubtedly of a degradingly selfish character, have endeavoured to circulate and keep alive rumours calculated to bring about the very condition of things which they pretended did exist and hypocritically professed to deplore. . . . That no grave evils have resulted is equally a matter of surprise and a cause for thankfulness.[98]

Hard times had played a part in the development of rebellion on the plains. Letters of those on the spot referred to rumors started by white men who wished to see a military force in the area to provide needed cash. These same conditions resulted in rumors of disturbances after the hostilities. No doubt these rumors received more attention following the insurrection even though there was less cause for rumor. Paul Sharp described a similar situation in the United States: "Army expenditures played such an important role in the region's economy that citizens constantly implored the government to expand its military commitments. They often pictured Indians as hostile and exaggerated isolated depredations into a state of warfare."[99]

There were murmurings of unrest again in the spring of 1887. Dewdney reported that he expected such rumors would continue for years to come.[100] However, he found a marked improvement in conditions, such an improvement that those who complained now said that the improvement was due to their outcry. They stated that this improvement "was forced upon the Department by pressure from outside."[101] They claimed that their clamor resulted in the dismissal of worthless agents and employees. Dewdney denied that the criticism of outsiders had forced the improvement in Indian affairs. However, Indian affairs appeared to be in a much better state than prior to the rebellion.

Dewdney's policies following the rebellion had relieved the immediate distress among Indians, Métis, and white settlers. He had imposed penalties on the rebellious Indian bands without the disruption of mass military retaliation, and he had continued to promote agriculture on the reserves. His conciliatory policy had encouraged the Métis to return to their settlements and had dispersed the nucleus of potentially explosive Métis at Turtle Mountain. The knowledge that the government of the Territories was aware of unrest and prepared to act to eliminate trouble restored the confidence of the settlers. These actions, the return to more normal conditions, and the attention which the rebellion itself had focussed on the area stimulated a renewed flow of settlement to the North-West.

# 4    The Bell Farm

*by E. C. Morgan*

NO single farming venture undertaken in the North-West Territories created more interest than the Bell farm founded at Indian Head in 1882. The round stone stable on the site of the headquarters of the farm, about two miles north of Indian Head on Highway 56, still arouses the curiosity of passers-by. It is the last vestige of a large farming enterprise which at its height encompassed a block of land almost ten miles square and represented an investment of several hundred thousand dollars. At times the venture appeared to be on the verge of success, but in the course of fifteen years it failed, first as a corporate enterprise and later as the personal farm of Major William R. Bell, whose name throughout was attached to it and who was its principal promoter and general manager.*

Born in Brockville, Ontario, on May 28, 1845, Bell, after gaining most of his education there, passed a part of his early years in the western United States. Then, with the gathering of Fenians at points along the Canadian border, he answered the call for volunteers and returned home to serve in the defense of his native province. Once again, in 1870, he took part in defending Canada from the threat of Fenian invasion and, in 1875, returned from military service with the rank of major of the Forty-first Regiment.[1] Soon after, it would appear, Bell returned to the United States where with partners he established the Bell-Kelso farm in Minnesota.[2] After leaving that state, Bell lived for a time in Winnipeg. No man was better qualified by experience or inclination to establish a large farming enterprise. Bell had already been a lumber merchant, a large-scale farmer, and a leader of men. The competitive spirit which had made him a top cricket player, a leading exponent of Canada's national game lacrosse, a crack-shot good enough to be named a member of the first Wimbledon team and a regular competitor at Bisley equipped him well for his latest and most ambitious venture.[3]

In 1881 Major Bell set out on foot from Brandon, Manitoba, to view

---

*This article appeared in *Saskatchewan History* for spring, 1966.

some of the country through which the Canadian Pacific Railway would pass. By this time the idea of establishing a large farm in the "New West" had been fixed firmly in his mind, and once he reached the fertile lands of South Qu'Appelle, he determined that this was the spot for it. He would form a company, raise sufficient funds, and acquire the land he had selected. Soon after his return to Winnipeg his ambitious scheme had become a reality with the acquisition of the land from the government and the Canadian Pacific Railway Company, and with the incorporation of the Qu'Appelle Valley Farming Company, with head office at Chatham, Ontario. His proposals to establish a farm were well received because both the government and the railway were anxious to encourage settlement. They saw in Bell's proposals an opportunity to advertise the North-West to prospective immigrants, to obtain immediate revenue from the sale of lands, and the promise of increased revenues through the activities of the company and the immigrants it would attract.

On February 10, 1882 Major Bell made formal application for permission to purchase the even-numbered sections of land owned by the Dominion government in the tract of land he had selected for the farm.[4] Approximately 23,000 acres in a nine-mile-square area were involved. The purchase price of $1.25 an acre was to be payable one-fifth in cash and the balance in four equal instalments. In return for the grant Bell promised "to place thereon, before the harvest of 1888, one hundred and twenty-eight families per township, that is to say, two hundred and eighty-eight families on the whole nine miles square."[5] He also promised within the same period to have 20,000 acres of land under crop and to expend not less than $600,000 on improving the farm. The government had previously been informed by the Canadian Pacific Railway Company that it would sell to Bell all the odd-numbered sections that he required.[6]

The Minister of the Interior, in recommending acceptance of Bell's proposal in a memorandum to council on February 28, 1882,[7] attached two conditions to the proposed agreement. He recommended that interest at six percent per annum payable with the annual instalment should be charged on the unpaid balance. He also recommended that in each of the years 1882-1886 the company be required to place twenty-five settlers on the even-numbered sections and cultivate 4,000 acres of land or forfeit for every settler under the number of twenty-five 160 acres, and for every 160 acres less than 4,000 acres cultivated forfeit another 160 acres. In supporting Bell's proposals the minister pointed out that by selling the lands to the company, the government would realize the same returns from the lands as they would if the lands were made available for homesteading and pre-emption. The only financial advantage to the government was that the money would most likely be obtained sooner from the company than from individual settlers. The scheme, the

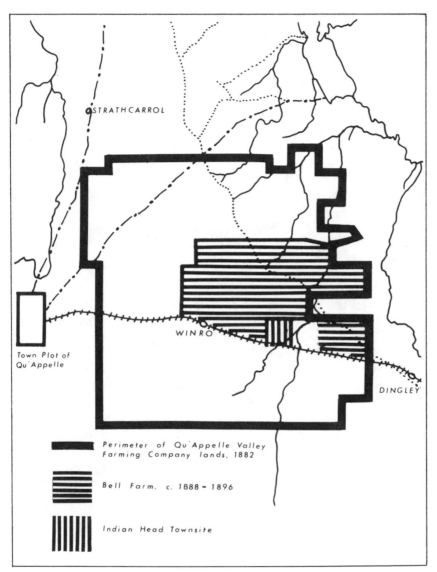

STRATHCARROL

Town Plot of
Qu'Appelle

WINRO

DINGLEY

Perimeter of Qu'Appelle Valley
Farming Company lands, 1882

Bell Farm, c. 1888 - 1896

Indian Head Townsite

minister believed, would advertise the Canadian West and it would probably aid immigration. Bell's proposals promised to place on the land settlers who probably would not be able to come without some form of assistance.

On April 3, 1882, Order-in-Council Number 427 was passed authorizing the sale of government lands to the Qu'Appelle Valley Farming Company Limited.[8] Agreement was also reached for the purchase of 29,111 acres of land from the Canadian Pacific Railway. The

47

railway agreed to sell the land at $1.25 per acre, which was the same price as that charged by the government. However, the railway price was conditional on the company cultivating and cropping one-half the land within five years.[9]

An indenture made on June 7, 1884,[10] and signed by officials of the Qu'Appelle Valley Farming Company and of the government, describes in detail the lands granted under the Order-in-Council passed on April 3, 1882. These lands, falling within townships 18, 19, and 19A, range 12; townships 18 and 19, range 13; and townships 18 and 19, range 14, all west of the second meridian, amounted to 23,658 acres, "more or less." Thus, statements to the effect that the company's holdings totalled 64,000 do not appear consistent with the facts. A true figure would approximate 53,000 acres, made up of railway lands totalling 29,111 and government lands totalling 23,658 acres.

On May 12, 1882, the Qu'Appelle Valley Farming Company Limited, with capitalization of $600,000, was incorporated under the Canada Joint Stock Companies Act, the capital consisting of 6,000 shares, valued at $100 each. Of the original twenty-four shareholders, three men, the general manager, William R. Bell, with 1,100, the president, John Northwood, with 1,000, and the secretary-treasurer, H. J. Eberts with 500, held 2,600 shares.[11] The only subscriber from outside of Canada was J. H. Burwell of St. Paul, Minnesota.

On June 25, 1882, breaking commenced on the company's lands. As the railway was still 200 miles to the east the company did not have time, if it was going to get any breaking done in the spring of 1882, to transport the necessary men and equipment to the site. The company therefore allotted a contract to Messrs. Seims and Armington to break 3,000 acres

Notman Photographic Archives, McCord Museum

*Bell Farm, Indian Head*

*Main office*

*Main stable and Bell's patent portable granaries*

for them. By the end of the first season the contractors had only been able to complete breaking 2,567 acres at a total cost of $9,919.98.[12]

Besides the land work, an early beginning had also been made on an ambitious building program so that by the time of the first annual meeting of the company, the president, John Northwood, was able to present the shareholders with a most encouraging report. During that first season, the two-storey main farmhouse, of stone construction,

49

containing sixteen rooms and measuring thirty-four feet by forty feet, with a wing measuring twenty-three feet by forty-four feet, had been occupied. Also complete was the main stable, of circular design, measuring sixty-four feet in diameter, having two box stalls, twenty-nine single stalls, stableman's office, 4,000-bushel oat bin, and a hayloft of 100 tons capacity. Other buildings erected included an ice house, cow barn, chicken house, and four stone and two frame five-room cottages, measuring twenty-five feet by thirty feet, each with adjacent stable for three horses. The president went on to outline plans for additional buildings, some of which were already under construction, and to advise the shareholders that extra implements and horses were in transit to augment the thirty-two horses and equipment now on the farm. Besides these undertakings, an artesian well had been sunk at the main house, and trees bordered the house and garden and the road to the railway station. Expenditures to date, the president said, had totalled approximately $91,000.

Thus it is not surprising that the president had begun his report on a note of optimism: ". . . we need not fear," he said, "to look back to the promises made at its [the company's] inception, nor to meet the subscribers, who, on the faith of those promises, put their money into the shares of the Company."[13] Northwood told his listeners that by judicious management, "grave difficulties" in occupying the land, and in gaining the public's confidence, had been overcome. He expressed the company's pride in having established the largest farm in the North-West, having the "greatest and finest" buildings and the "largest and best" equipment. Northwood also made reference to "pretended" squatters and expressed his belief that this problem would soon be overcome. He mentioned that the board of directors had under consideration a plan to encourage "students from the Motherland" to settle on the farm to learn the principles of agriculture. In conclusion, he advised the shareholders that for convenience the head office would be moved from Chatham to Winnipeg, and that early in 1883, the directors passed a resolution confirming the popular usage of the name, the "Bell Farm," for the property of the company.[14]

In a letter dated June 13, 1883, J. Gordon, Dominion-lands agent at Regina, indicated that the improvements forecast in Northwood's report were being carried out at a rapid pace.[15] By that date, 4,320 acres had been broken, and of this acreage, 1,920 acres had been sown to Red Fyfe wheat, 1,600 acres to oats, and a large field to potatoes and roots. Men employed then numbered eighty-two, and the horse population had reached 100. Seventy buildings dotted the farm, including twenty-seven cottages, which were situated on various sections. Gordon's letter is a clear statement that the momentum built up in 1882 and the first months of 1883 continued, despite the opposition to the enterprise which had been manifested by the squatters, the public generally, and one of Winnipeg's leading newspapers.

Conflicting statements in two letters written by Gordon, the Dominion-lands agent, are illustrative of the contradictions which characterized reports relating to activities on the farm. In the second letter, dated December 31, 1883,[16] Gordon advised the Minister of the Interior that the area cropped in 1883 consisted of 1,200 acres of wheat and 1,000 acres of oats, while in the letter of June 13, he had given the acreages as 1,920 and 1,600 respectively. By December 31, according to Gordon, buildings on the tract numbered 106, and 7,000 acres had been broken. Gordon's December letter states that on April 1, 1883, a number of laborers and their families, seventy-five horses, and several carloads of implements and machinery had arrived at the farm.

The magnitude of the farming operations required the establishment of a detailed plan for carrying out the work. Gordon's letter of December, 1883 and an interview which Major Bell granted the *Pall Mall Gazette*,[17] on his visit to England early in 1885, give some insight into the method of operating the farm. The company's operation was unique for its time, in that it was carried on with all the refinements of big business. Like the factory system of mass production, large amounts of land, labor, and capital were combined, and this labor needed no farming experience, since qualified overseers directed each phase of the operation. The farm was broken into five divisions. Each section within a division was further subdivided into three equal portions of 213 acres. On each 213-acre allotment was placed a cottage, stable, and granary, plus three horses, ploughs, wagon, and self-binder. This force, however, proved insufficient to crop the entire 213 acres in the one season, and any additions would not, it was thought, warrant the increase in the cost of production. Thus each 213-acre farm was again divided into three parts, of which two-thirds were to be sown each year and one-third left fallow. In this way the danger of exhausting the soil would be avoided, and through more thorough cultivation of the cropped portion, better yields could be expected. After seeding was completed, the farmer prepared the uncropped portion for the coming spring. In harvest time the farmer was joined by two additional laborers for stooking the grain cut by the self-binder. After this operation had been completed, the extra hands were then transferred to a threshing-machine crew. One machine was placed at the disposal of four farms, the working force of which combined to thresh their respective crops. Threshing completed, the farmer then began preparation of one-half of the area from which he had raised his crop. This, along with the portion ploughed between seeding and harvest, made up the acreage required for the ensuing season's operations.

51

In his interview with the *Pall Mall Gazette,* Major Bell expressed confidence in the enterprise, and his high hopes for the future of the North-West. He also described his methods of supervising the operation. All the latest innovations were used, and not the least important of these as far as Bell was concerned was the telephone. The telephone enabled him to command the entire operation from the main farm. And command it he did as the following remarks would indicate: ". . . every man must carry out my orders, right or wrong; if he does not, off he goes." Again, in reference to his foremen, "Local matters are left to them; imperial concerns are reserved for me at my telephone." On the completion of the day's work, the foreman received individual reports from the men employed in each division as to the daily progress, the hours worked, and supplies needed. The foreman in turn relayed this information to Bell. "The telephone," Bell explained, "enables us to annihilate space, machinery, to economize labor."

As for any large business, Bell considered the keeping of adequate records an absolute necessity. Thorough accounting methods were used on the farm, for as a corporate enterprise the farm could only continue operations if it showed a profit. Indeed to Bell, bookkeeping was not merely desirable, but perhaps the most important of all the farm's operations. "Why, it is the conclusion," he said, "of the whole matter. Depend upon it that in these days farming can only be made to pay by being placed on a thorough business basis." Therefore it is not surprising that the cost of production was carefully recorded. In determining the net profit per acre, labor and maintenance and a depreciation of twenty percent on stock and implements were counted. The amount for maintenance included such items as repairs to machinery and feed for the stock. All things considered, Bell estimated the cost of raising a bushel of wheat to be thirty-four cents, which did not, however, include the cost of delivering the grain to market. Each evening, following the receipt of the foremen's reports, the Bell farm became "one vast bookkeeping establishment." The headquarters staff then undertook the tabulation of these daily reports into weekly, monthly, and annual returns. All told, there were twenty-seven main entries, such as wheat, implements, flax, oats, roots, telephone, wood, and so on. These entries were further broken down into three sub-entries: Man, Maintenance, and Horse. This last process involved the apportioning of each expenditure thus summarized, either to capital account or to the three staples, wheat, flax, and oats. It was then an easy step for Major Bell to determine the cost of production by dividing these totals by the output. According to a "Labor Return" which appears with the interview, the expenditure in 1883-1884 on wheat included $6,913.77 for men, $2,892.37 for mainte-nance, and $3,072.50 for horses, while for "Implements" the outlay was $952.42 for men, $330.94 for maintenance, and $17.00 for horses.

The information that Major Bell was obtaining from his bookkeeping must have been somewhat disturbing, for indifferent crops in 1883 and 1884, squatters' claims, and unforeseen financial outlays for current undertakings and new developments soon were to place the future of the enterprise in doubt. However, in spite of the many problems confronting it, the company entered 1884 with continued optimism. In his report to the second annual meeting held in Winnipeg in January, 1884, the new president, Edgar Dewdney, Lieutenant-Governor of the North-West Territories, was able to announce the completion of many new improvements and additions to programs begun in 1882 and 1883.[18] Two barracks, cottages, a blacksmith shop, a horse infirmary, additional cottages with stables valued at $800 each, a stationary granary of 4,000 bushels capacity, and fourteen 1,000-bushel portable granaries of circular design had been added. The ambitious program of fencing, tree-planting, sinking of wells, and bridge-building had been continued, and the erection of an elevator at the railway station was under consideration. The gross expenditure in 1883 was set at $162,341.66, making the amount spent since the company's inception a total of $244,719.96.

A number of settlers anticipating the opening of the lands for homesteading had squatted on lands eventually sold by the government to the Bell farm. The refusal of the squatters to give up the lands they claimed by right of settlement had developed into a protracted dispute which created a great deal of ill will against the company. Newspapers carried conflicting reports on the situation, and there were premature announcements of the settlement of the problem. Early in 1884, *The Leader* carried a report to the effect that Mr. T. C. Johnstone, solicitor for the squatters, had succeeded in reaching a settlement with the company.[19] The squatters, sixteen in number, were to vacate their holdings and to receive from the company a cash payment sufficient to cover their interest in the lands and the improvements thereon. This value was to be set by arbitration, and the squatters were to be entitled to homesteads and pre-emptions elsewhere and to receive patents after one rather than the usual three years. J. Gordon, Dominion-lands agent, Regina in his report for 1884[20] advised the Minister of the Interior that he had visited Indian Head and had been successful in persuading the interested parties to refer the matter to arbitration. The squatters, he said, had chosen Mr. George Taylor, M.P. for Gananoque, and the company, Mr. John F. Wood, M.P. for Brockville, to represent them. The arbitrators, wrote Gordon, had visited the lands involved and had persuaded the company, and all the squatters but one, to accept a settlement under which the company would pay the squatters the actual value of their improvements. The squatters would be allowed homesteads upon any public lands open to settlement, and government approval would be sought in order that the period in which the squatters had resided on and cultivated lands within the company's tract would be credited to the requirements on their new homesteads.

On October 10, 1884, the directors of the company met to discuss the terms of the proposed settlement. The directors agreed to accept the terms of the proposed award and pay the amount to Gordon. He in turn was to pay the amount agreed on to each squatter who, by written agreement, accepted the award. One "die-hard" refused to accept the award and he was allowed to remain on the land.[21] Gordon was able to advise his minister that while in Calgary, in November, 1885, he had "partly effected a settlement of some of the Bell Farm squatters upon new locations."[22] In all, the company paid a total of $7,125 to settle the squatters' claims. This was broken down into an original payment of $2,810 and a payment of $4,315 under the terms of arbitration, the latter payment being made on November 15, 1884.[23]

Despite the unpleasantness and the difficulties created by the squatters the company continued to expand and diversify its operations during 1884. In that year an elevator, having a capacity of 50,000 bushels, was constructed, and the first load of grain was put through it on October 13, 1884.[24] The elevator, built at a cost of $12,000, was meant to serve not only the company, but the local farmers, at a charge of about two cents per bushel. Other new buildings completed during 1884 were an implement house, measuring 50 feet by 150 feet, and a large brick hotel costing $12,000.[25]

Although the newspapers reported "admirable crops" in 1883,[26] and "splendid" crops averaging thirty bushels to the acre for wheat and forty-five to fifty for oats in 1884,[27] the company was not happy with the results of the first two seasons. The company president reported that "owing to unfavorable weather, their crops have been seriously deficient during the last two seasons, and that, to add to their difficulties, the prices of cereals have ruled low."[28] The company had nearly 7,000 acres under cultivation in 1884, but an early frost had damaged a major portion of the crop, making it unfit for market.[29] By the end of 1884 the crop reverses forced the company to seek some adjustment in the terms of its original agreement with the government.

The company placed its case before H. H. Smith, inspector for Dominion lands, asking that the conditions of cultivation and settlement as imposed by the original Order-in-Council be withdrawn and that it be granted patent to the lands.[30] In return for this concession it agreed to pay the instalments of the purchase money remaining unpaid, with interest, and to carry out the original terms with respect to cultivation. Furthermore, Bell would immediately visit the United Kingdom to induce people to settle in the North-West and especially on the company's lands and also to obtain students for an agricultural college the company would establish at Indian Head. The patents to the land would enable the company to arrange mortgages so they could raise the money they needed to continue the farming operations.

In submitting the company's request to the Minister of the Interior with his recommendation that it be accepted, H. H. Smith gave a summary of the development of the farm. He pointed out that:

> ... the Company entered upon their undertaking with great energy, and up to this time have accomplished more than they undertook to perform; that the "Bell Farm" has been looked upon as the model farm of the country, and has undoubtedly done much to direct attention to the North-West Territories.[31]

Since starting farming the company had spent about $400,000 on cultivating and improvements and broken about 14,000 acres. Among the improvements were ninety buildings including houses, barns, granaries, shops, an elevator, and an hotel besides bridges and dams. The company had placed 106 settlers on its land as compared to the 72 which would have been required of a colonization company, and it had cultivated 140 percent more land than would have been required of homesteaders. The company's total investment per quarter section was $1,338 which far exceeded the value of improvements on the average homestead at the time patent was granted. The proposed agricultural college would, in Smith's opinion, prove a "valuable agent in inducing immigration" by advertising the possibilities of the country. Smith's recommendations in the company's favor met with the approval of the government, and an Order-in-Council was passed on March 2, 1885 authorizing the granting of patents to the land on the company paying the instalment money remaining unpaid, plus interest.[32]

In fulfillment of the company's promise, Major Bell went to England in March, 1885. There in a published interview[33] he was reported to have described the North-West as a veritable paradise for farmers. In his opinion the Canadian farmer had many advantages over his British counterpart, among them being the availability of cheap land, the lack of investment in manure, excellent implements at low prices, a protective tariff, and wonderful climate. To Bell the question for English farmers was "Can they hope to compete with Canadian wheat produced at a cost of 22s. to 23s. a quarter. If not why do they not come over and join us in Canada? ... The wheat trade of the world is inevitably falling into our hands." Bell concluded by discussing Britain's colonial policy as it affected Canada and suggested that "Any price ... was worth paying in order to preserve to the British Empire the granary of the world."

In the interview Bell made no reference to the proposed college, which had first been alluded to in the first annual report of the company's president and which Bell, in a letter to the Minister of the Interior on March 6, 1883, had referred to as being in operation. The college became the subject of a series of conflicting newspaper reports.

55

The editor of the *Qu'Appelle Vidette* took a cynical view of the proposed college.

> It is said that the large hotel here is to be made use of as an Agricultural College. How happy some of our farmers would be if they could only get hold of a pupil paying one hundred pounds premium and five dollars a week for his board. This college will be in connection with the Bell Farm. But a good many people seem rather doubtful whether a thorough knowledge of scientific farming is likely to be acquired on a farm of which the manager is an ex-lumber merchant, and the foreman an ex-policeman.[34]

The *Nor-West Farmer* in March, 1885 also announced that the company was considering the conversion of the farm into a college and that Major Bell was in England in the interests of the movement, and in May, 1885, the same paper reported that the necessary capital for the project had been obtained in England.[35] In April, 1886, the *Qu'Appelle Vidette* stated that it was "spoken of by many as a settled fact we are to have an agricultural college here" and added, "The news is almost too good to be true."[36] The Regina *Leader* reported that Professor Tanner of South Kensington, England, who had visited the farm in 1883, was busily engaged in locating the college at Indian Head,[37] but in August, 1886, the *Qu'Appelle Vidette* asked the question "Where is Professor Tanner? He is long past due."[38] The proposed college remained just that. As it transpired, any need for the company to honor this undertaking may have been removed by the action of the Anglican Diocese of Qu'Appelle in founding St. John's College at Qu'Appelle in 1885. This institution, with the same objective of training young men from the old country in prairie agriculture, was in operation in 1885.[39]

Early in 1885 the company announced that a contract for a grist mill had been awarded.[40] By March the lumber had arrived from Winnipeg, and the mill complex, including a brick engine room measuring sixteen feet by twenty-four feet, a shipping house measuring sixteen feet by forty feet by ten feet, and the mill itself, measuring thirty-six feet by forty-eight feet and four storeys high, opened for business in June, 1885. The honor of owning the first public grist to be ground into flour went to Chief Jack of the Assiniboine band located south of Indian Head.[41]

The hopes for renewed development in 1885 were shattered by the North-West Rebellion. The outbreak of fighting disturbed a good deal of the plans for continued expansion. A number of teams used for working the farm were placed on military transportation services, Bell himself was in the field, and the farming operations were largely neglected once the conflict began. It is inconceivable, of course, that Bell acted without the company's approval, and there is evidence to indicate that Bell served both its interests and his own. In any event, Bell was actively engaged as a Transport and Supply Officer and as a contractor. Appointed to the former position by Major General Middleton, effective April 1, 1885, Bell received $5 a day, for a total of $610, on termination of his pay on July 31, 1885.[42]

As a transport contractor, Bell was active as a partner in Bell, Lewis, and Company. During the rebellion this firm transported a total of 834 tons and 642 pounds of supplies from Troy to such points as Touchwood, Houghton, Humboldt, and Clarke's Crossing, for which it received $108,161.46.[43] The company, whose address was given as Lachine, Quebec, also received a cheque in the amount of $1,474.57 from the Commission on War Claims, for services not included in the above settlement. This figure was the net amount of the claim after the commission had deducted charges for rations and forage supplied to the company by the government.[44] The Qu'Appelle Valley Farming Company was also involved in transport services, according to the *Qu'Appelle Vidette,* which stated that the company's claim against the government for transport services was about $34,000, an amount which was separate from the claims of Bell individually or of Bell, Lewis, and Company.[45]

The involvement of Bell and of the company in the rebellion had jeopardized the future of the enterprise. In his letter to the Minister of the Interior in November, 1885, Boyle wrote,

> I regret to say, the outbreak . . . occurring in March last, just prior to seeding time, withdrew from work on the Bell Farm, the chief portion of the staff of working power in men and horses, and in consequence, the Company were able to cultivate and crop only a small portion of the land ready for seeding, thereby entailing a most serious loss on lands upon which a large sum of money had been spent in preparation the preceding season, a loss more fully apparent from the statement hereinafter made.[46]

In the statement which followed he advised the minister that the expected immigration in 1885 had been delayed by the unsettled conditions, that only about 1,000 acres were put into crop, out of an intended 8,000 acres, and that much of the remaining 7,000 acres of lands plowed at a cost of $30,000.00 had reverted to their natural state. As the profit on the cropped acreage had averaged $6.40 per acre, Boyle placed the total loss at little short of $45,000.00 on the farming operation, and even by offsetting this loss by the profit on transport services, the company, he said, had still lost $25,000.00.

Boyle went on to review the misfortunes which had beset the company since its inception. He drew to the minister's attention the difficulties the company had experienced with the railway company. Under the original agreement the railway lands, totalling 29,111 acres, were to be purchased at $1.25 per acre, the same price as the government lands. However, Boyle said, following the company's entrance on the

*Harvesting, Bell Farm*

lands, the Canadian Pacific Railway Company had forced it to pay "a much enhanced price for a large block of their lands known as sections reserved within the mile belt." Under these new terms, the company had already paid the sum of $65,440.00, but before granting title, the railway company was demanding an additional $9,881.00.[47] This meant a total payment of $75,321.00, instead of the $36,389.00 originally agreed to, and thus a loss of $38,932.00, which sum Boyle stated, would have enabled his company to cultivate an additional 7,000 or 8,000 acres.

In addition to the payment to the railway company, Boyle stated that the company had paid the government $5,120.00 for section 24, township 18, range 13, the Indian Head townsite, which land was originally within the tract taken possession of on April 29, 1882; $7,125.00 to squatters; and the first two instalments to the government, in the amount of $13,244.21. It is clear from the foregoing that the company had been unable to conform to the conditions as set out in the Order-in-Council dated March 2, 1885 and thus had not been able to acquire the patents for the land. Obviously the patents were needed so the company could mortgage the land, as Boyle wrote: "We must have money to go on with and we can raise it only on our land. To do this we must have title and unless this be given without further expenditure we must stop." In beginning his letter Boyle had remarked, "I have to meet the shareholders of my company early next month, and a very great deal will depend, as to our future operations, upon the decision you may arrive at." The company was obviously in a desperate financial position.

Within a year the government granted the application of the company for patents to the land acquired from the Crown, and titles were issued to the company in the period October 26, 1886 to April 16, 1887.[48]

In the spring of 1886 the principals in the company had been able to secure a mortgage from Winnipeg financiers,[49] and it is likely that this capital, together with the proceeds of the sale of the Indian Head townsite to the Canada Northwest Land Company,[50] enabled the company to settle with the government and to finance farming operations during 1886.

The refinancing program in 1886 was apparently facilitated by a manoeuvre which involved the formation of a new company, the Bell Farm Company Limited, with Winnipeg as its chief place of business. It was incorporated under the Canada Joint Stock Companies Act on May 19, 1886, with a capitalization of $475,000. Included among the corporate members of the new company were William Robert Bell and Herman Joseph Eberts, two of the major shareholders in the original company, and William Lewis Boyle, who had been its president in 1885. The stated objects of the new company paralleled to a marked degree the objects of the Qu'Appelle Valley Farming Company.[51] In a indenture dated July 21, 1886,[52] the old company conveyed all, or most, of the Bell farm to the new company, comprising not less than 40,000 acres of farmland together with the lots still held in the Indian Head townsite, including the mill, mill office, and elevator situated thereon, all for the consideration of $1.[53] A later statement indicates that the Bell Farm Company acquired all the horses, machinery, and other property, and assumed the liabilities, of the old company, which thereupon ceased to have any "real or personal interest" in the North-West Territories.[54] The principal liability assumed by the new company was the mortgage to Lord Elphinstone and his Scottish associates to secure $150,000 of debentures,[55] which had been obtained all, or in part, as early as 1884.[56] A meeting of the shareholders of the Bell Farm Company Limited, held in Winnipeg on August 7, 1886, approved a by-law enabling the company to issue $50,000 of debentures and to pledge certain properties in repayment thereof.[57] This amount, and the lands involved, were set forth in an indenture entered into on the same day, between the company and Messrs. Arthur F. Eden and Joseph B. McArthur of Winnipeg.[58] Signing on behalf of the company were William Lewis Boyle, president, and H. J. Eberts, secretary-treasurer. The new company, saddled with the combined mortgage debt amounting to $200,000, would require most favorable conditions to succeed, but these were not forthcoming, and financial difficulties continued to plague the enterprise.

At intervals, in the period 1886-1888, the *Qu'Appelle Vidette* reported that the farming staff had been reduced but that back salaries had been paid and everybody was happy,[59] that a number of the farm's horses had been seized directly from the equipment to which they were harnessed,[60] that Major Bell had brought "part of $38,000 with him" and would pay all hands, ending "an awful lot of growling,"[61] that the farm employees had been out on strike and many were now jobless,[62] that following a "hasty" visit by one of the company's directors back wages would be paid immediately,[63] and, finally, that "Some time ago the directors sent word to discharge all the men employed on the farm, and that they would no longer be responsible for their wages."[64] The general tenor of the *Qu'Appelle Vidette's* reports is supported by court records. Major Bell and the new company were frequently involved in litigation, usually in the role of defendants. During 1888 the company was sued by local tradesmen to whom it was indebted for repairs and other sundries, by laborers for back wages, and by banks for recovery of loans.[65] In April of that year the sheriff, acting on writs of execution issued on behalf of several creditors, seized a wide range of chattels, among them forty-one binders, sixty "Giant" engines, six separators, thirty-eight seeders, twenty-one sulky and fourteen gang ploughs, nineteen disk harrows, forty-seven spring tooth harrows, thirty-eight wagons, and 140 cords of wood.[66] This action was the beginning of the break-up of the Bell Farm Company, which was completed the following year.

On April 11, 1889, the Supreme Court of the North-West Territories ordered that the Bell Farm Company Limited be wound up under provision of the Winding Up Act and appointed a liquidator.[67] The same order confirmed that the Qu'Appelle Valley Farming Company was already in liquidation. In the process it is evident that both Major Bell and William Lewis Boyle acquired sizeable portions of the company's lands. Just when Bell started farming in his own right is not clear, but he may have commenced in 1888, perhaps under an agreement of sale or lease from the company. Certainly he severed his connections with the Bell Farm Company, as its general manager, in the spring of 1888 and filed suit against the company for recovery of moneys owing him. In his statement, Bell claimed $6,371.47 comprised of salary owing him while general manager of the farm from August 1, 1886 to April 3, 1888 and for promissory notes issued to him by the company and its predecessor in 1885 and 1886.[68] The company did not defend the action and the court rendered judgement in favor of Bell in the amount of the claim. Apparently Bell was able to enter into some arrangement with the company which permitted him to commence farming on his own account in 1888.[69] The size of Bell's own farm was said to be 13,000 acres in 1888,[70] although another account, seemingly exaggerated or possibly only an inversion of figures, stated that the major had purchased 31,000 acres.[71] Years later the *Winnipeg Free Press* reported that more than half the company's holdings had been purchased in 1890 by the English syndicate headed by Lord Brassey and that the balance of the farm had been rented by Major Bell, who in 1891 "extended his possessions by purchasing about 14,000 acres from the company, which then ceased to exist."[72]

More precise light on the timing of the disposition of the Bell Farm Company's lands, following its entry into liquidation in 1889, is revealed through an examination of land titles. William Lewis Boyle, late president of the Bell Farm Company, cited as a banker of New York City, acquired 17,436 acres of land from the company for payment of one dollar, assuming at the same time the mortgage of $50,000 owing Arthur F. Eden *et al.* He registered title thereto, October 22, 1889, but transferred to the Canadian Co-operative Colonization Company Limited title to some fourteen sections thereof within a month, on November 11, 1889.[73] Major Bell acquired approximately 19,700 acres from the company or its Scottish creditors which were registered to him on May 31, 1890 but he on the same day transferred title to some 7,000 acres to the Canadian Co-operative Colonization Company.[74] The latter company, which had acquired land from both Boyle and Bell, was founded by Lord Brassey, to whose name title to these lands was eventually transferred in 1895.[75] No attempt has been made to trace the subsequent disposal of the lands still held by Boyle. Major Bell in 1890 was owner of at least 12,700 acres, albeit they were encumbered by the mortgage to Lord Elphinstone and Sir George Warrender, the Scottish associates, for $143,500.[76] Whether or not Bell acquired or leased other Bell Farm Company land has not been ascertained but the established 12,700 acres, located north of the Canadian Pacific Railway tracks and virtually surrounding the town of Indian Head, is fairly close to the acreage suggested in the above press reports and offered at auction in 1896 when the farm was closed out.[77]

Thus, for the last six or seven years, the Bell farm, once an incorporated enterprise, was the personal operation of the man who had been its promoter and general manager. Greatly reduced in size, it was still of bonanza proportions and still fated to lose money, although there was some respite in the initial stages. According to the *Western World*,[78] in 1888 Bell raised a wheat crop averaging twenty-seven bushels to the acre on the 2,100 acres under crop, which, selling at $1.05 a bushel, netted him $20.00 an acre clear profit. In 1889, a dry year, only 1,000 acres were seeded, with the wheat yielding an average of nineteen bushels per acre. Perhaps it was the weather which deserved the criticism, but in 1889, the editor of the *Farmers' Advocate* visited the farm and later wrote:

> The Bell Farm shows up to poor advantage this year. A great deal of grain has been sown twice on stubble land, and it, without exception is very poor. I saw a number of eastern farmers who were so discouraged after seeing Mr. Bell's crop that they have gone back home again without buying. This is a case where the fault rests entirely with the farming; for, wherever the grain was sown on summer fallowed land the crops are good.[79]

Although 1890 saw the farm yield an average of twenty-three bushels of wheat per acre on 1,700 seeded acres, the abandonment of the summerfallowing program which, as general manager of the original company, Bell had instituted as early as 1883 is perhaps symptomatic of the various difficulties which had beset the farm from the beginning.

Beginning in 1891 Major Bell's plans included the placing of families in their cottages which stood on each 200 acres. Under this system Bell hoped to employ thirty-five to fifty men under his direct supervision and further to diversify his operations by breeding Clydesdale horses from the stock he had already shipped in from Scotland.[80]

With the beginning of his own venture, Bell appeared to find more time to engage in outside activities. He was a consistent winner of prizes at the Indian Head Agricultural Society's annual show, particularly in the heavy-draught-horses class, and at the shoots held in conjunction with the annual meetings of the Assiniboia Rifle Association. Bell also found time to star in cricket matches and to engage in politics. For a period of years he held the position of president of the Indian Head Liberal Conservative Association and the same position with the Indian Head Board of Trade after its formation in 1893. He was also president of the Assiniboia Rifle Association, a position to which he was re-elected in November of 1895, the year in which it is often said he left the area.

It would seem that Bell's fortunes were on the upswing after he began in 1888 to farm on his own. Good crops for a few years got him off to an encouraging start. But the misfortune which seemed to follow his farming efforts struck again in 1893, when a fire destroyed the elevator, office, engine house, flour mill, and a carload of ties belonging to the Bell farm. In addition, the fire destroyed 1,400 bags of flour and 1,300 bushels of wheat. Of the loss, set at $25,000, only $4,000 was covered by insurance.[81] This setback was followed in 1894 by one of the worst crop years in the area's history, a drop in wheat prices to thirty-five cents in 1895, and the death of his first wife on October 14, 1895.[82] Whether it was financial difficulty or the effect of the hard blows he had suffered in the previous two years is not known, but it was probably a combination of both which was responsible for the events which took place in 1896.

On February 8, 1896 the Scottish investors filed, in the Supreme Court of the North-West Territories, a statement of claim against William Robert Bell in the amount of $124,810.33, for settlement of the loan assumed by Bell in May, 1890.[83] Bell did not contest this action, and on April 4, 1896 the court awarded judgement of $124,131.99 to the plaintiffs.[84] With this award, the Scottish investors and other creditors[85] who had been issued writs of execution against Bell proceeded to seize and dispose of Bell's property. On May 30, 1896, property consisting of seventy-three horses, thirteen cattle, an elevator, and household furniture went on the auction block.[86] The local paper and the people of the district welcomed the breaking up of Bell's holdings. They claimed the action would benefit the town and district by enabling small farms to be established.[87] The sale of goods was followed, in the fall, by notices of land sales. The advertisement in the *Qu'Appelle Vidette,* September 10, 1896, was captioned, "Mortgage Sale of Valuable Farm Property Commonly Known as the Bell Farm." It listed approximately 13,000 acres of land for sale, the offer being repeated in the December 10, 1896 edition. The ultimate disposition of this land has not been traced, but it appears that the creditors did not recover their investment at least until 1903, when the writs were returned to the court.[88] It is clear, however, that Bell's farming operations at Indian Head had come to an end in the spring of 1896, and therewith ended a chapter in the history of prairie agriculture. The extent of Bell's personal losses has not been ascertained, and it is not known if he recovered anything from the debacle of 1896. He probably had other resources upon which to fall back.[89] For a time he was reported to be in eastern Canada,[90] but eventually he settled in Winnipeg where he died in 1913.

As a business venture the Bell farm had proved a failure. Had it survived only a few years longer, rising prices, wetter years, improved varieties of grain, and the general buoyancy of the wheat-boom period might have enabled it to realize the financial expectations of its promoters. Undoubtedly it retarded settlement within the area it encompassed, but this was a temporary disadvantage which was probably offset by the number of settlers it attracted through the international attention it focussed on the area. It had provided valuable facilities for the Indian Head district, especially the grain elevator and flour mill at a time when they were sorely needed. The settlement pattern it proposed, of many farm laborers employed on a "bonanza" estate, was not welcomed in the district and did not become popular or successful elsewhere in the region. It should be noted that some of the employees brought in by the company were numbered among the most successful permanent settlers of Indian Head.[91] In its initial success the Bell farm had demonstrated the fertility and productivity of the prairie soil when this fact was still little recognized in the outside world. It had also demonstrated the advantage of summerfallowing as a dry-farming technique. While it illustrated some of the problems inherent in large-scale operations, in its extensive employment of heavy machinery and its concentration on wheat production it portended future successful trends in Saskatchewan agriculture.

# 5 Yorkton During the Territorial Period, 1882-1905

*by Jane McCracken*

THREE important phases in the evolution of Canada's National Policy directly affected the early history of Yorkton. In an attempt both to defray the debts incurred in the construction of the Canadian Pacific Railway and to help populate the vacant North-West lands, the Prime Minister, John A. Macdonald, introduced the colonization-company scheme into the government's National Policy. One of the colonization companies, the York Farmers' Colonization Company, had its land reserve in north-eastern Assiniboia. Despite the company's endeavors to inject life into its reserve, York Colony floundered. Realizing that the colonization-company scheme was a failure, Macdonald felt that colonization railroads would serve as the means by which the government could fulfill its dream of a populous West.*

The future of Yorkton and York Colony was dependent upon the completion of the colonization railroad, the Manitoba and North Western Railway, to the hamlet. Once the track was completed to Yorkton in 1889, the effect the railway had on the growth of Yorkton is notable. As the terminus of the Manitoba and North Western Railway, Yorkton attracted a small trickle of pioneers, and in 1894, Yorkton reached village status. Following the adoption of new, vigorous immigration policies by the Department of the Interior, thousands of immigrants flocked to the Canadian West at the turn of the century. The pattern of their settlement was dictated by the railroads and Yorkton became the distribution point for thousands of Ukrainian and Doukhobor immigrants. The village grew and prospered from the business gained through the influx of immigrants, and in 1900, Yorkton was incorporated into a town. The unceasing flow of immigrants into the Yorkton area doubled the population of Yorkton within the first five years of the twentieth century.

To weld the country into a viable economic unit, the Prime Minister

---

*This article originally appeared in *Saskatchewan History* for autumn, 1975.

pivoted his government's national policy around a transcontinental railway line. Macdonald perceived that the railway would serve a dual purpose. Besides linking British Columbia with the eastern provinces, it would traverse the wide prairies, opening the land for settlement. The ratification of the contract with the Canadian Pacific syndicate in February, 1881 necessitated new land regulations which divided the land into four belts. The even-numbered sections in all four areas were open for homesteads and pre-emptions; the odd-numbered sections in class A could be purchased from the Canadian Pacific Railway. The odd-numbered sections in classes B, C, and D sold at prices ranging from $2.50 an acre to $2.00 an acre.

The construction of the Canadian Pacific Railway engendered great interest among Ontario businessmen. Expectations of a massive rush for land led to wild speculation in business enterprises, and when Macdonald let it be known that the government would set aside land reserves in belt D for corporations willing to promote the settlement of the land, the Prime Minister's office was flooded with applications. The land regulations of December 23, 1881 stipulated that the land would be sold to the colonization companies at $2 an acre, to be paid in five equal annual instalments. The companies had to settle two colonists on both the odd- and even-numbered sections of their respective reserves within five years. If a company fulfilled its contract, it was granted a rebate of $120 on the purchase price for each bona fide settler. As an additional bonus, the company was promised a further rebate of $40 for each bona fide settler if the tract was settled within the five-year period. In locating two settlers on each section, a company earned a rebate of $1 per acre, which reduced its purchasing price by a dollar.[1] The odd-numbered sections, then, could be sold at prices ranging from $3 to $20 per acre.[2]

The opposition press and party were very critical of the colonization-company scheme. However Macdonald was confident that the scheme would be a success. As land in the American Mid-West was taken up, the flow of immigration would be diverted into the Territories. The Prime Minister was equally confident that the scheme would defray the expenses incurred by the Canadian Pacific Railway.

> By this year, there will be 10,000,000 acres granted to colonization companies, ... which means the eventual payment of $10,000,000 into the Treasury besides the proceeds of such other casual sales as are made during this year. So that in one year we may fairly say we have got half of the whole $25,000,000 that we are pledged to pay the Canadian Pacific Railway.[3]

The colonization companies would act in much the same way as the railway companies had in the United States, which Macdonald asserted were "the best immigration agents."[4]

65

However, the enthusiasm displayed by businessmen for the scheme slowly dissipated. The contracts that the companies had to sign with the government dictated strict duties to the companies. Discouraged, many investors dropped out of the scheme. The companies then began to encounter difficulty in raising enough money to meet the first instalment payment. The dwindling enthusiasm for the scheme was made apparent when only 27 of the 106 companies were able to meet the deadline.

One of the companies which was able to meet the first instalment payment was the York Farmers' Colonization Company. In March, 1882, a small group of eleven men met in Toronto to organize a colonization company. Confident that a great deal of money could be made, the directors of the York Farmers' sought also to open the virgin North-West to the land-hungry farmers of York County in the Toronto area. Hoping that the Ontario farmers would be attracted by land that reminded them of Ontario, the York Farmers' Colonization Company applied for a land reserve in the parkland region of the district of Assiniboia. York Colony, as the company called its tract, consisted of townships 22, 23, and 27 in range 2; townships 25, 26, and 27 in range 3; and township 26 in ranges 4 and 5, west of the second meridian.

Soon after the York Farmers' received its tract, the company made appeals to those living in south-western Ontario, and in the spring of 1882, the managing director of the York Farmers', James Armstrong, accompanied J. J. Smith, W. F. Smith, William Meredith, and C. J. MacFarline to York Colony. These first pioneers were soon followed by seven additional men from Ontario. These settlers spent the summer building some type of shelter for the winter and clearing the required ten acres of land as stipulated by the homestead law. Some homesteaded near York City, the capital of the colony, while others took up homesteads in the Wallace district.

With the coming of winter, most of the settlers returned to Ontario. Only five men decided to remain in the colony that first winter. No doubt that first winter was a trying one. Isolated from the rest of the world, the five survived on a diet of flour, oatmeal, tea, syrup, dried apples, and some salt pork. After the long winter, two of the five men set out for Fort Ellice to replenish their depleted supplies.

During the winter months, the York Farmers' Colonization Company had been busy preparing pamphlets and booklets advertising York Colony. The company offered easy terms of payment for purchasers of an odd-numbered section and claimed that the prospective settler would be choosing his land in an already settled and prosperous tract. The advertisement of the York Farmers' painted both York Colony and York City in glowing terms. The company claimed that York City already had been established and could offer the colonist everything he needed from a general store, to hotels, post offices, and hardware stores. The company

66

continued with promises of the early completion of a saw mill, grist mill, a brickyard, a church, and a school. However, the settlers arriving in the colony in 1883 must have been surprised to discover that the company had exaggerated conditions in York City. York City, in fact, had little to offer the settler. Instead of the developed nucleus of a town, the pioneers "only found a station house and a primitive tent for a store."[5] However, by the end of 1883, the efforts of both the company and the settlers were beginning to show signs of bearing fruit. A. E. Boake established an emporium for agricultural implements and Joel Reaman built the Queen's Hotel, a combined stopping house and general store.

Unquestionably influenced by the company's advertising campaign, an encouraging number of land seekers arrived in the colony in the late spring of 1883, augmenting the number of settlers in the colony to 158. The York Farmers' Company established a ferry across the Qu'Appelle River, and a stagecoach brought a weekly mail delivery to the colony. Cash advances were made to the settlers, and the company employed settlers to haul freight from the Canadian Pacific Railway[6] for the dam and proposed grist mill. The York Farmers' also intended, as soon as the town plot was surveyed, "to make free deed to each bona fide settler . . . of a building lot . . . the conveyance to be perfected when the settler had completed his homesteading obligations as required by law."[7]

By the autumn of 1883, the speculative fever that had caught the imagination of the businessmen declined, and it was obvious that depression had returned once again. The westward movement of settlers almost came to a halt and despair reigned among the colonization companies; it was clear that the companies would not reap the lucrative profits they had initially anticipated. The York Farmers' Colonization Company then hoped to recuperate some of its financial outlay by improving York Colony to make it attractive enough to retain those pioneers already settled there. Nevertheless, deterioration in morale was apparent. Economic difficulties led to a modest degeneration of the harmony which had characterized the relationship of the company and the settlers at York Colony. The company became involved in two lawsuits with the settlers and in one of these the company was the plaintiff.

In a memorandum to the Minister of the Interior in 1884, James Armstrong enumerated three reasons for the failure of the York Farmers' to attract more settlers and to retain those colonists who had already settled in York Colony. The morale of the farmers was lowered when the crop of 1884 again suffered from early frosts, and the settlers, for the third consecutive year, were forced to buy seed grain for the next year's crop. Armstrong also did not hesitate to point out that York Colony could not survive without railway facilities. But with the failure of the Canadian Pacific Railway to build a branch line and with the main line situated as it was, seventy miles south of the colony, York Colony was doomed to stagnation. However, the managing director was most critical of the opening of the even-numbered sections in the Mile Belt for homestead entries. Situated near the railway line, these homesteads were being occupied by the small trickle of settlers who moved to the North-West.

Despite all the troubles and setbacks that the York Farmers' had suffered during the previous two years, the company looked forward to the 1885 season, hoping for a steady increase in immigration to the North-West. But these hopes were soon dashed by the outbreak of the Métis Rebellion in 1885. Frightened, the colonists at York Colony demanded protection against the Indians from the nearby reserves. The Minister of the Milita sent Major T. C. Watson to Yorkton to organize a home guard and to build a stockade. The York Farmers' Colonization Company again demonstrated its concern and interest in the settlers and in the future of Yorkton, by donating three town lots for the stockade. The enclosure, christened Fort Watson, was a proper stockade in every respect, having an inner sod embankment, four bastions, loopholes for the rifles, and an outer ditch.[8]

Although the feared Indian attack never materialized, the home guard had two encounters with the Indians. The first occurred on April 20 when Little Bones' band pitched camp on the Little White Sand River opposite Fort Watson. Major Watson offered them tobacco, tea, and pork, which the Indians accepted. When Major Watson refused to give the Indians more supplies the Indians began to raid a few of the settlers' homes. The home guard then marched to the Indians' new camp on Cussed Creek and persuaded the Indians to return to their reserves, after promising them provisions from Reaman's store. By June, the Yorkton area appeared quiet and Major Watson returned to Ottawa.

The morale of the settlers was lowered further in 1885 when drought and early frosts ruined the chances of a good crop. Armstrong felt that it was the company's responsibility to improve the colony to make it attractive for the settlers. The grist mill, which was ready for operation in 1886, was an important part of the company's plan of retrenchment. But because of the poor harvests, the grain was not a marketable commodity.

The York Farmers', by the end of 1885, was in deep despair. The rebellion drastically affected immigration to the prairies; the number of homestead entries throughout the North-West dropped from 3,753 in 1884 to 1,858 the next year. The rebellion proved to be the climax to numerous setbacks and put the finishing touches on the government's fruitless first attempt to have the northern part of the Territories developed by land companies. Rather than attempt further colonization of their tracts, the various colonization companies became more interested in extracting from the government the best possible cancellation of their settlement commitments. As early as the autumn of 1884, the company directors had met in Toronto to discuss mutual problems and had drawn up a draft petitioning the government for relief from their colonizing duties. The companies requested a reduction of a dollar on the purchase price of two dollars per acre for the odd-numbered sections, plus patents for land in proportion to the expenditures of the companies.[9]

With the outbreak of the rebellion, the companies increased the pressure on the Minister of the Interior, D. L. Macpherson, for a satisfactory settlement, but negotiations floundered over the price of the land. Then, in July, 1885, the acting minister, A. W. McLelan, suggested that the colonization companies be divided into two groups — those which did little to attract settlers or develop their tracts and those companies which had made an honest attempt to fulfill their settlement duties. Of those companies in the latter classification, only seven companies had brought out more than 50 settlers,[10] the York Farmers' Colonization Company, with 164 settlers in York Colony, being the most successful.

Meanwhile, Macpherson resigned as the Minister of the Interior, and the new minister, Thomas White, kept the colonization companies waiting for another year. He finally decided that the purchase price should be left at $2 an acre for all companies, but that those companies in the second category should be allowed a rebate of $160 per bona fide settler and should be given credit for the expenses incurred in the development of the reserves. This credit could be applied to the purchase of land at the rate of $2 per acre. On December 22, 1887, the York Farmers' was granted 51,358 acres chosen from the unoccupied odd-numbered sections within the colony.[11]

The essential reason for the failure of the colonization companies and the York Farmers' in particular lies with the failure of the government to build branch railway lines. The Canadian Pacific syndicate received thousands of square miles on either side of its proposed track, effectively cutting off the reserves of the colonization companies from direct access to the only railway line. The companies' tracts, situated as they were, could have been successful only if there had been a steady and heavy influx of immigration. The few settlers who did venture to the North-West, though, homesteaded near the railway once the Mile Belt was opened. Without settlers, the colonization companies were economic abortions.

As early as 1879, Macdonald had recognized the value of the colonization railroad policy, but such a policy was not seriously entertained until 1883, when it was evident that the colonization companies could not fulfill the objective of the Prime Minister. The

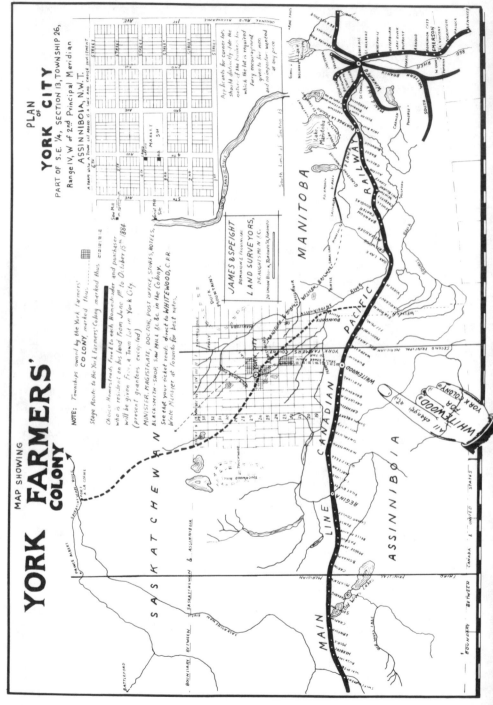

Deputy Minister of the Interior, in 1879, had recommended that the sale of land in Belt E at the purchase price of a dollar an acre to the colonization railroads would prove to be of mutual advantage to both the government and the railroads.[12] However, the colonization railroads soon began to harass Ottawa for free land grants, such as the Canadian Pacific Railway had received, in lieu of their purchase price of one dollar per acre. Under pressure, Ottawa finally agreed to grant 6,400 acres of land to the railway companies for each mile of track laid.[13] Although such a land-grant system could have produced admirable results, it proved only to be a cheap method by which the railway companies could extract lands from the government. These lands, all too often, were held by the railways for speculation. The worst offense, though, was the persistence of the railroads in demanding North-West lands for Manitoba railway mileage; more than half the acreage granted to the colonization railways lay in the Territories, although less than 24.4 percent of the track was laid in the North-West.[14]

The Portage and Westbourne and North Western Railway Company planned to run a line from Portage la Prairie to Prince Albert, which entitled the company to a very large land reserve enveloping the Yorkton area. (In May, 1883, the railway changed its name to the Manitoba and North Western Railway Company.) The free land reserve earned by the company, however, was not enough to secure financial success and the company harassed Ottawa with appeals for relief. Although the contract stipulated that fifty miles of track had to be laid each year, these appeals resulted in either an extension in time for railway construction or a reduction of the annual mileage to only twenty miles of track. Eventually, only 225 miles of track were completed, 52.59 miles of which lay in the Territories. The company, however, received 71.7 percent of its land grant in the North-West Territories.[15]

Although the Manitoba and North Western Railway reached Minnedosa in 1883, it was not until 1888 that the railway reached Saltcoats, sixteen miles southeast of Yorkton. In debt, the officials of the railway decided to halt construction of the line and make Saltcoats a divisional point. The directors of the York Farmers' Colonization Company, who had considerable interests in Yorkton and in the surrounding district, applied pressure on the railway officials to have the line extended to Yorkton. The railroad was surveyed and graded as far as Yorkton, but in the summer of 1889 the Manitoba and North Western Railway diverted its track four miles south-west of Yorkton. Unfortunately, the cause of this diversion of the line is unknown.[16]

Yorkton, like all other frontier settlements, desperately needed transportation and communication lines to connect it to the main line of the Canadian Pacific Railway. The citizens of Yorkton were aware of the importance of the Manitoba and the North Western Railway to the

71

future of the community and realized that Yorkton could not survive the four-mile diversion. A few shrewd businessmen felt that it would be more expedient to move the townsite south to the railway tracks, than to try to force the unnatural relationship of the hamlet to the railway. The first to move from Yorkton to the railway tracks was John Thorton, who established a general store there. Others, realizing that direct access to the railway line was necessary, soon followed. Donald Livingstone built a rival general store and John Mann established a livery stable just east of Thorton's store. The first hotel was owned and built by Thomas Ruttle, who also established a machine shop in the new community. All these businesses were located on Front Street which ran parallel to the tracks.

With the establishment of Broadway Avenue, which ran west off Front Street, men of enterprise and ambition located along the second business street. Thomas Collacott established a blacksmith shop on the south side of Broadway and later, in 1895, established a hardware store on the corner of Broadway and Third Avenue. George Betts built a second livery stable and feed barn on the corner of Broadway and First Avenue. J. J. Smith built the first lime kiln near the new townsite; he then built a brickyard, a general store on Argyle Street, and a grist mill on Front Street. William Dunlop was appointed Deputy Clerk of the District Court in Yorkton in 1890. Later, he established a farm-machinery-and-implement shop and was able to build up a large real-estate business. But by far the most enterprising and ambitious businessman was Yorkton's "merchant prince," Levi Beck. When he moved to Yorkton in 1889, he and his wife established a boarding house. This small enterprise was the beginning of his "empire." Over the next two decades, he established an implement store, a butcher shop, a general store, a harness shop, a confectionary, a bake shop, a lumberyard, and a flour and feed business.

Hoping to avoid the drought and early frosts of the prairie regions, a small trickle of pioneers moved northwards along the Manitoba and North Western Railway to the parkland belt of Assiniboia. The railway, with Yorkton as its terminus for fifteen years, had an immediate impact on the settlement. At a public meeting held in the schoolhouse on Argyle Street on July 15, 1894, it was announced that Yorkton had reached village status.[17] The pressure for municipal incorporation came from the citizens, who, accustomed to the municipal system as they had known it in Ontario, demanded the adoption of the same in Yorkton.

Over the next few years, a civic consciousness grew among the citizens of Yorkton. Convinced that Yorkton had a prosperous future, men such as J. H. Nelson, W. P. Hopkins, Dr. T. A. Patrick, J. J. Smith, William Simpson, Thomas Collacott, and others all contributed actively in the discussions and decisions made at the annual meetings. Drainage

*Livingstone Street and Broadway Avenue, Yorkton, 1900*

ditches were dug; all street and road crossings were graded and gravelled; the nuisance grounds were established outside the village limits; and three ladders and two dozen buckets were acquired for protection against fire.

There were other indications to suggest the development of the village. The first church structure in Yorkton was the Methodist church, built in 1893. Later, in 1899, the trustees of the Methodist church felt that the growing membership demanded a larger building. Also in 1893, the Presbyterians decided to build their own church. The Anglicans shared religious services with the Presbyterians until 1897 when they felt their membership was large enough to support a separate church. The Baptists, however, did not have a regular church building. The first services were held in a tent in 1897 and, later, in a hall over a store on Broadway Avenue. In 1896, the first printed weekly newspaper, the *Yorkton Enterprise,* was established by James Peaker. And in 1898, thirty-eight businessmen met to form the Yorkton District Board of Trade to encourage immigration to and industry in the village.

The stimulus that the village received from the Manitoba and North Western Railway was also reflected in the development of the Yorkton district. Although the settlers in the 1800's had hoped to establish grain farms, natural disasters such as early frosts, drought, and gophers led to discouragement. The farmers, though, learned to diversify their farming operations. They turned to stock raising, and the ranching industry throughout the Yorkton district experienced rapid expansion until after 1900.[18] In 1901, Yorkton claimed that "the number [of cattle for export] leaving Yorkton exceeded that of any shipping point in Manitoba or the Territories, excepting, of course, Winnipeg, totalling an aggregate of 5,400."[19] The farmers of the Yorkton district also raised dairy cattle and prompted by the territorial assembly, a number of the merchants and farmers formed a company, the Yorkton Creamery Association, to manufacture butter and cheese.

As part of the government's policy for the development of the Territories, the colonization railroads succeeded where the colonization companies failed. The York Farmers' enterprise was unsuccessful because York Colony lay seventy miles north of the only railway line. The Manitoba and North Western Railway was the catalyst which prompted the success and development of Yorkton and the surrounding district. Only five years after the completion of the railway line, Yorkton grew from a small settlement to village status. But the village could not parallel the growth rate of other prairie towns without an influx of settlers. What was needed desperately in the 1880's for the colonization companies to be successful, and what was needed at the end of the nineteenth century, was the heavy and unceasing flow of immigrants from Europe and the repatriation of Canadians from the United States.

Prior to 1896, Canada's immigration policies had been highly selective. The Conservative government classified immigrants to Canada as either "preferred" or "non-preferred." Immigrants from Great Britain especially, but also those from Scandinavia and western Europe, were classified as "preferred," whereas east European immigrants were labelled as "non-preferred."[20] However, this was only one reason why the government was unable to attract the numbers of immigrants it sought. The depression years of the 1880's had severely limited the funds needed for an extensive publicity campaign of North-West homesteads, with the result that few Europeans immigrated to Canada.

Changes in tempo and in policy came in 1896 when Clifford Sifton became the Minister of the Interior in the new Laurier government. The federal election coincided with the gradual upswing in the Canadian economy, and therefore Sifton was able to undertake an intensive advertising campaign of the Canadian West. Immigration agents were established in Britain, Europe, and throughout the United States. Pamphlets, folders, and maps were freely distributed by the agents. However, most of the nations of western Europe discouraged emigration. This left the "non-preferred" countries of eastern Europe. With its high density of poverty-striken farmers, the Austro-Hungarian Empire was the most promising of these countries. Head agencies were established in the Ukrainian provinces of Galicia and Bukowina to facilitate Slav immigration to Canada.

In Austria, the land reforms of 1848 had left the ex-serf personally landless; instead, the land belonged to the commune or village. This reduction in social status, along with the low acreage yields, the political subjection of the Ukrainian people, and the heavy taxes, rendered the

Slavs highly susceptible to the offers of the Canadian government. Between 1896 and 1914, 170,000 Slavs immigrated to Canada.

The Ukrainian immigrants were divided into groups. At Saltcoats, a minority was allowed to remain, but the majority was transferred to Yorkton. Two Ukrainian colonies were established in the Yorkton district, one at Beaver Hills and the other at the Crooked Lakes. Through hard work, perseverance, and the practice of strict economy, the Ukrainian settlements at Beaver Hills and the Crooked Lakes progressed favorably. During the summer months, the men in the colonies left their homesteads to find employment on the railway construction gangs of the Canadian Northern and the Pacific Grand Trunk. The Manitoba and North Western Railway also hired these immigrants, and in 1898 the men from the Crooked Lakes earned nearly $10,000 in cash from that railway.[21]

The Ukrainians represented the largest influx of immigrants into the Yorkton area, transforming the district. Once a British and Canadian area, Yorkton became the commercial centre for a large immigrant population.

Another group to settle in the Yorkton area were the Doukhobors who emigrated from Russia due to the sect's political differences with the Tsarist government. The Canadian government set aside a total of forty-five townships throughout Manitoba and the Territories as Doukhobor reserves. Due to the Doukhobor conviction of the injustice of violence, the Canadian government granted the Doukhobors exemption from military service. However, this military exemption was the only immunity they were granted. The government informed the Doukhobors that they were to conform to all other Canadian laws, including the homestead law.

Three major blocks were set aside for the Doukhobors in the Territories: one at Devil's Lake, known as the "South Colony," forty-five miles north of Yorkton; one at Rosthern; and the third at Thunder Hill. The Doukhobors cultivated their reserves in the name of the commune, not in the name of the individual.

Like the Ukrainians, the Doukhobor men worked on railway construction gangs during the summer months. It was not long before economic inequalities among families became apparent. Those men who earned a great deal of money soon began to oppose the communal ownership of land, machinery, and livestock, and by 1900, nearly a third of the Doukhobors had broken away from the commune to work their quarter sections as their own personal property.

Prior to 1902, the Doukhobors caused few problems. But in that year, religious fanaticism caused the Community Doukhobors to leave their reserves in October in search of the "promised land." They marched south through Yorkton to Minnedosa. There, starving and frozen, the

*Group of Doukhobors at Yorkton*

Doukhobors allowed the police to load them onto a train bound for Yorkton. The 1902 march had widespread ramifications. The Doukhobors had procrastinated on the registration of their homesteads for fear that the registration and the taking of the oath of allegiance would subject them to military service. Therefore, some contemporary observers regarded the 1902 march as a political move on the part of the Doukhobor leaders to force the government to concede its demands for the registration of their homesteads.[22] The march also brought into focus the sharp dissension and rivalry between the Doukhobor factions.

By 1903, differences between the Doukhobors and the Canadian government reached a critical point. Protesting the government's insistence on the registrations, a small group of Doukhobors staged a nude parade through Yorkton. Parades and hunger-strikes became commonplace after 1905 when Frank Oliver, the new Minister of the Interior, gave the Doukhobors the choice of registration or confiscation of their homesteads. Refusing to comply with the regulations, the Community Doukhobors had their homesteads confiscated in 1907.

A combination of Sifton's immigration policies, the upswing in the Canadian economy, and the demand for Canadian wheat on the world market resulted in the astounding growth rate of Yorkton and its hinterland. In 1894, Yorkton had been incorporated into a village. In 1900, Yorkton had a population of 600 and the village was incorporated into a town; by 1905, the population figure had jumped to 1,200. The reason for Yorkton's growth is not far to seek. The pattern of settlement of the immigrants was dictated by the railroads. The Manitoba and North Western served as the means of transportation and of employment for the immigrants. Yorkton flourished with the business engendered by the Doukhobor and Ukrainian immigrants. The merchants in Yorkton did all they could to outfit them adequately at a reasonable cost. As the main centre of the area, Yorkton soon became a major distribution centre, with a trading area extending "beyond Melville to the south, beyond Sheho to the west and as far as settlement extended to the north."[23] Yorkton's future was now well established.

In 1900, the new town council had a number of projects to undertake. Yorkton's rapid growth demanded further sanitation measures and greater fire protection. Additional purchases of equipment for the volunteer fire brigade were made in 1900, but by the next year the brigade had to request that the town council purchase more sophisticated equipment to meet the needs of the growing town. After purchasing a ladder truck and a fire engine, the council also decided to place a telephone in the home of the fire chief. The town arranged that the telephone exchange, owned and operated by a jeweller, Thomas Paul, would relay a fire alarm to the fire chief and to the members of the brigade.

Despite increased sanitation measures, a typhoid epidemic broke out in town in the autumn of 1901. Alarmed, the citizens recognized the need for a hospital, and the board of trustees accepted the offer of the Victorian Order of Nurses to build a cottage hospital. When completed in October, 1902, the Queen Victoria Cottage Hospital had on staff four

*Doukhobors camped at the Immigration Hall, Yorkton*

77

doctors, a dental surgeon, and two nurses. In 1903, the inspector of hospitals reported that although the operating room was "exceedingly well equipped," there was need of an isolation ward. The town council, however, procrastinated, and only when an epidemic diagnosed as diphtheria broke out did the council pledge to undertake immediately the construction of the isolation hospital.

Yorkton's success in attracting new industries was due to the promotion of the town by the board of trade. In turn, the board of trade's success at inducing new industry to come to Yorkton was dependent upon railway facilities. The board was able to convince the Canadian Pacific Railway, which had purchased the Manitoba and North Western Railway in 1898, to facilitate the traffic on the line to Yorkton by increasing the weekly number of trains.[24] However, receiving little encouragement from the merchants in town, the board faded from sight in 1902.

The defunct board had its duties shouldered by the town council. The council was well aware of the importance of railway facilities to the town's future, and when, in 1903, the council learned that the Grand Trunk Pacific Railway intended to build a line through the parkland belt, the council called a public meeting to discuss the possibility of inducing the company to build its line through Yorkton. At this point, the board of trade was revived, and its new directors were determined to place Yorkton in the forefront by persuading railway companies to build their main line or branch lines through Yorkton. The board was successful in having the Grand Trunk Pacific Railway build a branch line from Regina to Yorkton.[25]

The colonization railroads were to act as immigration agents. However, they were unable to promote the rapid development of settlement, and the new Liberal government took the initiative by creating new immigration policies which, combined with the scarcity of land in Europe and the United States, favorable world-wide economic conditions, and a substantial demand for wheat on the world market, led to the rapid growth of the Canadian West. The founding and growth of Yorkton during the territorial period illustrates that the development and settlement of the Canadian West was initiated by federal government policies. Yorkton was founded by a colonization company; its survival was assured by the Manitoba and North Western Railway; and its expansion was due to the arrival of east Europeans who homesteaded in the Yorkton area. The early history of Yorkton demonstrates clearly the intimate relationship between private enterprise, the settler, and the government.

# 6    The Harmony Industrial Association:

## A Pioneer Co-operative

### by Gilbert Johnson

IN the beautiful valley of the Qu'Appelle River a short distance above its confluence with the Big Cut Arm Creek, some eight miles east of Tantallon, stands a verdant grove of maples. May their branches spread, for they shelter the very cradle of the co-operative movement in Saskatchewan. Here is the site of the Hamona community, a Rochdale of the West, a Brook Farm on the Canadian plains.[1] The quietness of a sanctuary prevails over the spot today. The ruins of a couple of stone buildings are all that remain to indicate that it was once the site of human habitations. More than half a century ago this part of the valley was astir with the activities of men and women working under the inspiration of a great ideal.*

In the summer of 1895 a group of people met at Beulah, Manitoba, for the purpose of establishing for themselves a new order of society, an economic commonwealth within the framework of a Victorian political state, a co-operative refuge in the midst of a competitive world. They belonged to no particular religious sect or racial group. The only bond of fellowship was a burning faith in the co-operative way of life. The frontiers of settlement are commonly regarded as areas where individualism reigns supreme, so that a co-operative community on the Canadian prairies in the 1890's seems at first sight a strange incongruity. But history demonstrates that the lure of vacant lands on the far horizon has attracted both the acquisitive and the idealistic, both the money makers and those whose object is to found a new society nearer to their hearts' desire.

The Hamona community owed its origin to the idealism and organizing capacity of two brothers, J. E. and W. C. Paynter, members of an Ontario family which had settled at Beulah, Manitoba, about 1878. Another leader was Samuel Sanderson, of Oak Lake, a Quaker whose family years before had helped escaped slaves coming north by

---

*This article originally appeared in *Saskatchewan History* for winter, 1951.

"underground railway" to find new homes in Ontario. The impulse which led them to found a co-operative community was the Christian concept of brotherhood and the ideas of the English and American social reformers of the late nineteenth century. Such books as William Morris's *News from Nowhere,* Robert Blatchford's *God and My Neighbour,* Edward Bellamy's *Looking Backward,* and John Ruskin's writings were influential in preparing their minds for the venture.[2] "I became convinced," J. E. Paynter later wrote, "that something could be accomplished for the good of humanity by organizing those interested into a colony to demonstrate to the world what men could accomplish by working co-operatively instead of competing against one another."[3] He was the most articulate member of the group and discussed the project with many people in the course of his travels as agent for the Miniota Farmers' Mutual Fire Insurance Company.

In 1895 the two brothers prepared a draft constitution for the proposed colony, and a meeting of those who had become interested in the project was convened in the schoolhouse at Beulah in June of the same year. Here the constitution (printed at the end of this article) was adopted, clause by clause, and officers were elected as follows: president, S. W. Sanderson; vice-president, W. C. Paynter; secretary, W. C. Vincent; treasurer, W. B. Gurney. Shortly thereafter Robert Greer was elected vice-president and W. C. Paynter became secretary-treasurer.

The object of the organization, which was named The Harmony Industrial Association, was stated in the following terms in the preamble of the constitution:[4]

> Feeling that the present competitive social system is one of injustice and fraud and directly opposed to the precepts laid down by "Our Saviour" for the guidance of mankind in subduing all the forces of nature and the evils springing from selfishness in the human heart, we do write under the name of the "Harmony Industrial Association" for the purpose of acquiring land to build homes for its members, to produce from nature sufficient to insure its members against want or the fear of want.
> To own and operate factories, mills, stores, etc. To provide educational and recreative facilities of the highest order and to promote and maintain harmonious relations on the basis of co-operation for the benefit of its members and mankind in general.

Proposed capital stock of the association was set at $100,000, divided into 500 shares of $200 each, four percent dividend to be paid annually on shares. The total annual profits of the organization were to be equally divided among the members in proportion to the number of days' labor performed. The four-percent-interest provision was discontinued after the first year or two as being "an unbrotherly custom, absolutely forbidden by the Laws of the Bible."[5] In the event of a member

80

withdrawing from the association it was provided that he should be repaid in cash, stock, and implements in proportion to the amount of these he had brought into the colony, together with accrued profits.

To qualify for membership applicants were required to be of good moral character and well informed in the principles of co-operation and able to pass an examination in that subject.

Article 5, section 6, of the constitution reads:

Every member shall surrender his natural freedom which leads him to disregard the rights of others, for the sake of civil or social freedom, which, being based on the principles of right and justice, has regard for his rights and the rights of all.

Sections 7 and 11 provided that:

The Association shall in no way interfere with the free exercise of individual tastes, desires, and preferences in all social, religious and domestic affairs.
A man's endowments fix the measure of his duties and the employee of great endowments who does not do all he might shall be considered a less deserving workman than the employee of small endowments who does his best.

Politicians should ponder section 13:

No member shall vote for himself for any office and for any member to ask another to vote for him, shall be evidence sufficient to show that he is unworthy of public trust.

The modern family allowance system was anticipated in article 16:

Each child shall receive a graduated sum per year until 18 years of age, the amount to be determined by the Board of Directors.

Each member was guaranteed employment, whenever possible, in the kind of work for which he showed preference. All members were to receive the same compensation for each day's labor performed.

The Paynter brothers were responsible for the selection of the site of the colony, which was on the projected line of the Great North West Central Railway and at a point where there was good water, plenty of timber, building stone, light loam soil, and "fine water powers which can be utilized for manufacturing and lighting by electricity." "These things," it was declared in the prospectus, "freely supplied by the hand of nature ... with industry and skill may be made to contribute to our comfort and prosperity."

Building operations on the Qu'Appelle were started in the fall of 1895,[6] although, for a couple of years longer, some of the members continued to operate their holdings at Beulah in the interests of the association. In the fall of 1898 the Beulah interests were abandoned, and all the members moved to Hamona, as the colony was named.[7]

The delay in moving to the new site appears to have been connected with the problem of securing free homesteads while operating as a co-operative farming unit. When the association was formed, the prevailing regulations of the Dominion government under The Dominion Lands Act required that a homesteader should reside on his quarter section while performing his homestead duties. But the members of the association wished to have their houses grouped in a small village in order to carry out their industrial projects and to facilitate social intercourse. This difficulty was overcome by J. E. Paynter, who, after the general election of 1896, took advantage of his acquaintance with the new Minister of the Interior, the Hon. Clifford Sifton, to make representations on behalf of his associates.[8] The result was that at the spring session of Parliament in 1898, Sifton introduced an amendment to The Dominion Lands Act which made special provision for homesteaders who wished to engage in co-operative farming.[9] Upon application by a co-operative farming association, the minister might reserve a block of odd- and even-numbered sections within which the members could secure homesteads without residing on their own quarter sections, providing that their length of residence and improvements as members of the co-operative were equivalent to those which applied to homesteaders generally. One unanticipated result of this new provision of the act was that in the following year it provided a method for dealing with the wishes of the Doukhobors who were anxious to settle and farm on communal principles.[10]

While the membership of the Harmony Industrial Association was much smaller than had been hoped for, there were in the colony at one time ten families and a number of single men, probably about fifty persons in all. The homes were grouped in the form of a village, with both rent and fuel free to all. There was a blacksmith shop, a carpenter shop, and a laundry. A bunkhouse for single men was also provided. A community kitchen was operated for a time, but the experiment does not seem to have been very successful and was later abandoned. An important institution was the co-operative store where goods were purchased with scrip issued to all members for services rendered. Lime kilns were operated, and this product formed an important source of revenue for the colony. However, difficulties in transporting the lime to markets beyond the adjacent settlements imposed limitations on this industry.

Contacts were established with other co-operative societies. The group at Hamona subscribed to *The Social Gospel (Christian Commonwealth)* published by a co-operative community in Commonwealth, Georgia. More important were their relations with the Ruskin Colony on the Fraser River in British Columbia. An interchange of products on a barter basis was arranged between these two co-operatives, the Hamona

Association sending flour and butter and receiving lumber and salmon in return. The balances arising from the trading were settled periodically by cheque.

The children were instructed by a qualified teacher with a farm kitchen for a classroom until the Hamona School District Number 451 was organized in 1897 and opened in 1898. The social and cultural life of the colony was not neglected. In winter there were sleigh rides, tobogganing, card parties, concerts, and singsongs. A sort of forum was usually held on Sunday afternoon, at which topics of interest were discussed. Various members took turns conducting religious services. During the summer there were picnics and outdoor sports. One of the first sports days in the district is said to have been held at Hamona colony.

Owing to its small membership, the association was unable to launch many of its proposed industries and social services. Nevertheless, the colonists seem to have suffered less from the depression of the nineties than did many individual homesteaders, and they certainly enjoyed amenities of life denied to their more isolated neighbors. People who were members have since testified that the years spent in the colony were among the happiest and most educative of their lives.

About 1900 the members decided to dissolve the association. Difficulties had arisen due to the attitude of some of the later members who wished to extend the practice of communal living beyond the limits envisaged by the founders, and there was considerable disappointment when the railway line through the settlement failed to materialize. The winding up and distribution of the assets was accomplished without any conflict or court action and in a manner quite in keeping with the brotherly spirit which had animated the founders. Most of the houses and buildings were purchased by the members and removed to their respective homesteads.

To some of these devoted co-operators and their descendants, the dissolution of the colony only meant that their activities were transferred to wider fields of co-operative endeavor — to the Comrades of Equity, the Saskatchewan Co-operative Elevator Company, the Saskatchewan Co-operative Creameries Association, the Saskatchewan Grain Growers' Association, and the Saskatchewan Municipal Hail Association. Today the Hamona colony is but a few heaps of rubble and a fading memory. The vine here planted perished, but from its seeds there issued new life and growth.

## CONSTITUTION AND BY-LAWS

ARTICLE 1:

(Section 1) Feeling that the present competitive social system is one of injustice and fraud and directly opposed to the precepts laid down by

"Our Saviour" for the guidance of mankind in subduing all the forces of nature and the evils springing from selfishness in the human heart, we do write under the name of the "Harmony Industrial Association" for the purpose of acquiring land to build homes for its members, to produce from nature sufficient to insure its members against want or the fear of want.

To own and operate factories, mills, stores, etc. To provide educational and recreative facilities of the highest order and to promote and maintain harmonious relations on the basis of co-operation for the benefit of its members and mankind in general.

(Section 2) The capital stock of the Association shall be $100,000 divided in 500 shares of $200 each.

(Section 3) Four percent dividend shall be paid annually on shares. The total annual profits shall be equally divided among the members of the Association in proportion to the number of days' labour performed for the Association.

(Section 4) The stock certificates shall not be transferable except to the Association or its duly qualified members and no member shall be allowed to hold more than five shares, one share of which shall admit to qualified membership, ten percent of which SHALL be paid in cash, and no member shall have more than one vote in the Association.

(Section 5) All members upon being admitted shall sign the constitution, obligating themselves to comply therewith and that they become members and receive stock under the conditions set forth in this constitution.

(Section 6) No members can withdraw their property until three years and then only upon giving six months notice prior to the 1st day of November in any year, to the Secretary of their intention to do so.

(Section 7) The Association may pay a member, withdrawing in cash, stock and implements, in proportion to the amount of these things brought in, along with profits accruing to said member during the time he or she was a member.

ARTICLE II:

(Section 1) Qualification of members: Any person may become a member of this Association by fulfilling the following requirements:

    a) He or she must be of good moral character.

    b) Must be well informed in the principles of co-operation and be able to pass an examination in this branch as hereinafter provided.

    c) Must be in health, not under 18 years of age, with willingness and ability to aid in the promotion of the Association's object.

    d) Must receive a two-thirds vote of all members present and voting.

ARTICLE III: OFFICERS, THEIR ELECTION AND DUTIES.

(Section 1) The officers of this Association shall be a President, a Vice-president, a Secretary and a Treasurer (both offices of Secretary and Treasurer may be held by the same person), a Board of Directors consisting of thirteen members elected by a majority vote of all members present voting, for a term no longer than one year and subject to conditions in Section 5, Article 3, of these by-laws; and Superintendents of the following departments.

a) Department of Finance.
b) Department of Public Works.
c) Department of Education and Recreation.
d) Department of Manufacture.
e) Department of Agriculture.
f) Department of Distribution.
g) Department of Sanitation.
h) Department of Cuisine.

(Section 2) The President, Vice-President, Secretary and Treasurer shall be selected from among the board of directors and shall be elected at any regular meeting by a majority vote of members present and voting, for a term of no longer than one year, and subject to conditions in Section 5, Article 3 of these by-laws.

(Section 3) The Treasurer shall be Superintendent of the Department of Finance and shall not be required to give bond.

(Section 4) The superintendents of the different departments shall be elected by a majority of the members of the Association present and voting, for a term of no longer than one year and subject to conditions in Section 5, Article 3 of these by-laws.

All officers and superintendents of the Association shall hold their respective offices for a term no longer than one year or until their successors are elected, but they may be re-elected to the same positions.

(Section 5) On petition of 25 percent of the stockholders the President shall call a special meeting of the Board of Stockholders, not later than three days after the said petition shall be served on him, for the purpose of initiating new business or rejecting or approving any action of the Board of Directors or any officer. The President shall post three notices of such meeting in prominent places.

ARTICLE IV: DUTIES OF OFFICERS.

(Section 1) The duties of the President shall be to preside at the meetings of the Board of Directors exercising the prerogatives usually devolving upon such officer; to call all meetings of stockholders to order, state the object of the meeting and allow the stockholders to choose their own chairman; he shall see that all rules and regulations are enforced at the request of members of the Association; he shall give them such information as they may require, and he possess, of the affairs of the Association; make a semi-annual report to the members concerning the same.

The President shall sign all orders of the Treasury for money and shall have general management and control of the affairs of the Association.

(Section 2) The Vice-President shall perform the duties of the President in his absence and at all times aid him in the execution of the same.

(Section 3) The Secretary shall keep a record of the proceedings of the meetings of the stockholders and the Board of Directors, preserve the books and records of the Association and keep an accurate account of the business transactions thereof.

(Section 4) The Treasurer shall be the custodian of the Association's funds and keep an accurate record of all funds received and paid out by him.

He shall pay no money except by order of the President countersigned by the Secretary. He shall make a financial report quarterly or at such times as may be required by the stockholders.

His report shall be examined by an auditing committee consisting of three members of the Association and he shall perform any other duties incident to the nature of his office.

Duties of Superintendents

(Section 1) The duties of the Superintendent of the Department of Finance shall be such as are defined as the duties of Treasurer.

(Section 2) The duties of the superintendent of the Department of Public Works shall be to have charge of erection of all the Association buildings of whatever kind or description and the proper maintenance thereof and the grading, paving, etc., of the Association's streets, alleys and other public works.

(Section 3) The duties of the Superintendent of the Department of Manufactures shall be to have general supervision of the manufactories of the Association.

(Section 4) The duties of the Superintendent of the Department of Agriculture shall be to have charge of the farming and stock raising operations of the Association, care for forestry, lawns, gardens, boulevards and parks.

(Section 5) The duties of the Superintendent of the Department of Distribution shall be to have charge of the distribution of food, clothing and manufactured goods of all kinds.

(Section 6) The duties of the Superintendent of the Department of

Sanitation shall be to exercise a general oversight of the healthful condition of the homes of the members, factories, and other buildings belonging to the Association, to give instruction in the laws of hygiene and furnish medical treatment and medicine to members and their families without charge.

(Section 7) The duties of the Superintendent of the Department of Education and Recreation shall be to have general supervision of the educational facilities of the Association, to provide instruction and elevating entertainments and in general devote his energies to the moral, mental and physical well being of the members and their children.

(Section 8) The duties of the Superintendent of the Department of Cuisine shall be to have general charge and supervision of all hotels, restaurants, co-operative kitchens, etc.

ARTICLE V: GENERAL.

(Section 1) Each member of the Association shall be guaranteed employment whenever possible and in that branch of service which he prefers, subject, however, to conditions hereinafter provided.

(Section 2) A day's labour shall consist of not more than ten hours or such number under 10, as the Board of Directors may determine.

(Section 3) All members of the Association shall receive the same compensation for each day's labour performed or for a proportional amount for each fractional part thereof.

(Section 4) All orders of foremen and superintendents must at all times be obeyed.

(Section 5) The foremen of each department shall keep the working time of employees and report same weekly to the Secretary.

(Section 6) Every member of the Association shall surrender his natural freedom, which leads him to disregard the rights of others, for the sake of civil or social freedom, which being based upon the principles of right and justice, has regard for his rights and the rights of all.

(Section 7) The Association shall in no way interfere with the free exercise of individual tastes, desires and preferences in all social, religious and domestic affairs.

(Section 8) The Association shall furnish all teachers, books, apparatus and necessary appliances for the most thorough instruction of the children of the members in such lines as they show most aptitude.

(Section 9) The Association may fix a monthly rate of maintenance on residences based on the actual cost of construction.

(Section 10) The Association shall be entitled to all benefits to be derived from things produced, discovered or invented by any of its members provided said Association renders such support, aid and assistance desired and necessary to its construction and development.

(Section 11) A man's endowments fix the measure of his duties and the employee of great endowments who does not do all he might shall be considered a less deserving workman than the employee of small endowments who does his best.

(Section 12) The question of special incentives to call out the best endeavours of employees being one of great importance, the Board of Directors shall devise a system of preferment, and the system, which shall be subject to the approval of all the members by a majority of the members present and voting, shall be such as will best promote the interests of the Commonwealth.

(Section 13) No member shall vote for himself for any office and for any member to ask another to vote for him, shall be evidence sufficient to show that he is unworthy of public trust.

(Section 14) Each member shall be entitled to the use and occupancy of a residence lot.

(Section 15) All employees under 18 years of age shall be classed as apprentices and their compensation shall be determined by the Board of Directors.

(Section 16) Each child shall receive a graduated sum per year until 18 years of age, the amount to be determined by the Board of Directors.

(Section 17) Every member shall furnish the Secretary with a list of members of his family.

(Section 18) The school age of children shall be 18 years.

(Section 19) No member of the Association shall be permitted to allow his children to grow up in ignorance.

(Section 20) There shall be kept in the office of the Secretary a register in which the names, ages, and sex of each family shall be recorded.

(Section 21) No official of the Association or the Association in its organized capacity, shall loan the Association's funds.

(Section 22) Whenever a member of this Association fails to comply with the by-laws of this Association or fails to perform any of the duties or discharge any of the obligations imposed on him or her as a member of this Association, he or she shall thereby subject himself or herself to the penalty of suspension from the Association. When a member is suspended he or she shall drop from the pay roll and shall, for the time of suspension, be entitled to none of the privileges and benefits of the Association. When in the opinion of five members of this Association a member has made himself or herself liable to suspension under the laws of this Association, said five members shall prefer charges and specifications of offence or violation of duty by said member.

These charges shall set out the acts and doings of said member and wherein it is claimed these acts and doings are a violation of by-laws of the Association.

These charges and specifications shall be in writing and filed with the Secretary of the Association, who shall make a copy thereof and deliver it to the member charged, and notify him or her to appear at a time fixed not less than five days after notice — before a called meeting of this Association to try said member on said charges and specifications. Said meeting shall hear the proof on both sides and investigate the charges and specifications and then vote by ballot on the charges as a whole.

The question voted shall be "innocent" or "guilty." If a majority of the members present vote that the said member is "guilty" then the President shall submit to a vote of the meeting the question of "for what time suspended?" and the time of suspension having been determined by a majority vote of the members present at said meeting, the President shall declare the offender suspended from the pay roll and all privileges of the Association for a time determined by the meeting and the same shall be done.

(Section 23) The stockholders shall in the first week in January and the first week in July elect a board of examiners whose duty it shall be to decide upon the qualifications and fitness of applicants for shares of stock. Such board shall immediately after organize by the election of its Chairman and Secretary and formulate a standard of examination. Such board of examiners shall serve six months and report its findings in every case to a meeting of the stockholders.

(Section 24) No debts shall be contracted for the Association by any officer in excess of cash on hand.

(Section 25) A majority of the Board of Directors shall constitute a quorum for the transaction of business.

(Section 26) Any rules or regulations in any way conflicting with these by-laws shall be considered null and void.

(Section 27) No member shall be allowed to disclose any of the business affairs of the Association to parties not members.

(Section 28) It shall be the duty of any member to abide by any motion carried at a regular meeting of the Association or Board of Directors and in case of refusal he shall subject himself to the penalties provided for an infraction of the by-laws.

(Section 29) These by-laws may be altered or amended at any regular meeting of the members by a two-thirds vote of all members present and voting, provided such alteration or amendment has been presented in writing two weeks previous to the time of such change.

*The constitution concludes with a list of eighteen parliamentary rules for the conduct of meetings. Todd's Manual was to govern all questions not covered by the rules listed under this heading.*

# 7　From the Pampas to the Prairies:

## The Welsh Migration of 1902

*by Lewis H. Thomas*

*We have found a better land*
*In the far South,*
*It is Patagonia.*
*We will live there in peace,*
*Without fear of treachery or war,*
*And a Welshman on the throne*
*Praise be to God.*

THE singers voices rose, strong and buoyantly, on a Liverpool wharf on a day late in May, 1865, as 153 Welsh folk made ready to board a small chartered sailing vessel, the *Mimosa,* with the Welsh dragon flag at her masthead, which was to carry them to a no-man's-land across the Atlantic under the tenuous and remote control of the Republic of Argentina. The emigrants, the hoped-for vanguard of a movement of thousands, were the actors in a drama which had been stage-managed by a few ardent Welsh nationalists, bent on creating a Welsh state where their language, cultural achievements, customs, and non-conformist religious traditions would be preserved free of the compulsions of the British political and religious establishment and the blandishments of the assimilative nationalism which had absorbed so many Welsh migrants to the United States earlier in the century.*

Although the Welsh nation has its origin in the Celtic population of pre-Roman Britain, Welsh nationalism "is a very modern thing, little older . . . than the second half of the nineteenth century."[1] As in Europe, intellectuals played a decisive role in its origins, with their enthusiasm for native customs and literature. The nationalism of the Italian Mazzini, the Hungarian Kossuth, and the Irishman Thomas Davis aroused sympathy and admiration throughout Wales.[2] One of the fathers of Welsh nationalism was the Rev. Michael Daniel Jones (1822-1898), a Con-

---

*This article originally appeared in *Saskatchewan History* for winter, 1971.

gregational minister who in 1865 was the principal of the Congregational College at Bala, Merionethshire. In the *Dictionary of Welsh Biography* there is the following summation of his personality and achievements:

> He was a born fighter and could not bear opposition. He was ... the father of the nationalist renaissance in Wales; he loathed the English-worshipping Welshman, and it has been said that "the credit should be given chiefly to him and to Emrys ap Iwan (Robert Ambrose Jones) for transforming Welsh patriotism into a vigorous practical nationalism."[3]

Jones' mother had been evicted from her home by a Tory landlord because of her son's activities, and it is not difficult to understand that to him England and everything English were anathema. As a young minister, he had spent three years serving a Welsh congregation in Cincinnati, Ohio. He gained an extensive knowledge of the position of Welsh settlers in various parts of the United States and of the inexorable process of assimilation among the small, widely dispersed settlements of his fellow countrymen. It was here that he first heard talk of the opportunities of Patagonia.[4] A few years after his return to Wales the Argentinian government began to advertise for settlers from Britain and Europe,[5] and this was followed in 1861 by the establishment of a Welsh colonization society in Liverpool, the chief British embarkation centre for trans-Atlantic migration.

The organizers of the colonization society were young Welshmen, one of whom had lived in the United States, where the original Patagonian project had languished. Lending their prestige and influence to the society were a member of the British Parliament, a High Sheriff of one of the Welsh counties, a prominent land-owner and military officer (Captain Thomas Love Jones-Parry), Lewis Jones, a journalist with oratorical gifts, and Michael Daniel Jones, whose wife's money financed the society.[6]

Michael Jones and his associates realized that to attain their objective the colonists would have to erect psychological and physical barriers to assimilation. The former required self-discipline, zeal, and emotional commitment. The latter required physical isolation in a sparsely populated region beyond the reach of British jurisdiction. Such an area was not easy to find in the latter half of the nineteenth century, but it did exist in Patagonia, a country inhabited by a few nomadic Indians — a lonely land to which both Argentina and Chile asserted claims.

Charles Darwin had described Patagonia as a sterile area, but more favorable descriptions had appeared later in books of travel.[7] A pamphlet compiled by Hugh Hughes, secretary of the colonization society, purported to demonstrate that Patagonia was a fertile land with a climate and topography not dissimilar to that of Wales.[8] On the basis of some brief comments which Captain Fitzroy of the *Beagle* had made thirty years earlier, the committee selected the valley of the Chubut River, some 400 miles south of the nearest white settlement as the site for the colony.

To confirm their choice the committee dispatched Lewis Jones and Captain Love Jones-Parry to Patagonia in 1863. Despite the importance of their mission they spent only three days in the Chubut area, and then returned to Buenos Aires and negotiated an agreement with Dr. G. Rawson, Minister of the Interior, to reserve land for a group settlement.[9] Although this agreement was not ratified by the Congress, which disliked the idea of a large Protestant British colony in Patagonia, Rawson was prepared to assist the Welsh by means of individual land grants, surveys, and negotiations with the Indians to relinquish native rights. But at no time did he favor the creation of an autonomous Welsh state.

During 1863 and 1864 "Lewis Jones and other members of the Liverpool Commitee went around Wales describing the Vale of Camwy [Chubut River area] as a paradise."[10] The original group of settlers were drawn from various locations in both north and south Wales. Most of them were non-conformists in religion. Though nationalism may have been an influence, poverty was probably the primary cause of the migration. "They were largely coal miners, quarry workers and farm dwellers."[11] Only three or four were practicing farmers, and most observers stress that the lack of farming experience was a serious handicap[12] which was ignored by the promoters of the project. Nevertheless the hardships and failures of the first few years in the Chubut were not unlike the experience of many farmers moving from well-watered, well-treed areas to the semi-arid plains region of North America.

After a two-month ocean voyage the settlers landed at the nearest embarkation point, New Bay, some forty miles from the mouth of the Chubut. Some weeks later they moved to the lower Chubut valley and established the townsite which they named Rawson. Here, on September 15, an Argentine government party arrived to formally assert the sovereignty of the republic in Patagonia. The assistance which the government had given and was to continue to extend to the Welsh was not entirely disinterested,[13] since Chile also claimed the region. By exercising its administration and supporting what was to become a successful settlement, Argentina's claim was successfully asserted in a boundary treaty in 1881. But the dream of a Welsh state in the New World was doomed from the start, leaving the preservation of the Welsh language and culture to the devices of communal action and family discipline.

The first settlers had arrived at the wrong season for preparing the land and planting crops[14] and were only rescued from starvation by the timely assistance of the Argentine government. The Indians also befriended the Welsh, teaching them the use of the bolas and the lasso and other hunting techniques suited to the pampas.

The following year a crop was planted, but it came to nothing due to the lack of rainfall, and the settlers again faced starvation. Again the government came to their aid, supplemented by the supplies received from a British destroyer of the South East Coast of America Squadron. The next year was also depressing, so much so that the colonists contemplated leaving. About this time (1867) one of the settlers tried irrigating his crop and this met with marked success. In the following years the practice spread, and many miles of canals were built. Although later crops suffered from climatic variations the settlers produced their own food and eked out a living by hunting.

Encouraged by reports of good wheat crops, more Welshmen arrived in the 1870's from the homeland and from the United States, and by 1875 the population had more than doubled. The 1880's saw still further economic progress as a result of the perseverance and hard labor of the colonists. They soon had plenty of horses, and agricultural machinery was introduced. Alfalfa was grown, and livestock production flourished. Their wheat won gold medals at international exhibitions in Paris and Chicago.[15] In 1885 a consumers' co-operative was established. To facilitate exports, a railway company was chartered in the United Kingdom which built a forty-five mile line from the Chubut Valley to Port Madryn on New Bay, with government assistance. Lewis Jones imported a press and established a newspaper.

In 1882 Michael D. Jones visited the colony and was impressed with its progress and the retention of the Welsh language, although he was disappointed with some evidences of intemperance and decline in religious fervor — both characteristic products of the frontier experience. In negotiations in Buenos Aires he secured an extension of the powers of the municipal-type government of the Chubut area. On his return to Wales, he avoided picturing Patagonia as a land of milk and honey, and stressed only the need for good workmen in a variety of trades.[16]

In 1888 an offshoot of the Welsh colony was established about 360 miles inland in the piedmont below the snow-capped Andes. To reach it, many miles of rugged and barren country had to be crossed. It was originally called the Sixteenth of October settlement, to commemorate the date in 1884 when the Chubut area achieved territorial status, and it was to play an important role in the final boundary settlement of 1902 which favored Argentinian claims. In this region sheep and cattle did well. It is the locale of the last episode in Richard Llewellyn's novel *Up Into the Singing Mountains* and of *And I Shall Sleep Down Where the Moon is Small,* sequels to *How Green Was My Valley.* This westward migration was motivated by the lack of suitable land in the lower Chubut

Valley, which was affecting the prospects of new immigrants and young men born in the settlement.

As the years passed, Argentinians began occupying the area north and south of the Chubut Valley, and Italian settlers arrived in considerable numbers. But Welsh immigration practically ceased by the late 1880's. These developments resulted in the Argentine government tightening its administrative authority in Patagonia. A garrison was established, and in the 1890's the settlers began to complain of harassments by territorial officials. Complaints regarding peculation and arbitrary action voiced by the colonists were not exaggerated, according to the British ambassador at Buenos Aires. Writing to the Foreign Office, he stated that they "throw an ugly light on already pretty well-known methods of administration".[17]

The disputes with the government were mainly over three issues — land titles, education, and service in the army. Many settlers encountered interminable delays in securing titles to their land. As far as education was concerned, the Welsh from the start had provided their own schools, where Welsh was the language of instruction. In the 1890's the government at Buenos Aires decreed a policy of assimilation, and Spanish-speaking schoolmasters displaced the Welsh.[18] This was a blow at the root of the colony and seemed to presage its extinction as a Welsh community. It is interesting to note that this coincided in time with the action of the provincial and territorial authorities in the Canadian North-West, who were applying the same policy to the French-Canadian settlers.

The third issue involved compulsory military training for the young men born in the settlement. As citizens of Argentina they were subject to compulsory military service. The Welsh did not object to the training, but since it took place on Sunday it violated their conscientious scruples, nurtured by generations of evangelical convictions. When the president of the republic visited the settlement in 1899 he agreed to a change of day.

Beyond these three specific issues, the familiar enemy, assimilation, lurked. As one English traveller who visited the Chubut about 1900 put it:

> In 1865 the Welsh, in deep sorrow, left their own land to escape the tyranny of the English law, as they considered it, which sought to force upon them the English language. . . . And flying from Scylla they will fall (and to some degree have already fallen) a prey to Chrybdis. But it is a very pleasant Chrybdis, typified by a dark-haired, dark-eyed, lissom maiden, who will bear them sons no longer of the old purebred Welsh stock but of a mixed race. And so the effort of the forefathers, who fared overseas to found a new home, shall be made null and void.[19]

Then in 1899 disaster struck. From the first days of the settlement the main problem had been the lack of rainfall, but in that year the rains were torrential, and the raging Chubut River swept everything in its path. Many settlers, including Lewis Jones, lost all their possessions. The miles of canals, so painfully constructed, were destroyed. Another flood, in 1901, was almost as destructive. This disaster, coupled with the new policies of the Argentine government, led many of the colonists to consider migration to South Africa or Canada. The Canadian government immigration agent in Cardiff, who visited the colony in 1901, in a lengthy interview with a Liverpool newspaper, made the following comments on this point:

> The original idea of forming and building up a Welsh colony has been entirely abandoned, and it is sorrowfully admitted by the leaders that all hope for the success of that idea must be given up. . . . The Welsh in Chubut, generally speaking, realize that they have made a mistake in departing from under the British flag. They now feel that, although the British form of government may not be ideally perfect, it's by all odds the best form of government to live under.[20]

A measure of the disillusionment of many, if not all of the settlers, was the curious proposal which two colonists delivered to the Foreign Office in 1899.[21] They argued that Patagonia had been claimed for England by Sir John Narborough in 1670 and that the area was a no-man's land until the arrival of the Welsh in 1865. Following the hoisting of the English flag by Narborough, no flag had flown on this remote territory until the red-dragon flag of the principality had been raised. The two representatives asked that the Chubut Valley be made an independent state under the joint protection of the United States and Great Britain. The comment on the proposal by the law officer of the Foreign Office was brief and terse: "A nomadic detachment of Welshmen cannot, by 'squatting' on the desolate coasts of Patagonia convert the land so occupied into an integral part of the Queen's dominions."[22] The same answer in less precise terms was given by Lord Salisbury, the Foreign Secretary, to the Welsh members of Parliament who had put down questions on the reports of hardship and alleged discrimination suffered by the colonists.

Among the significant events of the years following the establishment of the colony and until after the turn of the century were the periodic visits to Port Madryn on New Bay by British vessels of the South East Coast of America Squadron. The commanders of these ships brought material aid in the early years, and their reports to the Admiralty, which in due course reached the Foreign Office, were notable for their keenness of observation and realistic appraisal of conditions in the colony. These visits occurred whenever morale was low and were warmly welcomed, and probably played a part in modifying the earlier Welsh hostility to the British government and the British Empire.

In 1896 a census indicated that there were 2,500 Welsh in the Chubut Valley, and in 1902 it was estimated that there were about 200 in the colony in the Andean piedmont. By this latter date opinion among the Patagonian Welsh had crystallized regarding their future. The majority were determined to stay and make the best of the situation; this group included farmers, storekeepers, railway officials, and government employees. The minority view favored migration to one of Britain's overseas possessions. A member of the staff of the British embassy in Buenos Aires, who visited the colony in 1902, wrote:

> I do not think that there can be said to be any dividing line between the Welshmen who are content to stay where they are on the one hand and those who intend to emigrate on the other. There are honest, hard-working, and intelligent men in both classes, they have all been through the mill alike, and the labour and ingenuity they have shown in engineering and working the irrigation canals reflects the greatest credit on all.[23]

It is at this juncture that developments in Patagonia and Canada intersect. The great wave of migration to Canada from Europe, the United Kingdom, and the United States had begun in the 1890's and was to continue unabated until the beginning of the First World War. The Immigration Branch of the Department of the Interior had launched an extensive campaign extolling the opportunities in "the Last, Best West." As a consequence the Canadian prairies were emerging, socially speaking, as a mosaic of peoples drawn from many distant lands. Canadian government immigration agents were active in several countries. As early as 1892 the agent in Liverpool had established contact with the Patagonian Welsh and had arranged for a few to migrate to the vicinity of Winnipeg and along the line of the Manitoba and North Western Railway.[24]

In 1897 an agent was appointed for Wales, W. L. Griffith, with headquarters in Cardiff.[25] Although Griffith had some success in promoting migration, he found that despite the hardships of life in the principality it was difficult to induce people to migrate to Canada because of "the unexpected but passionate attachment to home of these persons, the prejudice against emigrating, usually shown by the feminine portion of the family, the discreet but strong influence of the 'landlord' and his friends, the publication from time to time of unfavourable letters from unsuccessful emigrants to Canada, the competition, energetic as it is, of Victoria, Queensland, Western Australia, Tasmania and the Cape...."[26] To counter these prejudices the federal government arranged a visit to the West in 1899 by three prominent Welshmen — David Lloyd George, M.P., W. J. Rees, a J.P. and prominent citizen of

Swansea, and W. Llewellyn Williams of Cardiff, a distinguished barrister and writer. The visitors were favorably impressed,[27] and after the flood in the Chubut Valley, Lloyd George advocated that the Patagonian Welsh be encouraged to migrate to Canada.[28]

From 1899 to 1901 Griffith and officials in Ottawa and Winnipeg actively pursued the project of promoting a movement from Patagonia. In the summer of 1901 Griffith and W. J. Rees were sent to the Argentine to provide the Canadian government with precise and accurate information on the situation, and also to supply the prospective emigrants with information on opportunities in western Canada and to determine how many would be prepared to move. They were accompanied to the colony by Ernest Scott, secretary of the British legation in Buenos Aires. Scott remained longer than the other two, extending his investigations to the Andean settlement. He subsequently submitted a very full report to the Foreign Office in London.[29]

Meanwhile the Transvaal, with Lord Milner's encouragement, was also wooing the discontented Welsh. That country had the attraction of a more moderate climate than Canada, and the colonial government appeared to be interested in promoting irrigation in part of its territory. Such a move would have had the advantage of financial assistance from the British treasury, which Chamberlain, the Colonial Secretary, refused to extend to a group migrating to a self-governing colony. But Milner encountered difficulties in preparing for the migration, and although correspondence on the subject continued until the summer of 1905, nothing came of the proposal.

In February, 1902, the delegation of Welsh members of Parliament and other prominent Welshmen, whose representations to Chamberlain had been rejected, formed a committee of twenty-four, with Griffith as secretary, to raise funds to assist a migration to Canada. They raised about $10,000 but did not attain their objective of $30,000. However, on the basis of the funds at their disposal and the promise of a contribution by the Canadian government of one pound per head, the committee arranged with the Pacific Steam Navigation Company to bring the migrants to Liverpool, where they were to board an Allan-line ship for Quebec. The committee induced the Canadian Pacific Railway to provide a special low fare of five dollars from Quebec to Saltcoats, Assiniboia.[30]

In April, 1902, an advance party of about thirty Patagonian Welsh arrived in Winnipeg where the commissioner of immigration provided free transportation and a guide to take them on an exploratory visit to the area north and south of Grenfell, Assiniboia. The party was not impressed with the land in this part of the North-West Territories and returned to Winnipeg, whence they were sent to the area south-west of Saltcoats on the line of Manitoba and North-western Railway, which had

Public Archives of Canada C31·96

*Welsh Patagonians leaving Liverpool for Canada aboard the* Numidian

been acquired by the C.P.R. It appears that this district impressed them more favorably, probably because there was available land closer to the railway. Here the Department of the Interior reserved for the Patagonian Welsh all vacant even-numbered sections in townships 21 and 22, in ranges 3 and 4, west of the second meridian.[31]

On May 15, 1902, about 230 Patagonian Welsh bound for Canada sailed from Port Madryn to Liverpool on the Steamship *Orissa.* Most of them had been farming or ranching in Patagonia, but there were a few carpenters and a blacksmith. They had lived in the Argentine for varying lengths of time — some were relative newcomers, while others had grown up there.[32] The Argentine government was disappointed by their decision to emigrate, but was no doubt satisfied by the determination of the majority to remain in the territory. A few of the migrants remained in Britain because of sickness or other reasons. Two hundred and eight left Liverpool for Canada on the Allan steamship *Numidian* on June 12.

The Department of the Interior's reservation provided an ample choice of homesteads of 160 acres each. The Dominion Lands Act required an entry or registration fee of ten dollars, and title to the land could be secured in three years provided its requirements for residence and cultivation were met. But the Canadian government was not prepared to go much further than this. Many of the migrants had been forced to sell their properties in Patagonia at a small fraction of their value and had requested that free passage, a bonus payment of five dollars per head, and loans be provided. This the government refused, since it had already made a payment to the committee in London which had raised funds to assist the movement. Tents to shelter the immigrants, however, were made available until they could build houses, and assistance was to be given in securing employment. It appears that the Canadian government had the impression that the immigrants would all possess sufficient funds to make a fair start in the West. A carload of flour was sent to the settlement in December, to be distributed during the winter to those in need. In general, the government was well disposed towards the Welsh settlers, but was unwilling to make concessions which it was denying to other immigrant groups and individuals.

A few Welsh girls obtained employment in Winnipeg, and hospitalization was secured there for a number who were sick. On June 27, 197 of the immigrants left Winnipeg by train for the settlement, "in charge" (as the commissioner of immigration in Winnipeg put it) "of the Rev. [David G.] Davies, who has been truly a leader and father among his people in their emigration."[33] They detrained at Saltcoats, which was about fifteen miles from the centre of the reserved area.

By the early autumn of 1902 the *Manitoba Free Press* reported that the settlers had been busy since their arrival in erecting homes and stables, digging wells, and breaking land for the spring crop. Some had put up as much as forty tons of hay. A few of the dwellings were built of logs, but the majority were sod houses "skillfully plastered and white-washed."[34] This was the typical first house of thousands of other prairie pioneers. The press report indicated that, with a few exceptions, the majority of the Welsh were delighted with Canada and with the fertility of the soil. The change in climate may have been the chief problem of adjustment for the settlers.[35] Despite some hopeful predictions, no further reinforcements came from Argentina to join the arrivals of 1902. This group of prairie pioneers therefore numbered about 250 souls in all. In the summer of 1903 it was reported that all available homestead land had been taken up.[36]

The new settlement was known as Llewellyn, and this name was given to the first school district (Number 807) organized in February, 1903. Since the majority of the immigrants and their children spoke only Welsh and Spanish, teaching in English posed a problem for a time. In February, 1904, we find the school board reporting that they had secured the services of Mr. Moses Williams who had a certificate from London University. "A knowledge of the language [Welsh]," they stated, "is an absolute necessity to teach in this school for the first two or three years."[37] In January, 1904, Glendwyr district (Number 991) was organized, and in October, St. David's (Number 1141). At about the same time church services were also organized.

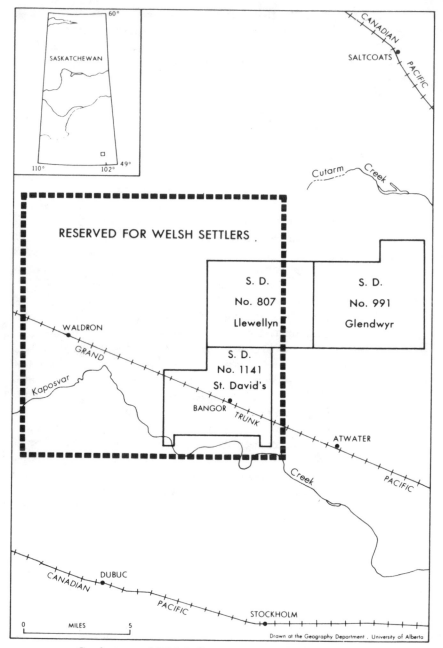

*Settlement of Welsh Patagonians in Saskatchewan*

The construction of a C.P.R. branch line about six miles south of the settlement in 1904 improved marketing arrangements, and Dubuc and Stockholm became market towns for the Welsh for a few years. Then in 1907 the Grand Trunk Pacific was constructed through the middle of the settlement, and the village of Bangor was established.

The Welsh seem to have done as well as most other pioneers in the park-belt region of the Canadian prairies. Whether they would have done better if they had settled in southern Alberta, in the ranching country or in the irrigation blocks being organized by the Canadian Northwest Irrigation Company, is problematical. The era of large ranches had ended, and many of them were being broken up to make land available to small stock raisers and farmers. Probably most of the best grazing lands were already under lease. Occupancy of the irrigation lands would have posed no problems to these pioneers of the Chubut Valley, but the lands were expensive and would have involved a fairly heavy debt commitment. The manager of the irrigation company had made a tentative promise to accept fifteen or twenty families on a trial basis,[38] but the suggestion was not followed up.

By the time of their migration to Canada these Welsh folk had abandoned the illusion that they could preserve their nationalism intact. They saw the inevitable pressures of assimilation which had appeared, and were to continue, in Patagonia. In coming to Canada they asked for no guarantees of language rights or of self-government. This is not to say that a community devoted to socio-religious homogeneity cannot successfully resist assimilation, as the German-speaking Hutterite communities in western Canada have proved. But the Welsh, unlike the Hutterites and Doukhobors, had changed with the changing times and had no further desire to isolate themselves in a British Dominion. Welsh church services and eisteddfodau were vital institutions in the lives of the first generation, but their political opinions did not prevent them from participating on Britain's side in World War I. They and their children soon became English-speaking, and their grandchildren, now widely dispersed by a changing agricultural economy, know little if any Welsh. The Patagonian Welsh became part of the western Canadian mosaic, but they made their chief contribution to the nation as successful farmers and builders of a community, cherishing the values of their nationality in family traditions and outlook, and not in the form of exclusive and intransigent assertions of national identity.

# 8     Bannock, Beans, and Bacon:
## An Investigation of Pioneer Diet
### by Edith Rowles-Simpson

*MORE than 217 Saskatchewan pioneers contributed informa-*
*tion for this article. Most of these contributors answered questions contained*
*in an eight-page questionnaire entitled "What Did Western Canadian*
*Pioneers Eat?" compiled by the author and the archives office. It was*
*impossible to include here all the information so generously contributed and*
*the questionnaires are carefully stored in the Saskatchewan Archives office,*
*University of Saskatchewan, for permanent reference.*

*Much of the detail for this article was taken from the questionnaires*
*answered by pioneers of the period 1880-1899, but all replies were used in*
*some way. All quotations, unless otherwise indicated, are from the*
*completed questionnaires.\**

In the early years, when there was no railroad west of Winnipeg, all
goods were hauled in carts and wagons drawn by ponies. In the early
summer the trails were bad and due to late arrivals some shortages
would occur. One time coal oil was so scarce that $10.00 a gallon was
charged for it by the only dealer who had any in stock . . . No one
carried heavy stocks. . . . much business was done by barter. Quality
in many cases was not as good as now. Jams and marmalades
contained little of the fruits they were supposed to contain, and today
would not sell. Prices were high in the early years on heavy goods. In
1880 and until the railroad reached "Troy" the freight rate from
Winnipeg was $10.00 a cwt. From 1880 to about 1892 all spices
reached retailers in wooden boxes containing five pounds and were
sold in bulk.

Such are the recollections of George Ballantine, who, as the youngest
of seven children, came to Prince Albert with his mother in 1880. Prince
Albert in that year was still the largest settlement in the Territories and
Mr. Ballantine, who by the time he was eleven was working in a general
store, had an unusual opportunity to observe the problems of pioneer

---

*This article originally appeared in *Saskatchewan History* for winter, 1952.

merchandising and particularly the characteristics of the foodstuffs which were handled.

In settlements like Prince Albert and Regina in the 1880's the stores carried quite a wide variety of foods, as is illustrated by the following advertisements culled from the local papers:

### ASHDOWN'S

| Canned Meats | Assorted Teas | Java Coffee |
|:---:|:---:|:---:|
| Sugar | Oatmeal | Tobaccos, etc. |

**At Lowest Prices**

Best XXXX flour always on hand.[1]

### REGINA TEA HOUSE

TEAS [six varieties listed].

IN CANNED GOODS Oysters, Lobsters, Jams, Jellies, Pickles, Peaches, Apricots, California Pears, Apples, Pine Apples, Pears, Tomatoes, Boston Baked Beans, Yarmouth Corn, Corned Beef (all sizes), Tongue, Roast Beef, Honey, Maple Syrup, Mince Meat, Coffee in Milk, Condensed Milk, etc.

IN PROVISIONS Hams, Bacon (smoked and dried), Bulk Goods, Corned Beef, Cheese, Eggs, Sausages, Flour, Bran, Oats, etc.

IN GROCERIES Sugar (Granulated), Paris Lump, Crushed, Bright Yellow, Low Yellow; Syrups, in tins and kegs; Tobaccos, Chewing and Smoking (all kinds); Cigars (all grades); Biscuits, full assortment.[2]

Large settlements such as Prince Albert and Regina may have had stocks of varied provisions, but settlements were few and far apart, and so the stores could not be depended upon as the only sources of food for the settlers. Nature provided an abundance of wild fruits and game, and the settlers supplemented these very soon by producing crops and raising livestock. One of the most interesting reports of growing food on the southern plains is that of Mr. and Mrs. Anthony Neville, who spent the winter of 1883 in Regina, moving to their homestead ten miles from what is now Lumsden in March, 1884. Mrs. L. M. Purdy of Balcarres, their daughter, relates the story. She writes:

By 1885 father and mother had land prepared so we planted a large garden and as soon as early vegetables — lettuce, radishes, young carrots, etc., were fit to use we took a buckboard load to Regina once a week. We found our best market at the N.W.M.P. barracks, where our buckboard would be surrounded by men hungry for fresh vegetables. We sold to the houses too, and often the women would ask if we would trade for sugar, rice, tea, or other things issued to them in larger quantities than they cared to use. More than one summer we got enough of the finest cut loaf sugar to do all our canning and preserves. The tea was the compressed kind, looked much like plug tobacco. We got plenty of rice, too.

There was a small hospital at the barracks, and meat and bread were issued to the amount needed if the hospital were full, so there we often got a big piece of fresh beef. They saved their dry bread, supposed to be for our chickens, but it was kept in clean cotton bags, and dry bread can be used in many ways. Mother used to put the meat into a big crock of buttermilk and if it were the least bit stale on the outside after a long drive home on a hot day, the buttermilk would sweeten it wonderfully.

Mother and I were real experts at finding and picking wild fruit, and the valleys near us provided a great quantity and variety. In 1889 we had a row of wild black currants in the garden and there was a grand crop of fruit on them and in the valley near. Mother and we girls picked twenty-four patent pails of beautiful currants and father took them to Regina and sold them for $2.00 a pail.

The year the C.P.R. was being completed mother used dried apples and wild raspberries and plenty of sugar and made many pails full of jam, selling it to the C.P.R. for twenty-five cents a pound, and the railway furnished the pails.

Father invested in a special variety of early potatoes, and got them on the market early and so was able to buy the things we needed to eat.

During several years we raised black hulless barley and had it ground to use for porridge and milk puddings. We also raised field peas for a few years, using them for soup and baking them like beans. We boiled wheat whole, ate with salt or sugar.

During several years, when we needed groceries, we would go with the wagon and pick buffalo bones and sell them in Pense, then buy flour, etc.

A typical shopping list for settlers in the earliest years (1883-1890) included sugar, tea, flour, dried apples, baking soda, salt, granulated oatmeal, rice, syrup, and perhaps coffee. Many of the settlers who arrived just after the transcontinental railway was built were able to secure land close to the railway, and so they were not far from a store and post office, but earlier settlers and later ones were not so fortunate. Mrs. H. Cudmore of Manor, now ninety years of age, tells of driving 100 miles from the station at Emerson, Manitoba, to their new home at Crystal City in the year 1881. (Crystal City is near what is now the border between Saskatchewan and Manitoba). We have numerous records of people going by ox team 50 miles or more to get supplies. No wonder they visited stores only once or twice a year! Mrs. Edith Kinneard Horn, now of Regina, whose parents set up housekeeping near Lumsden on section 14, township 21, range 19, west of the second meridian, in 1882, points out that she cannot say much about what was in the stores in the early years, for she did not get to town often. She lived only fifteen miles from

*Well-equipped pioneer kitchen*

Regina, but had to go there with oxen. Those pioneer women who lived further from the little settlements saw the inside of a store very seldom, the husbands having to do all the shopping. Eaton's catalogue, appearing for the first time about 1896, was a welcome shopping guide for these isolated homemakers.

On the long trek to their new homes settlers often used campfires for cooking their meals, and once they arrived at their destination the cookstove was soon set up. It was one of the most important furnishings in their new home. It served as a source of heat for the whole house, winter and summer alike, and from its oven came bread, roasts of meat, and dozens of cookies, puddings, and pies. On the stove the kettle or coffee pot was constantly steaming ready to serve a hot drink on a moment's notice. If a stove was not among the settler's effects brought from his former home, the homesteader would have to purchase one as soon as he arrived. The majority of stoves bought in those early days cost less than fifty dollars. Fourteen of our correspondents tell of paying less than ten dollars for this important item.

Mrs. S. A. Mann of Piapot relates the story of a stove bought from the Wrought Iron Range Company in 1892 for $86.00. She says, "When the salesman brought this stove in a wagon he simply dumped it out and let it fall to the ground. He guaranteed it would not break. He also gave the customer a sledge hammer and told him he could have the stove if he could break one of the lids." Those earliest settlers who could recall the maker of their first cookstove mention such names as Copp Brothers, Home Comfort, Majestic, McClary, Gurney, and Souvenir. Eaton's catalogue of 1907 offers the Kitchen Queen for coal and wood, with six holes, high shelf, and reservoir, for $41.85. Other cookstoves listed in the same cataogue are the Peerless for $48.00, Huron Chinook for $27.00, the Matchless, and the Gem. The Gem without reservoir for $12.00 is the cheapest stove listed; it is said to be of "cold rolled steel especially adapted for settlers."

We know that outdoor bake ovens have been used in many parts of Saskatchewan, but only four of our correspondents mention them. Cooking over open fireplaces indoors was quite uncommon, but there were some cases where it was done. We need more information on these two matters.

Wood from the river valleys and the hills was the fuel used by most of the pioneers. From Tantallon, Mrs. A. Kingdom tells of burning poplar and oak in the earliest days. Those who lived out on the prairies away from the rivers had to depend on buffalo chips for fuel. Mrs. Howard Burdett, living twenty miles north of Stoughton in 1889, writes, "Green wood was hauled from a wooded ravine and dried in the oven in forty below zero weather." We are told that "some anthracite coal was brought to Regina very early, and in 1891 lignite coal was available."

*Outdoor bread oven, Waterhen River, 1927*

Few people used coal in the earliest years because they lived so far from the railways, and besides, coal had to be paid for with money, whereas wood could be secured for the labor of cutting and hauling it. Sometimes the haul was a long one. Robert John Hogg tells of getting wood from the Turtle Mountains, a distance of thirty-five miles, about the year 1893, and others had an even longer haul.

Local coal mines were not uncommon in the south. Those living near Estevan, the Cypress Hills, and other surface coal mines were lucky. Some farmers had a coal supply right on their own land, but others had a long haul to make. Nelson Spencer of Carnduff relates how they used oxen to haul coal from Estevan, sixty miles away, about the year 1883. In spite of local coal mines and coal being shipped in, wood continued to be the common fuel for all pioneers except those living on the pairies far from natural wood supplies. These settlers had to depend upon coal, no matter what the price, once all the buffalo chips were used.

When selecting a site for the farmstead the wise farmer chooses a location near water. Pioneers with any experience in farming tried to do this, but they were not always successful, because shallow wells are comparatively scarce on the prairies. More than 60 out of 217 replies tell of a water supply one-quarter of a mile or more from the house. Twenty-one of these had to haul water in barrels more than a mile, and one person tells of hauling water eleven miles. Summer and winter, water was a necessity and many hours of hard labor were spent in melting snow in winter, hauling water in summer, and digging holes in the hope of locating water near to the farmstead. The government invested in well-drilling machinery, and by 1890 the North-West government owned no fewer than four well-boring machines which were to be used, under carefully drawn rules and regulations, for putting down wells in the North-West Territories.[3] We sympathize with Mrs. Jordens, who had many difficulties to contend with in the early years, not the least of which was about the year 1883 when they had water that was so alkali they mixed it with powdered ginger to take off the harsh taste.

Tea was the usual hot beverage in the early days. Brands of tea which were used included Red Rose, Gold Standard, McClary's, Blue Ribbon, and Ceylon. These were often put up in fancy tin tea caddies of one-, three-, or five-pound size, but the cheapest and commonest way to buy tea was in bulk. The stores bought the tea in chests lined with lead paper and the tea was weighed out in brown-paper bags. The price seems to have been about thirty-five cents a pound whether it was green or black. One householder reports buying green tea dust at ten cents a pound in 1890.

Coffee was not used as commonly as it is today. Those who told of using it were about equally divided in their purchase of coffee beans and ready-ground coffee. A few bought green beans and roasted their own. Substitutes for coffee were fairly common, which would indicate that those who were fond of using coffee found it too expensive to buy. Barley, roasted and put through the food chopper, was the usual substitute; but rye and wheat were also used. One housewife reports using toast to make a synthetic coffee. Cocoa is occasionally mentioned as a beverage, but water and milk took second and third place after tea and coffee.

Then as now meat was one of the cook's chief concerns. Pemmican, used by the Indians and explorers, was not used very much by the settlers; only one of our correspondents mentions it. Mrs. Joe Keys, now of Keystown, tells us that her parents at Wolseley in 1886 had as their meat supply "pemmican and the odd deer."

John Wilson, whose father settled at Saltcoats in 1883, when asked how his parents got fresh meat, replied, "With a gun." Though the buffalo disappeared from the plains shortly after the C.P.R. was constructed, there was still a variety of other game to be had. Around Prince Albert and Battleford, the occasional moose or bear was brought in, in addition to the smaller game. From the early settlements in the south we have reports of antelope, deer, badger, and porcupine being used as food. The variety of wild fowl was greater than today, prairie chicken, ducks, and geese predominating. Mrs. Keys writes, "About 1896 the wild geese came by hundreds and were plentiful for years." Reports have been received of eating crane, grouse, partridge, plover, snipe, and wild turkey. Mrs. J. Wilkie, an 1889 bride in the Wilkie settlement, near Pense, states, "The game improved after grain was planted." John R. Bird of Broadview, who came to the West in 1882, tells us that "the meat supply in the early years was rabbit, more rabbit and still more rabbit, prairie chicken, duck and sometimes deer." He adds that they could have fresh meat every morning out of a snare. He gives as typical menus for the years 1882-1886:

*Breakfast* wheat porridge with a little molasses (no sugar), toast, rabbit stew, tea, no milk.

*Dinner* rabbit, potatoes, bread and tea.

*Supper* more rabbit, potatoes (fried if we had grease), bread, tea.

Settlers raised their own meat as soon as possible after getting established. Nelson Spencer of Carnduff tells us that weanling pigs were worth fifty cents to a dollar each about 1883. Everyone butchered their own meat in the fall if they had anything ready. Pork was the most common meat used, beef came next, fowl was always a standby, and very few people mention using lamb or mutton. Fresh meat was available all winter because it could be kept frozen, settlers soon learning to cut meat into useable sizes before freezing. For summer use meat had to be preserved. Some housewives fried out pork, placed it in crocks, and covered it with fat. This fresh meat, stored in the cellar, would last for several months. Salt was the most common preservative for meat. Some used dry salt, but pickling, followed sometimes by smoking, was the favorite way for preserving pork. Beef, too, was often pickled, though corned beef never became as common as pickled pork. Mrs. George Johnson, who set up housekeeping at Langenburg in 1890, reversed the process of cold storage in winter and pickling in summer. She had a deep well for keeping the meat fresh in summer, and she pickled meat for winter.

In the *Regina Leader* of March 15, 1883, the following advertisement appeared:

P. BONNEAU, corner of Lorne and Eleventh Avenue, dealer in groceries and provisions; on hand about twenty tons of fresh buffalo meat.

This must have been one of the last occasions when buffalo meat was available. A few people, no doubt, bought meat occasionally in the early years, but few of our correspondents mention the store as a source of fresh meat. At Wolseley the storekeeper kept corned beef in brine in barrels, and customers took their own container to the store to bring the dripping meat home. Mr. George Ballantine, of Prince Albert, states, "We bought beef and pork from farmers, prairie chicken, wild ducks, geese, moose and deer from the Indians."

The "beef ring," an arrangement whereby neighbors took turns providing a carcass of beef to be shared among the members of the ring, was not common in the earliest western pioneer days. Only two beef rings are reported before the year 1900. We have records of seventeen rings organized before 1910, an additional eighteen started between 1911-1915, and approximately fifty rings reported operating after 1915.

Some early settlers made use of the abundant supplies of fish in lakes and rivers. The most interesting fish story comes from Sam H. McWilliams of Moose Jaw. He writes:

> In the spring of 1885 father rented a farm ten miles east of Moose Jaw, one mile south of the Moose Jaw River. Early in the spring dad took the shot gun and went to the river to hunt ducks. The spring freshet was on and in one place the river bed was narrow. The suckers trying to get upstream were so thick their fins were sticking up out of the water. Dad found a net made out of slender willows hid in the bushes. It was made on the style of the old wire fly net with a cone inside so fish couldn't get out again. It had been made by Indians. Dad placed it in the water where it was shallow and wide. He built a wall of stone on each side out to the snare so the fish had to go into the net. The next morning it was packed full, three or four barrels full. They were cleaned and salted for summer use. Each neighbour did the same until all were satisfied.

Several other early settlers report that they made a practice of taking fish in the spring and salting it for future use. One writes,[4] "Every spring for years we took suckers, salting some for later use, and we often went to Long Lake for pike and pickerel, salting and smoking these." Mr. and Mrs. Joseph Hamilton, who started housekeeping at Pense in 1891, write, "In the early years the men went to Little Arm and caught fish, cleaned and put it in brine and then nailed it on the west side of the house to dry." The kinds of fish mentioned were usually suckers, pike, pickerel, mullet, and goldeyes, but in the north they had whitefish, trout, and other varieties. Not all the early settlers used fish. One early settler says,[5] "We had very little fish, as fishing on the river takes time." Many settlers after about 1890 tell of buying frozen fish in winter and we conclude that some people caught fish and sold it to augment their income. Mr. C. A. Atkinson, now of Brooksby, tells of taking 400 pounds of fish from the Carrot River during the winters 1908, 1909, and 1910.

It was not easy in the early years to get a supply of fresh vegetables. Mrs. L. M. Purdy, quoted before, tells us that in the winter of 1883 the only potatoes available in Regina were frozen. Many of our earliest correspondents tell us that one could rarely get potatoes from the store, but had to get them from neighbors. Many people brought a generous supply of potatoes with them from the East, and as soon as possible they started gardens. The first gardens were not always successful, because seeds were often not suitable, and growing conditions differed from those the gardeners had been used to. Gradually the settlers improved the garden crops by keeping their own seed potatoes, peas, and beans, saving the first tomato that ripened and using it for seed, and adapting their methods of cultivation to the new conditions. At Prince Albert in 1881

*Working the potato patch*

the Ballantine family grew enough potatoes, cabbage, carrots, turnips, and onions to last for the winter. In the summer of 1883 A. B. Potter south of Whitewood grew his first crop of potatoes. In 1884 Robert Laidlaw of Summerberry also grew potatoes, and we have records of potatoes and other vegetables being grown near Regina and Saltcoats that same year. Good gardens soon began to appear elsewhere. Mrs. Cudmore, who settled at Crystal City, Manitoba, in 1881, says they always grew their own vegetables right from the earliest years. Mr. Lindeburgh, born near Punnichy in 1885, echoes the statement. As every pioneer knows, the popular place to grow potatoes was on the fireguard and, as you approached the tiny shack, there was usually no gate to bar your way, but as you slowed your horses to cross the fireguard you could inspect the potato patch, which gave some indication of the settler's size of family and farming ability.

Mrs. W. Curry, of Burrows, just east of Whitewood, who settled there in 1888, writes: "When people grew potatoes, they always made sure to keep seed. Newcomers got their seed from the earliest settlers. We could always grow good gardens here and did. Rhubarb was very useful in the making of pies and as fruit."

Many people refer to using mushrooms and lambs quarters about 1900. Mrs. Taylor of Paynton, who came west as one of the Barr Colonists, writes: "Lambs quarters were a favourite green. I well remember driving four miles to Mr. Peter Paynter's, an old settler, to pick a large sackful, a week's supply, and how good it tasted. We soon grew a supply on our own farm. Mushrooms and wild strawberries were in abundance in the early years."

111

How to preserve fruits and vegetables in the earliest years taxed the housewife's ingenuity. Mrs. Ed. Wilson, of Bienfait, points out that with no sealers, fruits had to be preserved in a heavy syrup. Crocks and jam jars were used, and wild fruit was abundant. There were strawberries, raspberries, saskatoons, currants, cranberries, buffalo berries, and gooseberries, the only limits on the amount to be preserved being the problems of buying sugar and picking wild berries. Some gardens soon helped to provide food to be preserved. Wild fruits were transplanted into home gardens, rhubarb patches were established, and wonder berries and citron were grown. If sufficient sugar could be spared, delicious citron preserves could be made.

The problem of buying sugar was serious; it was not only a matter of cost. Mrs. A. B. Potter, who arrived in Whitewood in 1884, says there was no white sugar to be bought. Mr. George Ballantine makes the same statement, adding that it was either yellow or brown sugar, and a ten-pound sack would cost $2.25. In 1880 there was no corn syrup; it was sugar syrup and came in twenty-five-pound wooden pails at $5.00 a pail. Other early settlers corroborate these statements. No doubt this sugar syrup was molasses, a by-product in the manufacture of cane sugar. Molasses, and later corn syrups, were staples in the cupboard. The earliest brands of syrup, Beehive, Rogers, and Edwardsburg, soon became well known, and from about 1890 no cupboard was properly stocked without a five- or ten-pound pail of syrup. Mrs. Frank Davis, who settled at Glen Adelaide in 1896, writes, "We used mostly maple sugar and we made it."

Mrs. Purdy's mother had been reading about the new method for preserving food by canning, and in 1885 she tried it out. Without proper jars and rubbers it was not easy to preserve food successfully by sterilization, but in spite of this, the idea spread, and other housewives were soon canning food. Among the earliest to preserve food by canning were the John Wilsons in 1886, the Nelson Spencers in 1888, Mrs. Jas. Geddes in 1891, and Mrs. Mary Elizabeth Roe in 1893.

Seventy-three housewives tell of drying peas for winter. Saskatoons, corn, and beans were each dried in more than forty homes. Other foods preserved by drying included apples, pumpkin, plums, raspberries, meat, fish, herbs, peel, and kale.

Pickling and brining vegetables were common practices, and in order to make pickles many pioneers made their own vinegar. Mrs. Jordens, at St. Hubert Mission, reports that her family made vinegar in 1885 "by using a mother of vinegar borrowed from a neighbour, adding sugar and water to fill a bottle."

Explorers in the West may have managed sometimes without flour, but as soon as homes were established flour became a necessity. Ogilvie's seems to have been the best-known flour in the earliest years, and it was at first shipped in from the East, usually from Brandon. Other brands of flour used by the pioneers were Strong Baker, Five Roses, Royal Household, Purity, Harvest Queen, Four X, and Lake of the Woods. Local mills were established early. Some of the locations were Prince Albert (Kidd's Mill), 1875; Regina, 1880's; Cannington Manor, 1882; Millwood, Manitoba, 1885; Fort Qu'Appelle, 1885; Virden, Manitoba, 1886; Wolseley, 1886; Lumsden, 1890's; and Gainsboro, 1900. Millwood must have been a busy spot in the autumn. The Wilsons, living forty miles from Whitewood, took their grist sixty miles to Millwood as early as 1886. The Currys, settling in Burrows in 1888, took their wheat ten miles to the mill. There were loads of wheat from Valley View, now Tantallon, hauled thirty miles to Millwood. It was about twenty miles for the Langenburg people, and in 1890, oxcart or sleigh was used for the trip. Mrs. Emily G. Barker, of Churchbridge, states that from 1892-1897 they took their grist thirty miles to Millwood from Kinbrae (now Liscard) and brought back six or eight bags of Ivory Straights. It was usual to take a load of wheat and exchange it for flour, bran, and shorts. A year's supply of flour was what most pioneers hoped to lay by. They were aware that newly milled flour did not make as good bread as that which was aged about ten months, so it was important to lay in a good stock. Modern millers are permitted to use improvers to age the flour rapidly, but in the 1890's there was little knowledge of cereal chemistry.

Some farmers were not within reach of a local mill and so they had to sell their wheat and buy flour. Some of these farmers were able to buy a year's supply but one pioneer,[6] settling near Stoughton in 1889, says, "We bought Harvest Queen, a second grade flour at about $2.00 for ninety-eight pounds; only one sack at a time was bought, for that was all we could afford."

To those of us who now live in the "Wheat Province" it seems strange that only about half the settlers who came before 1900 used wheat for making porridge. Some soaked the whole wheat overnight and cooked it slowly for hours but most people cracked it or ground it; sometimes they used a coffee mill, but more often a hand grinder or crusher. Many mention that they prepared wheat for the household in the same chopper that was used for preparing feed for the livestock. One careful housekeeper points out that, when preparing wheat for the family, both the chopper and the wheat were first carefully cleaned. Mr. Sam H. McWilliams writes, "I remember, as a boy of ten years, pounding wheat on a smooth flat rock with a hammer to make porridge for the family, not once, but many times." Mr. Gus Lauttamus of Tantallon states that they bought Four X flour but ground their own whole-wheat flour with millstones. Some of the whole-wheat flour produced in this way was made into porridge. A few people had wheat prepared for porridge-meal as part of their grist. Some of those who did not use

113

whole-wheat porridge in the early years tell us that they learned to use it later.

Out of forty-one samples of typical breakfast menus served before 1900, thirty-seven include porridge, usually oatmeal porridge. One hardy pioneer tells of porridge made from shorts, while another states that they usually ate cornmeal mush with molasses. Milk usually accompanied the porridge and often brown sugar or molasses, rarely white sugar.

Bread-making was one of the housewife's heaviest tasks, for she not only made bread for her own family, but often for the bachelors living near. Mrs. Emily Barker, living at Churchbridge since 1890, describes a wooden trough for mixing bread dough, large enough for twenty-four loaves. The pioneer breadmakers needed a cheap, reliable source of yeast, and no less than seventy-five of our informants used hops. The storekeepers kept a supply of hops on hand, but once the housekeeper had made her first purchase of these she tried to keep her own supply of yeast on hand, growing it in a jar of potato water, flour, and sugar. She often called this yeast mixture "starter." Thirteen of our contributors state that they made salt-rising bread. According to one of our correspondents who knew how to make both salt-rising and hops bread, the salt-rising bread was not as nice as the other, so she taught many of her neighbors how to use hops. When yeast cakes were available in the stores they were the "Royal" brand and came in round cakes in little round cardboard boxes.

Substitutes for bread were bannock, flapjacks, and biscuits. Mrs. E. Borwick, now of Meskanaw, writes: "In early days you could always get suet and we used it for puddings — some rendered and used it to make bannock; my husband had always been used to bannock; when he was a boy they used nothing but. He was born in Manitoba and his mother and father before him." Flapjacks were made of flour, baking soda, sour milk, and salt. The hot iron griddle or frying pan was rubbed with a piece of fat pork and the flapjacks were browned, turned, and browned on the other side. They were a staple for breakfast for many westerners for many years. The dough which we today bake in the oven as biscuits was, in the early days, often baked on top of the stove, either on a griddle or right on the stove lids, turned and browned (or blackened slightly) on both sides. It made a light and filling hot bread.

Most housewives used baking soda and sour milk or buttermilk for leavening their baking. Tartaric acid, rather than the cream of tartar we use today, was at first on the shelf to be used with baking soda in recipes where sour milk, molasses, and other acids were not present. Twenty-one of our replies tell of the housewife making her own baking powder. A recipe from an early cookbook suggests the following recipe for baking powder:

Ground rice — five ounces.
Carbonate of soda — three ounces.
Tartaric acid — two ounces.

Self-rising flour is not a new development. Mrs. Neville[7] used to make prepared flour in the early days, sifting weighed quantities of flour, tartaric acid, and soda.

Though condensed milk was available in the earliest years and has been the standby of prairie bachelors, the pioneer housewives seem to have used it rarely; instead they wanted to own a cow. This was not always easy. Robert John Hogg of Carnduff tells how, when he was eleven years old, he worked out to earn a cow for the family. In 1893 he could earn only fifty cents a day, so it took a long time before enough money was accumulated to make the necessary purchase. Once a cow was acquired, its contribution to the family was highly prized. Mrs. Purdy writes, "In July, 1883 we bought a cow and kept her milking two years before she freshened."

Neighbors were generous about supplying milk for newcomers; many are the records of "getting milk from the neighbors until we got a cow." An ingenious method in winter for sending milk to a neighbor was to pour what could be spared each day into a pail, allowing it to freeze and adding more the next day. The solid container of frozen milk could then be delivered without fear of spilling. Everyone made her own butter, and if there was any surplus, it was traded at the store. Mrs. Purdy tells how one year, when butter was 12½ cents a pound, and Regina could not buy all that the farmers were making, her mother made cheese and sold it for the same price as butter. She did well, for she was able to make twice as much cheese as she could have made butter. Many pioneers made pressed cheese, and they sometimes prepared their own rennet from the stomach of a freshly slaughtered calf. In addition to making cheddar or Canadian cheese one settler tells of making Edam cheese and another made Dutch cheese. Cottage cheese or curds was a common item on many menus.

Establishing a poultry flock was not an easy task. Mrs. Horn, now of Regina but born at Lumsden, says, "Our first chickens were hatched under a prairie chicken." Mr. and Mrs. A. B. Potter set up housekeeping at Montgomery P.O., N.W.T., about twenty miles south of Whitewood, in 1884. They had two hens with which to start their flock. In spite of the ravages of mink, coyote, and badger, poultry flocks increased and egg money was added to butter money to help buy groceries. Since poultry flocks were not adequately housed and fed, the hens usually stopped laying in winter. Housewives packed eggs for winter using a variety of ways to do this. Salt, in spite of the way it hardened if allowed to get damp, seems to have been the most common material for packing around the eggs. Oats, other grains, and bran were next in popularity. Three people mention using sifted ashes. Greasing the eggs, then wrapping them in paper or packing them in crates was the method used by twenty-two people. Lime water and brine are also mentioned, but they were not common. Waterglass, once it was introduced, was the most popular preservative, but it was not available in the earliest years.

Most housewives made their own soap, collecting wood ashes in a barrel during the winter in order to make their own lye for the spring soap-making. Water was poured into the barrel of ashes and allowed to drip out of the bung-hole at the bottom. The liquid collected was a lye solution ready to be mixed with the accumulated fat for the soap-making. The merchants, of course, handled laundry soaps, and before 1890 the brands available were Royal Crown, Sunlight, Fels Naptha, Dryman's, Comfort, and Pearl. Royal Crown seems to have been by far the most commonly used commercial laundry soap.

Our records show that there have been many changes in the merchandising of foods. In the earliest years stores stocked very little besides staples, and the supplies were kept in bins or barrels to be weighed or measured out to the customers. Even the brown-paper bags are different now. Some people recall that the paper bags were "once made like envelopes; the bottom corner had to be folded to make the bottom rectangular." Butter used to be sold to the storekeeper in rolls wrapped in butter cloth or packed in crocks. Lard was packed in casks. For the customer butter and lard were gouged out of the container with a circular motion of the knife, the pieces often being sold on chipped plates. Dried apples and later other dried fruit might be seen in the store in open containers where the customer could, and often did, help himself to a sample as he stood waiting for his order to be filled.

Granite cooking pots, tin milk pans and dippers, and heavy pottery dishes were the common kitchen utensils in every houshold. Heavy iron pots, dutch ovens, and frying pans brought to the West by the settlers are probably still in use today. The butter bowl and paddle for working butter were of wood, and sometimes a wooden butter table with a heavy wooden arm something like a rolling pin was made for working butter. The housewife often had to manage with woefully inadequate equipment, but she learned to improvise here as well as in her cooking.

Mrs. Purdy has submitted menus typical of what her mother served in the winters, about 1885:

*Breakfast* porridge or mush, milk and brown sugar, sometimes hash or cold meat, warmed potatoes, bread, butter if we had any, stewed or canned fruit.

*Dinner* stewed rabbit with dumplings, potatoes and another vegetable, sometimes plain pudding or pie.

*Supper* variable — a hot soup, pancakes, Johnny cake with syrup, sometimes a steamed pudding, fruit, bread, hot biscuits, perhaps potatoes cooked some tasty way, often raw onions.

Mrs. A. Bishop of Broadview came to live in the West in 1885, when she was only six years old. There were five in the family. The father had helped to build the C.P.R. as far as Wolseley. Mrs. Bishop remembers that typical menus for their meals were:

*Breakfast* porridge made of ground wheat.
*Dinner* potatoes, and one other kind of vegetable, sometimes meat, bread and butter.
*Supper* bread and milk, sometimes boiled wheat with milk and no sugar.

Mrs. Mary Elizabeth Roe started houskeeping at Pense in 1893. She gives as typical menus:

*Breakfast* oatmeal porridge, fat bacon, eggs, bread, butter and tea.
*Dinner* fat pork, potatoes and other vegetable and apple pie.
*Supper* rice and egg or canned salmon or hash, buttermilk pancakes and syrup.

Mrs. Jos. Keys writes, "The breakfasts in 1886 consisted of porridge, milk, tea for the older ones, some white bread, some molasses or syrup; and the other two meals differed slightly with perhaps a small quantity of meat or fish." Mrs. Keys was one of the children in a family of nine, the children ranging in age from two to twenty-three. She tells how, in 1886, she helped to serve the first Christmas dinner for their family in what is now Saskatchewan. She says: "The menu was little different from any other day. The older members of the family were away from home working."

Mrs. Ida Hanna (nee Keys) of Keystown writes: "As to shortages in early days, if the year was poor, as many were then, it meant practically no vegetables for the winter, and often not enough potatoes, although after 1887 I think we always had some. In that case, canned tomatoes were used more than anything else to help out."

John Wilson of Springside, who, as a boy of seven, settled with his family at Saltcoats in 1883, answers the question, "Were you ever reduced to almost starvation level?" by the following statement: "Only once when the snow was so deep that we could not get out. We divided the flour up and each one got just a slice of bread three times a day, but we always had rabbits which helped a lot. It was six miles to the nearest house. The man there walked over on his snowshoes to see us. He came the next day and brought some flour."

Mrs. Ed. Wilson was a tiny child when her parents settled at Oxbow in 1892. She writes: "My father was an Anglican clergyman and I used to go with him through the country and met some pretty slim menus. I remember once it was a sort of porridge made of flour and water." One is impressed, when reading replies, at the number of times courage and ingenuity were required of our western pioneers. Many were the

117

privations they endured. Mrs. Mary A. Jordens, married in 1887, tells of living on an Indian reserve at Fort Pelly for three years. For three months she had to cook on an open hearth, baking bannocks in front of the hot coals. Potatoes were cooked in an open kettle hanging on an iron bar over the fire. They had no cow until 1889, and the baby, until a year old, had nothing but mother's milk. Most pioneers did not suffer as many privations as Mrs. Jordens, but nearly all can mention at least one occasion when they were very short of food. It is quite remarkable how many of our contributors assure us that, once established, they were never short again. They often tell of neighbors helping one another, and over and over again we are assured that if a person was willing to work, there was no need to go hungry, even in the early years, in this land of plenty. In 1883, shortly after the founding of the *Prince Albert Herald*, a correspondent wrote a letter to the paper stating that westerners had to live on little else but salt pork and beans. In repy an indignant westerner had the following article printed as a rebuttal in the *Prince Albert Times*, January 31, 1883:

> Two or three gentlemen of Prince Albert gave a quiet little supper to a few friends the other evening at Dobb's Hotel, when the following menu was served —

## MENU

*Oysters*

Oysters Raw          Oyster Soup

*Fish*

White Fish Broiled          Anchovy Sauce

*Entrees*

Curried Eggs          Risole of Chicken Joints

Roast Beef          Boiled Turkey, Oyster Sauce

*Game*

Ptarmigan, Broiled on Toast

Prairie Chickens

*Pastry*

Plum Pudding, Brandy Sauce

Peach and Plum Tarts

*Jellies*

Wine and Ornamented

*Dessert*

Apples  Pears  Plums  Nuts  Raisins

Crackers and Cheese

Tea          Coffee

Mrs. Jordens, recalling Christmas, 1886, writes: "There were mother, father, Frank Jordens (my fiancé), Napoleon, Midas, Virginia, Erica, Victoria, Almira, baby Frederick and myself. We had roast pork and chicken with onion gravy, and a large plum pudding made from directions brought from England by Frank. It had to be boiled six hours steadily. We had doughnuts and raisin pies at other meals."

Mr. and Mrs. George Johnson settled at Langenburg in 1890. The earliest Christmas menu that the nine surviving members of their family can remember was "Roast goose with raisin filling; vegetables, Christmas cake; coffee. The Christmas cake was raised with yeast and had in it peel and raisins. It was a sort of raised fruit loaf."

Mrs. Alexina Morrison, aged eighty-seven years and now living at Carlyle, remembers serving the following menu, Christmas 1899, to her husband and a few bachelors from neighboring farms: chicken, head cheese, vegetables, potatoes, pies, apples, cakes.

The pioneers always had room for one more at the table and as a result western Canadian hospitality has become a tradition. What the menus were depended upon resourcefulness of the breadwinner and his helpmate, but in spite of shortages the early settlers seem to generally have had enough to eat.

# 9    Pioneer Church Life in Saskatchewan

## by Christine MacDonald

THE importance of their religious heritage to many of the early settlers in the Saskatchewan area is evident from the Saskatchewan Archives questionnaire on pioneer churches. This is one of the series of questionnaires which the archives circulated a few years ago to early settlers of the province. We must bear in mind that a large proportion of the 300 who filled in the questionnaire were people who themselves or whose parents had been closely connected with pioneer church activity. It is of some significance, however, that, in speaking of the time which elapsed between the arrival of the first settlers in their districts and the first church services held there, approximately sixty-five percent reported that services, of a kind at least, had begun within a year and most of the remainder indicated that religious activity had started within five years.*

To a number of districts came groups of people of common ethnic and religious backgrounds, accompanied by their priests, clergymen, or lay preachers. Mr. Louis Demay reports that the first settlers in the St. Brieux district journeyed from France with their missionary priest who became as well their postmaster and immigration agent.[1] In the Leofeld and Annaheim districts, which belonged to St. Peter's Colony, with headquarters at Muenster, Benedictine fathers arrived with the settlers.[2] The Mennonite colonies around Drake and Rosthern were served from the beginning by homesteader clergymen.[3] Many of the members of the Primitive Methodist Colony at Pheasant Forks, settled in 1882-1883, had been local preachers in England, and by adopting the old Methodist circuit plans these men were able to provide services to the whole colony.[4]

However, it was not just in colonies such as these that newly arrived settlers showed their interest and concern in carrying on the religious activity they had been accustomed to in their former homes. Methodist

---

*This article originally appeared in *Saskatchewan History* for winter, 1960.

services, for instance, were held almost immediately after settlement began in the Eastview district near Pasqua in 1891, reports Mr. Thomas E. Allcock,[5] and in the Meadow Bank district, according to Mr. William A. Harrison.[6] In the Northlands district[7] Presbyterian services began with settlement and one month after arrival of the first people in the Paynton area.[8] Mrs. James Bews notes that her husband, a Presbyterian minister who came as a homesteader with those who first took up land around what is now Tyvan, held services in his own home and in the homes of others.[9] Mass was celebrated almost immediately after the first Roman Catholic settlers came to Vossen[10] and to Kenaston.[11]

Services were held in a great variety of places before churches were built. One hardly needs to mention the use of schoolhouses as this occurred at some time in the history of almost every country congregation for periods varying from a few months to many years, as in a district near Togo where people met in the school from 1906 to 1952.[12] Summer services in the school are still a part of life in some prairie farming communities. Only one questionnaire indicates that the trustees would not allow church services in the school and here, in time, a community hall was built on the understanding that it could be used for services by any denomination in return for contributions to its up-keep.[13]

In the earliest days of settlement, homes were very widely used, if we can generalize safely on the results of the questionnaire. Many reported that the first services in their region, or the first of their own denomination, were held in houses of homesteaders or ranchers, often their own or their parents'. This practice was not confined to the very early years. Mr. A. G. Carter says that Protestants in his district (midway between Wadena and Elfros) met in the Milligan home from about 1915 to 1928.[14] Many of the houses were of a truly pioneer variety — sod and log. Mrs. Peter McLellan reports that the first Presbyterian services in the Clare community near Arcola were held in her father's home, at that time a one-room log hut into which fifteen people could squeeze. If more than fifteen attended, they had to stand outside at the open door.[15] At Paynton, writes Mrs. William Taylor, "In 1903 services were organized and held at our home, a log house 17 by 19 with two rooms. Democrat seats, boxes, boards and four chairs comprised the seating. Even the cookstove, well black-leaded, cold and covered with newspaper, seated four back to back. We children often sat on it. About sixteen to twenty was the usual number although sometimes thirty."[16] In several districts where people customarily met for church in a school or even in a small church building, with the onset of winter the congregation moved to houses either because of heating difficulties or to save some of the members from too long a journey in cold weather.

With services in homes there were bound to be distractions. Mr. W.

S. Rattray remembers "when I attended church and a flock of pigeons were in the attic of the house and they were *not* quiet."[17] "In Moosomin," writes Mr. Victor C. McCurdy, "I attended church in April, 1883 in the home of Mr. Struthers, an American fur trader. During the service Mrs. Struthers climbed up a ladder to reach a pan of bread and put it in the stove oven."[18]

Homes and schools were by no means the only meeting places for communities lacking church buildings. Services were held under trees, in tents, granaries, lumberyard offices, in or above stores, in hotel parlors or dining rooms, Orange or Oddfellows halls, town halls, railway station waiting rooms, and even in stables. An interesting progression was described by Mrs. T. C. Johns.[19] The first service in the Zelma area, she writes, was held in the dining tent of a railway camp in 1908, the second in a house to which the minister brought a hand organ. In the village, church was first held in a butcher shop. The congregation then proceeded for services to the living quarters of the flour mill, the owners of which rejoiced in the luxury of an organ. Attendance increased, necessitating a move, along with the organ, to the livery barn loft where services were held until fall when the loft was filled with feed. Thereafter, from 1907 to 1909 when the church was built, a boxcar provided accommodation for the congregation. Another barn turns up in the questionnaire sent in by Mrs. Thomas Goldsmith.[20] Their first services, led by a minister from Whitewood eight miles away, occurred in a barn owned by a real-estate company. Here the horses were "put up" underneath while the congregation sat in the loft. Mrs. Goldsmith recalls that it was very cold in winter but, she says, "Attendance was good." A rather startling location was the setting for the first Presbyterian services in Wiseton — the poolroom.[21] That the owner and operator of the poolroom was Roman Catholic is an indication of the good feeling which must have existed there between people of different faiths.

In a newly settled area, Sunday school, taught either in a home or at the school, was often the first form of religious activity. In general, Sunday school or catechism classes were either continued or begun following the organization of church services, and in several cases where services were held during the summer months only, Sunday school was carried on the year round. Almost all of the questionnaires stated that religious training for children was provided in the community during the summer months at least for several years, if it did not continue indefinitely. Several reported that the first Sunday school was held in their own home, with their father or mother as teacher, or indicated that they themselves had taught or had taken some responsibility for the Sunday school in their district or town. Classes in homes were usually attended by all the neighboring children regardless of differences in parental denominations, and in several towns, even after church groups of two or more denominations were established, the children were sent to a union Sunday school. In Yorkton, said Mrs. W. S. de Balinhard, who belonged to an Anglican family, she first attended Sunday school in her mother's home, then went to a union Sunday school which was organized in 1893 with a prominent Methodist as superintendent.[22] A union Sunday school was started in Moosomin before 1883, according to Mrs. Marion Anderson.[23]

A rather intriguing figure emerges from the questionnaire sent in by Mrs. Joel Anderson, who deals with the Willowbrook area.[24] "Before any church was built or services held in homestead days," she writes, "Mr. W. R. Sutherland travelled around driving a team or a buggy and took the gospel to the homesteaders' children. He drove from homestead to homestead where there were children, taught them a lesson, and gave them the Sunday school quarterlies. He had me study the lessons every Sunday then told me to write down the story of the lesson from memory.... People used to call him Sunday School Sutherland. He used to stay overnight wherever he happened to be by evening. He came along one day when my father was digging potatoes and I was picking them up. He just sat in the buggy by the potato patch and asked me questions on the previous lessons. I remember how pleased and surprised my father seemed because I could answer the questions." "Sunday School" Sutherland appears also in the questionnaire completed by Mr. W. S. Rattray, who refers to him holding services at Saltcoats until the Anglican church was built about 1899. Mr. Rattray remarks, "Mr. Sutherland would have service in any house and the people were glad to have him any time."[25]

That the children of Saskatchewan pioneers were not always paragons of good behavior at Sunday school is demonstrated by a story told by Mr. Charles Davis who lived in what is now the Meota area. The Sunday school teacher at Parkdale school around 1912 was always accompanied by her husband. The rest had better appear in Mr. Davis's own words. "She did the teaching. He simply drove to and fro and slept soundly during the lessons. I remember on one occasion the elder children tied his laces together, then stuck a pin in his rear."[26] One can imagine that instruction came to an explosive end that day!

The hardships of pioneer life were often shared with the settler by priest, minister, and student missionary. Many were homesteaders or farmers as well, combining missionary labors with work on the land. St. Elizabeth Mission, near Gravelbourg, for example, was established around 1910 when Father Wilhelm took a homestead and built a small house and chapel from which he also served Grismerville, Gooding, and St. Boswells.[27] A few added even a third occupation, that of schoolteacher, as did the Methodist minister in the early years of settlement in the Norquay area, who homesteaded and taught school in the Arabella district and held services at Mellmore school,[28] and the Rev. C. B. Kerr, a Presbyterian minister who was the first teacher at Hutton school near Redvers.[29] Others no doubt had a similar experience to that of Father Sinnett who looked after the Roman Catholics in the LeRoy-McGuire area. According to Mrs. John C. Knaus, Father Sinnett lived at first in a shack through the cracks of which rain leaked in summer and snow blew in winter.[30]

Long drives are still the order of the day for clergymen or student ministers with country appointments, but whereas they now travel by automobile, in those days they went their rounds by horse and buggy, on horseback, and sometimes on foot. Almost everyone with a village or country charge was responsible for at least two other appointments. Mrs. J. R. Aikenhead's story of the student minister at Melfort who held services at six appointments, three each Sunday, is by no means unusual.[31] Many of the student ministers in what is now the Arcola area, says Mrs. Peter McLellan, "walked as much as twenty miles on Sunday leaving [Sunday] morning or after Sunday service for as many as three or four services in the day. They might get a drive at times."[32] For the first ten Sundays in his field, Mr. William J. Scott, a Presbyterian student missionary-homesteader in the Elbow country around 1908-1909, walked thirty miles. When he acquired a broncho his labors were no easier as he had to take on another preaching point.[33] Mrs. James Bews reports that when she and her husband, Rev. James Bews, were homesteading halfway between Glidden and Eatonia around 1911-1912, his territory extended from south of Kindersley to the South Saskatchewan River and from what is now Madison to the Alberta boundary.

What was involved in keeping up with such a program is described in a story told by Mr. George Shepherd. "In the spring of 1910," he writes, "I worked for Jim Bott who was farming about ten miles N.E. of Craik. . . . What I principally remember is the long drives that the minister made to cover his charges on Sunday. The minister was Ben Bott, the brother of the man I was working for. As I recollect Ben Bott preached the morning service in Craik and at the end of the service he had a horse and buggy waiting and jumped in and drove out to the Rosehill district. He would be due for Sunday dinner at Jim Bott's and we would be watching for him coming. As soon as he drove into the farmyard I would take his horse to the barn while Mrs. Bott would have the meal all ready for us. The afternoon service over, the minister would hitch up his horse and buggy and drive about nine miles to Girvin. He would get supper there and then conduct the evening service for the Girvin people. After that he would drive back to Craik — a total of around thirty miles of driving."[34]

Roads and means of transportation being what they were, getting to and from church was very often a highly uncomfortable procedure for both minister and congregation. One elderly lay preacher early in the century used to drive to service at Lorlie school in the Pheasant Forks district with an umbrella fastened to the front of his cutter as a protection from the bitter winds in winter.[35] Mr. Richard B. Lloyd, who farmed in the Indianola district near Aneroid remembers a Baptist minister, Mr. W. H. Walker, also a homesteader, who took over the services in the school from 1912 until the village of Aneroid was put on the map in 1914. "I recall that the life of the pioneer minister was not exactly a bed of roses," he writes. "On Sunday Mr. Walker would hitch a team to a stone-boat and drive six miles to church. He was very faithful, and many days we have watched his coming on the stone-boat, with it pounding the horses' heels on each down slope, skidding sideways, landing the reverend gentleman in a snowdrift with his books flying in various directions. I think St. Peter must have reserved a special corner for Rev. Walker."[36]

Sparsity of settlement meant long treks to church for many people and lengthy trips for the clergy when visiting parishioners. Mr. Jacob Smith recalls twelve mile walks across the prairie[37] and Mr. Anton Riederer, drives of twenty-seven miles to Mass.[38] Others drove up to eight or ten miles by stone-boat, wagon, buckboard, buggy, democrat, sleigh, or cutter, with oxen and horses providing the motive power. The priest from Kuroki, in making his monthly visits to Roman Catholics in St. Front from 1912 to 1919, for a considerable period was met at Clair and driven by wagon twenty-five miles to his destination.[39] The Norwegian Lutherans in the Neewin district near Norquay were initially looked after by clergy from Winnipeg who travelled by train to Kamsack and from there were taken by horses to the homes of the families they wished to visit.[40]

The contribution of laymen to religious life in the early days is worthy of note. Mention has already been made of the Primitive Methodist Colony at Pheasant Forks where services were conducted for many years by Methodist and Congregational lay preachers. It was not at all unusual for a homesteader or farmer in a newly settled locality not yet served by clergy of any Protestant denomination to undertake services on his own initiative, as did the father of Miss Gladys Saloway the first Sunday after their arrival,[41] or, his interest in church matters being known, to do so at the request of his neighbors, as did the father of Mr. D. H. Maginnes in the Ermine district.[42] At Wild Rose, which in summer was supplied with student ministers, a lay minister carried on church meetings and Sunday school through the winter.[43] In very few questionnaires is there any indication of local feeling against laymen officiating. In one place, it is reported, they were stigmatized as being "holier than thou" but this was an unusual attitude.

Mr. Charles Davis has an amusing reference to performances of one very lively and enthusiastic layman whose ministrations he at one time

*"Going to church in the West," North Battleford area, 1912*

enjoyed. "Mr. B —— would roar like an enraged bull, pawing the floor with his feet, thumping the Bible till the church seemed to tremble and creak in protest. Nobody ever fell into a nod when Billy B —— was acting clergyman. No, Sir!"[44]

Money was a scarce commodity to most pioneer country folk. As might be expected many congregations in the larger towns and in a few of the smaller, especially those connected with the major Protestant denominations, adopted fairly early a plan of systematic giving such as weekly envelopes, and in numerous cases became self-supporting within a relatively brief period. But almost all Protestant church groups in the country and in villages were largely dependent for their finances (as many still are to a degree) on outside help — grants from church headquarters such as the Home Mission Boards of the Methodist and Presbyterian Churches, or the Anglican Synod — or on missionary societies such as the Church Missionary Society of the Anglican Church. These grants were supplemented by local contributions which might consist only of small collections taken at the Sunday services plus what the ladies' aid or similar women's organizations could raise. Attempts by some country congregations to use envelopes were unsuccessful because the ability to give depended too much on the harvest. Consequently in general the main canvass for funds took place in the fall after the crops were in.

The most unusual and perhaps most interesting method of raising church funds revealed by the questionnaires was adopted at the Anglican mission at Cumberland in the early years of the century. Mr. Norman

Irving, who came to Cumberland in 1904, reports that extra money was raised by the collection at Easter of furs which were traded for cash at Hudson's Bay Company and Revillon Frères Compagnie stores.

Different patterns of church giving emerge from the questionnaires sent in by members of the Roman Catholic Church, and of the Mennonite and Swedish Baptist Churches. Membership fees were paid yearly by Mennonites at Rosthern[45] and monthly (after 1916) by Swedish Baptists at Earl Grey.[46] Generally the basis of support for the Roman Catholic Church was a specified sum per quarter section, usually ten dollars, or a percentage of salary or earnings. In addition, of course, as in almost all the churches, collections were received at services, either regularly or for special purposes.

Women played their part in helping to support the churches. The means by which they made their contribution were very much the same as now — chiefly bazaars and affairs at which food was the main attraction. In the questionnaires, box socials, pie socials, and bean socials are mentioned fairly often. Oyster suppers were at one time featured by the Presbyterian ladies in Moosomin[47] and Drinkwater,[48] while the Baptist ladies of Halcyonia sold strawberries and cream at ball games.[49] At Carlea national loyalties were sometimes catered to. Mrs. Jean Hill mentions March 17 Irish stew suppers and January 25 haggis suppers. The delectable dish to which all people of Scots ancestry are supposed to pay homage was made by Mrs. Hill.[50] That autumn institution, the fowl supper, appeared on the scene quite early in our history, but with some differences in menu and methods of serving, and especially in price.

Saskatchewan Archives Board

*Ladies Aid refreshment booth*

127

"Help yourself" was the usual style, and twenty-five cents the price. Salads, except the humble potato salad, were few or non-existent, the emphasis being on homegrown vegetables, pies, and cake. In general the assortment of food was smaller, although not the quantity. The suppers at Cumberland could hardly qualify as "fowl suppers" since the bill-of-fare consisted of bannock, lard or bacon, and tea,[51] but no doubt the enjoyment and good-feeling associated with such affairs were there. Nor could the suppers at Grenfell, which for many years were called "tea meetings," at which the *pièce de résistance* was cured ham, but they were in the tradition.[52] A few of the people who answered the questionnaire look back with some nostalgia and a trace of bitterness to the suppers of former days. "In earlier days," writes one, "Farmers [supplied] their own food and ate normally. Today the customers are town guys who haven't had any dinner. It used to be help yourself and break even. Now [it is] dished out to show a profit." And another comments that they were "more sociable then. . . . In early days no one ate a whole pie."

Some less universally accepted money-making activities point up varying attitudes among the different denominations. Card parties, dances, and raffles of donated articles, farm produce, or animals were quite acceptable to Anglicans and Roman Catholics, but not to Methodists and Presbyterians, who nevertheless did not frown on auctions of such donations.

Three other methods may be mentioned. Mr. L. V. Kelly tells of plays and concerts held in Rocanville.[53] The financial difficulties of the church brought out some latent and outstanding talent, he says, some of the actors participating being ex-members of the legitimate stage. In 1903, to help with the building of Bethel Methodist Church in the Grenfell-Broadview area, the ladies' aid adopted the "talent money" system, giving to each member ten cents at Easter with the expectation it would be returned with increase at Thanksgiving.[54] But the most practical idea was that of the Anglican ladies of Shaunavon during the homesteading era. They made money by patching the bachelors' overalls, mending their socks and shirts, and cutting their hair, services which must have been highly appreciated.[55]

The importance of a church building to give "visible expression of the existence of a local congregation"[56] was early recognzed by the Canadian church leaders. Makeshift meeting places could not satisfy for long. The Presbyterian and Methodist Churches established building funds to make available, through their mission boards, long-term loans to new congregations, while the Anglican Church evolved a scheme to provide their new western parishes with churches at the least possible cost to the local people. Plans were developed for very simple structures which became facetiously known as "Canterbury cathedrals,"[57] the specifications being so explicit, even to the number of shingles and the

*Church under construction*

amount of shingle nails required, that they could be followed by any local carpenter. Hauling and construction work was to be done by voluntary labor and the cost of materials borne by mission societies in England. Several of the questionnaires bear witness to the working out of this system. Those reporting on the building of Anglican churches during the years 1905 and 1907 at Ashley, Lashburn, Meskanaw, and in the Newnham district (near LeRoy)[58] all refer to the use of a pattern supplied by Bishop Lloyd or Synod or Diocese, while the descriptions and dates given for nine other Anglican churches clearly identify them as belonging to the same plan. Money for the building of the Anglican church in Marshall, according to Mr. William Hodgson, was collected in the Fartown district of Huddersfield, England, three of the families homesteading near Marshall having come from that district.[59] Not all the building funds came from England however. At Ashley, each family contributed $25 towards the $250 which the plan estimated for materials. The Lashburn church was built with money donated by a remittance man who had been left a fortune and who also donated a rectory and a hospital. The first Anglican church in the Meota district was built of lumber obtained by working at Gordon's Mill, Birch Lake, eighteen miles away, the men donating 4½ percent of their earnings for extras.[60]

The building of churches by voluntary labor under the direction of a local carpenter or someone with building experience was not confined to the Anglicans but was common to all the denominations represented in the questionnaires. For Beaver Creek Norwegian Lutheran Church near Gronlid, home materials and resources were used as far as possible — local men hauled the logs, seats were homemade, and a local carpenter built the chancel furnishings.[61] The Roman Catholic church serving the LeRoy-McGuire area was also a log building, built in 1907 by volunteer labor, with donations for lumber for roof, floor, windows, and pews, the altar being made by the priest, Father Sinnett, and the pews by church members.[62] In 1888 at Wishart, a Presbyterian church was built of field stone by local members under the supervision of a hired stone mason.[63] The stone for this church, says Mrs. Hugh Cossar, was hauled from the surrounding district, the lime from Gordon's Reserve. A "moonlight lathing bee" was long remembered here, the men putting on lath while the women puttied windows by lantern light.

A few of the very early church buildings owed their erection to energetic clergymen. Mr. A. L. Dixon, who came to Maple Creek in 1883, reports that the Methodist church, a frame building which seated about 100, was built largely by the minister, the money being provided by local subscriptions with help from the mission board. And at Fort Qu'Appelle, writes Mr. William Kennedy, the Presbyterian church, built of field stone in 1884, was both designed and mostly built by the minister, Alexander Robson, who had originally been a stone mason.[64]

Evidence of the interest taken by Anglican individuals and congregations in England in their western Canadian counterparts is found not only in their contributions towards the building of churches but also in the many gifts or donations towards the furnishings of churches. These might include furniture, books, altar vessels, or vestments, as at Abernethy's Christ Church (built in 1885 and still used), where the furniture and linens came from England,[65] or the Anglican church in Ermine, built in 1913 under the supervision of a Welsh clergyman and designed like his church at home.[66] Here the altar furnishings and communion service were donated by his friends in England and Wales.

Some members of churches of other denominations also reported donations from outside their district. For instance, vestments for the St. Brieux Roman Catholic church came from France,[67] and the platform furniture for the Methodist churches at Eatonia[68] and Semans[69] was doated by the T. Eaton Company. However, judging from the questionnaires, such gifts were comparatively infrequent.

A majority of the churches erected by the settlers around the turn of the century and which figure in the questionnaires were frame structures, but during that period and earlier log churches were not uncommon. Examples may be drawn from all the main denominations. The Presbyterians at Clare, near the present town of Arcola, built two, the first in 1885 which was burned by prairie fire the following year and the second in 1895 which was used until the railway came through in 1900.[70] At Wallace, the Presbyterian church, built in 1893 of poplar logs hewn inside and out, was used until about 1911.[71] Roman Catholic churches at Annaheim (1903),[72] St. Brieux (1904),[73] and Vossen (1905)[74] were all of log, the logs for the Vossen church being hauled from the bush by oxen. Other log churches were the Anglican churches at Kutawa (1892),[75] and Winthorpe (1909 or 1910),[76] Lakeside Methodist Church at Sheho (1906),[77] and the first Methodist church at Red Deer Hill (1884),[78] which was distinguished also by a thatched roof, and the Lutheran and Swedish mission churches at Ohlen (1896),[79] all the lumber for the roof of one of these having been ripsawed by hand and the joists hewn by hand.

An unusual structure for this country was the Lutheran church built in 1893 at Edenwold.[80] With adobe walls, the only material bought was lumber for the roof. This church's first clergyman, a man from Germany, had earlier built an adobe house on his homestead with the help of members of his congregation. A small sod Presbyterian church, seating twenty-five, once used at Tullisville might also be mentioned.

As one would expect, the furnishings in numerous pioneer churches were at first makeshift or homemade. The planks and backless benches which were described by several as the earliest seating accommodation in churches of their communities must have added considerably to the discomforts of pioneer life. Let us hope sermons were not too long, as the refuge of slumber would certainly be denied congregations under those conditions! Several churches were furnished with pews and even an altar made by members of the congregation or by an individual who might be the local carpenter. Among those in this category we find the first Anglican church in the Meota district,[81] the Roman Catholic churches at St. Front,[82] Vossen,[83] and at Mazenod[84] where the pews were so well made they are still in use; the first Lutheran church at Edenwold,[85] where all the furniture was made by the local carpenter; and the Methodist church at Waldeck[86] where, says Mrs. H. C. Calverley, the furniture was made by her grandfather.

Log or simple frame structures with makeshift or homemade furniture were not the only churches built in country districts or in the small villages during the early years. Some quite substantial churches still in use were built in the 1890's. The present Anglican church in Wapella, a stone building, dates from 1891.[87] Moffatt Presbyterian Church near Wolseley[88] and Forest Presbyterian Church in the Cottonwood district near Regina,[89] both built in 1892, and Kenlis Methodist Church[90] in the Blackwood district, built in 1897, are now used as United churches. Kenlis Church, says Miss Lottie Meek, a brick building, seated 150 people and was fully furnished from the beginning

*Stone church and rectory at Fort Qu'Appelle, 1903*

with pews and pulpit, cocoa matting in the aisles, and red carpet on the platform.

One of the most significant aspects of church life in the West was the degree of co-operation which existed among people of various Protestant denominations and the trend towards church union. Of this there is abundant evidence in the questionnaires. In earliest days, frontier conditions frequently made co-operation essential if any services were to be available at all. As suggested before, often the first religious activity in a newly settled region consisted of Sunday school for the children taught by one of the parents in his or her own home, or gatherings in a home or school for informal services conducted by one of the homesteaders who might or might not be a clergyman as well. Generally, all the neighbors who had had church connections before coming west or who had any interest in a church would be there. As Mrs. W. S. de Balinhard of Yorkton put it, "We attended any service that came along."[91]

When a school was built and perhaps later a church, and a student missionary or clergyman belonging to one of the major Protestant denominations began to hold services, the same or a similar situation often prevailed since the first missionary or clergyman in the community would usually gain the support of all. Mr. C. Evans Sargent, for several years a student missionary for the Presbyterian Church, describes the congregations at his five preaching points as including "Anglicans, Presbyterians, Methodists, Baptists, Norwegian Lutherans, German

Saskatchewan Archives Board

*Interior of an early Anglican church*

Lutherans, Seventh Day Adventists, one Christian Scientist, two or three Roman Catholics, one Jew, one Marxian Socialist, and one Mormon," with "at times a fairly good attendance of the Round Church."[92] As the years passed, different forms of co-operation developed among people of various denominations. In some districts or villages covered by the questionnaires, services were provided by one denomination alone for many years, as in Meskanaw[93] and in Newnham district near LeRoy,[94] where only Anglican services were available; or Longlaketon[95] where the Presbyterians held sway until union in 1925; or Mellmore district near Norquay[96] where everyone attended the Methodist services. Sometimes a single church building would be used, alternately or at different times in the same day, by two or three congregations, as at Lockwood where the Methodists met in the early afternoon, followed by the Lutherans, and finishing off with the Presbyterians in the evening,[97] or in Sheho, Tuffnell, and Foam Lake[98] where the Presbyterians and Methodists shared churches. Alternate services by different denominations in schoolhouses were very common. In several places, these services were supported by the same group of people, financially as well as by attendance. This was the situation, for instance, at Paynton[99] and at Perth school near Rocanville,[100] where Presbyterians and Anglicans supported each other's efforts; in the Blackwood district (from 1889 to 1897)[101] and

133

in Melfort[102] (until churches were built) where Presbyterians and Methodists co-operated; and at one of the schools in the Senlac district,[103] where Methodists and Anglicans helped each other as late as 1917 and after. Sometimes there was co-operation between different denominations in the building of a church. At Lashburn, says Mr. W. T. McMurdo, Presbyterians held services in a church built by general subscription but sponsored by the Baptists.[104] Mrs. George Wilson reports that in Rocanville the Methodists helped build the Presbyterian church in 1900, both using it for a time until the Methodist church was built with some assistance from the Presbyterians, and finally, when the Anglican church was erected in 1911, many of the other churches contributed towards it.[105] The use of a church by another denomination until they could build one of their own was not at all unusual. This was done in the early days of Maple Creek where the Presbyterians held services in the Methodist church until the construction of their own in 1894[106] and in the Moffatt field near Wolseley where the Methodists used the Presbyterian church.[107]

The pressure towards co-operation and union was, of course, strongest among the Methodists and Presbyterians. Many pioneers felt there was no need to perpetuate denominational differences in a new country so that when, in 1904, the leaders of the Methodist, Presbyterian, and Congregational Churches began negotiations concerning a possible union, the movement in the West became intensified. The need for consolidating resources was felt at church headquarters as well as locally. Small and scattered populations and shortage of money meant that relatively few charges were self-supporting with the result that "non-intrusion policies" covering many mission fields were adopted and carried out by arrangements between Methodist and Presbyterian sudents of missions in order to save mission funds. Reflection of this trend is evident in the questionnaires, although not always as specifically stated as it was by Mrs. D. A. Moorehouse who, in writing about Wallard, refers definitely to a union arrangement between Presbyterians and Methodists for services in the school beginning about 1912.[108]

In new villages and towns many Methodists and Presbyterians, finding it hard to determine any substantial differences and impossible to support services and ministers of their own adequately or even at all, became convinced of the advantages to be gained by joining forces. As time went on, more and more union congregations were formed, until by 1921 over 1,000 union churches had been established in the prairie provinces.[109] It was not surprising therefore, with the example before them of union arrangements which worked, that when union was finally voted upon most Methodist, Presbyterian, and union congregations in the West gave it overwhelming support. Illustrations in the questionnaires of union churches formed before 1925 when the United Church came into being include those at Frobisher,[110] which in January, 1909 became the second union church in Canada (Melville, established November, 1908 being the first); Semans[111] where amalgamation took place in 1913; and Zelma,[112] organized in 1917.

Revival or mission services were a feature in the life of comparatively few communities represented in the questionnaires. Mention is made of yearly or five-yearly retreats or special missions, some lasting two or three days, in a number of Roman Catholic parishes, and no doubt they were held in other parishes as well. Travelling evangelists at one time or another held meetings for the Methodists in the Estevan district,[113] at Hawarden,[114] and in the Moosomin district[115] which was visited by the team of Crossley and Hunter about 1892. There were Free Methodist revival meetings lasting from one to two weeks in the winter at Mount Green.[116] At Chickney yearly summer camp meetings were important events as they brought together everyone from a large area around.[117] Mr. Sydney Chipperfield describes these gatherings as follows: "In the early days . . . about once each summer a camp meeting would be held. This would be in a nice bluff or clearing and people would attend with wagons and buggies and of course some came walking. About four or five local preachers would take part in the service. A wagon would be drawn up and the speakers would use the wagon as a platform. The services used to start about half past ten and continue until about four to five o'clock."

Mr. E. C. Watson tells an entertaining story about some revival meetings in the Wishart district.[118] "One of the resident members of this district conducted revival meetings at times," he writes. "This man, so they and himself said, had been a very wild character and one of the bare-fisted fighters. He would visit a place or home, hold a little service, argue about the scriptures [and] also give some good points on boxing. [He] was a very strong man and weighed over 250 lbs. when not fat. He had a voice when he preached that shook the church and I remember babies all crying. I have seen this man referee a boxing match."

That the church was the centre for social life was the almost unanimous opinion of those who commented on this aspect of pioneer life. For homesteaders and farmers in the earliest days, church services, whether held in houses, schools, or church buildings, often provided the only community activity. Long and hard work, distances between dwellings, limited and slow means of transportation, and lack of money restricted energies and opportunities for activities outside the home. Sunday was the one day and church the one opportunity in the week to meet neighbors and friends. Here people could gather before and after the service to talk — the women about clothes or recipes and no doubt the neighborhood gossip; the men, while hitching up oxen or horses, about the past week's farmwork, animals and crops, or even to do a little

*After Mass at Willow Bunch Roman Catholic Church, about 1916*

business. Bachelors found church attendance good for more than their souls since, as Mr. Hodgson of Marshall says,[119] very often invitations for supper were forthcoming. There was also the possibility of meeting any unattached pretty girls in the district.

Visits after church might be accompanied by food, especially when services were held in homes. Proceedings often concluded with tea at Tyvan, Mrs. James Bews reports,[120] and with supper and singsong at Mellmore, according to Mrs. A. B. Bjerke.[121] And, says Mrs. J. J. Meredith, when services she attended in a Battleford district school were held in the morning, the congregation would usually share lunch.[122] Mr. C. Evans Sargent tells of a Norwegian Lutheran family at one of his appointments who entertained the whole congregation, usually about twenty-five, to dinner or supper, depending on whether it was a morning or evening service.[123]

An added incentive for church attendance was provided for a time at Paynton[124] and Francis.[125] During the summers of 1903 to 1905 services were held in homes which were also the post offices. "In 1903," Mr. Harvey H. Linnen writes, "mail for Francis district came by way of Indian Head forty miles away and it was generally understood that any homesteader going to Indian Head during the week days was supposed to bring all the mail for the local districts of Francis home with him, then on Sunday ... to church service and distribute it [there]. In that way everybody for miles came to get their mail and attend service and to find out who was going to Indian Head the next week to take mail to post."

136

As populations increased so did church activities. In many places women's organizations such as ladies' aids, altar societies, women's associations and the like were formed and associations for young people such as Epworth Leagues and Christian Endeavour Societies. Money-making activities such as the bazaars and suppers mentioned before brought people together and concerts which very often followed these affairs provided opportunities for the display of local talent. Songs, dialogues, recitations, sometimes short plays, violin or accordion solos, or a speaker who might be a minister from a neighboring town supplied the entertainment. "The songs were mostly out of tune but everyone clapped regardless," says one pioneer, but others think the local concerts of early days were of better calibre than now. Annual Christmas concerts began early in the century in the Presbyterian church near Wishart, says Mrs. Hugh Cossar who remembers the highlight at one, the first gramophone in the district. "It was an old fashioned model with an attachable horn and really caused quite a sensation."[126] Mr. Hugo Bartel of the Mennonite community at Drake also recalls a memorable Christmas program. "For a tree they decorated a small poplar tree and put on home-made candles. The weather was very cold but the house was so full they took out a window to get fresh air."[127]

As purely social gatherings, church picnics seem to have been popular, although not universal. At Ermine[128] people were "too busy and scattered for picnics" and the Free Methodists at Mount Green didn't approve of them.[129] Unfortunate experiences early dampened initial enthusiasm at Bethel and Halcyonia. Picnics began for Bethel district Methodists in 1904 and continued until the 1908 gathering which was followed by sixty-two cases of typhoid fever.[130] Two attempts by the Baptists at Halcyonia, reports Miss Gladys Saloway, were "dismal failures," rain bringing disaster to the first and measles to the second.[131] However, these unhappy occurrences were exceptional, judging from the questionnaires. In some areas yearly picnics or outdoor socials began very early in the history of settlement — at Pheasant Forks in 1883,[132] at Longlaketon in 1889,[133] and in 1886 for the Baptists at Edenwold.[134] Here, says Mrs. Richard Miles, the first picnic followed a Sunday morning church service, the food being spread in one long column in the schoolyard to avoid any grouping into separate cliques. At this and following picnics, matters of importance to the congregation were usually decided.

Food, sports, and entertainment at a number of these affairs show something of a contrast with present-day church picnics. To begin with, they were not merely for the children but included the whole family, and indeed some appear to have been planned mainly for the pleasure of the adults. Horse racing was a feature at Brightholm,[135] Wild Rose,[136] and St. Brieux[137] where ox and cigar-smoking races as well provided variations, and at one village which should perhaps remain nameless to avoid a possible community feud, much beer, according to one reporter, added to the general excitement aroused by the races.

The national origin of some participants was reflected at Brightholm district picnics where tossing the caber added to the pleasure of the Scots, while cricket kept Englishmen happy at Paynton[138] and Wild Rose. Baseball, bathing, horseshoes, and the usual foot races were of course common then as now. A number of church picnics concluded with a dance in the evening, as at Winthorpe where the first Anglican church picnic in 1912 was attended by all within a ten-mile radius. Each woman brought a picnic basket, says Mrs. C. F. Sentance, and cooked food and lemonade were sold from a booth. In the evening the left-over food was taken to a farmhouse where the day closed with dancing and more refreshments.[139]

A few interesting variations in food consumed at early picnics emerge from the questionnaires. Rabbit, prairie chicken, and wild ducks were on the menu at the first picnic held for members of the Roman Catholic church at St. Front in 1922.[140] At their first picnic in 1911 the Beaver Creek Norwegian Lutherans of Gronlid fared well on moose-meat sandwiches, homegrown vegetables, pies from locally picked berries, and homemade ice cream.[141] Mrs. William Taylor has fond remembrances of twelve raspberry pies with cream which must have made the mouths water of Paynton picnickers in 1909.

Among the pioneers who answered the questionnaire are many who sometimes look back with a feeling of regret for the days that are gone. Overlooking the difficulties and discomforts of frontier life, they recall the good fellowship of early days, the comparative absence of divisions because of denomination or material possessions. They see with concern the decline in country districts of a sense of neighborhood and the gradual disappearance of the country congregation. Automobiles and better roads which have brought town, city, and weekend resort closer they regard as not unmixed blessings since church and social life can no longer find their centre in the immediate district. Mr. E. E. Lundell says: "It seems that the automobiles of today and the hardtop roads make neighbors farther away from each other. . . . I'll never forget the aroma coming from the prairies and wolf willows as we came walking to the school house services, and when I say we, I mean whole families." And, writes Mr. C. Evans Sargent, "In the pioneer days we were all like little boats tossing on the prairie ocean of dry land, taking a chance on success or failure in an unpredictable adventure. It was a simpler, more sincere and more neighborly life in the church as in other ways. Those early mission congregations seemed to me nearer the spirit of true worship than any I ever attended."

# 10 The Constitution of Saskatchewan

*by Evelyn Eager*

THE creation of the provinces of Saskatchewan and Alberta on September 1, 1905 was the culmination of a movement for autonomy which had its first official expression at the turn of the century. The North-West Territories Assembly in 1900 dispatched a memorial to the federal government requesting provincial establishment, and the next four years witnessed requests, demands, and intermittent communication between federal and territorial officials on the subject. Throughout, it was financial considerations which motivated the territorial agitation. The Territories had satisfied its immediate constitutional aspirations when it achieved responsible government in 1897, and it was the necessity to relieve its stringent financial situation which caused the Territories to urge provincial establishment.*

Finally, in September, 1904, Prime Minister Laurier promised that if his government were sustained in the coming general election, it would be prepared immediately afterwards to enter upon autonomy negotiations. In November, following the election and in compliance with his promise, he notified the head of the territorial government, F. W. G. Haultain, that the Dominion government was prepared to receive a delegation during the first week in January to discuss the granting of provincial status. Meetings between the two governments commenced on January 5, 1905, with the federal cabinet committee consisting of the Prime Minister; the Minister of Justice, Charles Fitzpatrick; Sir William Mulock, Minister of Labour and Postmaster General; and R. W. Scott, Secretary of State. Clifford Sifton, who as Minister of the Interior would normally have taken a prominent part in the negotiations, left for the south early in 1905 for reasons of health. Territorial representatives were Premier Haultain and his senior cabinet minister, G. H. V. Bulyea. In addition, Haultain had written in December to senators and members of the Commons for the Territories indicating that he was anxious to have their co-operation in Ottawa from the outset of negotiations.[1]

---

*This article originally appeared in *Saskatchewan History* for spring, 1962.

Details of the consultations were not made public, but negotiations apparently proceeded with dispatch. Upon conclusion of the conferences the actual drafting of the bills for the establishment of the two new provinces was left to the Minister of Justice and a cabinet committee. On February 21, with few of the members of Parliament absent and the visitors' galleries crowded, the Prime Minister introduced the bills in the House of Commons. The original intention was that the new provinces should come into existence on July 1. A prolonged and intense objection which was raised against the school clause, however, and the subsequent introduction of an amended clause delayed passage of the bills. Royal assent finally was given on July 20, with the acts to become effective on September 1. Inaugural ceremonies for the province of Alberta were held in Edmonton on that day, with the Governor-General, the Prime Minister, and other officials and guests, Mounted Policemen and horses then moving to Regina for similar ceremonies on September 4.

It was a gala day in Regina, with a program which demanded true pioneer stamina. Decorations in the city included four giant arches of wheat, oats, and evergreen, and gaiety and enthusiasm were evident everywhere. Special excursion trains brought "the greatest crowd ever met within Regina,"[2] and local bands were reinforced by others from points in Manitoba, from Wolseley, Rosthern, and the Indian Industrial School. A children's parade, reception of the Vice-Regal party, a "monster parade," and military and police reviews were features of the morning program. In the afternoon the Mounties presented their musical ride, and a sports program included "push ball" and lacrosse games, followed by a fireworks display and an inaugural ball at night. Interspersed throughout these activities were the usual speeches, addresses, presentations, replies, and other formalities associated with such an occasion. Of these, the significant constitutional act was the swearing into office of the Lieutenant-Governor, thus formally launching the government for the new province of Saskatchewan.

The Saskatchewan constitution incorporated the traditions and practices of parliamentary responsible government which had come to Canada from their British source. After the British parliamentary system and British common law became established in the North American colonies in the early years of settlement, they were adopted without question in the constitution of the new Dominion of Canada when it came into existence in 1867, as well as in the provinces first entering Confederation. Following the pattern thus established, the new western provinces accepted these features as a natural heritage and looked both to the Canadian government and to England for precedents, modifying and adapting them as necessary.

Just as the British parliamentary system rests in many essentials upon convention, so in the drafting of the Saskatchewan Act the tradition

*Inauguration day decorations on South Railway Street, Regina*

of omission, obscurity, and elasticity was observed in certain respects, revealing in form as in substance its ancient origins. The existence of a Lieutenant-Governor, as the representative of the sovereign within the province, was assumed, and to him the act assigned the duty of choosing persons to compose the executive council. No mention was made of the central figure, the Premier, who in practice heads that council, nor was the existence, or necessity, of political parties acknowledged. It is here that convention and tradition take over from the written act. The practice is observed that the Lieutenant-Governor chooses as Premier the leader

*Inauguration ceremonies. Seated, left to right, Sir Wilfrid Laurier, Mrs. J. H. McIllree, Lady Grey, Earl Grey, Lady Laurier, Lieutenant-Governor Forget, remainder unidentified*

of the party which has the support of a majority of members in the elected assembly. The Premier in turn chooses the other members of his cabinet, abiding by the unwritten law that any member so chosen must have a seat in the assembly or secure one within a reasonable time. Resting also upon convention is the practice that the cabinet must resign if at any time it loses the support of the assembly. The Lieutenant-Governor thereupon has the alternative, as circumstances may indicate, of calling upon the leader of the opposition party in the assembly to form a cabinet or of dissolving the existing assembly and calling an election.

Certain aspects of the Saskatchewan Act were pre-determined by the British North America Act of 1867 which had established the general constitutional pattern for the Dominion. One important feature of it, which was North American rather than British in origin, was the federal type of government. In contrast with the unitary system of England, whereby all power and authority is concentrated in the central parliamentary body, the British North America Act set forth the respective fields in which the Dominion government and provincial governments might each exercise exclusive control. The Saskatchewan Act stated that "the provisions of the British North America Act, 1867 to 1886, shall apply to the province of Saskatchewan in the same way and to the like extent as they apply to the provinces heretofore comprised in the Dominion. . . ." Among the powers thus coming exclusively within the jurisdiction of the province were the amendment of its own constitution, direct taxation for revenue and borrowing of money on the credit of the province, establishment and maintenance of various institutions, municipal organization, property and civil rights, administration of justice in the province, and "generally all matters of a merely local or private nature in the province." Education likewise came under provincial jurisdiction, subject to certain safeguards for religious minorities enforced by the Dominion government.

In accordance also with terms of the British North America Act provision was made for Saskatchewan representation in the Dominion Parliament. Membership in the House of Commons for Alberta and Saskatchewan was to remain as it had been for the Territories, so long as the present Parliament continued, with re-adjustment to take effect upon its termination. The representation for each province was to be determined upon the completion of the next quinquennial census[3] according to the formula of the British North America Act — that the number of members should bear the same ratio to its population as the number sixty-five bore to the population of Quebec. The province was to be represented in the Senate by four members, with provision for an increase to six after the next decennial census. This was in conformity with a suggestion advanced two years earlier by western members that the area west of the Great Lakes should be considered a division for purposes of Senate representation, with each of the four provinces having six members. The Prime Minister in debate explained that Senate representation was not based upon population but "upon purely arbitrary considerations having in view minorities, and that the great provinces should not override the smaller ones."[4]

One of the earliest points of agitation in autonomy discussion had been whether one or two new provinces should be created. Premier Haultain consistently advocated the establishment of a single province, which, he pointed out, would avoid the duplication of government machinery. He apparently had little or no support for his viewpoint among those gathered in Ottawa for the autonomy talks, although some were present who earlier had joined with him in advocating the creation of a single province. In the House of Commons his only support in this matter came from the Conservative members for the Territories. An agitation within Manitoba for the westward extension of its boundaries, which was renewed in 1904, contributed heavily in favor of the establishment of more than one new province. If the eastern portion of the Territories were to be annexed to Manitoba, it was sure to create a disturbance in the Territories as a whole, and especially within the area affected. On the other hand, if Manitoba's boundaries were not extended, and a single new province stretched from Manitoba to British Columbia, the great disparity in size would arouse sharp protest within Manitoba.

The only practical alternative therefore seemed to be the creation of two new provinces from the Territories.

Once the number of provinces was decided upon it was the dividing line between them which presented the main boundary question to be decided. There were certain other points of discussion, such as pressure from Saskatchewan for a port on Hudson Bay, and some difficulties had to be worked out in connection with ownership of land in the northern areas affecting the boundary there. The line between Alberta and Saskatchewan nevertheless provided the only real issue with respect to boundaries. During the week preceding the introduction of the autonomy bills, at a conference called by Haultain, a majority of the North-West members of Parliament and senators favored selection of the fourth meridian as the dividing line, which was thus included in the bill. Haultain argued for a boundary seventy-five miles further east, and Conservative members in the House of Commons advocated a line sixty miles east of the meridian so as to include all the ranching country in Alberta and thereby eliminate hardship resulting from laws governing a farming country conflicting with the needs of a ranching area. This argument was refuted, however, and the fourth meridian was established as the western boundary of Saskatchewan. On the east the line extended north from the Manitoba boundary to the second meridian which it followed to the sixtieth parallel of latitude, which formed the northern boundary.

The name for the new province was chosen with little dissension, with the choice lying between the titles of the two territorial districts from which the new political entity was formed, Assiniboia and Saskatchewan. Clifford Sifton preferred the name of Assiniboia, although he regarded the choice of relatively little significance since both names were identified with the history of the Territories. One factor which doubtless affected the decision in favor of Saskatchewan was the request of citizens of the northern district that there might be a province with that name, with no parallel request from the southern district of Assiniboia. Furthermore, the main waterway of the province was called the Saskatchewan River, a name taken from the Cree language and meaning "swift flowing." Historically the name had been known in the East before that of Assiniboia and also, through extensive advertising outside Canada of the "Valley of the Saskatchewan," the name suggested vast tracts of fertile land.

The establishment of a single legislative house, the legislative assembly, was accepted without question, to be composed originally of twenty-five members. The laws of the North-West Territories respecting the constitution of the assembly and the election of members were to apply until otherwise determined by the legislature and, until otherwise directed by the Lieutenant-Governor in Council, the seat of government

*F. W. G. Haultain*

was to remain at Regina. The "powers, authorities and functions" of the Lieutenant-Governor, both individually and as exercised with the advice and consent of the executive council, also were to continue in the same manner as prior to the coming into force of the act, subject to change by the legislature.

There was disagreement as to the boundaries of electoral constituencies, and this was linked with an agitation in certain parts of the province over the location of the provincial capital. Although immediate continuation of the capital at Regina was expected, the sudden and suspicious appearance at Ottawa of delegations from various parts of the Territories, ostensibly concerned with "bridge building," and local newspaper interest in the capital question, foreshadowed future controversy.[5] With Saskatoon and Regina as the two main contenders for the capital, the relative number of members in the north and in the south of the province would vitally affect the respective chances of success of the two centres when the permanent location of the capital was subsequently decided in the assembly. The question of electoral divisions was discussed at a conference of western members of the Commons and senators, and such members of the territorial assembly as were in Ottawa preceding the introduction of the autonomy bills. No agreement was reached and the matter was left to the Dominion Parliament. The schedule of constituencies proposed in the House of Commons in May of 1905 was scanned therefore with interest not only by the opposition with its eye on political advantage, and local communities with their usual quick jealousies, but also as it would affect the capital question. Twenty of the seats of the former territorial assembly fell in the new province of Saskatchewan, and their boundaries were changed no more than was necessary to add the five new seats required under the terms of the act. The final result was nine seats in the northern part of the province compared with sixteen in the south.

The great controversy which arose over the separate-school clause is a story in itself and will be dealt with here only in brief outline. The original wording of the clause permitting the continuance of separate schools in the new provinces was objected to by Clifford Sifton, Minister of the Interior. After the bill was presented in Parliament he immediately interrupted his rest in the south and returned to Ottawa, where he received support in his protests from other western members of Parliament. In prior discussions it had been generally agreed that the "existing system" of separate schools in the Territories should continue in the new provinces, and Sifton objected that the proposed clause opened the way to more extensive privileges than those presently in force. There was much confusion and misunderstanding in official circles as to the precise nature of the "existing system" of separate schools. There was also confusion concerning the possible effect of the proposed legislation on the extension of the scope of separate-school authority. Sir Wilfrid Laurier was reluctant to alter the clause, and a tense situation developed at Ottawa. Subsequent events included the resignation of Clifford Sifton from the cabinet, a threatened revolt, which did not materialize, of certain other cabinet ministers and members of Parliament, and the amendment of the disputed clause. The amended separate-school clause specifically ensured that privileges granted to separate schools in the new provinces should not extend beyond those presently included in

146

territorial legislation. This was the provision which Sifton and his supporters had insisted upon, and it constituted the terms finally enacted into legislation, although Sifton did not return to the cabinet even after gaining his point.

Meanwhile, the conflict and the confusion which was evident at Ottawa became multiplied many times over in a great public controversy respecting the school clause. Divisions were along both political and religious lines, with two by-elections in Ontario fought mainly on the issue. Protestant, and specifically Orange, objections were raised not only against the terms of the original clause but against the inclusion of any separate-school clause at all. Later, opposing Roman Catholic protests were raised against the amendment. Paradoxically, the storm raged mainly in the East, with the West accepting the settlement of its affairs with relative calm, in the main showing more concern about spring seeding than about separate-school legislation.[6]

Another subject of special controversy was the public domain. Section 21 of the Saskatchewan Act declared that "all Crown lands, mines and minerals and royalties incident thereto, and the interest of the Crown in the waters within the province under *The North-West Irrigation Act* 1898" were to continue under the administration of the Federal government "for the purposes of Canada." Although this was contrary to the viewpoint emphatically expressed earlier by western Liberal members that the public lands must be transferred to any new province created, all Liberal members of the Commons and Senate reportedly not only agreed to the change in principle, but even "were unanimous in urging upon the Government that the North-West would prefer to have the lands retained by the Dominion if the new provinces were guaranteed adequate revenues."[7] In view of the Territories' financial austerity, the suggestion of "adequate revenues" in lieu of lands doubtless had great persuasive powers, and the shift of western Liberals in their position was but the first of such reversals, one way or the other, which the members of both political parties employed with complete abandonment so long as control of the public lands remained an issue. More significantly probably, it appears also that the unanimity of agreement appeared only after it became evident that the decision to retain the lands under federal control could not in any event be shaken.

Questions relating to the public domain still remained to be settled when the Minister of the Interior left for the south early in 1905. This was an area in which Sir Wilfrid Laurier deferred absolutely to his minister, intruded the question upon the latter's temporary retirement from his duties, and accepted his decisions unquestioningly. In advising the Prime Minister in a letter of January 22, 1905 not to yield in the matter of public lands, Clifford Sifton set forth his reasons for advocating continued Dominion control.

147

... giving them to the Provinces would be ruinous to our settlement policy and would be disastrous to the whole Dominion [he wrote]. The mere report that the lands had been handed over and that there might be a change [in] the policy of administering them would cost us tens of thousands of settlers in the next two years to say nothing of the more distant future — The continued progress of Canada for the next five years depends almost entirely on the flow of immigration.[8]

As an alternative to straight Dominion ownership, Senator J. H. Ross of Moose Jaw, long a champion of western rights, proposed that the Dominion should hold the lands as a trust, retaining control of their administration but handing over the proceeds annually to the province. This he considered would sufficiently safeguard Dominion interests for purposes of immigration, but would give greater satisfaction to the people of the province and be of great importance politically.

Laurier favored the suggestion,[9] but Sifton did not approve. Ironically, although the proposal was not adopted, the Dominion in later years nevertheless faced those very difficulties which Sifton warned would result from acceptance of the plan. He stated that:

It involves setting up a fiction in place of a fact, *i.e.,* it involves an admission that the new Provinces were or ought to be constitutionally owners of the land. This is wholly untrue. The original provinces owned the crown lands. The Dominion owns these lands and decides now to erect provinces. — It is for the Dominion to say upon what terms. . . . To crystallize an assumption that the provinces are owners and entitled to the rights of a *cestui qui trust* is to set up an elaborate and untenable fiction.

Once a trust was admitted, he continued, it would not be possible to refuse the provinces the right to demand an account of everything from the beginning. "You may seek to limit the admission now but the future will see the limitations broken down. — You will lay the foundation for a perennial agitation in these new provinces for more," he warned. He dealt also with the immediate practical difficulty of seeking to make up an account, as it would be impossible to know what should be charged against the provinces in the land account and would cause every item to be "a subject of dispute and interminable argument." Furthermore, he predicted, as soon as the provinces were strong enough they would demand an adjustment of the account and would get it. His advice was that "the facts should be taken as they are — we should say to the provinces — You have no lands and we cannot give them but we shall provide a liberal revenue in lieu of it."[10]

Laurier accepted his minister's advice and in the House of Commons he stated that the lands belonged to the Dominion, while Sifton stressed the undesirability of any terms which might be interpreted as meaning that the lands belonged to the provinces. For that reason Sifton regarded the terms of compensation for lands as they originally appeared in the bills a mistake and expressed the opinion that they should be fixed arbitrarily instead of by reference to the acreage and price. By basing the compensation upon a calculated value of the land, as had been done, he stated, the Territories would claim this as an admission that the lands belonged to them beneficially at least if not in law. This already had been seized upon by Premier Haultain, he pointed out, and in the future, when seeking readjustment, the provinces would be able to say that by these terms the Dominion had admitted provincial right to the land, but the provinces had not accepted the Dominion valuation.[11] Sifton's viewpoint was taken to heart by the Prime Minister, and the act as finally adopted based compensation for lands on population.

The constitutional viewpoint which made it possible for the Dominion to withhold control of the public domain from the new provinces was in marked contrast to that which prevailed south of the border. In the United States the theory was maintained that, once admitted into the Union, each state then possessed equal privileges with all other states. A Supreme Court decision declared in 1899:

> This court has held in many cases that, whatever be the limitations upon the power of a territorial government, they cease to have any operative force, except as voluntarily adopted after such Territory became a State of the Union. Upon the admission of a State it becomes entitled to and possesses all the rights of dominion and sovereignty which belonged to the original states, and ... it stands 'upon an equal footing with the original States in all respects whatsoever.'[12]

In Canada, however, Parliament can exercise power, as it did in 1905, to vary the terms under which new provinces may enter. It was held to be constitutionally proper that the clause respecting separate schools might differ from that in force in other provinces or that the Dominion could retain control of the public lands even though this was not true of the older provinces.

Aside from the general question of lands, the matters of grazing lands and of water rights were specifically considered. There was some pressure from the West for grazing lands to be transferred to the province and, since this area would include the country capable of and requiring irrigation, it was further suggested that the transfer should include powers respecting irrigation. Sifton vetoed the idea of transferring grazing lands on the grounds that it would be impossible to distinguish them. He likewise advised that irrigation should remain under Dominion authority. Although admitting that this was in many ways undesirable, the "balance of desirability" he thought lay in that direction. Since interprovincial and even international questions would arise with respect to water rights, he considered that "by retaining the plenary power at

Ottawa you ensure the fact that a central body which for its own interest is bound to try and do justice to all parties will be able to adjust difficulties as they arise. In the case of the Provinces there would be no way of dissolving a deadlock should one arise."[13]

In addition to western dissent which probably occurred within the Liberal party in early stages of discussion respecting public lands, this question was one of the focal points of controversy between Liberal and Conservative members. Any qualms which western Liberals may have experienced privately were in no way evident in public and, in fact, what appeared to be a generous money settlement rendered it no hardship for any supporter of the government to endorse enthusiastically the entire agreement. Liberals therefore agreed on the necessity for continued federal control of the lands on "the highest grounds of policy" and as necessary for successful continuation of the immigration policy. Conservatives opposed the retention of control by the Dominion and also criticized the amount of the compensation allowance. Their leader, Mr. R. L. Borden, held that the people of the North-West were just as much entitled to control of their lands as were people in the eastern provinces, that they were interested equally with the Dominion government in the promotion of immigration, and that federal fears in this respect could be eliminated by a clause relating to free homesteads and the price of land. Haultain supported this stand, maintaining as he had from the first that control over the lands rightly belonged to the province, and protested also that federal control over irrigation invaded provincial jurisdiction in matters of property and civil rights.

The financial terms granted the new provinces were more liberal than had been at first contemplated and were widely agreed to be generous. The annual subsidy, based on the original terms of the British North America Act, was to be $50,000.00 for the support of the government and legislature, and a per capital subsidy of $.80 a head on an estimated minimum population of 250,000, to be increased according to population growth to a maximum population of 800,000. Quinquennial censuses were to be taken in addition to the regular decennial census, and at 2½ year intervals between, estimates of population were to be made on which subsidy increases would be based, in addition to the increases based on census figures. In the absence of a provincial debt, a debt allowance of $405,375.00 was granted, calculated on the basis of earlier debts taken over from other provinces. Clifford Sifton's suggestion that the debt allowance be readjusted on the basis of population increase, once at the end of five years and once at the end of ten years, as "a great and valuable concession,"[14] was not adopted, but instead the compensation in lieu of lands was arranged on a scale to be increased with population growth, as determined by the quinquennial census. The original payment as compensation for lands, on the assumed population

150

of 250,000, was to be $375,000.00 and could increase to a maximum of $1,125,000.00. An additional allowance in lieu of lands amounting to $93,750.00 was to be paid annually for five years for the construction of public buildings.

Provision had also to be made for two organizations which had acquired prior interests in the area, the Hudson's Bay Company and the Canadian Pacific Railway. Following the expressed wishes of the Hudson's Bay Company, the section of the act dealing with its rights was in the same terms as the corresponding section in the Manitoba Act of 1870 and read, "Nothing in this Act shall in any way prejudice or affect the rights or properties of the Hudson's Bay Company, as contained in the conditions under which that company surrendered Rupert's Land to the Crown." The Minister of Justice, one of the federal cabinet committee, had proposed that an amendment be added: "and all rights, privileges and properties conferred on the Canadian Government by the said conditions shall in so far as they relate to matters within the Legislative authority of the Province belong to and be vested in the Government of the said Province."[15] Representatives of the Hudson's Bay Company objected that, although the amendment allegedly was only to allow provincial governments permission to take land for roads as the Dominion government could do under the original surrender to the Crown, the language was in general terms and might cover other matters not then foreseen. As a result of their vigorous protests the amendment was dropped.[16] It is a matter of legal interest that, in view of the general terms in which the rights of the Hudson's Bay Company are stated, a strong case can be presented for the company being able, if it wished, to continue its ancient privilege to sell liquor within the province.

The right of the Canadian Pacific Railway Company to exemption from taxation, which the Dominion government had granted in 1881, was continued. This clause was protested by Walter Scott, member of Parliament for Assiniboia West and a prominent spokesman for the West, who, in the course of the disagreement between himself and the Prime Minister over the tax-exemption privilege, twice submitted his resignation to Laurier. The 1881 agreement which the Dominion government made with the Canadian Pacific Railway granted the company perpetual exemption from taxation on all its capital stock, rolling stock, and grounds, as well as a tax exemption for twenty years on lands granted by the Crown to the company. The latter provision had caused controversy during territorial times respecting the date when the twenty years commenced. The Canadian Pacific Railway held that it meant twenty years from the issue of patents for the land, and by delaying the issue of patents until it was ready to sell the various parcels of land, the company avoided any taxation. Territorial officials argued that the twenty years began at least upon completion of the road, when

151

*Walter Scott*

the land grant was thus earned, if not sooner, but court decisions were in favor of the company.

A Manitoba Supreme Court decision of March, 1903, however, that the Canadian Pacific Railway tax exemption did not apply in the Territories, brought expressions of doubt from Scott as to the wisdom of an early grant of autonomy. He contended that if this decision were upheld by the Privy Council it would be relatively easy to secure a relinquishment by the company of the exemption right. Scott, who earlier had supported autonomy, thereupon made explicit declarations in the

1904 election campaign that he would oppose any constitutional change until the tax-exemption situation became clear or unless Parliament, in granting autonomy, removed the burden of perpetual exemption. Scott took part in autonomy consultations at Ottawa, and while the bills were before the House he made private inquiries respecting the inherent power of a province to set aside such a right.[17] His support of immediate autonomy was based upon Laurier's "statement of . . . belief that it would at some time in the future be the duty of Parliament to cancel the tax exemption feature of the C.P.R. contract. . . ."[18] Scott therefore asked, "that the Government and the House ... concur in ... [Laurier's] statement and assurances in a tangible way by putting in black and white in the provincial charter the notice of intention to cancel these exemptions, — a notice to all concerned, to the Company, to the people of Canada, and especially to the people of the new provinces."[19] In Committee of the Whole on May 16 he proposed an amendment that the clause should include the words, "provided that the foregoing shall not prejudice the right of the parliament of Canada, by expropriation or otherwise, to obtain the relinquishment by said Company of the Company's rights under Section 16 of the contract aforesaid." When introducing the autonomy bills on February 21, Laurier had deplored the tax-exemption provision of the Canadian Pacific Railway contract and intimated future action to obtain its abrogation by legislation, mutual agreement, expropriation, or some other method, but the government nevertheless would not agree to write the amendment into the act. It was rejected in committee and again when Scott moved amendment on the third reading. On both occasions Scott sent his resignation to the Prime Minister for transmittal to the Speaker but both times it was refused.

Laurier's rejection of the amendment resulted from Canadian Pacific Railway objections. After the amendment was first proposed, the Prime Minister informed Canadian Pacific Railway officials that he was disposed to accept it, but first desired their views.[20] The president of the company, Sir Thomas Shaughnessy, immediately expressed sharp disapproval. He asserted that the contract between the government and the Canadian Pacific Railway created a solemn obligation which nothing should be done to impair. He said that the proposed amendment was "valueless to accomplish any practical result," but he considered that it was "objectionable as impliedly declaring the Government's right to deprive the Company of some of its charter rights, and as suggesting the intention of the Government to do so at some future time."[21] Scott on the other hand had urged upon the Prime Minister that:

> the limitation upon provincial autonomy involved in these exemp-
> tions is intrinsically a very serious matter. ... I think. ... you are
> depriving the province of an asset almost equal to the amount which
> at the outset you are proposing to pay the provinces in lieu of the

153

public domain. Were the matter not so serious it would be really laughable to consider the enormous noise which has been made over the education clause which merely asks the provinces to do what they would be pleased to do of their own accord, in contrast with the almost entire lack of any mention of this tax exemption limitation which unquestionably does not leave the provinces free to do as they would do except for this restriction; if the North-West school districts and municipalities and Legislatures were free to tax the C.P.R. I think we may depend upon it that they would exercise the right.[22]

It was his own public declarations on the matter, however, which Scott eventually saw as barring him from accepting the provision, rather than the terms of the clause itself. In addition to the definite stand which he had taken in the election campaign, he had stated in effect on the floor of the House that if the amendment were not accepted, he would resign. When Scott submitted his resignation a second time, however, Laurier put pressure upon him to withdraw it. With the turmoil over the school clause still raging, he pointed out that the reason for Scott's resignation probably would be misinterpreted and the Prime Minister promised Scott that whenever the exemption came to be burdensome he would take appropriate action in the matter.[23] Scott agreed therefore to let his resignation stand in abeyance at least until the end of the session or until the school agitation died away. He assured the Prime Minister furthermore, that "in conjunction with your statement respecting the tax exemptions, the terms are in my opinion quite satisfactory."[24] Nevertheless, at that time Scott intended eventually to have his resignation go into effect on the basis of the declarations which he had made.[25] When he became leader of the Saskatchewan Liberals later that year and shortly after was selected Premier for the new province, his resignation was accepted for that reason, without the original cause for its submission becoming known to the public. Ironically, Scott later realized that what he had considered a necessity for his resignation did not exist, as evidently no one had interpreted his statement in the House as meaning that he intended to resign.[26]

In addition to providing a permanent form of government, the Saskatchewan Act contained clauses of only temporary applicability, concerned with the immediate problems of establishment and to provide for the transition period until the new legislature could act. Properties and assets of the North-West Territories were to be divided equally between Alberta and Saskatchewan, with the two provinces jointly and equally responsible for all debts and liabilities of the Territories and with provision made for the appointment of arbitrators in case of any disagreement in these matters. Following the precedent established at Confederation and also when other provinces were created, no provision was made in the act for interim expenditure. It was pointed out that the provincial authorities would have the funds and could expend them, but

154

would have to obtain an indemnity for such expenditure from the legislature when it met.[27] The law courts, officers, and laws were to continue as they existed until changed by the provincial legislature. Societies or associations regulating the practice of professions or trades also were empowered to maintain their existing rights during the interim period.

The authority for the passage of the Saskatchewan Act was set forth in the preamble. After Manitoba was established in 1870, doubts had arisen respecting the power of Parliament thus to create new provinces, and as a result Imperial legislation was passed in the following year specifically ensuring that right. Under authority of this legislation of 1871, the framers of the Saskatchewan Act pointed out,

> it is enacted that the Parliament of Canada may from time to time establish new provinces in any territories forming for the time being part of the Dominion of Canada, but not included in any province thereof, and may, at the time of such establishment, make provisions for the constitution and administration of any such province, and for the passing of laws for the peace, order and good government of such province and for its representation in the said Parliament of Canada.

Despite this sanction the constitutionality of the Saskatchewan Act came into question even before it was passed by Parliament. Although the 1871 legislation firmly established the right of the Canadian Parliament to create new provinces, opposition members questioned whether it had the right substantially to alter the terms of entry from those which existed in other provinces. Inclusion of the separate-school clause and the withholding of public lands, they contended, were unconstitutional because they encroached upon the rights of the new provinces. Even persons who upheld the right of Parliament to include these provisions in the act expressed some anxiety for a statement or decision confirming their view. While the autonomy bills were still before the House of Commons, the Minister of Justice, later Chief Justice of the Supreme Court, pointed out to the Prime Minister the advisability "of obtaining in some form an authoritative declaration to the effect that this Parliament has the power and possibly the duty to deal with the educational clauses of the new bill in the way that we have done." He added that he was "firmly convinced that in law our position is unassailable and would be so held by the Privy Council."[28] No such action was taken, however.

The question was a major issue in the first Saskatchewan election, in December of 1905. Haultain and his followers campaigned as members of a newly formed Provincial Rights party, maintaining that autonomy terms represented an invasion of provincial rights and that the Saskatchewan Act should be submitted for judicial review. This Haultain promised to do if he came to power. Scott upheld the constitutionality of

155

the act and defended its terms, deploring the disruption in provincial affairs which would result from Haultain's proposed course of action. Following a bitter campaign in which controversy over the separate-school clause played a prominent part, Scott won sixteen of the twenty-five seats. Despite his victory, Premier Scott was anxious to allay the doubts that had been raised. Shortly after the election he tentatively suggested to his Liberal counterpart in Alberta, Premier Rutherford, that the Alberta and Saskatchewan governments join in a request to have their respective acts submitted to the Privy Council for a decision as to their constitutionality.[29] Premier Rutherford did not receive the idea with any enthusiasm and suggested as a more desirable alternative the ratifying of the acts by Imperial legislation if any doubts still existed.[30] Laurier, although expressing a keen desire to remove "this unfortunate controversy," nevertheless agreed with the stand taken by Rutherford and doubted the wisdom of again opening the question.[31]

Premier Scott nevertheless proceeded to take means within his own province to check the opposition cry of unconstitutionality. In the legislature on May 22, 1906, his supporters passed a resolution addressed to the Governor-General of Canada, preceded by a recital explaining that the Saskatchewan legislature had no doubts of the power of Parliament to pass the Saskatchewan Act and that the terms and provisions of the act had been approved at the general election in the province on December 13, 1905.

> And whereas nevertheless doubts have arisen [the resolution continued] and are expressed by a political party respecting the constitutionality of certain of the provisions of the said Act; And whereas it is desirable that these doubts should be removed and that the constitutionality of the said Act and of the several provisions thereof should be finally determined; We do therefore humbly pray that Your Excellency will be pleased to take steps to have submitted to the Judicial Committee of the Imperial Privy Council the question of the constitutionality of The Saskatchewan Act and of the several provisions thereof.[32]

Members of the Provincial Rights opposition in the legislature, although upholding the request itself as the course they had advocated, objected to the wording of the preamble and moved an amendment to strike out the reference to "a political party" and to substitute a statement declaring merely that a difference of opinion existed. The amendment was defeated and the motion passed on a straight party vote. Commenting on the matter later Haultain acknowledged the dilemma in which the resolution placed his party. "[We] could not have supported the resolution as it was brought in and forced through the House, without stultifying ourselves," he wrote, "and there is no doubt it was brought in in that form for that purpose."[33] No action was taken at Ottawa, and knowing the view of the Prime Minister on the matter, it is unlikely that Scott expected that anything would be done. The resolution nevertheless served what was doubtless its intended purpose of cutting the ground out from under the opposition, and the cry of "unconstitutionality" eventually died away.

The outcome of a reference to the Supreme Court in 1926 which upheld the constitutionality of the Alberta Act, however, applied equally to Saskatchewan. In connection with an agreement between Alberta and the Dominion respecting natural resources, the constitutionality of section 17 of the Alberta Act, the separate-school clause, was questioned. The matter was referred to the Supreme Court, and the act was held to be *intra vires*. In his judgement the presiding judge stated:

> It seems to be as plain as words can tell that, at the time of the establishment of the province of Alberta, the Parliament of Canada had the power to define and regulate the legislative powers which were to be possessed by the new province. . . . I cannot find, either in the British North America Act of 1867 or of 1871, anything expressed or implied which limited the power of the Parliament of Canada in 1905 to define the constitution and powers of the provinces which were at that time established and constituted within the Territories.[34]

Saskatchewan shares with the other provinces of Canada the right granted by the British North America Act to amend its constitution "except as regards the Office of Lieutenant-Governor." Also, the Saskatchewan Act left the details and sometimes the main outlines of government functions and procedures to be enacted by the provincial legislature. During the first session of the provincial assembly, legislation was passed respecting the organization and functioning of the executive council, the legislative assembly, the public service, and various government departments. The next legislature provided for the establishment of a new judicial system. In subsequent years amendments were made to these and other statutes relating to the machinery and powers of government. Amendments in some instances became necessary due to provincial growth and development; at other times they eliminated provisions which experience had proved unsatisfactory. Party policy and political advantage have been the reason for other amendments, and upon occasion special circumstances have necessitated temporary change. Such legislation, initiated, added to, and changed from the first meeting of the Saskatchewan legislature to the present, fills out the form of government structure of which the Saskatchewan Act is the framework and nucleus.

# 11 The "Magic City on the Banks of the Saskatchewan":

## The Saskatoon Real Estate Boom, 1910-1913

*by R. Rees*

ONE of the least attractive features of the European settlement of western Canada was the speculation in land which attended the settlement. Although the speculation was as regrettable as any other expression of greed, it would be naive, in view of the rapidity and mass nature of the settlement, to have expected more restrained behavior. The speculation affected both urban and rural land but was heaviest in the growing towns and cities where land was scarce. In all cases it was based upon expectations of growth. During the first decade of the century, boom conditions prevailed throughout the prairies. The success of the settlement plan had occasioned a huge influx of population — Saskatchewan recording a fivefold increase between 1901 and 1911 — which coincided with the expansion of the wheat economy. After the middle of the 1890's, wheat prices had moved sharply upward, transportation charges declined, and farm productivity increased rapidly.[1] By 1910 it was evident that the prairies were destined to become one of the great wheat-exporting regions of the world and westerners were understandably optimistic about the future. As service and distributing centres, the towns were expected to share in the general prosperity.*

In general the highest optimism was reserved for those towns which were situated at the junction of railways lines, it being an article of faith in the early West that intersecting lines guaranteed a community's growth. An interesting case in point was the experience of the small town of Warman, situated fourteen miles north of Saskatoon. In 1906 it found itself at the junction of the Canadian Northern and Prince Albert lines. The latter was then operated by the Canadian Pacific Railway which paid no attention to the Canadian Northern's schedule, thus enforcing long delays at Warman. To accommodate the passengers, three large hotels were built, and in anticipation of future growth, lots were surveyed up to a mile from the town centre, some of them selling at high prices.

---

*This article originally appeared in *Saskatchewan History* for spring, 1974.

*Canadian National Railway station, Saskatoon, 1913*

For promotional purposes a map was prepared showing Warman as a great centre with Saskatoon as an insignificant settlement fourteen miles to the south. Two years later the Canadian Northern bought the Prince Albert line and ran the trains to suit the schedule of its main line. Passenger delays were eliminated and Warman remained a small town.[2]

The local events leading to the Saskatoon boom were also connected with the railways. By 1908 the city could boast the services of all three transcontinental railway companies — the Canadian Pacific Railway, the Canadian Northern, and the Grand Trunk — and commercial interests began using the slogan "Hub City," the first of a series of unfortunate destiny labels. A year later the city succeeded in its bid for the University of Saskatchewan, so that by 1909 it had acquired those functions which were to form the basis for its subsequent economic growth as a distribution and marketing centre for central Saskatchewan and an educational and institutional centre for the whole province.

Given these circumstances, there were ample grounds for confidence in the city's future, but business interests and city "boosters" foresaw only unlimited growth and prosperity. In doing so they were responding to the excessive optimism which seems to have characterised not just western Canada but the whole of the western world before the outbreak of the First World War. The brashness of the period and the general belief in wealth and material progress as an unequivocal good were described by George Orwell in *Such, Such Were the Joys.*

There never was, I suppose, in the history of the world a time when the sheer vulgar fatness of wealth, without any kind of aristocratic elegance to redeem it, was so obtrusive as in the years before 1914. It was an age when crazy millionaires in curly top hats and lavendar waistcoats gave champagne parties in rococo houseboats ... the age of The Merry Widow, Saki's novels, Peter Pan and Where the Rainbow Ends. .... The goodness of money was as unmistakeable as the goodness of health or beauty, and a glittering car, a title or hordes of servants was mixed up in people's minds with the idea of actual moral virtue.[3]

Although, in western Canada, the manifestations were somewhat different from those in England, the ethos in both places was virtually the same. The West's particular contribution to the vulgarity of the period was the boastful, extravagant statement. The *Saturday Press*, for example, in its building-and-development supplement, November, 1912, described Saskatoon's growth between 1904 and 1912 as "the greatest example of town and city building in the world's history," and an advertisement placed in an eastern newspaper claimed that the city was "the eight year old wonder of the British Empire."[4] Unfortunately, the hyperbole was not confined to Saskatoon. Civic boasts reverberated throughout the province. The following appeared in a full-page advertisement in a Regina newspaper in 1912: "The Eyes Of The World Are Upon Regina The Capital And Wonder City Of This Mighty Province Whose Growth Can No More Be Stemmed Than The Waters Of The Sea."[5] Prince Albert, which seemed to be as certain of its destiny, was to become a northern metropolis. Hydroelecteric power generated by the placid North Saskatchewan would make it "The White Coal City," and a railway to Hudson Bay, "The gateway to Europe." A publication sponsored by the board of trade in 1910 predicted the usual roseate future, to be enjoyed by a population of half a million, and ended with this remarkable panegyric:

> Hear ye the roar of enginery and motor, the buzz of wheel, the hum of pulleys, the symphony as sung by power applied to drill and saw and hammer. Note ye the flow of material into the city and the stream of finished product that leaves by train going to build the homes of the sturdy men who are tilling the prairie.[6]

The combination of high emotion, created by these gospels of growth, and belief in the unlimited potential of the West was an ideal matrix for the growth of speculative fever. To trigger the growth only an inflow of capital was needed. This final prerequisite was provided through the initiative of the boards of trade and the real-estate companies. Financial houses and the general public both at home and abroad were alerted, by a flood of promotional literature, to the golden opportunities awaiting the investor in the western cities. At the time there were large supplies of mobile capital in Britain seeking profitable ventures overseas, and the Canadian prairies were regarded as a favorable area for investment.

160

In some of the promotional literature extraordinary claims were made. A group of Saskatoon real-estate promoters predicted a population for the city of 400,000 to 600,000 by 1940 and even the mayor, in 1910, foresaw a population of 100,000 "in a few years."[7] In 1912 a full-page newspaper advertisement underlining the city's attractiveness as a location for industry predicted that "Winnipeg will be a Chicago and Saskatoon will be a Minneapolis and St. Paul with a million people."[8] Prospective industrialists were promised cheap sources of power in the form of natural gas — vast bodies of which were "known to exist" within the vicinity — and hydroelectricity, which was to be generated by harnessing the South Saskatchewan River. To advertise the agricultural potential of the province and allay fears about the reported limitations of the prairie climate, the president of the board of trade grew sub-tropical plants outside his office. With similar intent photographs were taken of bumper crops of onions, potatoes, and cabbages and distributed widely. Fortunately, the zeal was leavened by a little gentle caricature: postcards using trick photography to show giant cabbages and enormous wheat stalks ridiculed the excessive claims of the prairie boosters.

However, gentle caricature was no match for the zeitgeist. When reality itself is inflated, the caricaturist is disarmed. Capital flowed into the West — "a continuous tide of British gold,"[9] according to Elbert Hubbard, the famous inspirational essayist who visited Saskatoon in 1912 — and the cities boomed. Saskatoon's boom began in the fall of 1910 and ended in the summer of 1913. Since its general history is fairly well documented[10] only its salient features need be mentioned here. Like all speculative booms it was characterised by inflated land prices and totally unrealistic subdivision. The surrounding prairie was used as a seedbed for real-estate fantasies. Land — some of it still not built upon — was subdivided into lots in a radius extending six miles from the city centre, with the mayor recommending that the radius be lengthened to ten miles. In all, about 15,000 acres outside the city limits were surveyed into town lots, most of them selling at prices above their present value. By 1913, even allowing for an expansion of the city's boundaries in 1911, it has been estimated[11] that there was enough subdivided land outside the city limits — approximately sixty quarter sections — to accommodate a population of half a million in detached houses.

To administer to the speculative fever, the number of real-estate firms in the city mushroomed from 8 in 1908 to 257 at the height of the boom in 1912. Today there are 58. According to Elbert Hubbard, many of the real-estate boomers were Americans, some of them, presumably, being professional town promoters who had participated in the booms of the American West and Mid-West. Although cash did exchange hands, most of the transactions were in "futures," the buyer making a small down payment, holding the remaining debt in the form of a mortgage.

Lots exchanged hands frequently — on occasion several times during a week — making large profits for both local and foreign investors.

Inflationary pressures, however, were not confined to real estate. In 1911 the board of trade had advertised the city's population as 17,000 whereas the Dominion census in October of that year found it to be only 12,000 and as if to add insult to injury gave out a figure of 30,000 for Regina. The inevitable reaction, in view of the wound to an abnormally sensitive civic pride and the danger of a loss of credibility in the financial houses, was an outburst of righteous indignation. The census finding, expostulated the mayor, "is absolutely unreasonable, unbelievable and absurd."[12] Shortly afterward the board of trade organized a retaliatory citizens' recount which restored the figure to a respectable 18,000.

The essence of the boom was the hallucinatory real-estate promotion. One of the more interesting of these concerned the building of the industrial "city" of Factoria. The scheme was conceived by a Chicago syndicate which bought a 470-acre development site about two miles north of the city boundary. Manufacturing was to be based primarily on the natural resources of the site: a spring of water, "the purest in Canada"; limestone; clay; and sand. "It's the natural resources that make Factoria a reality — the water — the clay — the sand,"[13] intoned the head of the syndicate who proposed to utilize them in a brewery, a lime kiln, a brick-and-tile factory, and a glass-and-bottle works. The development was also to include a flour mill, a farm-implement factory, and a sixty-six room hotel. A few of the plants and a tarpaper hotel were actually built, but the project, which called for $1,000,000 worth of industries and a population of 2,000 within a year, collapsed with the end of the boom.

Another well-known industrial promotion of the period was the formation of the "Industrial League" which, in spite of the rhetoric and swollen expectations attending its inception, sounded a more realistic note. The promoters of the league recognized that the limits to Saskatoon's service and distributive function would be set by the population of its hinterland. By 1910 free homesteads were already scarce and the rural areas were filling up with settlers. With the completion of settlement, argued the promoters, future growth would depend on industrial development.To bring this about they proposed to create a rotating fund — started by citizens' contributions — which would be used to help industries to locate in the city. Once in production, shares were to be sold and the money invested in new plants. The scheme was greeted enthusiastically, and within a few days, $1,000,000 had been pledged to the league. After a few months the *Saturday Press* offered this encomium: "Today, after a test of a few months . . . it would appear that the Industrial League had sounded the chanticleer call that signalled the dawn of the sun of industry upon the prairie west, and particularly upon

*Tax office, City Hall, about 1913*

Saskatoon."[14] Further allurements to prospective industrialists were the offer of free sites in "Cordage Park" and the provision of cheap Slav labor to be brought into the country by an incorporated company with the Dickensian title of "Toil Corporation Limited." Fortunately, perhaps, the league also died with the boom.

As if intent on providing another intoxicant for an already overstimulated populace, city council adopted during the boom years a novel and, in the judgement of orthodox economists, a naive system of taxation: Henry George's "single tax." In its pure form, the "single tax" is a system of taxation by which a community raises the whole of its revenue through a tax on land alone, exempting improvements. The justification for the scheme is that the value of land is created by the community, which should, therefore, receive the benefits. Through placing a heavy tax on land Henry George hoped to nullify the advantages of ownership, his ultimate objective being the effective elimination of private property in land. It is ironic, therefore, that the scheme should have been adopted at a time when fortunes were being made from land sales. However, it was precisely to prevent speculation that the "single tax" had been adopted since, as George and his supporters argued,[15] the heavy tax on land would force its owners to put it to use. Among the benefits expected to accrue from the scheme were that commerce and industry, unburdened by taxation, would flourish;

*East side of Second Avenue looking south, 1910*

that land prices would be kept down; and that scattered developments, seeking cheaper sites in outlying areas, would be prevented. The latter was a particular problem on the spacious prairies. In arguing for the centralizing influence of the "single tax" upon the location of buildings, the Winnipeg commissioner noted that "throughout the prairie country there appears to be a great tendency to build in scattered disconnected sections away from the heart of the city thus greatly adding to the expense of constructing and maintaining local improvements."[16]

In western Canada the history of the adoption of the "single tax" — or, more precisely, a modified version of it since it was never adopted in its pure form — began in British Columbia in the 1890's and from there the practice spread to Alberta and Saskatchewan. In Saskatoon concessions to improvements were first made in 1911, the assessment being reduced from sixty percent to fifty percent of their fair actual value. Further reductions to thirty-five percent and twenty-five percent were made in 1912 and 1913. Land, on the other hand, was assessed at its full value.[17]

The effects of the "single tax" system on the development of Saskatoon were assessed by the city commissioner in a special report in 1917.[18] He found that few of the expected benefits actually accrued. The system not only failed to prevent speculation but, in the commissioner's opinion, actually encouraged it by adding to the general excitement through offering potential developers the prospect of an almost tax-free future. In addition, it proved to be a difficult tax to collect and, in part,

164

*Twenty-first Street, about 1910*

accounted for the enormous arrears of taxes in 1917. The commissioner could also have added that it failed to prevent scattered developments. On the positive side it did encourage owners to develop their property but to such an extent that the supply of buildings exceeded the normal demand. In 1917 Saskatoon, like many other western cities, was embarrassed by an oversupply of buildings. The commissioner concluded his report with an appeal to council to spread the burden of taxation by reducing the assessment of land values by twenty-five percent and by increasing the assessed value of improvements from twenty-five percent to forty percent of their fair actual value. These changes, he offered, would both broaden the tax base and spread the burden of taxation according to the recognized principles of ability to pay and benefits received.

Although in essence the boom was a chimera sustained by rhetoric and financial promises, it was not without substance. Profits made from real-estate speculation were invested in downtown buildings such as hotels and office blocks, some of the latter, which were expected to be part of a crowded development, having windows on only one or two sides. In addition, hundreds of houses and large numbers of churches, schools, and other public buildings were built to accommodate and serve the growing population, which doubled, approximately, during the boom years. Between 1909 and 1912 the annual value of building permits

*Five-span steel bridge over the South Saskatchewan River at Saskatoon, 1913*

increased from $1,000,000 to $7,000,000.[19] Money borrowed by the city on the strength of its dangerously inflated[20] — owing to the extensive subdivision and high land values — revenues was used to build roads, sidewalks, street lighting, water mains, and sewers. In his budget statement of 1921[21] the city commissioner estimated that these improvements could have served a population twice the current (1921) size of the city.

Judged solely by quantitative standards Saskatoon could justifiably claim to be a "wonder city." But in the qualitative sense the case was otherwise. Considered generally, the architecture was dull and undistinguished and the general layout — standard gridiron or checkerboard — unimaginative. In his study of architecture in Canada, Alan Gowans[22] points out that the western cities had the misfortune to be built during the least attractive period of Canadian architecture; the Late Victorian, which persisted here until the 1920's. By the beginning of the century, Victorian design had lost its earlier inventiveness with the result that the centres of the western cities were dominated by uninteresting, basically utilitarian buildings. But in western Canada in 1913 it was quantity rather than quality that impressed. One overwrought citizen, who was as overwhelmed by the sight of his city as the ancient Sumerians had been with theirs, mused, as they had, upon the possibility of supernatural origins: "And when you look up and see the stately residences and massive public buildings lining its banks you wonder if you are in a dream city or can this really be the little village of yesterday. Saskatoon has risen like a magic city on the banks of the Saskatchewan."[23]

The "magic city," nevertheless, had a physical reality, and to control its development, council, in 1913, appointed a city commissioner, having adopted a commission form of government in 1911. Given the prevailing mood it wasn't a responsibility that could have been entrusted to an ordinary man. The commissioner, Mr. C. J. Yorath, who arrived in May, 1913 with an A.M.I.C.E. and ten years of planning experience in England, had "the makings of what Mr. Elbert Hubbard would call a hundred point man" and combined "the cultured accent of the English cosmopolite" with "the broad forehead and deep eyes that go with intellectuality and the sauve manner that goes with culture."[24] Although, to judge from his reports, Mr. Yorath was an intellignet and a sensible man, he was, inescapably, a victim of context. His public statements reflect the general optimism which, although it had subsided by the summer of 1913, still maintained its public front. In an address to the real-estate board in June, 1913 Mr. Yorath could still say: "I believe the high optimism of Saskatoon is justified. We are on but the threshold of our greatness. In the centre of the greatest wheat growing province of the dominion ... we are very favorably situated."[25] In his remarks alluding to the future planning of the ciy, the models he used were Washington and Paris.

Although he was to condemn the irresponsible subdivision and the rash spending of council during the boom years, Mr. Yorath, ironically, is remembered for a map which now serves as a memorial to the boom since it mirrors the spirit of the period and shows much of the subdivided land outside the city limits. The map was produced in 1913 at the request of council, who wanted guidelines laid down for the city's future development. In spite of the restrictions imposed upon it by previous subdivision, the map is an interesting document since it is a melange of then-current planning theory and practice. Mr. Yorath's taste, as revealed by the plan itself, by his favorable references to Washington and Paris and by an example of a city plan used as an illustration in his annual report for 1917, was for planning in the grand manner. The ideal city was to be laid on a foundation of broad tree-lined avenues, spacious public parks, and monumental buildings occupying vantage points on elevated ground or at the heads of avenues. The principles of baroque planning had been revived at the end of the nineteenth century by the planners of the influential Chicago World's Fair in 1893.

Owing to the pre-existing subdivision Mr. Yorath could only superimpose baroque features upon the gridiron network. His additions included broad avenues and boulevards and, where space was available, parks. The avenues and boulevards, in addition to improving the appearance of the city, were designed to serve practical needs: the diagonal avenues were meant to provide easy access between the centre and the periphery, and the encircling boulevards, the main inner one

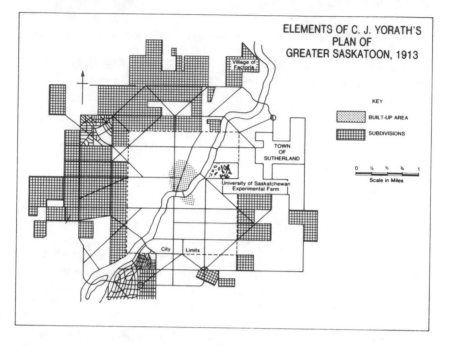

corresponding fairly closely to today's Circle Drive, to connect peri-
pheralpoints. Mr. Yorath was a severe critic of the gridiron layout which
he condemned on the grounds of its wastefulness and its impracticality. It
was wasteful in the sense that the streets, being nearly all of the same
width, were costly to maintain, and impractical in that it did not channel
traffic. In a grid system any street can be a through street. In his 1917
report Mr. Yorath demonstrated the advantages of a curvilinear street
pattern woven into self-contained residential neighborhoods providing
recreational, shopping, and educational facilities for the local community. His models were the neighborhoods in the newly built English
garden city of Letchworth.

Commissioner Yorath's ideas, however, were never implemented.
Instead of directing the future growth of Saskatoon, he was, on the
contrary, to spend much of the term of his appointment, from 1913 to
1921, restoring the city's financial base. Political instability in Europe,
together with doubts raised about the financial viability of the western
Canadian municipalities, stemmed the flow of money in the spring of
1913. Denied sustenance, and exposed to sober appraisal, the boom
quickly subsided. In the fall of 1913 Henry Howard of the Investor's
Guardian in London issued this warning:

> I think that Saskatoon, under its present conditions, will have quite
> reached the limit of the credit to which it is entitled, even if it has not

already exceeded it. It seems to me that a debenture debt approaching the sum of $8 million is a serious matter for a young community whose assessment value was only $40 million in 1912. The progress made by Saskatoon during its life of ten years is remarkable but it must be remembered that it takes a reasonable time to develop a city and that a forcing process is always an expensive matter.... There is a fine framework of a city in Saskatoon but, like that of a slender stripling, it wants filling up. If, of the very large number of vacant lots which obtruded themselves upon my notice in the majority of streets in Saskatoon, a fair proportion are built on and occupied in the next few years, then Saskatoon might have a reasonable expectation that its future calls on the market would receive respectful attention.[26]

The next few years, however, saw little building. In 1914 the value of building permits amounted to only $500,000, compared to $7,000,000 in 1912, and in 1915 reached the all time low of $20,000.[27] With the collapse of the boom the reckoning was severe. Several years later the commissioner was to describe the financial condition of Saskatoon in 1913 as "the most deplorable of any city in the West."[28] Yet surprisingly, and perhaps undeservedly, the city in the long run was to benefit from the boom. The owners of surveyed prairie lots, who were either unable or unwilling to pay the taxes, forfeited them through default. As a result, by the time of the Second World War, Saskatoon found itself in the fortunate position of owning most of the unimproved land within the city limits. Anticipating the rapid post-war expansion and anxious to avoid the historic pattern of speculation, spiralling land values, and disorderly development, council established a real-estate committee to dispose of the land. The committee decided to sell the land on a lease-option agreement which stipulated that the purchaser build on the land within one year of the purchase date. Title to the land was not transferred until the contract obligation had been fulfilled, thus eliminating the possibility of a quick re-sale. To encourage large scale, co-ordinated development, contractors were offered land for one-half of the assessed value on condition that at least ten houses be built. Industrial property sales were conducted in the same manner.[29]

Since 1957, the real-estate committee, in collaboration with the planning department, has pursued a policy of continuous land acquisition using the revenues from its land sales. In doing so it has been able to maintain a reserve of land sufficient to meet its development needs for fifteen to twenty years ahead. As a result Saskatoon has been able to achieve the most orderly physical expansion of any city in Canada and, through its domination of the land market, has been able to stabilize land prices. Today Saskatoon, which sixty years ago was described as a "speculative boomer's paradise,"[30] is one of the few cities in North America where land speculation is no longer a major problem.

# 12    The Elevator Issue, the Organized Farmers, and the Government, 1908-1911

*by D. S. Spafford*

THE "elevator issue" of 1908-1911 was a significant event in the political history of Saskatchewan. It occasioned a far-reaching debate on the principles of public ownership; it presented the first threat of a serious breach between the Liberal party and the organized farmers; and it ended in what became one of the most important achievements of Saskatchewan's co-operative movement. The issue has left its students with a number of questions which might be subsumed in one: how was the government able to fly in the face of the farmers' demands for public ownership of grain elevators — and do so in apparent confidence that it would be vindicated?*

Correspondence in the ministerial papers of Hon. Walter Scott[1] adds to our knowledge of the issue. Of the Premier's own part in the issue it reveals much: that he was unsympathetic to the farmers' plan, both on its own merits and because of the diagnosis of the farmers' problems which it implied, and that the co-operative program which was recommended by an independent commission in 1910 was an idea entertained and actively promoted by Scott well before the commission was established. Equally remarkable is what the correspondence and contemporary newspaper reports suggest about the farmers' role in the issue. The farm leaders, it is made evident, had serious doubts about the plan they were promoting among their followers and ostensibly urging upon the government. The farmers' advocacy of public ownership gives the impression of being, in fact, less a reflex of collectivist doctrine than the calculated tactic of a pressure group.

The agitation for publicly owned grain elevators gathered force early in 1908 when conventions of the Grain Growers in the three prairie provinces gave approval to what became known as the Partridge Plan, named after its author, E. A. Partridge of Sintaluta, Saskatchewan.[2] The plan called for Dominion ownership of terminal elevators and provincial

---

*This article originally appeared in *Saskatchewan History* for autumn, 1962.

ownership of inland elevators. A meeting of the Premiers of the three provinces was called by Premier Roblin of Manitoba and took place at Regina in May.[3] The meeting produced only a suggestion that the railways be pressed to make certain reforms. When this proposal was rejected as "totally inadequate" by the Interprovincial Council of Grain Growers and Farmers' Associations (a liaison group which had been formed in 1907), a second meeting of the Premiers, this time with representatives of the farmers, took place on November 26, 1908, again at Regina. The Premiers' formal reply to the Interprovincial Council in late January, 1909, stated that their respective administrations were not prepared to participate in a system of provincially owned elevators without a monopoly position which could be acquired only by amendment of the British North America Act. "It was thus sought," Patton writes, "to place the onus of the elevator issue upon the federal authorities."[4]

The Interprovincial Council stated publicly that legal monopoly was not necessary for the financial soundness of the Partridge Plan; there is evidence, however, that the farmers' delegates at the November meeting had privately agreed that it was.[5] In any case, the constitutional issue brought an end to the interprovincial phase of the farmers' campaign. The Grain Growers decided to apply pressure to the governments singly.

In November of 1909 the Saskatchewan Grain Growers' Association formally petitioned the Scott government for publicly owned interior elevators. The campaign was now squarely in Scott's own political arena and its intensity began to arouse his concern. "The agitation in the Province is producing an effect upon the Members of the Assembly," he wrote in early December, "most of whom insist now that some steps must be taken in the direction of meeting the demands of the Grain Growers."[6] Further, now that the provinces were acting independently, Scott risked being pre-empted in a popular solution to the farmers' demands. Roblin, by letter, attempted to divine Scott's intentions while remaining remarkably silent concerning his own. Scott replied on December 13 that his government, "deeming discretion the better part of valor," would probably consent to the appointment of a commission of inquiry, "to try to devise a plan to do what the Grain Growers want done in a way, if possible, to leave the Government free from the more obvious dangers inherent in a system directly operated by the Government. I am hopeful that we may not be driven into a system of direct Government ownership."[7] On the following day the Saskatchewan legislature agreed unanimously to the establishment of an elevator commission. Two days later, on December 16, the Manitoba government indicated that it would go ahead with government ownership.[8]

The resolution passed by the Saskatchewan legislature called for the

171

establishment of a commission to examine proposals for "the creation and operation of a system of elevators" which would accomplish the objects of the farmers. The opposition party expressed concern at its generality, specifically at the lack of explicit reference to *government* elevators. The concern was highly pertinent. The Premier was determined, privately, that government ownership should be avoided if at all possible; publicly, he observed an impartiality which befitted a question about to go to an independent commission.[9] Nor, indeed, did he think he would be driven to public ownership. The executive of the Saskatchewan Grain Growers' Association had informed him in confidence before the resolution was passed that it was, in Scott's words, "quite willing to consider any alternative scheme that may be suggested to serve the same purpose" as the farmers' plan.[10] The Grain Growers' secretary, F. W. Green, made the same admission when he appeared before the legislature's committee on agriculture and municipal law in early December to state the farmers' case for public ownership. This flexibility on the part of the Grain Growers' leaders was of some significance to Scott because he had an alternative plan in mind.

Scott's plan was to establish farmers' mutual elevator companies with financial assistance from the government. His correspondence reveals that he had been entertaining the idea several months before the commission came into being.[11] He took the trouble to introduce the idea into discussion when the legislature created the commission, using as a vehicle a letter which he had received a few days before.[12] Later, he was to call his reading of the letter "a hint [to the legislature] as to what might be expected"[13] — though it was not put forward as a "hint," and it is unlikely that the legislature understood it to be one. The plan had the virtue of avoiding public ownership. Moreover, it had precedent to commend it. Scott wrote late in 1909:

> It is universally agreed that a system of elevators directly owned and operated by a Government would be attended by grave economic and political dangers. There is much to be said in favor of the principle which we have already applied in our rural telephone legislation and also with regard to the so-called Government Creameries, that is to say, the granting of a measure of Government aid sufficient to make a locally owned system financially possible and leaving the responsibility of the maintenance and operation upon the local communities.[14]

On February 26, 1910, the cabinet reached a decision on the personnel of the elevator commission. It was to be made up of F. W. Green, secretary of the Saskatchewan Grain Growers' Association; George Langley, Liberal M.L.A. for Redberry; and a political economist, Professor Robert Magill of Dalhousie University, Halifax.[15] Langley was a director-at-large of the Saskatchewan Grain Growers' Association. As

*George Langley*

a farm leader who was also associated with the governing party of a province, he had been a logical choice as intermediary in the negotiations between the Premiers and the organized farmers in 1908.

Probably neither Langley nor Green — but especially Green — was desirous of serving on the commission. The Premier wrote to Langley at the time of appointment that he could see that Green "was fearful of accepting appointment, — afraid, I suppose, that his position in the [S.G.G.A.] Executive might be weakened."[16] The Saskatchewan Grain Growers' Association had re-affirmed its support of public ownership of internal elevators in convention just two weeks before, and as a member of the executive and a director, respectively, Green and Langley were committed to the Partridge Plan.[17] They surely must have been aware of

173

Scott's opposition to public ownership. Even more to the point, both had been acquainted with the Premier's alternative plan and had indicated approval of it. Scott wrote two weeks before the commissioners were appointed,

> Langley thinks the Grain Growers will be quite satisfied if the suggestion [aid to farmers' companies] can be carried out and Fred. Green . . . in private discussion with us expressed himself as thinking that such a scheme if it could be worked out would be a good deal safer and more satisfactory to all concerned.[18]

Scott gave much attention to the selection of a political economist. He asked advice of President Murray of the University of Saskatchewan who discussed a number of candidates (including Magill) and who recommended, in order of preference, Adam Shortt, then with the Civil Service Commission at Ottawa; Professor J. A. Commons of Wisconsin; and a Professor McVey of North Dakota. Shortt was approached first[19] and though he was willing to serve, he found he could not be spared from his work in Ottawa. Scott personally interviewed Commons, Professor O. D. Skelton of Queen's University, and, finally, Magill, whom he eventually selected.

By his own account, Magill was a strong supporter of public ownership. "My attitude is simple and constant," he wrote to Scott after the commission's report was completed.[20] "I believe in public ownership of public utilities, when the conditions of successful operation exist. . . . No one has ever heard me oppose the principle of public ownership." He had so often advocated that principle, he stated on another occasion, "that some have called me a 'socialist'."[21] His fellow-commissioners were also avowedly sympathetic to public enterprise. Langley probably leaned the furthest left of any member on the government side of the House, though it was a distinction won in relatively conservative company. Both he and Green had been associated with working-class political movements in England before emigrating to Canada.[22] Altogether, it was a commission that might be expected to produce a rather less conservative report than it did.

In the report,[23] dated October 31, 1910, the commission rejected public ownership and recommended instead a system of co-operative elevators owned and operated by the farmers and assisted by generous loans from the government. The commission's recommendations were translated, with only a few minor changes, into law in March of the next year with the creation of the Saskatchewan Co-operative Elevator Company. The legislation provided for the construction, or acquisition, of elevators when fifteen percent of the necessary capital stock had been subscribed by a "local," the government advancing the remaining eighty-five percent.

Saskatchewan Archives Board

*F. W. Green at steering wheel; E. N. Hopkins next to him on front seat;*
*E. A. Partridge at left back; Harry Darrel in bowler hat; Moose Jaw, about*
*1909*

That its recommendations bear such a close likeness to Scott's idea inevitably raises a question about the commission's independence. To call it "Scott's idea" is, perhaps, to prejudge the matter: the idea had occurred to others, as the Premier's correspondence shows, and it already had been applied to two services — creameries and rural telephones. Supposing the idea did originate with the Premier, there is no reason why the commission should have disqualified it on that ground. Scott may have played his cards too cleverly, if not with outright impropriety, by appointing two of the commissioners in the knowledge that they looked with favor on his alternative plan. Yet, his first reaction to the news of the commission's findings displayed surprise enough to suggest that he did not regard such findings as a foregone conclusion.[24]

The commission pointed out enough specific difficulties in the plan submitted by the farmers to make its rejection a reasonable, if still an arguable, decision. Indeed, in the light of the subsequent success of the co-operative elevator program in Saskatchewan and the abysmal failure of public ownership of elevators in Manitoba, the decision must appear a wise one. The report had one curious aspect. In its summing-up, the commission stated that two formidable handicaps to a plan such as the farmers proposed were the likelihood of political interference and — "perhaps the greatest obstacle to the development of public ownership" — "a general disposition [on the part of the public] to exact the utmost possible from the public treasury while not giving the utmost return."[25]

175

To find such arguments presented over the names of three professed advocates of public enterprise is somewhat surprising. Was their reversal in the report a matter of convenience rather than conviction? One is led to ask this question by the knowledge that the commission (or Magill, at least) had a more fundamental objection to the farmers' case, one which, significantly, received very little prominence in the report itself.

The farmers' case for government-owned elevators was based on a belief that monopolistic practices in the grain trade were depressing their receipts from marketed grain. Green and Langley, for their part, were in doubt whether public ownership represented the best possible solution to the farmers' problem. Magill had doubts of a more important kind: he did not consider that the problem itself was at all as serious as the Grain Growers claimed.

> As a student [he wrote to Scott] I was and am very much surprised to find so little grounds for real complaint. I expected to find a far worse state of matters than really exists at present. I believe that a strong combine would however soon have developed — a combine such as up till now does not exist in the grain trade in Canada. This is the only reason (apart from politics) which I, for one, would recommend even a loan.[26]

In other words, the problem was not serious enough to justify so stringent a remedy. The commission's review of the farmers' complaints amounted to a discreetly put debunking exercise,[27] reflecting Magill's assessment of competitive conditions in the grain trade and suggesting, incidentally, that his assessment was at least passively concurred in by the other commissioners. It was a point of view which, given too much emphasis, probably would have lost the farmers' confidence in the commission.

Magill's correspondence reveals the not-altogether-comfortable position of the farmer-commissioners whose personal allegiances, public statements, and private convictions were being ground between the millstones. Langley, Magill said, "loved to play the role of a member of the House, a close friend to the government, a champion of the farmer, and above all he wanted to avoid the fate of John Miller."[28] Green had been recalcitrant at first, "due to the awkward attempt he made to work with us and yet not break with Partridge."[29] Indeed, he came close to dissenting on the findings. According to Magill:

> Mr. Green devoted some time to gathering information about the operation of the Manitoba elevators, and *this resulted in his agreeing to the report.* Had it not been for this, I have little doubt that there would have been two reports. Further that information coupled with some which I had personally received enabled me to write about provincial ownership in a way which otherwise would have been difficult. I assure you that Saskatchewan should be pleased that the Manitoba people went in as they did. If it was possible to have some of the features & experiences of the Manitoba elevators fully written

up in your province, your people would hesitate about following the example.[30]

Once the report was signed, its acceptance by the Saskatchewan Grain Growers' Association executive and the membership became a matter of considerable importance to Green and Langley. Its rejection would have amounted to a vote of non-confidence in them, both as commissioners and as farm leaders. An unmistakeable note of triumph is detectable in Langley's scribbled account of the reception of the commission's report by the Saskatchewan Grain Growers' Association executive:

> You may be interested to know how the G.G. Executive received the report — Well on the whole favourably; there was a sort of Glumness on the part of Durrell & Evans and Partridge was by instinct hostile but both Green and I felt more than Satisfied. I asked Green how he regarded the reception & his reply was we have them treed sure thing.[31]

Because his role as the farmers' spokesman was more clearly defined, Green found himself in a position rather more awkward than Langley's. When the Grain Growers next met in convention, Langley rose to the occasion with a persuasive and confident speech in support of the recommendations of the commission. Green spoke to the same purpose, but in apologetic tones. When the commission was established, he said, there had been "no question in his mind" but that he would press for public ownership. When he said before the legislative committee in early December of 1909 that the Grain Growers were not inalterably wedded to public ownership, he had been using a stratagem "to get the government into an attitude favorable to taking over the whole system of elevators as he was instructed to do."[32]

Among Scott's reasons for opposing the farmers' scheme, perhaps the most important was a belief which he shared with Magill that the farmers tended to take an unduly pessimistic view of their situation. There "never was a moment in the last twenty years when there was less need for haste," he told the legislature when the resolution to establish the commission was introduced. Never had there been less "robbery" than at the present time, when the farmers had the protection of the Manitoba Grain Act, when they had the benefit of the Saskatchewan Grain Growers' Association, and the Grain Growers' Grain Company, and when the railways were beginning to give reasonable service.[33] That a "material lessening of the actual grievances" of the farmers should be attended by a considerable increase in the agitation for government action was, to Scott, a perplexing state of affairs.[34] He thought he detected in it some self-interested activity on the part of the Grain Growers' Grain Company which, he said, "has been simply coining money under the one cent commission rule. [Its leaders] think they see a secure position for their business with a system of government transferring and storage warehouses covering the wheat country."[35] Moreover, of the grievances still outstanding, at least some had to do with rail, rather than elevator, services. He considered it significant that in southern Manitoba, where there was fairly active railway competition and boxcars could be had without delay, there was also, as he understood, relatively little support for public ownership of elevators.[36]

Scott found the farmers' petition unconvincing in another respect. He believed that the Grain Growers' commitment to the Partridge Plan was more apparent than real. At their convention each year, the Grain Growers voted overwhelmingly in favor of the Partridge Plan. Yet, in negotiations with the government, they showed a surprising readiness to compromise. Mention has been made of the Saskatchewan Grain Growers' Association executive's admission that it would accept an alternative scheme and to the favorable hearing which Green and Langley gave to Scott's proposal.

More significant, Scott was able to recollect a meeting with executive members of the Grain Growers as early as April, 1908, at which he was told "unanimously and freely that they lacked confidence in the Partridge scheme."

> When I wanted to know why then did they agree to it in convention they said that some action was needed and they had no satisfactory alernative to present. They wanted me to find a satisfactory alternative if possible which would be free from the dangers of government ownership.[37]

The Premier stated it as his belief that when Green had admitted before the legislative committee that the Grain Growers were not inalterably committed to public ownership, the Saskatchewan Grain Growers' Association secretary had "correctly expressed the view of every man in his Association outside of Mr. Partridge."[38] Scott went on to say that, apart from the joint conference of 1908, no deputation of Grain Growers had ever met the government and "candidly and directly" urged government ownership. He said, "They complained of grievances. They wanted action. They wanted a remedy. But they never directly urged government elevators."[39] On first sight at least, Scott's claim appears to overlook the Saskatchewan Grain Growers' Association's petition of November, 1909, in which government ownership was represented as the only feasible remedy for the difficulties of the farmers. But the petition was a public statement, and the Grain Growers' public stance was, as Scott was aware, quite a different article from the private opinion of its leaders.

Scott may have had other reasons for his opposition to the farmers' plan: the enormous cost of such an undertaking, perhaps, and the dangers inherent in a program which involved priorities and left his government open to charges of partisanship. Regarding the last point, he once made reference to "the dangerous features of a system on the one hand liable to political manipulation and, on the other hand, as regards location of elevators and management, in which a Government would be always subjected to undue local pressure."[40]

To attempt to disentangle from these considerations Scott's views of public ownership as a theoretical principle would not be a productive exercise. But it would be a mistake to think that he had no such views. Professor Fowke has pointed out that, in turning down public ownership of elevators, Scott's action was consistent with "the one well-established collectivist economic principle in the national field in Canada" at that time, namely the principle which "sanctioned the use of public funds and public credit for developmental purposes" with the proviso that "public ownership and management should be avoided at almost any cost."[41] Sir Wilfrid Laurier's attitude to the elevator question, as he expressed it in Regina, was that he was "not a believer in government ownership of utilities, but in this case he saw no serious objection to it if no other methods could be adopted to bring about a more satisfactory state of affairs."[42] It may be said with some assurance that as a matter of political philosophy Scott, too, preferred the "other methods" to public ownership.[43]

But what appears to be more relevant to an understanding of the elevator issue than the Premier's own political inclination were the views which he attributed to the farmers. Scott may not have been indifferent to the ideological cast of his elevator policy but he believed that the farmers were. His belief finds clear expression in the following statement: "The farmers of Saskatchewan have always been mainly interested in obtaining an effectual remedy against unfair conditions in the grain trade regardless of whether such remedy meant government elevators or some other and safer scheme."[44] Langley pressed a similar interpretation upon the Grain Growers' convention of 1911.

> But do not forget this [he told the delegates]: these public ownership schemes were not intended to bind us to a fetish in any way at all. They were all proposed as a means of ridding us from the evils that attended the marketing of our grain. I want to point out distinctly that public ownership was not the end we were aiming at.... Therefore, when Mr. Partridge gets up and says it was public ownership we have been striving for, he is wrong. We were only advocating public ownership because that was at the time the best remedy we could see against the evils of private ownership.[45]

It may be argued that this interpretation of the farmers' interests was only a convenient rationalization for rejecting public ownership. Yet, to the extent that one can attribute the result of an election to the outcome of a single issue, one may say that Scott was prepared to stake the good health of his government on his belief that the farmers would settle for something less than public ownership of elevators. His intuition, if such it was, was vindicated: there was a day of suspense,[46] but the 1911 convention of the Grain Growers eventually accepted the commission's report. Once the co-operative elevators were in operation, no more was heard of public ownership.

A remarkable parallel exists in the telephone question of 1907-08. The Saskatchewan Grain Growers' Association urged public ownership of rural service upon the government in 1907. The government turned it down in 1908 and proposed instead a program of mutual companies. The decision went not only unprotested but, as far as one can tell from newspaper reports, unmentioned at the next Grain Growers' convention.[47]

If Scott was right and the farmers did not in fact prefer public ownership over other solutions to their wheat marketing problems, then how can one account for the remarkably strong campaign waged on its behalf? The answer appears to be that the Grain Growers or, more accurately, their leaders, used public ownership as a club to hold over the government's head. The farm leaders, despite their own misgivings about the Partridge Plan, rallied the farmers to its support in an attempt to force the government to take action. They left the government to determine the kind of action to be taken, with the understanding that in default of its finding a satisfactory alternative, public ownership would be adopted. No way of putting the question, it must be said, was better calculated to loose the inventive genius of the Scott government.

At one time or another in the first decade of the province's history the Grain Growers advocated the socialization of railways, terminal and interior elevators, municipal abattoirs, telephones, and various natural resources. "Taking it altogether," J. A. Maharg, the president of the Saskatchewan Grain Growers' Association, said in 1911, "the opinion of the Grain Growers has been most favorable to Government ownership. . . ."[48] But the Grain Growers did not, he added, support it "as a matter of principle," but in each case went "into the merits or demerits thoroughly before taking a step." Certainly, there were some among the Grain Growers—Partridge, for one[49]—who supported public ownership as a "matter of principle." For others, co-operatives or effective government regulation would have done as well. The comparative ease with which the Grain Growers were dissuaded from their stated goal of public ownership in both the elevator and telephone issues suggests that the latter group predominated. Flexibility was one of the most valuable assets of the Grain Growers acting as a pressure group, but it was a flexibility tempered by an astute recognition of the uses to which a doctrinaire stand could be put when occasion demanded.

# 13  The French-Canadians and the Language Question, 1918

*by Raymond Huel*

ON February 27-28, 1912, representatives of Saskatchewan's French-Canadian community assembled in Duck Lake to form *l'Association Catholique Franco-Canadienne de la Saskatchewan* (A.C.F.C.), an organization dedicated to defending and promoting the ethnic and religious rights of French-Canadians. For the province's French-Catholic population, the moment to unite and organize was indeed opportune, for within ten months the separate-school issue, dormant since the first provincial election of 1905, would again reappear on the scene. Separate-school controversies have had a crucial impact on French-speaking minorities because such disputes inevitably bring forth the thorny question of language. French Catholics erect a separate school to ensure instruction in and the teaching of their maternal language which they consider indispensable to the preservation of their faith. Consequently, French-Canadian schools have become *de facto* linguistic schools, and this peculiar status has fanned the flames of the burning separate-school issue. In Saskatchewan, French-Canadians and their schools would become ideal targets in the rapidly rising offensive to make the province's population truly homogeneous: as Catholics they would bear the brunt of the attack on the separate-school system; as French-speaking Catholics determined to preserve their ancestral language, they would be singled out as fifth columnists striving to prevent the true Canadian character from emerging in Saskatchewan.*

Ironically, the genesis of the controversy which re-emerged in 1913 was neither religious nor ethnic but financial. Once raised, however, it did not long remain at that level. On September 14, 1911, Judge McLorg of Saskatoon dismissed an appeal by the Town of Vonda against a Court of Revision decision concerning the assessment of separate-school supporters. In upholding the lower court's decision, McLorg ruled that each ratepayer exercised the option of supporting either the public or

---

*This article originally appeared in *Saskatchewan History* for winter, 1970.

separate school.[1] Previous to this judgement, it had been held that members of a minority constituting a separate-school district were legally compelled to support that school, but the School Act was not explicit in this respect.[2]

McLorg's judgement had serious implications for the financial status of any school district which contained both a separate and public school. In Kipling, for example, most of the Protestant ratepayers were exercising their option to support the Catholic separate school rather than their public school because the former had a lower rate of assessment.[3] Premier Walter Scott, who was also Minister of Education, felt that unless the law were clarified a similar situation could develop in any locality encompassing public and separate school districts. To prevent this possibility, Scott introduced an amendment, in the form of a proviso to the School Act, making it mandatory for the ratepayers of a religious minority to support their separate school.[4]

The Reverend Murdock MacKinnon, minister of Regina's Knox Presbyterian Church and Premier Scott's own pastor, was extremely critical of the amendment. He informed Scott that the proviso was radical and that it deprived "many intelligent Roman Catholics" of the "right" to send their children to the public school and to support such schools.[5] Scott replied that the proviso did not alter existing lgislation but merely made explicit that which had formerly been implicit.[6] This explanation failed to satisfy MacKinnon and, after the amendment had been assented to, he advised the Premier that the matter had not been dealt with satisfactorily and that he would discuss the issue from his pulpit.[7]

On May 24, 1914, MacKinnon made good his promise to discuss the issue from Knox's pulpit. He charged that the amendments were designed to whip Catholics "into line" and place the public school at a disadvantage. MacKinnon contended that it was the duty of government to unite rather than segregate the people, and he charged that the separate school, which the government had undertaken to foster, was the greatest enemy of the "unifying movement." He concluded his sermon by calling upon all lovers of "freedom, justice and fair play" to smite hard against legislation which was an insurmountable obstacle to the attainment of unity.[8]

Thus far, the issue was one of separate schools and their financing but in May, 1915, Scott introduced an amendment to the language clause of the School Act which added to the dimensions of the controversy. Previous to the proposed amendment, the cost of employing a "competent person," who was not the teacher normally in charge of the school, to provide foreign-language instruction in accordance with departmental regulations, was borne by a special levy on the parents who took advantage of such instruction.[9] In an attempt to provide proper support for foreign-language instruction, Scott introduced the following amendment to section 177, sub-section 3 of the School Act: "Provided that if the regular teacher is competent to conduct such course of instruction the board shall not be required to impose and collect such special rates."[10]

Reaction was not long in coming and provided grounds for Scott's opposition to merge. In a front-page editorial entitled "A Wedge for Bi-Lingualism," Regina's *Evening Standard and Province* "discovered" a sinister plot behind the amendment: the non-English majority in any school district could escape the extra cost of foreign-language instruction by engaging a teacher of their own nationality and, consequently, "competent" under the terms of the legislation. Alleging that pupils would not be exposed to English-speaking teachers, the *Evening Province* asserted that the amendment was a "deliberate" and "dastardly" attack on the public schools.[11]

During debate on the Consolidated School Act, the Conservative leader, W. B. Willoughby, stated that the public schools should not become a medium for teaching foreign languages and asked that the clause be withdrawn because it introduced bilingualism into the schools. The Premier replied that it was ridiculous for anyone to link the government with a policy of bilingualism because of this proviso. Rather than have this suspicion spread, Scott moved that the clause be withdrawn and the legislature unanimously concurred. Commenting on this "defeat," the *Evening Province* prided itself on having been instrumental in eliminating bilingualism from the public-school system, "the melting pot from which the second generation may emerge Canadian to the core."[12] The separate-school controversy and the language issue had coalesced to set the stage for the crucial debate on the language question in 1918.

The school controversy gained momentum with each succeeding month. On December 26, 1915, MacKinnon again discussed the school issue in a 100-minute sermon delivered before a packed audience which included Premier Scott. MacKinnon charged that the clerical school, which had been "blasted" out of Europe, had found fertile soil in Saskatchewan as a result of the School Act amendments and that it was perpetrating "non-Anglo-Saxon ideals and features." He accused the A.C.F.C. of having "attacked" the public-school system, and the French, Poles, Germans, and Ruthenians of using the schools to foster their own sectarian ends. MacKinnon maintained that Scott had used the power of the legislature to assist these groups in discriminating against that "great unifying agency," the public school. According to MacKinnon, it was the government's duty to foster assimilation by eliminating sectarian ideals and racial segregation.[13]

Thus, by 1916, a significant change had taken place in the separate-school controversy. What had begun three years earlier as an objection to legislation affecting the financial status of separate schools had, by 1914, shifted to an attack on the separate-school system per se and, by late 1915, transformed itself into an assault against the teaching of languages other than English. In January, 1916, the opening salvo in this new phase of the school question came at the meeting of the Provincial Conservative Association in Saskatoon. The Conservative leader, W. B. Willoughby, announced that his party would repeal the School Act amendments if it formed the next government. Referring to Scott's "attempt" to open the door for bilingualism, Willoughby declared that English should be the sole language of instruction in public schools. Two hundred delegates cheered themselves hoarse after this pronouncement.[14]

While the Conservatives were applauding, officials of the Grand Orange Lodge met with Premier Scott and informed him that the order would support the political party which favored the abolition of separate schools. The lodge also felt that the teaching of French should not enjoy a special status and that foreign languages should not be taught in the primary grades.[15] In February, a resolution requesting that every child be taught in the English language was passed at the Saskatchewan Grain Growers' convention.[16] In March, a resolution calling for an amendment to the School Act prohibiting the teaching of foreign languages in the first five grades was passed at the annual Saskatchewan School Trustees' Association (S.S.T.A.) convention held in Regina.[17] A few days later, the annual meeting of the Saskatchewan Association of Rural Municipalities passed a resolution endorsing the demands of the Grain Growers and Trustees.[18]

Against this background, the language question could not fail to become a prominent issue in the 1917 provincial election. The Conservatives criticized the government's educational policy with advertisements like the one in the June 16 issue of Regina's *Daily Post:* "Vote for the Opposition Candidate and Banish the Monster of Poly-lingualism from Saskatchewan Forever." Conservative rallies heard the same call, embellished with charges that the Liberals were taking refuge behind foreign elements in the province.[19] The Orange Order submitted a questionnaire to candidates asking whether they were in favor of non-sectarian public schools, abolishing bilingual teaching, repealing religious qualifications for members of the Educational Council, and the enactment of a law to require that all trustees be able to read and write English. If the candidate answered affirmatively, the lodge regarded him as a "suitable person" to represent the constituency.[20]

In spite of the tumult over the school question, the Conservative effort had little electoral result in 1917, and the Liberals were returned with a majority of fifty-one members on June 26, the largest majority ever recorded by a political party in Saskatchewan's history. Despite the overwhelming Liberal victory, the results of the June 26 election could not be regarded as a referendum on the educational issue. There was, within the Anglo-Saxon population, a certain segment which was not satisfied with the verdict and who, like the Reverend MacKinnon, would not let the matter rest until satisfaction had been obtained. On June 27, the day following the election, the *Daily Post* had already informed Premier William M. Martin, Scott's successor, that the people were looking to him to make English the sole language of instruction "by whatever means are found possible and most expeditious."

As a result of the coalescence of the separate-school issue and the language question in 1915, education had, by 1917, become a highly charged emotional subject whose repercussions, political and otherwise, were incalculable. The language question became a burning issue for the people of Saskatchewan in 1918. The cry of "English only in Saskatchewan schools" became the panacea for all the province's ills, educational and otherwise. A delicate matter under any circumstances, the language question came to Saskatchewan at a time when the issue would inevitably be heightened by incidents which were taking place outside the province. The events of World War I had serious repercussions on Saskatchewan's European minorities. Flag-waving and an overabundance of patriotic sentiment precluded any spirit of moderation or toleration for the teaching of foreign languages.

The conscription crisis in Quebec made Saskatchewan's French-Canadians even more vulnerable to censure. It was an era when everyone "saw red" and ascribed the sins of fathers to their sons. It was also a period when appeals to passion overruled rationality in an effort to ensure that Quebec, and all it stood for, would not be reproduced or perpetuated in Saskatchewan. The primary course in French became an inviting target for those who maintained that the French language did not, and should not, enjoy a special status in this province.

By 1918, there was a desire, on the part of a certain vociferous segment of Saskatchewan's Anglo-Saxon population, that English must be the sole medium of instruction in schools. In the course of its campaign, the principle of "English only" became much more than simply a problem affecting education; the maintenance of democracy, the Empire, and the Canadian nation in a curious way all seemed to require that English be the only language of instruction in schools. In its editorial of January 9, the Saskatoon *Daily Star* stated that while Canada was condemned in perpetuity to two languages, no sanction should be given to the teaching of foreign languages in Saskatchewan. If English were not the only language of instruction, it would be impossible to build the Canadian nation or make the privileges of Canadianism "clear and compelling" to all. The Saskatoon branch of the Sons of England placed an advertisement in the *Daily Post* drawing attention to their resolution requesting the repeal of all provisions permitting instruction in foreign languages. Calling upon the Grain Growers to endorse these resolutions, the secretary of the Sons of England, H. G. Buck, said that while soldiers were fighting overseas to safeguard democracy, it was the duty of those at home "to see that this province shall remain British, first, last, and all the time." The Regina Great War Veterans' Association also sent similar resolutions to the Grain Growers.[21]

The language question aroused a great deal of discussion at the Grain Growers' convention held in Regina, February 12-15. Reverend J. G. Shearer, honorary secretary of the Dominion Social Service Congress, received a tumultuous ovation when he declared, "For the future of our country, English as the one language in our schools is the essential principle of our great democracy."[22] The convention passed a resolution calling for the exclusive use of the English language and English readers in the elementary school.[23] Commenting on the proceedings, the *Daily Post* stated that the Grain Growers had placed the bilingual question on the plane it ought to occupy. "It is the united call of the people of the province for action on a question of great importance."[24] Both the *Morning Leader,* which had liberal tendencies, and the *Grain Growers' Guide* played such questions down by either ignoring the issue where possible or keeping comment to a minimum.

The attitude of the Grain Growers' convention, however, was simply a foretaste of what was to follow a week later at the school trustees' convention scheduled for February 20-21 in Saskatoon. On February 15, the *Daily Post* announced that 800 delegates had registered already and hinted that "alien trustees" were planning a surprise and would register en masse on the last day in an attempt to control the assembly. In its editorial of February 19, the *Daily Post* looked upon the trustees to voice the unanimous desire of the people for "English and English only." The more liberally minded editor of the Saskatoon *Phoenix,* however, complained that the forthcoming convention was developing "a great deal of unnecessary rancor," and warned that Saskatchewan's foreign population had to be properly and sympathetically understood if assimilation were to come about; it would not be hastened by "irritant assertions."[25] As events were to prove, few heeded this plea for moderation and toleration. For its part, the *Morning Leader* expressed the hope that the language question would be dealt with in "a broad statesmanlike" manner in Saskatoon. The editor had refused to assume a dogmatic position on the issue but, nevertheless, he reminded his readers that an "unquestioned ability" to speak, read, and write English was an essential prerequisite to the Canadian ideal and citizenship. He asserted that there was no place in this Dominion for aliens who refused to identify with the language, life, and institutions of Canada.[26] The editorial was much more moderate in tone than those of the *Daily Post* but its import was manifest — English must be the dominant language taught and used in schools.

For their part, French-Canadians prepared to make their presence felt at the convention. The A.C.F.C.'s official organ, *Le Patriote de l'Ouest,* reminded its readers of the events of the 1917 convention and urged every French district to send delegates; if the French understood their duty, they would have 200 to 300 delegates.[27] As the convention date drew nearer, the A.C.F.C. became alarmed at the "great offensive" that was being directed against bilingualism. Through the medium of the English press, the A.C.F.C.'s executive addressed an open letter appealing to the sense of fair play of English-speaking trustees. The executive deplored the racial campaign carried out on the eve of the convention and maintained that bilingualism was not contrary to the national ideal. The French would be attending the sessions to study the best means of perfecting the school system, and they wished to work hand in hand with English trustees to eliminate racial issues from the discussions.[28] Reverend S. P. Rondeau, who later became a prominent spokesman for the Ku Klux Klan,[29] replied that the racial campaign was being "forced" upon the English as a result of a movement to dominate Canada and make it French by undermining the public-school system and the "assimilative power" of the English language. Rondeau's concept of a "sane" educational policy was "one common public system and one regnant language, the English language, which has ever proclaimed equal rights to all and special privileges to none."[30]

An estimated 3,000 delegates attended the trustees' convention which, because of its size, had to be divided between Saskatoon's Knox and Third Avenue Methodist Churches. The Third Avenue Church was filled to capacity, and hundreds had to be turned away and the doors locked. A "concentrated rush" by those outside broke down the doors but few were able to find seats. Extremist English-speaking trustees were plainly in control of the February 21 sessions. President P. M. Friesen, himself, was not present because of the hostile reception accorded him the previous day when he called for compromise on the language question, and in the ensuing election, not one man with a foreign name was nominated for a high executive position.[31]

The most tumultuous session of the convention, however, followed the presentation of resolutions requesting that all trustees be British subjects, able to read and write English, that no language other than English be used as a language of instruction, and that no language but English be taught during school hours. Speaking to the resolution calling for English as the only language of instruction, President-elect J. F.

187

Bryant stated that it was necessary to forge the cosmopolitan population into a unified whole. Dr. J. M. Uhrich of Hague stated that the knowledge of an additional language did not affect one's loyalty, and he urged the assembly to act as Canadians and find a common ground. The audience burst into laughter when he referred to Belgium as "a radiant star in a storm swept sky." Father J. Libert, recently returned from the war and wearing the horizon-blue uniform of a French soldier, pleaded the cause of the French language in the name of the French and Belgians who were fighting overseas to defend civilization and liberty and who, upon their return to Canada, would be shocked to learn that an attempt had been made to prevent their children from learning French. "In the name of Belgium and France, I ask you to table this resolution." The audience laughed. Another delegate spoke enthusiastically in favor of English only and was applauded loudly.[32]

Discussing Libert's motion to table the resolution, *l'abbé* Sinnett of Lanigan stated that a country could speak more than one language and still be united. He contrasted bilingual Belgium, which had shown a high degree of patriotism, to Australia which had only one language and yet could be considered disloyal because she had refused to enact conscription. Pandemonium broke loose in Knox Church with cries of "Retract," "Put him out," "Get off the platform," and "Three cheers for Australia." Sinnett offered to retract the term "disloyal" if it had displeased the delegates but he was not given the opportunity to do so.[33] At this point, Emile Gravel of Gravelbourg asked the assembly if it would not make a distinction between the teaching of French and the teaching of foreign languages. From all corners came cries of "No!," "No difference."[34] The original resolution calling for English as the only language of instruction was carried almost unanimously "to the accompaniment of loud cheering and sustained applause."[35] Canada had been saved.

The next day's issue of the *Daily Post* might proclaim that the convention had made "a notable advance in the cause of a better school system," but for Saskatchewan's French-Canadians, its resolutions were bitter food. Bryant, himself, was well pleased with the results of the convention. He informed Premier Martin that, in view of the presence of over 3,000 delegates, the resolutions expressed the sentiments of the people on the language issue, and therefore, he "respectfully urged" Martin to enact the necessary amendments to implement the resolutions.[36]

Much to Bryant's dismay, however, the trustees' secretary John McCarthy, cast serious doubts on the legality of the Saskatoon convention. McCarthy claimed that only 100 delegates had been appointed duly by annual meetings of ratepayers; the remainder, who had been elected by boards of trustees, were not accredited delegates and, consequently, the elected executive was disqualified. He believed that the matter could be resolved only by having a meeting of qualified delegates to elect a new executive.[37] Bryant dismissed the secretary's charges as a "technical quibble" and the executive relieved McCarthy of his duties. The executive justified its actions in an open letter to school trustees which concluded with a stern admonition:

> To John McCarthy, who is a member of the Roman Catholic Church and to the Roman Catholic Church whose servant he is, we desire to say with all seriousness, hands off the free educational institutions of Saskatchewan or there will be trouble.[38]

For its part, the A.C.F.C. issued a public protest against the trustees' resolutions, describing them as "a direct violation of the rights of parents to have their own language taught to their children." The association felt certain that the resolutions would sow discord and hatred among the population and therefore were detrimental to the interests of Saskatchewan and Canada.[39]

As was to be expected, the French language press did not remain oblivious to the events that had taken place in Saskatoon. The convention was described as an orgy of fanaticism which even the most precise of terms failed to describe. *Le Patriote* claimed that a thirteenth resolution should be added to the twelve already passed: that all sensible people refuse to have anything to do with this "association of fanatics." *Le Patriote* also suggested that the S.S.T.A. change its name to the "Unschooled Orangemen's Association" and hold its meetings in the North Battleford asylum, the home of "infuriated fools."[40] The French-Canadian attitude towards the events of February 21 was poignantly voiced by Emile Gravel in an eulogy to the late Father Libert: *"La motion recommandant au gouvernement l'abolition de l'enseignement du français dans les écoles de notre province fut votée avec le même enthousiasme et le même plaisir qu'aurait pu causer la prise de Berlin."*[41]

Convinced that they could no longer remain within the S.S.T.A., the French-Canadian trustees formed a provisional committee to establish their own association, *l'Association des Commissaires d'Ecole Franco-Canadiens de la Saskatchewan* (A.C.E.F.C.). In April, the committee's president, Emile Gravel, and its secretary, Raymond Denis, appealed to all French-speaking school districts to join the new oganization whose primary objective would be the maintenance of the primary course in French. In addition, the A.C.E.F.C. would concern itself with issues directly affecting French-Canadian schools: textbooks, the recruitment of bilingual teachers, and appointment of bilingual inspectors.[42] In view of Quebec's "unreasonable attitude" vis-à-vis the war effort and the "difficult position" of the Martin government with regard to the language question, Denis asked Attorney-General W. F. Turgeon if he saw any inconveniences resulting from the formation of the A.C.E.F.C. Denis informed the Attorney-General that a convention would probably be held in the summer and that the French trustees would shelve all issues which could provoke criticism.[43] Turgeon replied that he did not anticipate any complications if the trustees followed the policy outlined by Denis.[44]

The trustees' convention acted as a catalyst on an already seething issue. In March, the Grand Orange Lodge reaffirmed its opposition to separate schools and urged the government to prohibit the use of foreign languages in schools.[45] While the sentiments of the lodge were to be expected, the resolutions of the S.S.T.A. were fortified by the support of the Saskatchewan Association of Rural Municipalities, one of the most influential and representative bodies in the province.[46] In turn, the Baptist Conference and the Anglican Synod of Saskatchewan also requested that English be the sole medium of instruction.[47] In September, the Joint Legislation Committee of the Sons of England and the Orange Lodge of Saskatoon sent out thousands of circulars urging the public to demand a "satisfactory settlement" to the language question.[48] The agitation, which was now province-wide, was producing tangible results. In November and December, Martin's office was buried under an avalanche of petitions requesting the termination of foreign-language teaching in schools.[49]

As Premier and Minister of Education, Martin was aware that a solution would have to be found for the troublesome language question and, early in 1918, he had already consulted with officials of the Department of Education. Superintendent D. P. McColl informed his superior that the provisions concerning the primary course in French had been a "bugbear" to the department and would continue to be so until it was given a more precise definition. As a solution, he suggested that the School Act be amended to subject the primary course to departmental regulations which would have the effect of being more specific.[50] The registrar, R. F. Blacklock, believed that departmental regulations should be amended to allow foreign-language instruction only after regular school hours.[51] Replies to a special questionnaire regarding instruction in the French language and the teaching of foreign languages, as provided for by the School Act and departmental regulations, revealed that French was being taught in seventy-seven schools, German in seventy-one, and Ruthenian in thirty-seven.[52] In August, three months before his office was inundated with petitions to terminate the teaching of foreign languages, Martin had already drafted an amendment to section 177: all schools were to be taught in the English language and no other language was to be used during school hours, but upon a resolution from the local school board, French could be taught as a subject of study for one hour a day.[53] Under Martin's amendment, English henceforth would be the only language of instruction.

Although prepared for the worst after the trustees' convention and the campaign of summer and fall, the A.C.F.C. would have been even more alarmed had it known the exact terms of Martin's amendment. The French-Canadians, however, were not taken completely by surprise. In September, 1918, Father A. C. Auclair, *Le Patriote's* director, informed Denis that the language question would be dealt with at the next session of the legislature; there were rumors that the status of the primary course would be clarified and that French would be recognized as a subject of study in all grades. Auclair stated that the Orangemen bore more of a grudge against the French than any other ethnic group. If an attack were directed against the French language, Turgeon would resign, but Auclair suggested he did not believe that this would settle the issue. Heeding the advice of Archbishop Mathieu of Regina, Auclair stated that it was important to work quietly in bringing pressure to bear on members of the legislature despite Walter Scott's advice to certain "political friends" to face the storm and let the Orangemen howl.[54] In spite of the fanaticism and passion already aroused by the language issue, *Le Patriote* felt confident that the members of the assembly would be honor bound to safeguard the constitutional guarantees accorded to the French language. Its editor, Donatien Frémont, optimistically believed that, on the eve of the peace conference in Versailles, there could be no talk of opposing the French and English in Saskatchewan.[55]

A government amendment, however, had to be more than Martin's own draft. It required cabinet backing, and in the weeks immediately prior to the opening of the legislature, there was much cabinet uneasiness over Martin's draft proposal. The Premier's decision to abolish the primary course was one important cause of the resignation of W. R. Motherwell, the Minister of Agriculture. To Motherwell, who aspired to federal politics and who was dissatisfied with Martin's stand on union government, the language question became the "last straw" which prompted his resignation from the cabinet. Writing to Scott, who was in the East, Motherwell explained that he could not support legislation which would leave fewer rights to the French than "rabid mad" Ontario had allowed with Regulation 17.[56] In caucus Motherwell was supported by Attorney-General Turgeon and the Minister of Municipal Affairs, G. Langley. Provincial Treasurer C. A. Dunning, Public Works Minister A. P. McNab, and Provincial Secretary W. E. Knowles, on the other hand, opposed Motherwell, while the Minister of Highways, S. J. Latta, was friendly "but almost neutral."[57] Motherwell's letter of resignation, dwelling as it did mainly upon his other reasons and only coming on page thirteen to "a strictly provincial issue" which had caused him to suffer "the agonies of a veritable Gethsemane,"[58] would seem to have glossed over the issue of the French language in order not to make Turgeon's position, already difficult because of his nationality, even more unstable.[59]

On December 13, Motherwell hopefully informed Scott that Martin might modify the amendment because some Liberals believed that the matter required greater consideration. In a postscript, Motherwell was able to announce jubilantly, "Have just had another caucus at my request as a private member & Martin has come through & granted what wanted — not to take anything away from the French — the boys when they understood the matter objecting strongly to his draft."[60] Motherwell also informed Sir Wilfrid Laurier of Martin's capitulation but asked that it be kept confidential; Motherwell described the Premier as "a very vacillating man" and claimed that his behavior was unpredictable.[61]

While Motherwell's resignation came as a surprise, in the sense that he had no vested interest in the matter, the person mostly likely to resign, out of personal convictions, would have been Attorney-General Turgeon, a French-Canadian, who was regarded by his compatriots as the representative of French Catholics in the government. For Turgeon, who, as Attorney-General in 1912, had assured the teaching of a primary course in the French language by his interpretation of section 136 of the School Act, the present proposal to abrogate that course must have indeed caused him also to suffer the "agonies of a veritable Gethsemane." Informing Scott of Motherwell's resignation, Turgeon stated that he himself had reached the same decision only after much hesitation and that he was not convinced of the wisdom of Martin's policy.[62] On December 16, three days after Martin's capitulation to Motherwell, Turgeon was still intent on this course and advised Archbishop Mathieu of his intention to resign. While the precise reason for holding to his intention after Martin's change of heart remains unknown, Turgeon may have felt that the Premier had not granted sufficient linguistic privileges to the French or, like Motherwell, he possibly feared that Martin might alter his decision to grant limited concessions to the French and revert to the provisions of the draft amendment. In any event, the news "literally sickened" the archbishop, who replied that, in the circumstances, Turgeon's resignation would be a calamity. *"Aussi je crois qu'il serait beaucoup mieux sacrifier cette première année qui remplacerait le cours primaire, que de vous voir partir, si réelement le gouvernement ne peut faire accepter cette faveur. . . . Fasse le ciel que vous restiez à votre poste au prix de n'importe quel sacrifice."*[63] So advised, Turgeon remained in the cabinet but he regretted the whole performance of the Premier over the language issue. Turgeon's remedy for the school question, "the curse of Canada" as he appropriately described it, would be to take it out of politics and place it in the hands of an "enlarged and better co-ordinated university."[64]

192

Saskatchewan Archives Board

*W. F. A. Turgeon*

While the French appeared to be hopelessly outnumbered in this relentless campaign to abolish the teaching of foreign languages, they, nevertheless, had a powerful friend in the person of Mathieu, a man who elected to work behind the scenes, preferring diplomacy and tact to bombast and bravado. Since September, the archbishop had been using his personal influence on behalf of the French-Canadian cause, an influence which was not to be underestimated and which Auclair had described appropriately: *"Il y a de l'acier dans son gant de velours."*[65] Mathieu had stressed the necessity of a quiet campaign and, consequently, the A.C.F.C. refrained from adopting the aggressive tactics of the Orange Lodge during this trying period. The A.C.F.C., however, was not inactive. During December, its *comité exécutif* met twice with Premier Martin and his colleagues to present and discuss French-Canadian representations, but unfortunately, no documents relating to the deliberations exist.[66]

Again in accordance with Mathieu's desires, the A.C.F.C. pursued an educational campaign among the "better elements" of the English-speaking population. Articles by "Canadien," in reality Mgr. Mathieu, dealing with the linguistic aspirations of the French and previously published in *Le Patriote,* were translated, printed in brochure form, and distributed to members of the assembly and other "influential citizens." This was an extension of the campaign, previously undertaken in 1917, to effect a *rapprochement* between the English and the French. The A.C.F.C. believed that the best means of countering the agitation for English only was to carry the arguments in favor of the French language to the public at large and convince the people that the French language enjoyed a special status throughout Canada.[67] It was a valiant but futile attempt, considering the circumstances, to convince Saskatchewan's English-speaking majority that it should accord to the French minority the same educational privileges exercised by Quebec's Anglo-Saxon minority.

In view of the agitation which had taken place throughout the year, the language question emerged as an inescapable issue in the second session of the fourth Saskatchewan legislature. On December 17, Premier Martin introduced Bill Number 31, An Act to Amend the School Act.[68] The difference between chapter 23, section 177, 1915 and the amended version was that the latter abrogated the provisions permitting instruction in languages other than English between the hours of three and four o'clock in the afternoon. English, henceforth, would be the sole language used during school hours with the exception of French which could be used as a language of instruction in grade one and which could be taught as a subject of study, for one hour a day, in subsequent grades.

This concession did not meet with the approval of the *Daily Post* and *Daily Star* who maintained that Saskatchewan's "salvation" lay in the establishment of one language — English — in the schools.[69] In Calgary, Reverend M. MacKinnon, serving as a chaplain in Military District Number 13, condemned the amendment for not going far enough: "French must go, Quebec failed us during the war.... Let all enlightened citizens speak, write and wire until French goes with German."[70] The Grand Master of the Orange Order supported MacKinnon's stand and urged that French be banned from public schools because the French spoken in Saskatchewan and other parts of Canada was "not French anyway."[71]

Dissatisfaction, however, was not confined solely to the Anglo-Saxon element. Presenting the views of the French community, Auclair stated that the new legislation was imperfect, as in the past, because the French language still enjoyed a status inferior to that of English. Only in the Province of Quebec did the French language enjoy perfect equality with English. Auclair claimed that the French were opposed to the removal of the limited privileges previously accorded to the teaching of European languages because the school system provided ample opportunities for teaching English as a common language.[72] While Auclair may have believed this, he secretly feared that the abrogation of these privileges would have a "fatal reaction" on French-Canadians because it would divide Catholics.[78] "Canadien" also complained that the new amendments offered less than the French had hoped for.[74]

The debate over the language question, however, became even more tempestuous in the assembly. On December 18, Martin moved second reading to Bill Number 31 in a speech that lasted over two hours and which even his staunch critic, the *Daily Post*, referred to as "the finest ever delivered by the leader of the government."[75] Martin justified the exception made for the French language on the grounds of the historical rights of the French people in Canada. Motherwell, Latta, and Dunning also presented stirring addresses on behalf of the French language.[76] Donald Maclean, as leader of the opposition, stated that the Conservative party was not going to make political capital over the school issue but, nevertheless, he maintained that the schools must serve as a means of unifying the people of the province into one "harmonious whole." He claimed that the present bill was merely a compromise and moved an amendment to make English the only language of instruction in elementary schools.[77] This motion was defeated forty-eight to four. During Committee of the Whole, the Conservative leader again unsuccessfully moved an amendment to make English the only language of instruction.[78] When the legislature reconvened on January 8, 1919, Maclean reiterated his opposition to the amendments because of the privileges accorded to the French language. He claimed that on purely legal grounds, the French had no stronger rights than any other non-English groups outside the province of Quebec; in Saskatchewan, there was no pedagogical argument, no "sane argument," in favor of compromise on the language question. A Conservative motion to refer the bill again to Committee of the Whole was defeated forty-two to seven.[79] By this time it was a foregone conclusion that the bill would be passed on the third reading. It went into effect on May 1, 1919.

The privileges accorded to the French language, as a result of the amendment, provided less than the French-Canadians might have hoped, but more than their worst fears suggested. Under the circumstances they decided to turn what was essentially a compromise — and perhaps a necessary one — to good account. Auclair and "Canadien" both urged their compatriots to enlighten public opinion and eliminate prejudices so that French Catholics might obtain full justice from the English-speaking majority. "Canadien" remarked, that since the half-hour of religious instruction could be given in French, French-Canadian children would be able to hear 1½ hours of French in each school day. He was convinced that *le doux parler* could still survive in Saskatchewan: *"avec ce qui leur est donné, nos enfants pourront encore apprendre la belle langue de leurs ancêtres: il ne tiendra qu'à eux de la conserver tout en apprenant et en sachant l'anglais dont nous comprenons tous l'utilité — même la nécessité — dans une province comme celle-ci."*[80]

Commenting on the language question, Auclair remarked that, in view of the excited state of public opinion, inflamed by fanaticism and passion, the French should have been prepared for the worse. In the end, however, the French had not fared too badly: the primary course had been restricted to one year instead of the customary two,[81] but French was recognized now as a subject of study for one hour in each school day. Auclair regarded the exception made for the French language as a step toward the eventual recognition of the equality of French and English. He interpreted the legislative addresses on behalf of the French language as evidence that the Anglo-Saxon mentality had undergone a significant change for the better and that this should be a source of comfort for French Catholics. Be that as it may, few, in 1918, were willing to concur with the views of Sir Wilfrid Laurier, a man who was fully cognizant of the intricacies of the French-English problem and who anticipated, by half a century, the findings of the Royal Commission on Bilingualism and Biculturalism:

> I quite agree, and we are all united that every child in Saskatchewan should be given an English education, but we are all agreed also that a French education can be imparted and ought to be imparted whenever possible. The man who speaks two languages is better equipped for life than the man who speaks but one. The truth is so obvious that none will dare dispute it. The apostles of one language and one language only, when pressed to the wall, always come back with the statement that it is impossible in the school to teach more than one language. I grant that in some places those of French origin are so few that it would be impracticable to do so, but there are many places where it is not only possible but easily feasible.[82]

# 14  C. A. Dunning and the Challenge of the Progressives, 1922-1925

*by J. William Brennan*

THE years following the First World War were difficult ones for the Canadian nation, and especially for its two traditional political parties. Disenchantment with the record of Laurier and Borden led the agricultural community, through its farmer organizations, to seriously consider independent political action for the first time. The goal was no less than the replacement of the existing governments in the prairie provinces and in Ottawa by administrations more receptive to the demands of western wheat growers. In Saskatchewan this did not come to pass. The new farmers' Progressive party failed to dislodge the Liberal government which had been in power since 1905. The one man, more than any other, who saved the Liberals from defeat was Charles Avery Dunning, the third Premier of Saskatchewan.*

Dunning's rise to prominence in the public life of Saskatchewan had been little short of meteoric. He had come to Canada as a lad of seventeen, ill prepared for the rigors of pioneer life on the prairies. He had filed on a homestead and had become a successful farmer, but had not been content to remain on the land. Dunning had joined the Saskatchewan Grain Growers' Association (S.G.G.A.) and had been chosen vice-president of the farmers' organization in 1911. In that same year he had become general manager of the newly formed Saskatchewan Co-operative Elevator Company. Dunning was then only twenty-six. During the next five years he had guided the "Co-op" as it developed a large system of grain elevators owned and operated by the farmers. In 1916 he left the secure world of business for the much more uncertain world of politics. Charles Dunning joined Premier W. M. Martin's government as Provincial Treasurer, and in six years, at the comparatively early age of thirty-seven, became Premier.

---

*This article is based on an unpublished Master's thesis by the author entitled "The Public Career of Charles Avery Dunning of Saskatchewan." The article originally appeared in *Saskatchewan History* for winter, 1969.

Saskatchewan Archives Board

*C. A. Dunning*

Dunning assumed the provincial premiership at a time when the wave of agrarian political agitation was at its peak. Prairie agriculture was depressed and the farmers were deserting the old parties for a new political organization of their own creation. Liberal governments in the other prairie provinces were disappearing, and Liberal representation from the West in the House of Commons had been virtually swept away by the Progressive tide in the first post-war general election.

In Saskatchewan the Liberal government had since 1905 carefully cultivated the support of the organized farmers by including prominent Grain Growers such as Dunning in the cabinet, and by never implementing legislation of interest to the farmers of the province without first consulting the S.G.G.A. Premier Martin further attempted to mollify the farmers' political movement by cutting all ties with the federal wing of the Liberal party in 1920, and by inviting J. A. Maharg, a Progressive M.P. and prominent farm leader, to enter the cabinet shortly before the 1921 provincial election.[1] The organized farmers had discussed provincial political action at their annual conventions in 1920 and 1921, but had not definitely decided to enter the provincial political arena.[2] The Grain Growers' Association, therefore, took no official part in the 1921 provincial campaign. The chief opposition was provided, not by the Conservatives, who had gone into a state of decline, but by a scattered group of Independents. In these circumstances the Liberals won handily.

From this point, Martin's political position steadily declined. In the course of the 1921 federal campaign he spoke on behalf of W. R. Motherwell, the federal Liberal candidate in Regina.[3] This aroused the ire of the Grain Growers, who had expected that members of the provincial cabinet would support the Progressives, and caused J. A. Maharg to resign a week before the election, charging Premier Martin with bad faith.[4]

Provincial political action was obviously to be an important issue at the next S.G.G.A. convention. After two days' discussion, the delegates finally agreed on a resolution authorizing the creation of a committee "to assist those Provincial constituencies that wish to take action, and support the declared principles of the Association, to organize themselves for direct Provincial political action."[5] The provincial Liberal party would have to face a direct challenge from the organized farmers. Premier Martin realized himself that he had lost the support of the farmers and made preparations to resign.[6] The only minister who could curb the rising tide seemed to be C. A. Dunning. Early in 1922 he was chosen as the new leader of the Liberal party and Premier of Saskatchewan.

Dunning's qualifications were impressive. As a freshman cabinet minister his political talents had been an unknown quantity, but his organizing ability and his shrewd political sense soon became apparent. On the hustings and in the legislature Dunning had proven himself a tireless worker and a match for any man in the give-and-take of debate. More important, from the standpoint of the government and the Liberal party, was Dunning's record as a farm leader. The Grain Growers and the Liberals had always maintained a close working relationship in the past; now the organized farmers could boast that one of their number

199

held the reins of power in the province. The strategy was sound, but had the choice of Dunning as Premier come too late to save the government? Clearly by 1922 there were many farmers who could not regard an avowed Liberal like Dunning as the best representative of their interests.

And indeed Dunning was an avowed Liberal. From the beginning he had tied himself and his fortunes to the Liberal party. When Dunning joined the Martin government in 1916, he must have been aware of the latent revolt against both of the old parties spreading through the farmers' movement. But he obviously had come to the conclusion that the welfare of the prairie farmers rested not upon the creation of a third party, but upon the influence they could bring to bear electorally upon an existing nation-wide political organization. It would be Dunning's task as Premier to convince the farmers that he was right.

The new Premier decided to meet the Grain Growers' political movement head on. In his acceptance speech at the convention which had chosen him as leader, Dunning announced that he had been chosen to head the provincial Liberal party. This did not mean, however, that he was "under marching orders from now on to go out and fight the farmers of this province." The bulk of the farmers of Saskatchewan, he believed, were Liberals. The bulk of the members of the Grain Growers' Association were Liberals. Just because "a number of very consummate politicians" were seeking to steal the machinery of the farmers' organization to use it for their own political purposes was "no reason why we should make the mistake of fighting the whole institution."[7]

Dunning's strategy was obvious. He would discredit the move to agrarian political action through the S.G.G.A. without seeming to discredit the S.G.G.A. itself. Only by such an approach, while at the same time disavowing, temporarily at least, any association with the federal Liberals, could the issue finally be resolved.

Dunning reaffirmed his political position in his manifesto to the people of the province issued shortly after he assumed office. His government intended to follow a "sane, progressive, Liberal" course in administering the affairs of the province, and he urged the people to support the government in carrying out its announced program. He addressed a special appeal to the S.G.G.A.

> It is my sincere hope that this farmers' organization, to which this province owes so much, and to which personally I owe a debt of gratitude for past opportunities of service, will not set up, either actually or by implication, a political test for membership. However that may be, I feel that on the basis of record and policies both myself and the government have at least an equal right to appeal for the support of the farmers of Saskatchewan with those who are opposed to the government in the legislature, whether they be members of the Grain Growers' Association or not.[8]

Premier Dunning soon discovered that his stress on the word "Liberal" was being misunderstood. He did not mean to suggest, as the opposition press charged,[9] that he intended to reverse the policy laid down by Martin in 1920 and re-establish the link with the federal Liberals. He had used the word to denote a certain set of political policies and did not intend, by defining his government as a "Liberal" government, to defend Mackenzie King's actions at Ottawa.[10] In any case Dunning took steps to mollify the Grain Growers. Soon after he took office, for example, he asked the S.G.G.A. executive for copies of all resolutions passed at the annual conventions since 1918,[11] presumably as a guide for future policies.

The immediate political problem for Dunning was a series of by-elections to be held in the summer of 1922. Dunning voiced a cautious optimism that his government would carry the contests with ease.[12] As events were to prove, his predictions were well-founded. Indeed, his caution was quite unnecessary, for, as it turned out, only two of the seats were contested by the Grain Growers. A farmers' candidate was nominated in North Qu'Appelle against J. G. Gardiner, the new Minister of Highways (and head of the Liberal party organization) but withdrew at the last moment. This Dunning regretted, for he had hoped that a convincing victory in a seat like North Qu'Appelle would scotch the efforts of a "political clique" to turn the S.G.G.A. into a political machine.[13]

The first open fight between the Grain Growers and the government was in Happyland, a constituency ravaged by poor crops and an area in which the radical Non-Partisan League had been active.[14] To counteract the charges of the opposition that he was out to fight the Grain Growers, Dunning pointed to his own record as a member of the executive of the farmers' organization and warned that the only result of political action by the association would be a decline in membership.[15] The vigorous campaign waged by the government in Happyland was not without results, for the Liberal was elected, but by a majority reduced from that of 1921.[16]

Dunning had reason to be grateful for the results of the first contests with the Grain Growers' political movement, especially considering the dire predictions that had been made in some quarters regarding the fate of his government. He confessed to Walter Scott that many had regarded it as "a last forlorn hope to attempt to stand against the wave of farmer political organization, particularly when, on assuming office, I made it perfectly plain that the Government would be a Liberal Government." The result in Happyland had, of course, changed all that, and he now expected to be able to carry on for "quite a time to come."[17] As events were soon to show, the Happyland campaign marked the transition from defensive to offensive tactics in the encounter with the Progressives. With his position secure, for the time being at least, it must have appeared to Dunning to be an opportune time to make a move towards re-establishing the link with the federal Liberals. The move was disastrous.

The federal constituency of Moose Jaw, held at the time by a Progressive, had been declared vacant due to irregularities in the 1921 general election.[18] Appeals were made to Dunning to actively assist in the campaign in the common cause of Liberalism.[19] Dunning remained aloof. He had been bothered by the 'flu and intended to go away for a short recuperative rest. (In fact, he had been advised to stay out of the province until after the campaign was over.) The Progressives had shrewdly nominated E. N. Hopkins, a long-time Conservative, in the hopes of wooing Conservative voters in Moose Jaw. There was some danger that the Premier might make a "characteristic fighting speech" which would play into the hands of the Progressives by alienating Conservative voters. However, "practically everybody else" would be going to Moose Jaw, under the expert direction of J. G. Gardiner.[20]

The co-operation of the federal and provincial Liberals was not enough. In a straight two-way fight with the Liberal candidate, W. E. Knowles, a former provincial cabinet minister, Hopkins won easily.[21] The vigorous campaign waged by the provincial Liberals on behalf of Knowles did not go unnoticed, however; the *Grain Growers' Guide* reported that five out of seven provincial cabinet ministers and seven Liberal M.L.A.'s had taken part in the campaign. Premier Dunning had been absent from the province, but, the *Guide* pointed out, his influence had been felt nonetheless. The newspaper disclosed that J. G. Gardiner, in a public address during the campaign, had announced that the cabinet had decided "it was time for a showdown with the farmers' political movement, and that the Moose Jaw by-election afforded the opportunity."[22]

This charge produced a quick reply from Gardiner that he had made no such statement.[23] Whether he had or not, the active participation of members of the provincial government in a federal by-election campaign indicated that Dunning and the provincial Liberal party, now apparently less concerned about the Progressive threat, were anxious to reunite the two wings of the party, even if this meant hardening the lines of opposition with the Progressives. If the Dunning government had hoped to enhance its own political position by taking this step, the defeat in Moose Jaw jarred these hopes considerably.

The return of the provincial government to active support of the federal party, after a separation of nearly three years, was bound to have repercussions in the provincial political arena. However, the reaction came, not from the Grain Growers' Association, but from a new quarter.

The Independents elected in 1921, and disappointed in their hope of support from the S.G.G.A., organized the Saskatchewan Provincial Progressive Association to contest a by-election in Milestone constituency. The guest speaker at the convention which launched this new party and chose a candidate for the upcoming contest was Harris Turner, editor of a Saskatchewan farm newspaper, *The Progressive* and an Independent M.L.A. Turner was a radical critic of the party system in general. While admitting that Premier Dunning was an excellent man, Turner observed that every time Dunning rose to speak in the legislature one could "visualize behind him the cogs, wheels, pistons and pinions of a menacing machine." A resolution was passed at the convention which viewed "with grave alarm" the close association of the Dunning and King governments and the active participation of members of the provincial party in the Moose Jaw by-election. To preserve the results already achieved by the federal Progressive party, it was decided that a provincial Progressive association should be established to organize the whole province.[24]

The Progressives, in forming a provincial party, had clearly thrown down a challenge to the Liberals, and Dunning was quick to respond. He had already dealt with the relationship of federal and provincial politics at the Liberal nominating convention held a week before the Progressives' meeting. Chastened by his abortive attempt to link the separated wings of the Liberal party in the Moose Jaw by-election, Dunning announced that it was a bad thing for a provincial government or a provincial party to be "bound hand and foot" to any federal party organization. He did not propose that his government become the "donkey engine" of the federal Liberals.[25]

Dunning also replied to the charge that he was leading a political machine. It was true that there was a political organization behind his government, but it was not a machine in the sinister sense of the word.[26]

Sinister or no, the Liberals' political organization was put to good use in the Milestone campaign. There were no real issues. The Premier and the other Liberal speakers stressed the government's record of economical administration. This was an aspect of government policy with obvious political merit at a time when the farmers were still suffering from poor crops and low grain prices. The Liberals left nothing to chance and in the last week of the campaign blitzed the constituency with speakers.

The result was a victory for the government, by the largest majority ever recorded in the constituency.[27] The Saskatchewan Provincial Progressive Association had lost the first round to the government, but there would most assuredly be other contests. The Dunning government had emerged from a difficult contest in a much stronger position.[28]

Dunning's prestige as a party leader and a politician could only be enhanced by such a victory.

The year 1924 was much taken up with talk of the Wheat Pool and prohibition, but for Dunning politics was not neglected either. In fact, 1924 was for Dunning and the Liberal party a most critical year.

Some events, of course, were hopeful. In January the S.G.G.A. decided to leave politics. The debate was short, and the majority large, on a resolution rescinding the action taken by the 1922 convention in authorizing political action. An attempt, by the way of a second resolution, to support the provincial Progressives was tabled.[29] The S.G.G.A. was clearly determined on a course of strict neutrality. A compelling reason for the desire on the part of the association to leave provincial politics was the loss in membership which had taken place. All along Dunning had believed that this would be the result as soon as the association got into politics. The newer, more radical Farmers' Union of Canada, committed to economic action only, was, by 1924, larger than the older farmers' organization.[30]

While the S.G.G.A. was leaving politics altogether, the new farmers' political party, the Saskatchewan Provincial Progressive Association, was taking steps to strengthen its organization in preparation for the next provincial election. A convention, presided over by Harris Turner, who had recently been elected house leader of the opposition group in the legislature, was held in Saskatoon in August. The provincial platform adopted at this convention expressed the opposition of the group to the party system. The Progressives were in favor of economy in administration, in part through a reduction in the number of civil servants, electoral and legislative reforms (a fixed term for the legislative assembly, the single transferable vote, and a reduction in the number of M.L.A.'s by one-third), co-operative marketing of farm products, completion of the Hudson Bay railroad, and Senate reform.[31]

Not long after their convention in Saskatoon, the provincial Progressives again met the government in an election contest. The resignation of George Robertson, the Independent member for Wynyard, to become full-time secretary of the Saskatchewan Wheat Pool, necessitated a by-election in that riding. Premier Dunning was faced with a difficult choice. The seat was hardly a "safe" one, since it had been held by an opponent of the government. He could defend a delay in calling the by-election by saying that he did not wish to mix politics with threshing. On the other hand, the fall session of the legislature was to be an important one. In a plebiscite held in July, 1924, the province had declared its opposition to a continuation of prohibition, and a new liquor bill was to be introduced in accordance with the wishes of the people. Indeed, Dunning had promised to call the legislature earlier than usual to deal with this very important matter.[32] To delay the calling of the by-election would deprive the people of Wynyard of a voice in the debate on the government's liquor legislation. This apparently Dunning did not want to do, for he announced that the vote would take place on October 20.[33]

The campaign was a relatively pallid affair, but the result left no doubt as to the popularity of the government. The Liberal won, by a majority of over 900.[34] A by-election in Cannington earlier in the summer had gone to the government by acclamation,[35] and now Wynyard had gone to the government as well. Premier Dunning had good reason to be gratified with the results. Since assuming office in April, 1922, Dunning and the Liberals had won nine successive by-elections. At a time when the Liberal parties of Alberta and Manitoba had long since succumbed to the attacks of the farmers' political movement, Dunning's Liberal government remained standing and, with the result in Wynyard, had actually improved its position in the legislature.

By this time the provincial Liberal leader was no doubt thinking ahead to the next general election, due by custom in 1925, by law in 1926, and either way not now far off. He might have regarded the impending elections with confidence, considering his success against the Progressives, had it not been for the political resurgence of the Conservative party. Leaderless since 1921, when Donald Maclean had retired to accept a seat on the Bench,[36] the party held a convention in 1924 to choose a new leader, Dr. J. T. M. Anderson, and draft a platform. The platform pledged a Conservative administration to economy in government, educational reform, assistance to farmers in marketing their products, and development of the province's natural resources. The convention denounced what it termed the "orgy of extravagance" of the Provincial Treasurer in his seven years in office and pledged the party, if elected, to reduce the "heavy load of debt" and "crushing burden of taxation" under which the province was laboring.[37]

Dunning did not take the threat of a reorganized and revitalized Conservative party lightly. He feared it might "absorb a certain number of the saner and more level-headed farmers and endanger his chances in three cornered contests."[38]

Early in 1925 the signs of an approaching general election became more and more unmistakable. As Provincial Treasurer Dunning devoted a considerable portion of his budget address to a rebuttal of charges that he had been on a "drunken bat of expenditure" since he entered the government.[39] After the legislature prorogued he undertook a series of speaking engagements throughout the province, appealing for a strong organization and sufficient funds to contest a general election whenever one was called.[40] Nominating conventions were held in many ridings, and Premier Dunning and his cabinet were kept busy addressing these meetings. Finally, on May 9, 1925 the Lieutenant-Governor, acting on the advice of the government, dissolved the Fifth Legislative Assembly and announced an election for June 2.[41]

Premier Dunning at once issued an election manifesto to the people of the province. He dealt at some length with the record of the government and appealed for the support of the electorate on that record. He pointed to a financial policy which, pursued through a period of acute depression, had placed the province "in an excellent position to take advantage of improvements in world conditions." He stressed the record of the government in support of co-operative marketing, in encouragement of agricultural and industrial development, in health and education, and in provision of telephone service through the largest publicly owned system in Canada.[42]

A week later the Progressives issued their election manifesto. They criticized the government for calling an election at a time when most farmers would be too busy with seeding to take part in the campaign or even to inform themselves of the issues by attending political meetings. The main issue before the voters was clearly whether the people of Saskatchewan were willing to tolerate any longer the "skilfully organized, expensive, patronage-fed organization" that had been constructed by the Liberals during their twenty years in power.[43] Great stress was laid on the need for economy in government, and in this the Progressive election manifesto was simply a restatement of the platform drawn up in 1924. The Conservatives, for their part, did not issue an election manifesto as such, but simply pointed to the platform drawn up at their 1924 leadership convention. The battle lines had been drawn.

The opposition parties were faced with great difficulties in the 1925 election campaign. There were fewer acclamations than in 1921, three as opposed to seventeen in the earlier contest,[44] which indicated that the opposition had put more candidates in the field. However, there was no strong opposition press to carry the fight to the government. The Conservatives had no daily newspaper to explain their views, although an editorial column, "The Conservative View Point" in the Moose Jaw daily, did present the party's point of view to the voters. Similarly, the provincial Progressives could count only on the support of the weekly *Western Producer,* edited by Harris Turner. In contrast the Liberals could rely upon the support of the editorial pages of the six daily newspapers in the four largest cities in the province. In an era when the newspaper was still the single most influential form of mass persuasion available to a political party, the lack of a strong press was a serious weakness for the Progressives and Conservatives.[45]

The predominant issue in the campaign was the record of the government, as must have been expected. Much was made by the opposition of comparisons of the financial state of the province in 1917 and 1925, after eight years of "reckless expenditure" by Dunning.[46] The Premier had already referred to these charges in his budget address, and during the campaign he continued to remind the voters that new services, such as the government-operated farm-credit scheme, or extensions of existing services, especially in education and welfare, had meant increased expenditures.[47]

Premier Dunning was very critical of the two opposition parties. They were a "double-jointed opposition" appearing to be all things to all men. They had not criticized the expenditures of the government in the legislature, although they had had ample opportunity to do so. Now they were accusing the Liberals of extravagance.[48] The Conservatives and the Progressives were united in only one thing — defeating the government. The voters deserved to know what either of the opposition parties would do if they should form the next government, but they were not being told. Dunning pointed to the expensive errors of government by "group" in Ontario and appealed to the electorate to support a continuation of "responsible government" by re-electing the Liberals on June 2.[49]

The voters of the province did just that on election day. Dunning and the Liberals were re-elected with fifty seats. The Progressives, without the support of either farmers' organization in the province, won only six and the Conservatives two.[50] The entire Dunning cabinet, with the exception of the Attorney-General, was returned to office. In contrast, Harris Turner, the most prominent critic of the government in the former legislature, was defeated in Saskatoon by Dr. Anderson, the Conservative leader.

The Progressives had challenged the dominant position of the provincial Liberal party but failed to unseat the government. No single factor caused the Progressive defeat in the 1925 general election. The generally capable administrative record of the Dunning government, the Premier's own personal popularity and political ability, the effective party organization managed by J. G. Gardiner, and the weakness of the farmers' political party in Saskatchewan — all accounted for the Liberal triumph over the Progressives. Dunning's own part in this victory must be weighed against these other factors.

The record of the Dunning government was a creditable one, considering the difficult economic situation which the province had faced. Surplus had followed surplus in the budgets of the war and post-war boom years. Depression conditions made Dunning's task much more difficult. Slight increases in revenue were not large enough to meet increases in expenditure, and a deficit of over $2,000,000 resulted by 1924. Only by stringent economies was the budget balanced during the next two years. However, Dunning's stress on the need for economy and retrenchment was in fact echoed by both the Progressives and

Conservatives during the election campaign. In terms of basic platform issues, then, the parties did not differ greatly.

The weakness of the Progressives could not be concealed. They were hampered by the lack of a strong organization. Neither farmers' association in the province was willing, at the critical time, to support the farmers' political party. In part this was indicative of a change in stress within the farmers' movement. The enthusiasm which marked the organization of the Wheat Pool undoubtedly led many farmers to look to economic rather than political reform for a solution of their problems. Much of the explanation of the failure of the Progressives to dislodge the provincial Liberals, then, must lie in the fact that for the Progressives, the 1921 general election was held too early, the 1925 contest too late. In 1921 the S.G.G.A. had not yet sanctioned a provincial farmers' party — this had come later — but by 1925 the S.G.G.A. had withdrawn from politics altogether.

The Progressives were also hampered by the return of agricultural prosperity. In 1921 the farmers' political movement seemed to pose a serious threat to the Liberal government. The appeal to farmers of a third-party protest movement dissipated as the drought and depression of the early 1920's was replaced by high prices and good crops later in the decade. The Progressive threat diminished accordingly. Lacking a strong issue with which to confront the government and lacking the support of the S.G.G.A., the Progressives were no match for the well-organized Liberals.

The role of the Liberal party organization headed by J. G. Gardiner should not be underestimated in assessing the causes of the Progressive defeat, yet this was the most difficult factor to evaluate. A party organization had been in existence since 1905, and its effectiveness was not allowed to diminish during the intervening years. It was not uncommon for the Liberals to offer a job or a contract, or a road or a public building in return for political support.[51] There is no doubt that "Jimmy" Gardiner was an effective political organizer. Harris Turner supposedly remarked during the 1925 provincial election campaign that if every government employee out canvassing the province in the interests of the Liberal party were obliged to wear a uniform, it would appear to an outsider that Saskatchewan was under the heel of an army of occupation.

In the last analysis, though, Dunning, not Gardiner and the Liberal "machine," must be given the bulk of the credit for beating the Progressives. It had been to Dunning that the provincial Liberal party had turned in the hour of its greatest peril.

He had been equal to the task. His handling of the Progressive challenge showed him to be an astute and capable political leader. Moreover, he was a forceful platform speaker — a result of his early activities in the Grain Growers' Association. When he became Liberal party leader in 1922, his former prominent association with the organized farmers served him well. It was Dunning, the former Grain Growers' leader, who alone could attack the farmers' political movement without appearing to criticize its foster parent, the S.G.G.A. It was not simply fear of schism and a weakening of the farmers' organization which caused Dunning to act as he did, of course, but also a desire, as a good party man, to keep the Liberal ship afloat in heavy seas. This latter desire also prompted Dunning to maintain Martin's break with the federal Liberals. The tactics worked. Once the S.G.G.A. withdrew from politics, Dunning's appeal to an agrarian electorate made the Liberals, seemingly, unbeatable. With the Progressives no longer a threat, he could now move to re-establish the old link with the Liberals in Ottawa. This was soon accomplished, and Dunning emphasized the new relationship by actively campaigning for Mackenzie King in the 1925 federal general election and by accepting a portfolio in King's cabinet.

It would be interesting to speculate on the fate of the provincial Liberal government had Dunning remained in Regina. As it was, the Liberals were defeated in 1929, by the resurgent Conservative party which had caused Dunning so much concern. For the Liberals, a near quarter century of uninterrupted political power would come to an end. Had it not been for the shrewd and capable Dunning, the end might have come four years sooner.

# 15 The Saskatchewan Farmer-Labor Party, 1932-1934:
## How Radical Was It At Its Origin?
*by George Hoffman*

MUCH of the writing which has been done on the early Co-operative Commonwealth Federation (C.C.F.) has emphasized its radical socialist nature. This holds true for both the national party and its Saskatchewan counterpart from 1932 to 1934, the Farmer-Labor party. Historians generally argue that both were radical and socialist at their origins in 1932 and 1933. They also maintain that the party broadened out and became more moderate, particularly after the mid-1930's, because of the political realities of the time.* They claim that it was necessary for the party to change its stand on certain issues because the original position was too radical for the majority of Canadians.[1]

One cannot seriously dispute that the Farmer-Labor party, founded in Saskatoon in July, 1932,[2] was a good deal more radical than the other major political parties in the province at the time. Judging from many of the policy statements of the United Farmers of Canada (U.F.C.), the Independent Labor party (I.L.P.), and the Farmer-Labor party between 1930 and 1934, it would seem that the new political movement which emerged in Saskatchewan was unmistakably socialist. In the spring of 1930, prior to the federal election held that year, the U.F.C. issued a program which called for, among other things, "the abolition of the present competitive system of manufacture and public ownership and democratic operation of public utilities and natural resources."[3] At the 1931 U.F.C. convention, proposals even more radical were put forward and accepted. One resolution which was passed condemned the capitalist system and called for social ownership and co-operative production.[4] Another, which was supported by the majority of the delegates, favored nationalization of farmlands and the implementation of a use-lease system of land tenure.[5] In the fall of 1931, when the Independent Labor party was established, a platform which contained similar proposals to those put forward by the U.F.C. was formulated. Included were planks

---

*This article originally appeared in *Saskatchewan History* for spring, 1975.

which called for the nationalization of banking, a planned economy, and a national health scheme.[6]

The first detailed Farmer-Labor party policy statement was adopted by the political directive board of the party in September, 1932. This program reflected the policies adopted earlier by the U.F.C. and the I.L.P. The preamble to the statement read:

> In the opinion of the organized Farmer-Labour Group in Saskatchewan the present economic crisis is due to the inherent unsoundness of the Capitalist system which is based on private ownership of resources and the capitalistic control of production and distribution.[7]

The party's stated objective was "the social ownership of all resources and the machinery of wealth production to the end that we may co-operatively produce and distribute for use and service rather than for private gain."[8] In order to achieve this objective the party called for such things as the establishment of a planned national economy, socialization of the country's financial system, social ownership, development, operation, and control of utilities and natural resources, and socialization of all health services.[9]

Thus there is no doubt that certain policies of the U.F.C., the I.L.P., and the Farmer-Labor party can accurately be described as socialist or radical. However, radicalism and socialism meant different things to different people. Walter Young's comments about the early C.C.F., that "there was no unanimity about what the new federation stood for," and that "socialism is susceptible of a wide variety of interpretation,"[10] hold equally true for the Saskatchewan Farmer-Labor party. The various programs which authors have described as radical or socialist also contained provisions which can hardly be described as such. Perhaps most significant of all was that throughout the formation of policy, the moderates at conventions and conferences were always in control. Their point of view consistently won out over that of radicals who wanted the party to take a stand further to the left. This was evident at every major conference in which Saskatchewan Farmer-Labor spokesmen participated. And nowhere was it more evident than at the 1931 U.F.C. convention, an event which frequently has been treated as a great triumph for the radical wing of the farmers' movement.[11]

The two radical resolutions concerning the capitalist system and the use-lease scheme which were passed at the 1931 convention did indicate that the organized farmers were moving in a socialist direction. The depression had made many of the province's farmers desperate, and they were willing to turn to new solutions. But despite this, a close examination of the proceedings of the convention indicates that the left wing of the U.F.C. was not in control and certainly did not dictate what

211

should or should not be passed. As much can be learned from the measures rejected at the convention as from those approved.

Early in the convention the following resolution was introduced:

> THAT legislation be enacted to prevent foreclosures, evictions or seizures until the next session of the Legislature, and that at that time the bill automatically come up again for reconsideration.[12]

Ben Lloyd[13] then moved an amendment to the resolution which stated:

> THAT legislation be enacted to prevent foreclosures, evictions or seizures and that until this legislation is enacted we instruct our members to organize mass resistance to foreclosures, evictions and seizures.[14]

The debate on the resolution and amendment indicated the degree of radical sentiment at the convention. H. E. Mills, a U.F.C. member from Colonsay and associate of Ben Lloyd, favored the amendment.[15] "I think the time has come," Mills argued, "to act exclusively in our own interests. If we cannot get the legislatures to act for us we must take it [sic] into our own hands."[16] However, other delegates strongly opposed the Lloyd amendment. Tom Johnson, a prominent figure in the provincial C.C.F. in later years, spoke against it. He referred to it as a direct incitement to revolution and anarchy and urged delegates to bring about improvement of economic conditions through proper channels.[17] Later in the debate Johnson reinforced his argument:

> I do not know if you have all realized what this [Lloyd's] amendment means. Just read the resolution and then read the amendment. . . . The resolution as amended would mean this that every single, solitary soul, whether he was worthy or not, would not be amenable to the laws. Mr. Lloyd's amendment means that there shall be a moratorium forever . . . That is what I object to. . . . I know farmers in my district who . . . for their own good and for their neighbors . . . should be evicted. Their farms are nothing but weed beds. That kind of farmer should be evicted and if you adopt that amendment that kind of farmer cannot be evicted.[18]

When the Lloyd amendment finally came up for a vote, it was defeated, and the original resolution was passed. The radicals suffered a clear defeat.

Certainly the most controversial proposal which emerged from the 1931 convention was the use-lease plan of land tenure. The U.F.C. executive brought forward a resolution which favored modifications in the system of tenure which existed in the province. Its resolution read:

> THAT no more Provincial lands or resources be alienated, that no more homesteads be granted or farm lands sold, but that "Use Leases" be instituted for all land and resources now owned by the Province and all titles permanently retained by the Province.[19]

212

H. E. Mills amended the resolution to include all land:

> THAT no more Provincial lands or resources be alienated, that no more homesteads be granted or farm lands sold, but that "Use Leases" be instituted and that all land and resources now privately owned be nationalized as rapidly as opportunity will permit.[20]

A long and hotly contested debate followed. When a vote finally was taken, the Mills amendment was carried by a narrow margin.[21] Thus the U.F.C. supported the idea that the government should "own" all land and that it be leased to the farmer.

The Mills amendment, which intended that the use-lease system apply to all land in the province, was more radical than the original resolution which stated that use-leases should be instituted only for crown lands. On the surface it appeared that the viewpoint of the radicals had won out. However, the arguments used in the debate modify such a view. Mills made the original amendment, but the majority of those who spoke in favor of it were not supporters of the extreme left. One example was Mrs. A. Hollis of Shaunavon who was certainly not known for her radical views.[22] In favoring the Mills amendment, she argued,

> if we believe in "Use Leases" . . . for the land which is not at present alienated from the Crown, I think we should go a step further and believe that the land which we are supposed to own, but which we know is practically owned by the big mortgage companies . . . as rapidly as opportunity will permit, become socialized.[23]

The use-lease plan was acceptable to delegates like Mrs. Hollis because they had become convinced that the times called for drastic action. They supported use-lease not because they questioned the right of private ownership of property, but rather because they viewed it as the only means of preventing the mortgage companies from seizing the land. In this sense support for the use-lease plan was very much in the old Progressive tradition.

Other delegates who spoke in favor of the Mills amendment also used arguments which in many ways were not radical to support their viewpoint. One delegate asserted:

> The use-lease will provide more incentive to improve land than the present system. In my opinion . . . this matter of the private ownership of property is just a state of mind. We imagine we are owners . . . The "Use-Lease" . . . will provide . . . that you can pass the right of your lease on to your next-of-kin. . . . There is no security at the present time, and there is that advantage behind the "Use-Lease" system. . . .[24]

Such statements were not arguments in favor of state ownership of the land. Many delegates maintained that the use-lease plan would not give the land to the government but in fact would ensure that each individual farmer would be given security of tenure on his land. In this way use-lease was viewed as a means of maintaining the traditional way of rural life in Saskatchewan. It was meant to preserve family farms, not to create state farms.

It was evident from the debate on the use-lease resolutions that it was not the extreme left of the U.F.C. who carried it through. The resolution was supported by men like Ben Lloyd, H. E. Mills, and L. P. McNamee, but they did not have the following to force through the proposal. Immediately after the passage of the use-lease plan, McNamee attempted to introduce another resolution which he said would deal with the "mortgage and interest phase of ownership."[25] His right to do so was challenged because the subject was not on the agenda. The delegates were asked by the chairman if they wished to allow the McNamee resolution to be introduced, and they responded in the negative.[26] It was clear that the convention was not controlled by McNamee and the men who shared his radical views.

Similar generalizations can be made concerning the program adopted by the I.L.P. in 1931. Most of the platform certainly cannot be described as radical. Proposals calling for a national health scheme, unemployment insurance, and improved labor legislation were clear indications of the party's moderate Fabian nature. M. J. Coldwell later recalled that Saskatchewan I.L.P. leaders read Blatchford's *Merrie England* and material from the National Labor College in Britain. He always maintained that I.L.P. doctrine was "very much a British socialism."[27] The program of the Saskatchewan I.L.P. owed more to Blatchford than to Marx.

Similar conclusions can also be drawn regarding the Farmer-Labor party's program. The provincial economic policy of the party published in the fall of 1932 contained some proposals that could be termed radical but also called for such things as the extension of co-operative enterprises, electoral reform, and retention of all existing social legislation.[28]

In addition, evidence suggests that some of the Farmer-Labor socialization proposals were supported by both leaders and rank and file of the party from what is not commonly accepted as a socialist point of view. The best example of this was the stand that many took on monetary reform. Socialization of the country's financial system was consistently advocated by the Farmer-Labor party prior to 1934. But it must also be remembered that a large number of people, socialist and non-socialist, believed that the improper functioning of the monetary system was at the root of the depression.[29] Supporting monetary reform, and even going so far as favoring the socialization of the financial system, did not necessarily indicate that one was a doctrinaire socialist in the West of the 1930's.

214

The popularity of monetary reform at this time ensured that the social-credit ideas of Major C. H. Douglas were given a serious hearing in Saskatchewan. The reaction of the Farmer-Labor party to social credit is interesting. As one would expect, some socialists in the party argued strongly against social-credit proposals. Wells Bentley, a veteran socialist from Preeceville, commented:

> the Douglas plan would still leave private ownership of the means of production, both natural resources and the tools of production. The only difference between this and our present system, being that the control of credit would be in hands responsible to the electorate instead of in the hands of irresponsible people as at present.[30]

However, not everyone in the party was critical of Major Douglas' ideas. Violet McNaughton, a prominent Saskatchewan Progressive in the 1920's and a supporter of the C.C.F. in the 1930's, favored this type of monetary reform. "I am becoming more sold to the Social Credit theory as the shortest road out of the present depression," she noted in 1932.[31] Mr. F. Gable, the principal of the Viscount school and an early Farmer-Labor supporter in that area, wrote to George Williams in 1933:

> At the request of a number of interested persons here last fall, I have carried on a series of meetings on Economics according to the C. H. Douglas school. . . . I think these meetings have predisposed a considerable number of people here to a large part of the Farmer-Labor platform, and fairly strong support may accordingly be expected at this point.[32]

Another supporter of the Farmer-Labor party from the Kerrobert constituency, where social-credit ideas were particularily popular, wrote to party headquarters and asked, "May the C.C.F. adopt the Douglas system as their [sic] economic policy . . . ?"[33] On the whole, there appeared to be considerable amount of support among the rank and file of the Farmer-Labor party throughout the province for the social-credit economic program.

More surprisingly, some of the leaders of the party also at times showed a clear sympathy toward the economic proposals of Major Douglas. This was particularly true of Frank Eliason, the party secretary. "While we have no fault to find with the principle which the Douglasites advocate," he informed E. M. Graham of Major, Saskatchewan, "it is as far as we are able to ascertain impossible to have any of the old parties put their program into effect and if it were put into effect, it does not go far enough and will simply be a patch on capitalism."[34] He expressed a similar point of view in a letter to a Farmer-Labor supporter from the Shaunavon constituency: "I see no essential difference in their [Social Credit's] final program and that of the C.C.F., and I cannot understand

215

why they do not whole-heartedly come out in support of our policy."[35] In addition Farmer-Labor leaders often stressed the monetary issue in their many public addresses throughout the province prior to 1934. M. J. Coldwell, who was chosen to lead the party at its founding convention, sounded very much like William Aberhart, when in a speech in Avonlea in 1933, he described the existing monetary and banking system as "the greatest racket on earth" and "the principle [sic] cause of a depression in the midst of plenty." "Bankers of the world," the Farmer-Labor leader went on, "control the destiny of the human race, and Sir Herbert Holt controls the destiny of Canada, not Mr. Bennett and Mr. King as most people think."[36]

Thus, while it is true that some within the party rejected the monetary proposals of social credit as being anti-socialist, others found no difficulty in seeing similarities between the economics of social credit and the financial policies advocated by the Farmer-Labor party. Eliason's views on monetary reform and social credit are particularly significant. No one had more influence than he in policy making or in the day-to-day running of the party prior to the 1934 provincial election.

The stand which the Farmer-Labor party took on monetary reform was an indicator of the great variation of opinion within the party. On this issue, as on so many others, the moderates, the reformers within the party, were very strong. The sympathy which many Farmer-Labor leaders and supporters had for social-credit economic ideas in the early 1930's showed that the party's support of socialized banking was not based entirely on socialist ideals.

An examination of various speeches and declarations of Farmer-Labor leaders on party policy in the early 1930's also generally reveals a moderate approach and attitude. George Williams, who was considered to be on the left wing of the party, serves as an example. In 1932 the party published a booklet entitled *What is this Socialism* in which Williams explained socialism Farmer-Labor style. In the foreword he pointed out that Canadians were not interested in any particular "ism" but that they wanted to be reasonably sure an economic system would work before they supported it.[37] His comments throughout the article illustrated the pragmatic, moderate philosophy of Farmer-Labor socialism.

> Socialism provides for the private ownership of personal property such as the home in which an individual dwells, or the personal comforts of life that are used in order to make life fuller and better. Socialism does not mean, as some people would have you believe, that if you have two shirts you must give one to your friend or share your house with a stranger. It does mean that no one will be obliged to go without a shirt or without lodging. These things — shirts, homes, radios, washing machines, brooms, mops, automobiles, a dress suit, a sewing machine, and chewing gum are personal property. Socialism not only recognizes the right to the possession

*George H. Williams*

and enjoyment of personal property, but wants to make it possible for people to enjoy a great deal of it.[38]

Williams' stand on the question of land nationalization was another indicator of his political philosophy. In addressing the founding convention of the national C.C.F. in Regina in 1933, he stated that "the basis of the C.C.F. land policy was a recognition of the family farm as the

217

*M. J. Coldwell*

fundamental unit. What we want in Saskatchewan," Williams said, "is the benefit of socialism for the farmers, that the products of the farmers' industry will be used for social purposes. . . ."[39]

M. J. Coldwell, on numerous occasions, also made statements and speeches supporting a moderate reform socialism. In one address he stated that he was definitely a socialist and then went on to say that to him "socialism meant simply putting into practice the principles of Christian brotherhood."[40] He constantly denied that the program of the Farmer-Labor party was in any way similar to the Russian plan.[41] In a

218

speech in Regina in January, 1934, he described Farmer-Labor policy as a middle way between communism and fascism and spoke favorably of the Roosevelt New Deal.[42] In general, Farmer-Labor leaders portrayed the party as a moderate, Fabian, reform-orientated movement, based on the principles of practical Christianity. A conscious effort was made to disassociate the party from anything that could be termed doctrinaire or Marxist socialism.

The leadership of the Farmer-Labor party was in fact strongly opposed to those within the party who attempted to spread the principle of Marxism. A great deal of difficulty was experienced with certain labor spokesmen who went into rural areas and preached such doctrines. One case in point was that of Fred Fix, a Marxist socialist and a member of the Melville branch of the I.L.P. In 1933 he travelled into rural areas to address gatherings on behalf of the Farmer-Labor party. When reports of these meetings reached headquarters, leaders quickly intervened, and he was no longer allowed to speak on behalf of the party. After one of Fix's speeches Williams wrote to Eliason:

> The boys from Young came over to my Viscount meeting and told me that Mr. Fix of Melville told the farmers around Young at the Mowhawk school that all the farmers would be collectivized. They would all live together and work 4 hours a day. It did a lot of harm and now we have to send an agricultural speaker to counteract it even then we will still lose some votes. . . . It seems that it is unwise for us to send industrial speakers to farmer meetings. . . .[43]

Eliason was even more explicit on the subject.

> The industrial socialist, whether he be Canadian, American, or European, will do us more harm than any other type of speaker that I can think of because they [sic] will not adhere to the principles as laid down by our annual conventions. As a matter of fact, they [sic] are absolutely opposed to a definite program of any kind and insist that we should only issue a manifesto. However, I point out to this type of people that the Saskatchewan farmers will not accept a manifesto but are clever enough to want to know just what this is all about before they decide [sic] to cast their vote in favour of our principles.[44]

Eliason continued and made some interesting general comments regarding socialism and the Farmer-Labor party:

> I have hesitated from the very beginning to style myself as a Socialist. I am of the opinion that I am on far safer ground if in reply to the question "Am I a Socialist?" I come back with the reply "That I am a supporter of the economic program which was laid down by the July convention of the Farmer-Labor Group and if that is Socialism then I am a Socialist and if it is Toryism then I am a Tory."[45]

Such statements clearly indicated the pragmatism of Eliason's ideas and his lack of enthusiasm for any dogmatic socialist position.

The relationship which existed in the province between the Farmers' Unity League (F.U.L.) and the Farmer-Labor party also throws considerable light on the ideology of the latter. The Farmer-Labor party was not only criticized by the two established parties and the right-wing press but also was attacked bitterly from the left. Throughout the early 1930's the Farmers' Unity League denounced it as just another capitalist organization.

The Farmers' Unity League was established at a conference in Saskatoon in December, 1930.[46] The meeting was called by the Farmers' Educational League, the radical group which had operated within the organized farm movement since the creation of the U.F.C. Among the delegates to the founding conference were such well-known Saskatchewan left-wingers as Fred Shunamen, Ben Lloyd, H. E. Mills, and Walter Wiggins.[47] The F.U.L. claimed to have a different outlook than other farm bodies, stressing the class division in agriculture and basing itself upon the poorer farmers.[48] It drew up a list of immediate demands including debt cancellation, organized resistance to foreclosures and evictions, tax boycotts, and a $1,000-per-year guaranteed income for all farmers.[49] Its founders decided that F.U.L. members would work both inside and outside of existing farm organizations.[50] They also voted unanimously to extend greetings to the All-China congress of Soviets which was meeting at that time in China and later declared complete support for the policies of the Soviet Union.[51]

There is little doubt that the Communist party of Canada played a direct role in the launching of the Farmers' Unity League. By 1931 many of its founders were open supporters of that party. As well, evidence of the direct connection between the league, the Communist party of Canada, and Moscow was brought forward during the trials of Canadian Communist leaders following their arrests in 1931. Among the various documents seized at Communist party headquarters in Toronto were instructions from Moscow on an agrarian program for the Communist party of Canada.[52] The party's agricultural policy was based on these instructions. In November, 1930 the party recommended that a left-wing agrarian organization to be known as the Farmers' Unity League be created. Tom Ewen, one of the Canadian communists arrested and brought to trial, testified that all farmers who were members of the Communist party went into the F.U.L. and that these men formed the leadership of the league.[53]

From the beginning the league was hostile to the United Farmers of Canada. Although it approved of its members working within the U.F.C., the purpose of such activity was to radicalize the existing farm organization and capture its leadership. The Communist party was said to have instructed F.U.L. members to participate within the U.F.C. as long as it would help in the eventual disintegration of the latter body as it then existed.[54] At the communist trials in Toronto in 1931, Tom Ewen was asked if it was the purpose of the F.U.L. to destroy all existing farm organizations. His reply indicated the official attitude which the league took toward the U.F.C.:

> Not to destroy them but to transform them into weapons of struggle in the interests of the membership of the farmers. The farmers in these oganizations, in United Farmers of Canada, for instance, find themselves in much the same position as the workers in the Reformist unions in that their interests are being sold out by those in command, by the leadership.[55]

The *Furrow,* the league's official publication, reflected this position toward the U.F.C. and later the Farmer-Labor party. In November, 1930 in an editorial critical of U.F.C. leadership, it asked: "Has the U.F.C. become a sort of 'windbreak' to shelter the government from the wrath of the outraged farmers?"[56] In March, 1932 the paper commented on the recent U.F.C. convention: "Radicalism in word, and reaction in deed, reached its peak in the convention of the U.F.C. just past. The delegates passed resolutions demanding a Co-operative Commonwealth and almost in the same breath provided careful safeguards for individual ownership of land. . . ."[57]

Similar attacks were made on the Farmer-Labor party and its leaders. In one editorial the *Furrow* referred to the C.C.F. as the third capitalist party in Canada and compared Frank Eliason to R. B. Bennett.[58] At the first national convention of the F.U.L. held in Saskatoon in July, 1932, the Farmer-Labor party was referred to as an organization which mouthed some socialist phrases but which in reality was a reactionary capitalist party. The party was condemned for advocating another method of preserving the capitalist system.[59] At times the F.U.L. viewed the Farmer-Labor party as its most deadly enemy. "Parliamentary reformism is social-fascist in essence, because it essentially places its faith in the capitalist class and has no confidence in the toilers . . . ," the *Furrow* wrote in 1934. "The so-called leftist in such a position is more dangerous than the milder demagogue and must be fought that much more strenuously."[60] F.U.L. spokesmen argued that Farmer-Labor leaders were the worst kind because it was difficult for the masses to view them as their class enemies. Or as one F.U.L. supporter put it in a letter to *The Western Producer,* "they lead up very close to what is needed but yet fail or refuse to take such steps and action that will lead to a complete solution of the farmers' and workers' economic problems."[61]

Despite this opposition to the leadership and programs of the U.F.C. and the Farmer-Labor party, the league did not condemn the individual

221

members of these two organizations. To the league the majority of members were "oppressed farmers" who were being misled by what the *Furrow* commonly referred to as the "Kulak elements" in the farm movement. The policy of the F.U.L. was to work within the U.F.C. and develop the class consciousness of the poor farmers and "rescue" them from their reactionary leaders.[62] The league's policy toward the Farmer-Labor party was even more ambivalent. In areas where there was some support for the league and perhaps where Farmer-Labor opposition to the league was also strong, it considered nominating a candidate to participate in elections. Thus it chose Walter Wiggins to contest the 1934 provincial election in the Pelly constituency, totally independent from and in opposition to the candidate of the Farmer-Labor party.[63] In other areas of the province, where circumstances were different, the league was more willing to work with the Farmer-Labor party. The best example was in the Elrose constituency where Farmer-Labor party and F.U.L. members seemed prepared to nominate a joint candidate.[64]

The position which the F.U.L. took presented great problems for the Farmer-Labor party. Leaders of the party decided that if it was to have any chance of electoral success, it had to disassociate itself clearly from the league. Like other democratic socialist parties, it attempted to distinguish its solution to economic problems from that of the communists. Farmer-Labor leaders argued that their party aimed to attain social justice for the farmers and workers by constitutional means, while the F.U.L. planned to use revolution as a means to gain its ends.

No one struggled harder against the Farmers' Unity League than Frank Eliason.[65] He condemned the league for the type of tactics it advocated. In a letter to *The Western Producer* he wrote:

> They oppose the Farmer-Labor policy because we aim to set up a new economic order by peaceful constitutional means. . . . we must keep cool heads, rally in support of the Farmer-Labor economic program and bring about a reorganization of society in a sane manner.[66]

On another occasion Eliason described the F.U.L. as having "no reasonable arguments to offer, no practical program to suggest." "They cry out in support of the poor," he wrote, "but when they are asked what should be done in a practical way towards finding a solution for these problems of the farmers, then they are void of any practical suggestions."[67]

Eliason was at the centre of the controversy with the F.U.L. which arose in 1932 over the situation in the Elrose constituency. The difficulty began in October, when a meeting was held by the local constituency committee of the U.F.C. to discuss nominating a farmer candidate for the next provincial election. No speakers from the central office of the Farmer-Labor party attended, but Cyril Harding of the F.U.L. was present. The meeting passed a resolution favoring co-operation between the F.U.L. and the Farmer-Labor party in the next provincial election. Five members of the Farmer-Labor party constituency committee were appointed to meet with league representatives to plan a united front. It also was decided that another meeting would be held in the near future at which a united-front program would be adopted.[68]

Upon receiving the minutes of the Elrose constituency meeting, Eliason immediately contacted members of the Farmer-Labor constituency committee and advised them of the danger of lining up with the league.[69] In addition, he sent each official a copy of certain extracts from the Communist party trials in Toronto which clearly indicated the link between the F.U.L. and international communism.[70] Eliason also wrote a special letter to the five members of the Elrose constituency committee who were appointed to meet with the league to plan a united front. He pointed out that a Farmer-Labor candidate must support Coldwell's leadership and subscribe to the economic policies laid down by the party.[71] His swift intervention in the affairs of the constituency effectively blocked the possibility of a joint U.F.C.-F.U.L. candidate. However, the constituency remained a problem for the Farmer-Labor leaders. Early in 1933 Eliason wrote to a party organizer who had been sent into the Elrose area by central office:

> The eyes of the Province are focused upon the Elrose constituency. The Liberals and the Conservatives would, of course, like to see a union of our forces in that constituency. They would then immediately tag us definitely with the Russian tag and it may mean a loss of many votes in the rest of the Province.[72]

Walter Young argues that democratic socialist parties, on occasions, harmed themselves by condemning the communists. He states that in some cases such attacks weakened the socialist front because in attacking communists, democratic socialists were denouncing enemies of the capitalist class, an action which often was difficult to justify to rank-and-file supporters.[73] However, this does not appear to be the case in Saskatchewan during the early 1930's. Support for a united front was not great among the province's farmers. Denouncing the Farmers' Unity League undoubtedly helped more than it harmed the Farmer-Labor party in its appeal to the electorate. The Elrose constituency was the only example prior to 1934 where there appeared to be any significant amount of grass-roots support for a united front of U.F.C. and F.U.L. farmers.[74]

The position which the Farmer-Labor party adopted toward the F.U.L. indicated that the party leaders were clearly anti-Marxist and anti-communist. There is no evidence that the leadership of the party seriously considered any type of co-operation with the F.U.L. Even George Williams, who at one time had been a close associate of many of the leaders of the league, strongly opposed any kind of alliance. Williams approved the stand taken by Eliason on the Elrose situation. After Eliason's decisive action, he wrote:

> I believe you did exactly the correct thing with reference to the Farmers' Unity League, only I believe you should go further. I believe you should send a copy of that letter ... to everyone of our constituency chairmen and to all Sect. Campaign Managers. The sooner you do this the better because they are going to try to horn in on all of our nominations.[75]

The evidence therefore suggests that the policies and leaders of the Farmer-Labor party from the earliest point were not as radical nor as socialist as is commonly believed. The party's policies, the views of its leaders, the attitudes of its leaders and supporters toward other reform movements, and its relations with the extreme left all indicate this. John Bennett and Cynthia Krueger, in their article on the early C.C.F., attempt to point out the pragmatism of its platform. They write, "The C.C.F. began compromising its radical doctrine the day after the Regina Manifesto was issued in 1933."[76] It would have been more accurate to say that a good deal of moderation, pragmatism, and compromise existed from the very beginning in the C.C.F.'s programs and in the minds of the men and women who formulated them and took them to the people. The generally held theory that the "radical fathers of the party" substantially moderated and compromised their ideas after 1934 needs to be seriously reassessed. Tommy Douglas was probably closer to the truth when he stated recently that his views were far more radical now, in the 1970's, than they were during the years of the depression.[77]

# 16    The Year We Moved

*by Mrs. A. W. Bailey*

DURING the 1930's we lived on a small prairie farm south of Regina. On the morning of June 22, 1937 my husband George and I rose earlier than usual as he had to be ready to leave at six o'clock when a neighbor was to call for him. Together they were going about 200 miles north of where we lived to look at land, with the intention of locating a farm. I was to stay behind to do the chores, and to help me we got a young lad about fourteen years old. The morning dawned as so many other mornings of the thirties dawned, with the hot, amber light of the sun, filtering through dust-laden air. Even this early in the morning there were not the fresh, dewy breezes that the southern prairies is famous for. We sat at breakfast and panted for air as we talked of moving to a place where there were green grass and shade. It would be a veritable heaven after so much dust and wind.*

When the Model A carrying the two men had disappeared over the hill, I poured myself another cup of coffee and wished I could have gone with them. They were to be gone three days and I knew they would be long days for me, but if they got land where things grew green and lush it would be worth waiting for. I tried to think what it would be like to live in another place. I had spent all my life in this district. My childhood home was only a mile away and the old school where I had taken my elementary grades was not much farther. My own children would go there if we stayed here. A feeling of compunction swept over me. Then I looked out at the fields and pasture where I could see one of our horses pawing the sand trying to get a mouthful of grass. Only the tops of the stones showed; the rest of them was buried in sand. Russian thistles were piled ten feet high in fence corners and held there by layers of sand which had blown across them. Some fences had gone down under the weight of the load on them.

As the sun got higher, the wind rose, sending swirls of dust high into the air. Topsoil was carried off fields, and sloughs, long dry, were cracked

*This article originally appeared in *Saskatchewan History* for winter, 1967.

225

*Dust storm in southern Saskatchewan, 1934*

wide open from the intense heat. Huge cracks showed in yards, roads, or any place where ground was packed with travel. To the west of us alkali from a dry lake rose hundreds of feet into the air when a whirlwind zig-zagged its way across barren acres.

At seven o'clock I called Bob, my helper, and together we went to the barn to do the chores. I milked while he fed the pigs and cleaned out the stalls. Then while he did the separating I made breakfast and got the children up and dressed. Later I went about the task of trying to clean the dust off the windowsills and floors. This was a daily, thankless job for no sooner was it cleaned off than it blew in again. No house, regardless of how well built it was, was immune to dust in the thirties. As I went about my work I thought ahead to the evening radio programs that we enjoyed so much. This night, June 22, was a special night, for Joe Louis was to fight James Braddock and it was to be broadcast. We had always enjoyed these bouts, and sometimes George and I had made little bets as to who would win. Louis was my favorite and I wished I had bet this time. It was much more exciting when a bet was made. Oh, well, I would have the pleasure of telling him about it when he got home.

The wind blew all day and by five o'clock it had reached almost gale proportions. Grains of sand hit against the windowpanes, and the windcharger howled and tugged at its moorings atop the roof, making the whole atmosphere reek of impending danger. But as the children and I sat down to supper, a strange silence fell over the countryside. The wind died down suddenly as if someone had thrown a switch and turned it off.

After they had eaten, the children went out to play while I did the dishes before going to the barn for the evening chores. I wanted to have my work done by eight so I could sit and enjoy the fight on the radio. Suddenly my son came running into the house, greatly excited. "Come quick, Mom," he shouted, "there's a big black cloud coming in the sky." He ran out ahead of me and pointed to the western sky where, sure enough, there was the blackest, most terrifying looking cloud I had ever seen, on the horizon. It was moving very quickly and the edge of it was literally rolling along. Panic rose in me. What should I do? Where should we go? The house was sure to be blown away and our nearest neighbor was a mile away. At the rate the cloud was moving I could never make it as I would have to carry the baby, and the neighbors might not be home anyway.

"Where's Bob?" I asked my son.

"Over there," he pointed, "fixing the pigpen."

"Go tell him to come quick," I ordered. Then I shut the door tight, picked up the baby, and yelling at the other two to follow, I ran for the dug-out barn we had made in the side of a hill. Already the shadow of the cloud was upon us.

The cows were standing by the barn waiting to be milked, so I let them in ahead of us.

"Go as far back as you can," I shouted to the children. "Get up on those sacks of feed and sit there." I fastened the door on the inside, picked up the baby, and made my way to where the boys were.

"We're safe here," I told them, marvelling at the calm of my voice which belied my inner feelings. Strangely, none of the children asked what was wrong or questioned why we were in the barn. They sat silent and still. By now it was pitch-dark in the barn and I knew the cloud was over us. Every second I expected to be lifted and carried in the air or to have the barn taken from over us.

I had no way of telling time but when I thought it was safe to do so I groped my way to the door and opened it just a crack to look out. It was like a vacuum outside, quiet and dark, yet I could hear pails and milk stools being hurled about. I went back to the others and reported it would soon be over, and then we would go back to the house. I was anxious to see what damage had been done, yet fearful of what I would find.

When it was light enough for me to see the forms of the cattle, I knew it was safe to open the door, so once again I looked outside. It was the strangest phenomenon I had ever witnessed. A cloaking silence enveloped the whole outdoors, yet dust hung in the air so thick it was clearly visible. Everything — land, air, sky — was a dull grey color. With the baby in my arms and the boys close behind me I went to the house. Our feet sank in sand almost to our ankles and we breathed and tasted sand, so held our hands over our faces as we walked.

As we neared the house I noticed that the door had blown open, and pots, pans, pails, and curtains were strewn all over the place. Dust was so thick on the floor that I had to use the scoop shovel to take it out. Such a mess! I knew now that the black cloud had been saturated with dust lifted from somewhere, maybe many miles from us, and carried along in a sort of vacuum, to be dropped along the way. The wind had been high up and the sand had cut out the sound, causing the eerie silence during the worst of it. It was the strangest storm I had ever witnessed on the prairie.

When I had most of the dust off the floor, I took the children and went and helped Bob do the chores. When the chores were finished for the night, I went about the job of getting rid of more dust and sand from the house. The bed clothes had to be taken out and shaken, and the mattresses had to be swept off before any of us could go to bed. As I did this work I consoled myself with the thought that soon we would be moving out of this dust bowl. After the others were in bed I remembered the fight and turned on the radio, but all I could get was the noise of static so I shut it off. Although it was still quite early on a June evening, it was very dark. I was afraid to go to bed in case another storm came up during the night and caught us unprepared. So I sat by the kitchen window until midnight and then I lay down on the couch with my clothes on. I was surprised when I awoke to find everything intact, and the sun trying weakly to brighten up the dirty old world.

Three days after they had left the men returned with stories of a land of milk and honey to the north of us. It was refreshing to hear about it and hard to believe that only 200 miles away, conditions were so vastly different. George had not located land but had looked at several places and was going back early in July to make a deal for one of them.

On July 8 George and my brother-in-law Ed left for the north again, and this time I knew that when they came back we would be moving within a short time. The big dust storm had convinced both of us that we were not satisfied to stay in this place any longer. I was alternately elated and remorseful at the thought of leaving the prairie. After all, it had been a good place to live until the thirties brought this desert-like era to us. I loved the hills where I went sleigh riding in the winter and horseback riding in summer just for the sheer joy of being outside. I thought of the many times I had ridden my saddle pony Dolly to the top of a high hill and let her graze while I sat on her back and looked for miles in each direction, seeing nothing much but more high hills. Each hill was different from the ones around it, but there is something about prairie hills that gets into the blood and makes one feel intimate with nature. I thought also of leaving our neighbors, some of whom I had known since childhood; of the dear old school to the south; and of my mother who would be alone if we moved away. These were some of the thoughts that told me to stay where I was.

Then I thought of our stock trying to get feed off the sand-filled pasture; of the fields, dry and cracked from lack of rain; of the dust we were breathing; and of the relief cheques that came each month and hardly kept us in food. How long would it last? What would it do to young men like my husband who wanted to get started in farming but did not have the means to get established? These were some of the thoughts that told me we would be better off to move.

When the men returned, each had located a farm and we were to move as soon as we could get ready to go. The farms were close to each other and that meant my sister and I would be neighbors. The days ahead were busy ones to be sure. We planned to take just what was necessary, which meant some of our stock had to be sold. There were arrangements to be made regarding the transportation of our few household possessions and ourselves. And of course through it all, the routine, daily tasks had to be carried out as usual. While going about my regular daily routine I often wondered just what living in a new district would be like. I had never been farther north than Regina which was only 100 miles away, so it was not any different than where we lived now. I wondered how far the school was from our new home, and when I asked George he said he had not thought to ask about the school. However, he said the district was thickly populated so there must be a school not too far away. He had also told me that the area was heavily wooded, so I wondered how the children would find their way to a school that was buried in a forest. And I remembered that I had read somewhere about bears living in heavily treed areas. My poor children would be eaten alive if they walked through the bush alone! George was sympathetic to my feelings but said we were going. "We have nothing to lose," he told me. "After all, it's not as if we ever got started in farming here."

Then he told me of the gardens he had seen, of the wild fruit that could be had just for the picking, of the wood he could cut for fuel and to sell, and of the game he could shoot for meat. He was familiar with the bush land as he had been raised in a similar environment in Manitoba and had never completely fallen in love with the wide open spaces of the prairie.

Even in our sparsely settled district, news travelled fast and soon cattle buyers were coming to buy any cattle we did not intend to take with us. We sold our few sucking calves for the princely sum of five dollars each, their mothers for just a trifle more. One calf was butchered for meat, and for several days I was busy cutting and canning the beef that would sustain us in our new home until winter when deer could be shot. There was no garden stuff or fruit, but I packed my empty sealers in anticipation of the wild fruit I would pick when I got to our "garden of Eden."

229

By the end of the third week in July we were almost ready to pull out. Our household necessities, the stock we were taking, and the few pieces of machinery we had accumulated so far were to be shipped by train. My sister and her husband and family were going by car while George and I and our baby would go by truck with some more delicate furnishings that we would need as soon as we got there. Our son would go with his aunt and uncle in the car.

The Sunday before we left some of our friends and relations dropped in to see us and to bid us farewell. Nearly all our things had been taken to the station so I cooked dinner on a little tin stove outdoors. The gods were good to us this last visit together, for the sun shone brighter than it had for many weeks. "Maybe it will change now and rain," someone said. I looked at George with a question in my eyes, but he said, "If it does we won't be here to see it. We're leaving on Tuesday come rain or shine." This expression — come rain or shine — had become somewhat of a standing joke during the thirties, and although it was always said in jest there was still the spark of hope in it too.

Late on Monday afternoon we were ready to leave. We were going to drive to the station with the team and wagon and then load them on the train, while we spent the night with friends. We were taking our little rat terrier with us, and our old collie, Mac, was to make his new home with a neighbor girl, Kathy, who had always showed a great fondness for him. The smile on her face when she led him away compensated somewhat for my tears. He was a good old dog! I knew he would have a good home with Kathy for she was as fond of him as I was.

There's something about a first home that is very dear to a person. George had built this little two-roomed house himself, and most of the things we had in it were either wedding presents or things from my childhood home that Mom had given me. It was almost like one of the family, and as we moved away from it I knew I just couldn't leave without becoming very sentimental. When we got to the turn that would take us out of sight of it I told George, in a husky voice, to stop. He thought I had forgotten something and was about to turn around when I said, "Just stop for a minute. I want to take a good look before we go over the hill." In those few moments I relived the past few years — years that would become lost to me now that I was moving away, except in memory. I got a lasting mental picture of the little home where my first two babies were born. The house that had sheltered us from the snow and wind and dust storms would stand lonely and silent now, with the mice playing in the rooms and the frost cracking the flowered wallpaper I had so recently put on the bedroom. I closed my eyes and said a silent little prayer for my first dear little home.

Tuesday morning was hot and windy. A small crowd had gathered at the station to see us off. Some were sincere well-wishers hoping we would have a good trip and that our new home would be happy and prosperous. Some envied us and openly wished they could go along. Others just shook hands and said nothing. Then men helped with the loading of the horses and wagon into the boxcar while the women talked and kept an eye on their children as the train was due any minute. Suddenly my son yelled, "There's Mac. There's Mac," as the old dog came running up to us with his tongue hanging out and his tail going back and forth in delight at finding us. I fell to my knees and put my arms around his shaggy neck and almost kissed him. "What will we do with him?" I asked George with tears in my eyes. "We should make him go back," he answered, trying to appear gruff, "but I suppose now that he is here we'll have to take him along with us." I knew he could no more have sent Mac back now than he could have sent one of the children. So Mac was put in the boxcar along with the other stock and possessions. How much better it would have been for him if we had sent him back where he could have lived out his life in peace and loving care, for when we got settled he developed the dangerous habit of chasing cars, and one morning we found him on his back in the ditch, cold and stiff, where he had been flung by a passing car as he bit at its wheels.

After the train had pulled out we arranged ourselves for our long trip. Ed, at the wheel of the car, took the lead and we followed in the old truck. We had quite a load in the back, made up of bedding, a bed, dishes, lamps, and other household articles for two families. The gravelled road was rough and the truck was uncomfortable, but we were young and going to a new land where dust storms were unheard of. Optimism was what we needed! Optimism like our forefathers had when they had done this same kind of thing. It was kind of exciting once we got going.

The hundred miles to Regina seemed endless. There is nothing more monotonous on a hot, windy day than driving along a prairie highway. Mile after weary mile with no change of scenery or temperature. Conversation was nil so my thoughts went back to the little house we had left. It would be unbearably hot in it now, with all the windows and doors shut tight. If I could have read George's mind, I'm sure I could have seen his thoughts were ahead of us in the lush, green, cool spot he had picked for our new home.

We stopped for coffee at a lunch bar at the Milestone turn off. It was nice to get out and stretch our legs and let the children run about. We enjoyed our pie and coffee and a freshening up in the washroom, and were soon on our way.

We arrived in Regina about noon and went to George's brother's home where we had lunch and a rest. Then we went downtown and bought a few things we would need on the remainder of the trip. At two-thirty we started out again for another lap of our journey. We felt

231

*A southern Saskatchewan highway in the thirties*

refreshed now and the road was so much better than what we had already come on.

Before we left home I had heard the men talking about the Qu'Appelle hill. They had made it seem something terrible, but I thought they were joking, as I had lived among hills all my life and had never seen one I would be frightened to drive down, and we had some pretty steep hills! Ed had thought it was dangerous to take any chances going down it with the old truck so he had mentioned it to George. But George was confident that he could manage it all right. He had driven down it several times before and was used to driving in a hilly terrain. But he was reckoning without the unstable condition of the truck. When I saw the sign announcing the approach to the Qu'Appelle hill, I felt some apprehension and automatically drew the baby to my breast, hoping we would come to no harm. Ed, who was following close behind honked his horn as a reminder for us to go carefully down the hill. I was glad there was someone near us.

Up, over, and heading down! The bottom looked a long, crooked way from us, longer, perhaps, than it would have been if I had not been alerted to it. To the right was the bank of the hill where the road had been carved out and to the left was a thick cable to warn motorists that there was a steep embankment that spelled danger. I was fascinated until I realized that the truck was going faster than it had been and also that it was swerving from side to side. Fear, cold and choking, gripped me and then George said, "She's away!" as he tried unsuccessfully to shift gears. The brakes had failed and the truck was out of control! It was then that I mercifully passed from consciousness.

232

When I came to, someone was putting cold cloths on my face. Someone else said, "She's waking up. Thank God!" I heard my son say, "We won't have to get a new Mom now, will we, Dad?" It was then I realized that they had thought I was dead, so I tried to get up, but was pushed gently back down by a strong hand. I learned later it was Ed who had taken over and bathed my face with cold water brought to the scene by a farmer who lived at the bottom of the hill and had seen the crash. He had done this before, he said, as there had been many accidents on this hill, and he had learned the thing he could do most to help was to bring a jug of cold water.

From somewhere an ambulance appeared, and people were hurrying to lift me into it. I had a feeling of mixed-up emotions and thoughts, just as blackness swept over me again. When I came to for the second time we were moving along smoothly in the ambulance. A great sweep of nausea hit me, and without being able to help myself I threw up on the floor of the ambulance. The attendant told me not to mind as they were used to that in their business. He made me as comfortable as possible, and soon we were backing up to the ambulance entrance of a Regina hospital. I was wheeled into the hospital on a waiting stretcher and laid on an examining table. A white-garbed doctor made a thorough examination for possible breaks or serious injuries; then I was put into a hospital bed until George came for me. He had followed us to the hospital in a car which had been at the scene of the accident and had brought the baby along for an examination. She had a very bad glass cut on her knee which would take some careful attention before healing up. Otherwise she was just shaken up. The doctor said I was to rest for at least two days before resuming the trip. George phoned his brother and made arrangements for us to spend another day and night there. My sister and her husband and family had gone on to their destination and had taken our son with them.

As the old truck was written off as a total loss, we had to get transportation to go on with our journey. George's brother helped us out by taking us and our belongings the rest of the way. I was very weak and had to stop often to rest. When we got to the Qu'Appelle hill, I saw where the truck had gone through the cable and spread itself out over the hillside. There was broken glass glistening in the sun and pieces of my suitcase and dishes. I was told I had gone out through the top of the truck when it crashed. If it had been a better truck I would not have gone out so easily. Of course, if it had been a better truck, the brakes would have held and we would not have had the accident — perhaps!

In the later afternoon we got to the town of Naicam, and as I was very tired we decided to get a room and spend the night. I also wanted to bathe the baby and change the dressings on her knee. I had not seen her wound yet and when I unwrapped the bandages and looked at it I

233

became sick again. There were two semi-circular cuts, one above the kneecap and one just under it. They were deep, raw-looking tears, and I was almost afraid to apply the white powder the doctor had given us for fear they would start to bleed. However, I finally got them dressed and got her to sleep. It took these cuts many weeks to heal over, and when they did they left a lifetime pair of scars. I had numerous small cuts and scratches that also left scars, but nothing as bad as those on our daughter.

The next morning we started out bright and early after a hot breakfast and were soon in the bush country that George was so anxious to get to. I was fascinated by the tall trees and the snug little farm homes still sleeping by the roadside. Everything was so green, and many yards showed clotheslines filled with pure white clothes hanging limply in the morning sun. I tried to remember when I had seen a sight like this on the prairie. Women had to take the clothes in almost before they were dry to prevent the grime from settling in them. And they were *never* left out over night!

Near the road were bushes which George told me were wild raspberry canes. "Could I have some?" I asked. I had never tasted a raspberry that wasn't in a jam pail and I longed for a fresh one. No sooner asked for than received. He picked a handful of the delicious fruit. Mm-mm-mm, they were really good! I got a thrill just thinking about being able to go out and pick this kind of fruit for myself. There were other fruit bushes growing near the road too. I was told they were gooseberries; pinchberries, so good for jelly; high-bush cranberries; and chokecherries. I knew what chokecherries tasted like for we had picked some when we went picking saskatoons in the Big Muddy every year. They had a lovely tangy taste that made you want more.

I commented on so many homes close to the road, and the men told me that is the way it was in the bush country as it was a hard job making roads through the bush. So the people built near the main road and their land lay to the back of the buildings. I compared this to the "roads" as we called the trails across fields and pastures back home. Nobody travelled on the square on the prairie.

We travelled on slowly, George pointing out things he thought would interest me. There were no windmills here as on the prairie. Reason? No wind to speak of! We could see no pastures or herds of cattle. This was because the pastures were small and consisted of uncleared bush land. Farmers kept only what stock they really needed, as feed was scarce and cleared land was needed for cereal crops. I learned later that the flies made it impossible for stock to stay in the bush during the day at certain times of the year. This meant that inside feeding was an almost year-round practice.

234

Soon we came to a knoll and George told his brother to stop the truck. Pointing ahead to a scattering of buildings on the side of a hill he said, "Well, there she is." I squinted against the rising sun and saw what appeared to be a small town laid out over a valley and on the hillside.

"You mean — you mean — that's Bjorkdale?" I stammered.

"That's Bjorkdale," he answered. "Your new hometown."

My new hometown! A million fears filled my mind at that moment. Could we make a living in this strange place? Did we do the right thing by coming here? It was all so different from the prairie. Mentally I went back to our little house. The sun would be shining in the east window now, right on the mirror above the washstand. It had often aggravated me, but it was something I knew well. Then the thought struck me — the sun was likely obliterated by a sand-filled cloud. The mirror was not there any more. It was packed away in the barrel with the dishes. I heard the words again that had made me decide to come here: "We have nothing to lose." It was right; we had nothing to lose. We would start from the beginning.

"It's kind of — pretty," I said. Then hopefully, "Isn't it?" Any assurance at all, even an affirmative reply to my question would have made me feel better then.

We started on then toward the little town in the valley, which lay sleeping and clean looking like a child who had been well scrubbed before being put to bed. We saw a building with a sign over the door telling us it was a general store, so George said he wanted to get some eggs for breakfast. I went in too, and a pleasant little woman came to the counter from a back room where a newly made fire was crackling happily in the cookstove. It smelled nice in the store and all at once I was hungry. We got our purchases and the woman asked us if we were new in the district. When we said we were, she welcomed us and said she hoped she would see us often. Later I asked George why the wood made so much noise as it burned, and he told me it was spruce wood and the noise was made from the little pockets of resin exploding as they got hot. It also exuded the pleasant aroma which had filled the store. I hoped we could burn spruce wood in our stove.

We still had six miles to go before reaching our new home. I was so anxious to see it! George had told me there were some log buildings on it and that the house was not too good but he could make it liveable by winter. There were many small sawmills close and he could work to pay for lumber. These small sawmills provided many farmers with winter work, which was a great help. They could either take their own logs to be sawed and then sell the lumber or work for wages in cash.

We went two miles due east from Bjorkdale, then made a ninety-degree angle to the north. The road was not too bad here although it was only a dry-weather road. It had been carved out of the bush many years before and was called the Peesane Road as it joined the towns of Peesane and Bjorkdale. We learned that this road was the topic for many interesting and sometimes heated conversations and that a petition was being circulated to have it built up and faced.

I had seen pictures of log houses but never in my life had I seen one that resembled the one that came into view as we ended our journey! It was so crooked that I wondered at it not toppling over. Nobody spoke as we turned into the yard and stopped in front of this questionable dwelling. First impressions are always durable and how I wished my first impression of this place could have been more welcoming. Weeds and underbrush grew up around the windows. The building logs had been longer than necessary for the size of the house but instead of them being cut to length they had been left their original length and weird arms stuck out at each corner, like giant interlaced ladder rungs. Trees, tall and straight, grew right beside the house, and it was impossible to see even to the road which was only a few rods away.

George, who had got out of the truck immediately and gone into the house, stuck his head out the door and said to me, "Aren't you coming in?" For reply I burst into uncontrollable tears. The baby followed suit out of fear and sympathy. No amount of cajolling on the part of the men could stop my sobs, which were filled with homesickness and self-pity.

While I sat in pure misery, George had gone across the road to where my sister and her family were settled. In a few minutes they all came running over, and I was so glad to see them that I cried more than ever.

"There's no use crying," my sister said. "We're here now and that's it. Even if we did want to go back we couldn't. We're still on relief, remember? Come over to our place and I'll make some coffee."

So that was my initiation to the bush country. After a cup of hot coffee and a chat with my sister, I decided it might not be so bad after all. One thing I knew for sure was that the more determined we were to stay and get properly settled the sooner we would have a home. The children, at least, were not fretting. They climbed trees and played hide-and-seek in the bushes, and came in with torn clothes and scratched knees.

The two things that I was not prepared to cope with were nettles and hornets. I had never seen either one before in my life, so when I got back to our house I plowed right through the weeds at the door and soon my arms were sore and swollen. I scratched them which made them worse than ever. George then told me that these weeds contained poison which irritated the skin, and until he could get them cut down I would have to watch both myself and the children when moving about the yard. In the meantime the horrid, burning lumps on my arms nearly drove me mad.

To get back to the house. As I said, it was crooked, but how crooked we did not know until we measured it inside. The bottom of the north wall was fourteen inches farther out than the top. This was the wall the door was in so when it was opened it swung back against the wall like a drunken sailor. The south wall was nearly as bad. There was a fairly good floor and the roof was shingled, which would give us protection from the rain. But the mud had fallen out from between the logs, leaving gaps big enough for the birds to fly through. There were a few planks laid across the timbers that were to be used for a ceiling, and we could see things fastened to the inside of the roof that were dark grey and round. I thought they were bird nests, but George told me they were hornet nests and that he would get rid of them as soon as possible. It meant nothing to me as I had no experience with hornets.

We put the day in by unpacking the stuff in the truck and placing it where we could use it. The men had salvaged as much of our belongings as they could from the wreck, and I had not questioned them as to just what had got broken. But when they unloaded it I was amazed to find things like the lamp glass intact and the bread pans smashed beyond use. The mirror was not even cracked but my small suitcase was in shreds. One end of our bedstead was badly bent and the other end was perfect. We straightened the bent end and it is still in use to this day. Most of our eatables were gone and some of my clothes were badly torn.

When we lit the lamp that first night, the hornets thought it was a signal for them to come to tea. In a swarm they invaded the table and whole room. I started to catch them and put them in the lamp but George told me to leave them alone as they had a very venomous stinger and if I got stung it might be dangerous.

"The first thing I'll do in the morning," he said, "will be to get rid of their nests."

"And how will you do that?" I asked.

"Well, it's easy, if you know how," he informed me. "I'll take a length of stovepipe, tie a piece of paper over one end, and then slip the other end over their nest. I'll slide it gently against the nest, the nest will fall into the pipe then I'll cover that end and dump the whole thing into some kerosene." When we put the light out and went to bed the hornets settled down and did not bother us.

But getting rid of their nests was not as easy as George thought it would be. He put the ladder against the wall and carefully made his way across the planks towards the nests with the prepared stovepipe in his hand. The hornets spied him first, and in a burst of profanity he threw the stovepipe out the open window and jumped to the floor, madly swatting at the furious enemy. He ran outside and flailed at them with his cap and arms. When they finally went back to see what damage he had done to their nests, he was already starting to swell in spots and moan

237

with the pain. For days his face was badly swollen. This was a warning for me and the children to stay clear of them. But we found out that the best time to get rid of them is at night as they are not active then. Kerosene poured into their nest after dark will kill them and discourage others from rebuilding in that spot. They were strictly a daytime pest. I could write many pages on this family's experience with hornets during the next few years. The neighbors became so used to seeing at least one of us with a lumpy jaw or an eye swollen shut that they would automatically say, "Baking soda will ease the pain," or "Try mud on it. That will reduce the swelling." So one time when our old cow, Inez, swung her head while I was tying her up and hit me on the forehead, raising a huge lump, our neighbor said, "Have you tried vanilla on that hornet bite?"

The next afternoon the men went to Bjorkdale to meet the train that was bringing our stock and machinery — and our dogs. How glad they were to see us and we were just as glad to see them. It was surprising what a difference it made to have our animals with us. All at once I felt that it would be home after all.

The next months were busy ones to be sure. There was the house to winterize, wood to take out for winter, feed to be found and brought home for the cattle. Here we were discouraged a bit by some of our neighbors telling us that prairie cattle would die on swamp hay. The well had to be cleaned out and a school found for our son who was ready for that step in his life. We were still on relief cheques and would be for a year. We also were to receive a clothing cheque in November for forty dollars. This was the allotment for four people for one year. As George intended working in the bush during the winter months most of the cheque would be used for warm clothing for him.

And so began the first of more than twenty-five years in a vastly different way of life. Two years after we left, the prairie made a come-back and the old-timers were glad they had stayed. They had many years of work behind them to sustain them over a period such as the "dirty thirties." For us — well, it's hard to say. We didn't have anything to lose by moving out, but still there is a bit of the hills in my blood, and sometimes in my dreams I can hear the coyotes howling and the ice cracking on the slough on a bitterly cold night. But this has been home for a long time, and who knows — if I were to move away from here I would likely miss many things too!

238

# 17   Relief Administration in Saskatoon During the Depression

*by Alma Newman*

DEPRESSION, drought, dust, and grasshoppers are the words which usually come to mind first in considering Saskatchewan history during the 1930's. The province was simultaneously subjected to the ravages of two unrelated phenomena, a world-wide economic depression and a prolonged period of drought, which combined to provide the blackest period in its history. The coincidence of depression with drought meant that the province suffered to a considerably greater extent than any other in Canada. The Royal Commission on Dominion-Provincial Relations discovered at the end of the period that the average per capita income in Saskatchewan fell by seventy-two percent, a decrease twice that of Nova Scotia,[1] and that the financial burden of the depression was five times that of Ontario and the Maritimes.[2] Moreover, while in most provinces the low ebb of depression had been reached by mid-1933, the worst years for Saskatchewan inhabitants were 1937-1938. Thus the suffering endured by the province during this period was both prolonged and intense.*

The responsibility for the provision and administration of relief in the urban municipalities of the province lay with the local authority. The provincial City and Town Acts had made these units of government responsible for health, police, fire, and street-illumination services. In addition the urban municipality had the duty of providing certain services for the protection of human life. These included the prevention and control of disease, the maintenance of hospitals, the provision of medical care or assistance to indigent persons, and direct relief to inhabitants.[3] In normal years, revenues enabled the urban municipality to fulfill these functions satisfactorily. However, the depression caused

*This article is based in part on an unpublished master's thesis by the author entitled "Urban Relief Administration in Saskatchewan in the Depression." The thesis was submitted in 1969 to the College of Graduate Studies, University of Saskatchewan, Saskatoon Campus. The article originally appeared in *Saskatchewan History* for spring, 1969.

the number on relief to increase dramatically, and costs rose proportionately. In 1936, the cities in the province advanced eighty-three times as much relief as they had in 1927.[4]

Obviously municipal finances could not bear these burdens. If unemployment relief became too great a strain, the municipality would appeal to the provincial government for assistance. Similarly in times of acute distress, the province could seek Dominion aid. However, throughout the whole depression decade, unemployment relief was considered to be primarily a local responsibility and problem. Financial help from the provincial and federal governments was offered only on an emergency basis. Both senior governments disclaimed the responsibility of administering relief in the average urban centre and refused to contribute towards administration costs. Saskatchewan municipalities and the provincial government constantly urged that the federal government should organize and finance relief, and initiate a scheme of national unemployment insurance. Throughout the whole decade, however, the federal government insisted that the administration of relief was a municipal responsibility. A letter to a Saskatchewan relief recipient in 1939 illustrates this point:

> The Dominion Government while assisting the Province of Saskatchewan, do not administer the granting of assistance to individuals. This is the responsibility of the Municipality in which you reside, who must decide to whom, to what extent and under what conditions assistance shall be granted.[5]

The fact that urban municipalities were held responsible for relief, combined with the hope that the depression would not last for long, meant that all Dominion and provincial assistance was considered to be on a temporary basis. Hence relief policies in the 1930's consisted of a veritable patchwork quilt of yearly enactments, followed by Dominion-provincial and provincial-municipal agreements, at annual or monthly intervals. Posterity has almost universally condemned the way in which the problem of relief was tackled. The Rowell-Sirois Commission concluded in 1938: "It is clear there was no co-ordinated or carefully planned relief policy in Canada in the Depression."[6] The governments simply adopted whatever method existed for dispensing temporary relief and "extended it *ad infinitum*."[7]

Prior to 1934 the Dominion government contributed a fixed percentage of relief costs. After September of that year a system of monthly grants-in-aid was instituted. The province was left to determine what proportion of municipal relief costs would be paid from this grant. Each branch of government tried to extract a greater portion of relief costs from the others. The constant interaction between the federal, provincial, and municipal governments and the attempt to shift responsibility from one authority to another meant that the average relief recipient was totally confused as to who exactly was in control. Numerous recipients referred to the system as that of "passing the buck," while an individual closely concerned with their problems contended that a "vicious system of shirking responsibility was instituted."[8]

Relief adminstration becomes even more complicated when the different types of relief and the various categories of recipient are considered. Fundamentally two types of unemployment relief could be administered by an urban municipality — public-works schemes created to absorb the unemployed, and direct relief, which consisted of the provision of the necessities of life: food, fuel, clothing, and shelter. The former of these methods was undoubtedly the more desirable, since it kept relief recipients in useful work. It was also far more expensive to operate than direct relief. Both labor and material costs had to be paid. In a prolonged period of depression it was not financially viable. Public-works schemes were, therefore, generally abandoned after 1932, when it was apparent that the depression was no temporary aberration. Direct relief was resorted to on an ever-increasing scale.

Normally four classes of relief recipient could be distinguished in a Saskatchewan urban municipality: residents; transients; the physically fit, single, homeless unemployed; and the physically unfit, single, homeless unemployed. The urban municipality was financially responsible for the relief of its bona fide residents only. These were persons who had a defined period of self-sustaining residence in the locality. Initially this was a six-month period. After September, 1934, the residence qualification was changed to twelve consecutive months. In 1936 it was altered further to twelve cumulative months in a three-year period. Transients were persons without residence qualifications. They were granted relief at the expense of the federal and provincial governments. The Dominion and provincial governments shared the costs of the relief of the single, homeless unemployed; the physically unfit were cared for in the urban centres, and the fit received relief in federal-government camps specially created for the purpose.[9] Although the municipality bore the burden of relief costs for bona fide residents only, it had to pay administration costs and medical expenses for both the unfit, single, homeless unemployed and the transients relieved through its offices by the Dominion and provincial governments. This proved a source of continual dissatisfaction to the municipality, and eventually some changes were instituted.

To the urban municipality the relief problem was a practical one requiring action. To those in need, the question of relief was neither constitutional, nor political, nor economic, nor administrative. It was simply a matter of where the next meal was coming from. A study of the relief problems in Saskatoon illustrates how the problems faced by an urban municipality were handled.

Initially in Saskatoon relief was directly controlled by the city council, working through the relief department, which consisted of a relief officer, assistants, and investigators. As the depression deepened and the numbers on relief increased, it became impractical for the council to superintend relief administration so closely. In the first half of 1932 it was estimated that at last fifty percent of all council meetings had been taken up with the consideration of relief problems. Moreover, the number of meetings had increased dramatically in this period. To the end of June, 1932, there had been fifty-four meetings compared with thirty-five for a similar period in 1931. Two standing committees, appointed to look after relief matters, had been meeting continuously.[10] Consequently, in October, 1932, the council decided to appoint a separate body, the Civic Relief Board, to superintend the administration of relief and investigate any complaints. The board consisted of eight persons: seven citizens and the mayor. They were appointed by the resolution of the council and had to submit a monthly report on the relief situation in the city to the council. The initial life of the board extended until June, 1934, after which date a new board was to be appointed annually.[11]

In the first few months of its existence the Civic Relief Board was allowed to determine various aspects of relief policy in Saskatoon. One of the primary concerns of the board was to keep relief expenditure to the minimum. In an early meeting it endorsed a policy of requiring relief recipients to repay the city for any assistance given, whether in kind or cash.[12] A little later the board asked the *Star-Phoenix* to insert a news item requesting all citizens who had any information concerning families who should not be on relief to pass it along to the board for investigation.[13] The board organized itself into a series of special committees, each one responsible for an aspect of relief policy. One of the most important of these committees was the one in charge of the relief store which the city operated. On the recommendations of this committee, changes were made in the commodities sold in the store. The board functioned in close association with the relief officer, who made a weekly report at meetings.

Relief administration under the Civic Relief Board, however, engendered dissatisfaction and unrest among recipients. The taxpayers on the board naturally adopted a parsimonious attitude towards relief. Their main concern was to keep costs down. Their penchant for thriftiness manifested itself when they decided that eggs and lard were to be supplied at the butcher's shop which the city operated, instead of at the relief store, and charged on the recipient's meat voucher. On this occasion the value of grocery vouchers decreased while there was no appropriate increase in the value of the meat voucher.[14] A month after this innovation the *Star-Phoenix* commented that "there was a 'feeling'" between the Board and the unemployed which should not exist."[15] In October, 1933, the council took stronger control of relief affairs when it passed a resolution enabling it to lay down policies which the relief board was *forced* to implement.[16]

Ill feeling, however, persisted. Consequently when the question of the appointment of a new board for June, 1934, came up, it was decided that the board should be discontinued and council once again took a direct charge of relief administration. Although control of direct relief reverted to the council, a Relief Appeal Board was created to lighten the burden of relief at council meetings. This board was to consist of the mayor and city commissioner serving in an advisory capacity, and two members of the council, serving on a rotating basis for three months each. The board was to meet every two weeks to hear the appeals of relief recipients who had complaints.[17] By 1935 the number of complaints necessitated weekly meetings.

As an appeal tribunal, the board could not hear delegations. This was a perpetual source of annoyance to the local associations of the unemployed with which Saskatoon abounded, since these could not represent their members. The most frequent appeal coming before the board was for reinstatement on relief. The appeal had to be made in writing forty-eight hours before the scheduled board meeting. This was to enable the relief officer to refresh his memory of a certain case history, so that he could make a verbal report to the board to enable it to judge the validity of the appeal. In many respects, the relief officer became the most important person at meetings, since it was invariably his department which had cut the appellant off relief. He was usually able to provide adequate justification for his action. Consequently few appeals appear to have succeeded.

Saskatoon was one of the few cities to have an appeal board. Its advantages were appreciated by T. M. Molloy, who described the board as follows to a complainant:

> The Appeal Board has among its members the Mayor, some aldermen, all persons not only capable of weighing all the facts in connection with such case, but who are interested in seeing that the relief costs of Saskatoon are kept to the minimum, and that persons on relief shall not suffer for want of assistance.

> I was informed, therefore, that when a case has run the gauntlet of the Relief officials, and has been reviewed by the Appeal Board, we may rest assured that no undue hardship will be caused any family by reason of the policy which has been adopted by the City.[18]

In actual fact the advantages of the appeal board were largely illusory. The unemployed could air their grievances to an official body, but few succeeded in reversing the original decision of the relief department. Throughout the later 1930's the unemployed associations asked that relief recipients be allowed to appeal their case *before* relief was discontinued, so that unnecessary hardship would be avoided. One such organization was advised that its request could not be acceded to as it was "impracticable to carry it out."[19]

It was inevitable that there would be complaints about relief. It was impossible to satisfy everyone. However, conditions in Saskatoon must have been particularly bad or the unemployed extremely well organized to account for the numerous associations of unemployed which grew up there in the 1930's. In 1936 there were nine such organizations in existence: the Ex-Service Men's Welfare Association, the Fraternal and Protective Association of Saskatoon, the Single Men's Association for the physically unfit, the Single Workers' Union, the Married Transient Relief Association, the Transient Relief Association, the Disabled Veterans' Association, the Transient Emergency Association, and the National Transient Union.[20] Unrest and organized associations on a substantial scale were to be expected in a large city. Saskatoon certainly experienced troubles in relief administration, most of which were concentrated round the person of the relief officer.

Both F. G. Rowlands, relief officer until 1933, and G. W. Parker, his successor, appear to have been unpopular figures. This was perhaps to be expected since the relief officer had wide powers, especially relating to the giving of relief on an emergency basis and to newlyweds or the partners of a common-law marriage.[21] Rowlands and Parker were both ex-army officers, who were occasionally lacking in "the milk of human kindness,"[22] although they were excellent administrators and organizers.

As early as December, 1930, relief recipients were urging that Rowlands be replaced. The Saskatoon Unemployed Association appeared before the council complaining that light and water had been cut off from the unemployed and suggesting that "in so far as the Mayor has continually stated that no one in Saskatoon should be permitted to go hungry, then we ask that Mr. Rowlands be replaced by a relief officer who will carry out the Mayor's wish."[23] The council refused to comply with this request at this stage. But a crisis was reached in June, 1933, when the Civic Relief Board discussed the lack of harmony between the various branches of the relief department, particularly the investigating department, and the relief officer. It was decided that three members of the board should interview Rowlands and request that he apply for two-month's leave of absence with pay, after which he was expected to resign.[24]

Rowlands lost no time over this. On June 2 the *Star-Phoenix* contained a small article on the resignation of the relief officer after fourteen years of service with the city. No reasons were given, but it was understood that there had been "disagreement with the Civic Relief

244

Board on matters of policy."[25] Rowlands' resignation was met by many protests, and the council was inundated with demands from citizens and relief recipients for a judicial inquiry. From this it must be inferred that the officer had been satisfying numerous relief recipients and applicants. However, he was not reinstated. G. W. Parker, who had started work in the relief office only the previous February, was appointed as his successor. Parker held the position of relief officer throughout the remainer of the 1930's.

Ironically, Parker seems to have been the cause of more troubles than his predecessor. Apparently he was an extremely vigilant relief officer who liked to initiate and control every action in his department. From the vast amount of correspondence and cases he dealt with, he was obviously dedicated to his job. However, he tended to apply relief rules and regulations with the precision of an army officer, rather than the understanding of a welfare officer. As one observer pointed out to the provincial Minister of Municipal Affairs, "Mr. Parker may be very efficient but he is also very severe and the constant complaint is that he refuses to see people."[26]

Recipients were cut off relief with insufficient warning and not allowed to discuss their case with the relief officer. One recipient complained that he had been working part-time with the approval of Parker to supplement his relief allowance. One day he went for his relief order and was informed that his relief had been discontinued. He naturally objected to the lack of adequate warning. Of all persons, relief recipients were the least likely to have any extras stored up for times of hardship. The appeal board met only once a week. As the angry complainant pointed out, "five or six days were a long time to starve."[27] Fortunately the board reinstated this man on relief. Parker's action, therefore, appears doubly reprehensible.

As his experience in relief administration increased, Parker seems to have become overconfident. From 1936 onwards the Provincial Bureau of Labour and Public Welfare had great difficulty in stopping the Saskatoon relief officer from challenging their rulings. Molloy wrote to City Commissioner Andrew Leslie in early April, pointing out that one cause of much trouble and inconvenience lay in the fact that Parker refused to take cognizance of the 1934 relief agreement which gave the bureau the right to determine government relief cases and stated that such cases were to be kept on relief until instructions were given to the contrary. No decision was to be made until after investigation, and this rested to a large extent on the facts supplied by the relief officer. In this respect Parker rendered splendid service; his investigations and reports were thorough and prompt. However, the bureau reserved the right to interpret and apply regulations.[28] Parker had apparently been telling people to return to certain municipalities, when he had received instructions from Molloy allowing them relief in Saskatoon as transients.

The relief officer failed to distinguish between the individual recipient and the municipality responsible for his welfare. Parker preferred to punish the relief recipient by refusing him relief, rather than granting assistance and recovering expenditure from the municipality concerned. In spite of numerous suggestions and warnings from the provincial relief department, Parker continued to pursue what he himself considered to be the right policies, even though they contravened the official ones. In October, 1937, a memorandum sent to W. Dawson, director of relief, indicated that difficulties were still being experienced with the Saskatoon relief officer:

> A terrific lot of correspondence could be avoided if Mr. Parker would give us the same co-operation as the relief officers of other cities are giving. Mr. Parker never considers a letter answered until it is answered in the way in which he himself wants it answered.[29]

Occasionally Parker became incensed at one particular individual, and concentrated his anger and annoyance on that person. Frank Eliason, the secretary of the United Farmers of Canada in Saskatoon, wrote frequent letters to Regina complaining about Parker's action in certain cases and asking for information. Invariably the provincial government referred these enquiries to Parker, who resented Eliason's constant intervention and tactics. Eliason was regarded by Parker as "nothing but an agitator, a trouble-maker" who apparently had "no idea of common courtesy with regard to minding his own business."[30] The fact remains, if relief had been administered with less severity, there would have been fewer complaints.

Parker appeared to adopt a very superior attitude towards aliens on relief. One Austrian on relief who wanted to return to his homeland applied to the Saskatoon relief officer for assistance. Considerable difficulty was experienced in assessing this case, especially as the applicant's English was poor. At one stage Parker dismissed the man as a foreigner and a liar and wrote to Molloy: "I certainly have no intention while I am in this position to have any unnaturalized Austrian defy the regulations of this office."[31] This type of prejudice again manifested itself in a later case. One Austrian complained to the provincial government about Parker's attitude towards aliens. Parker defended himself as follows:

> I somewhat resent from an Austrian the inference that I have not a right to express my opinion. In fact, as no doubt you are aware, I have not hesitated, nor do I intend to hesitate to express my opinion with reference to such people as Mr. [X].[32]

However, although the relief officer was entitled to express his own opinions, he was essentially the servant of the city council and for the most part he had to implement its policies.

Parker's anti-alien bias was really only the negative aspect of Saskatoon's policy of favoring British subjects or those in process of naturalization when recruiting men for employment in public-works schemes. A resolution was passed to this effect at a council meeting in June, 1930.[33] The city's initial response to the unemployment problem of the thirties was public-work projects. They hoped in this way to avoid placing large numbers of people on direct relief.

In the summer of 1930 the city embarked on a program of sewer-and-water construction and sidewalk- and lane-paving. This relieved the unemployment situation considerably and hopes were expressed that the problem had been surmounted.[34] Fall, however, brought increases to the relief rolls, and it was estimated that 1,500 persons would need assistance. Consequently the city made an agreement with the provincial and federal governments, whereby a new subway was built and a system of storm sewers completed between October, 1930 and June, 1931.

In 1931 the city sought permission to build a bridge as a relief measure at an estimated cost of $850,000. The Dominion agreed to pay $350,000, the province $140,000 and the city the remainder.[35] The Broadway Bridge should have been completed by May 1, 1932. Extensions were granted until August 15, 1933.[36] After this date there were no federal-government-sponsored public-works schemes in the city until 1939, when the Liberal government initiated a scheme whereby the federal and provincial governments paid for labor costs and the city paid for material expenditure other than the purchasing of tools and equipment. The project consisted of recovering stones from the river bed, and grading and ditching underdeveloped streets.[37] Once again the preference for naturalized citizens was apparent, with a resolution passed by council giving them first preference in the work.[38] However, for the greater part of the 1930's relief in Saskatoon was mostly direct aid.

Initially the City of Saskatoon adopted the policy of making relief recipients sign an undertaking to repay relief advanced to them. This was abandoned in November, 1933.[39] Thereafter relief recipients on the whole had neither to work for, nor repay, relief. The only recipients who had to perform any regular labor were those who had insufficient casual earnings to pay their own electric light and water bills. These cases were credited with forty cents an hour for work done, which usually consisted of woodcutting, and the city then paid their bills. In December, 1936, approximately 300 men were working eight hours each month to pay off their bills.[40] The only time the city demanded work from certain relief recipients was as a punishment for breaking regulations or making false declarations.[41]

247

Direct relief consisted of the provision of food, fuel, clothing, shelter, and medical care, although these were not necessarily given to all relief recipients. Each case was judged individually and relief given according to need. There were three main classes of relief recipients in Saskatoon throughout the 1930's: bona fide residents, transients, and families receiving relief at the expense of other municipalities through the civic relief office. The largest groups were the transients who were the responsibility of the Dominion and provincial government, and residents who were the direct responsibility of the city. Although financial responsibility for their relief lay in different hands, both groups were served by the same relief adminstration. Ideally there was to be no discrimination of treatment between transient and resident unemployed.[42]

Because of the scale on which relief was required in the city, the major preoccupation of the council was that costs should be kept to a minimum and that adminstration should be efficient. An early problem was to find a satisfactory method of providing food since most relief recipients needed this form of relief. Until 1932 the city used the relief system which had existed since 1921. By this, recipients were given food vouchers specifying certain goods. These were exchangeable at any local store. Unfortunately the system was open to abuses. Some merchants, in order to procure and keep trade, allowed recipients to purchase commodities other than those specified and made a profit by overcharging the unemployed for this privilege.[43] Moreover, there was the detailed work of issuing relief orders, receiving and approving accounts, and keeping extensive records in the city treasurer's department. In the 1920's when relief had been a minor concern in the city, this scheme had worked well. In the 1930's it was inadequate, cumbersome, and costly. Consequently, as a possible solution, council considered the idea of operating its own relief store at which all relief recipients would be required to deal. The city would keep costs to a minimum by being able to purchase goods wholesale. Corruption would similarly be reduced. The idea of establishing a relief store was discussed frequently at council meetings in 1931 and a committee set up to study the details.

Inevitably there was considerable opposition to the idea from both relief recipients and local merchants. The local Grocers' and Butchers' Retail Merchants Association claimed that it was unfair to their bona fide, tax-paying members for the city to set up in competition and monopolize the relief trade, which was becoming a major part of their livelihood. Moreover, it was an added injustice to merchants who had extended credit to relief recipients. If the city operated its own store, they would never be repaid. Petitions were presented to the council indicating that the establishment of a civic relief store would throw merchants on relief too.[44] The relief recipients argued that the store would prevent them from buying their goods at the cheapest price and would eliminate the small element of choice which the open voucher system had given them. The Saskatoon Unemployed Association suggested that cash relief or "face cash value" cards negotiable at any store would be more satisfactory to their members.[45] The council was prepared to try this. As a result, from November 13, 1931 onwards, grocery orders were issued to any store requested by the recipient and stated merely the total value of the order, allowing more freedom in the selection of food.[46]

However, the innovation did not work to the satisfaction of the council. After further discussion and investigation it decided to establish a civic relief store, which opened on June 1, 1932.[47] The council reverted from the food quotas on a cash basis to a commodity basis once more. In determining the list of foods and quantities, regard was had to the size of the family on relief and the ages of any children. Food was classified on a unit basis, with a maximum of sixteen units allowed to any one family. In terms of food, three units covered five quarts of milk, fifty cents worth of meat, and ten loaves of bread. A man and his wife were allowed eight units and would use the remaining five to purchase tea, sugar, vegetables, fruit, soap, and matches.[48] Throughout the history of the store, continual changes were made in the lists of available commodities, and numerous attempts were made by the Civic Relief Board to ensure that diets were properly balanced.

All modifications did little to alter the simple fact that relief recipients and local merchants did not like the store. The former complained of the lack of choice, the high prices, and poor quality of goods sold. Moreover, there was no delivery system. In the cold winter months, recipients from all over the city had to trudge to the store for their groceries, instead of being able to go to their nearest shop. One alderman asked if free street-railway transportation-passes might be given to families taking the larger orders to enable them to make their journey home more easily.[49] The request was refused.[50] Between May, 1932 and October, 1934, when the store was abolished, the council received regular delegations from relief recipients and local merchants asking for the abolition of the store. It was described as having been established "on a straight pattern from Soviet Russia."[51] This accusation marked a reversal of roles on the part of the administration and the unemployed. The former was accused of Soviet tactics instead of the latter. The Fraternal and Protective Association declared that Saskatoon was the only city in North America where the unemployed were subjected to such "demoralizing and degrading treatment" and contended that they were being treated "as convicts or a herd of cattle."[52] The city conceded that there was some ground for complaint. However, the store was continued because, for the city, it was cheap, efficient, and easily controlled. Substantial savings were made by wholesale buying. In

249

December, 1932, the net gain was estimated to be $1,122.54, and in January, 1933, $1,038.75 was expected.[53] This money could be used to defray other relief expenses.

Dissatisfaction with the store reached such a peak in early 1933 that the provincial government decided to investigate. This decision was sparked by the activities of A. W. Wylie, a grocer of the city, who sent an outspoken letter to Premier J. T. M. Anderson alleging that the city was making a profit on the relief store and charging the federal and provincial governments for this. As Wylie pointed out, "The time of depression has passed by, and in its place we have something very, very much more to be dreaded 'oppression' — think it over."[54]

Simultaneously the government was receiving a series of protest letters and petitions about relief conditions in Saskatoon. The unemployed sent a memorandum of their grievances, which included an attack on the Civic Relief Board and its practices. There was alleged discrimination in the distribution of food from the relief store. Some recipients had to line up; others received their supplies at home. The unemployed asked for cash or open vouchers, claiming that they could purchase on average twenty to twenty-five percent more from their allowances if this was granted. The Civic Relief Board was seen as the sole cause of all trouble, and violence was threatened if reform was not forthcoming.

One of the most interesting pieces of information sent to the government was contained in a secret supplement to a petition from the Fraternal and Protective Association of Unemployed Citizens and Taxpayers. This warned that the personnel of the relief board were a "number of the deepest died old Grits of Saskatoon, who will stop at nothing to bring discredit on the present administration."[55] The board was supposedly trying to get the unemployed to blame the government for the poor conditions in the city. These political ramifications to the discontent may have hastened government intervention. Whatever the motivation, the Saskatchewan Relief Commission, at the suggestion of Premier Anderson, organized an investigation into Saskatoon relief administration. The Reverend Thomas Bunting was appointed to go to Saskatoon on March 14, 1933 to meet the unemployed and attend a meeting of the relief board.

Bunting found conditions in Saskatoon far from satisfactory. People were not getting the proper proportions of food, and many went without for one and a half days before they received their next allowance. Bunting suggested that an open-voucher system for issuing food supplies might prove more satisfactory. The relief board appeared quite unconcerned about conditions and harsh in their application of relief regulations. Bunting went so far as to suggest that they be dismissed.[56]

This suggestion was never acted upon. The government could not interfere so directly in civic affairs. However, it could exert more subtle pressures to make way for a policy change in respect to the relief store. In September, 1933, T. M. Molloy attended a meeting of the relief board at which he informed the members that the policies of the federal and provincial governments with regard to relief in future were that "purchases should be through the regular channels of trade and that wherever possible Canadian goods should be purchased in preference to those from foreign countries."[57] Eventually the council decided to allow relief recipients to purchase their groceries through regular trade channels. As of October 1, 1934, the relief store ceased to exist.

Before closing the store council held a plebiscite, in September, 1934, among the relief recipients to ascertain the preferred method of obtaining food relief. There were three choices offered by the plebiscite: the relief store, the open-voucher system, or cash. Three hundred and sixteen out of the 371 persons voting favored the cash system, and so the council implemented this policy. Although this undoubtedly pleased the majority of recipients, there remains the strange fact that only ten percent of the approximately 3,400 eligible to vote in the plebiscite took advantage of the opportunity to register their opinions. The *Star-Phoenix* suggested that the relatively small vote was due to effective picketing by the Saskatoon Worker's Associations. "Throughout the week every effort was put forth by the pickets to prevent the jobless from voting. 'There is a catch in it,' was the contention of more than one who took part in the boycott."[58] This would indicate that the relationship between the unemployed and the civic authorities was far from harmonious.

The institution of a cash allowance for food relief proved permanent and gave greater satisfaction to recipients and merchants than any previous system. Initially, money equivalent to the retail price of food required was given to recipients once each week. In February, 1935, the council decided to give allowances once every two weeks to give the recipient greater purchasing power and to economize in relief adminstration costs.[59] From January, 1936 onwards, Saskatoon used the Dominion government *Labour Gazette* retail-price index to calculate food costs and determine increases or decreases in allowances. There were periodic manifestations of discontent as to the amount of money being given. In June, 1939, the Central Council of Unemployed and Welfare Associations requested that the food allowance be increased fifty percent for a two-week period on the occasion of the visit of King George and Queen Elizabeth, "to enable those on relief to properly observe this momentous occasion."[60] This request was refused. On the whole, however, the unemployed in Saskatoon found cash relief preferable to any other. Some recipients boasted about conditions in the city after October, 1934. Lorne Lynne, when addressing the Prince Albert strikers in 1936, informed them that their standard of living was forty percent below

Saskatoon's and that the Saskatoon unemployed had never struck because they were able to make the city authorities see their point of view.[61]

If the city had solved the problem of food relief, there still remained three other important aspects of policy to be dealt with: clothing relief; the relief of the single, homeless unemployed; and the relief of non-resident families in the city. Dissatisfaction with the provisions made for clothing came from numerous relief recipients. The problems of providing adequate clothing appeared only gradually. Most relief families could manage for a while. Eventually the day would come when there were no more cast-offs, and the family was forced to seek the assistance of the Clothing Relief Bureau. Initially clothing relief in Saskatoon was organized by six service clubs. They worked on a voluntary basis and collected money and secondhand clothes, wherever they could. As the numbers on relief increased and the need for clothing became more pressing, the clothing bureau, which the service clubs had formed, sought financial assistance from the city council. On July 1, 1931, they asked for, and received, a sum of $165 a month to pay the salaries of officials needed to operate the bureau on a full-time basis.[62] This grant was increased to $200 per month in October of the same yar.[63] In the early years of the depression the bureau had complete control of clothing relief and it appears that its administration was efficient. It evolved into a miniature relief department with a filing system to keep track of every case in the city. The bureau served as a clearing house for the good works of service clubs, women's organizations, churches, and private individuals. In addition the bureau co-operated with the relief department officials and did follow-up work that they had neither the time nor the resources to undertake.[64] Eventually, however, it was necessary for the council to make a regular grant to the bureau for the purchase of clothing, bedding, and footwear, on a scale large enough to meet the demands of relief recipients. Greater contributions necessitated stronger central control. Consequently in June, 1933, the bureau was abolished and a Clothing Relief Depot established, administered by the city rather than the service clubs.

Inadequate clothing relief was a perpetual complaint of the Saskatoon unemployed. Toward the end of the 1930's they demanded that a cash grant, equivalent to twenty-five percent of the food allowance, be given to enable relief recipients to purchase their own clothes rather than being forced to take the offerings of the civic depot. Women especially resented the garments given to their families. The regimentation of the styles, the cheap quality of the material, and the lack of variety were the standard complaints. Matters reached such a state in mid-1938 that a delegation of women appeared before the council asking for cash for clothing. They contended that the use of the clothing depot was placing a large percentage of citizens in a position of pauperism, reducing their initiative and self-respect. The most deplorable fact was that children were "growing up in this system of regimentation and general drabness" and being forced into "inferior positions" since their clothing marked them as children on relief.[65] In the following year the council sought the permission of the provincial government to give the desired cash for clothing.[66] The government agreed and on April 24, 1939, the Clothing Relief Depot was abolished.[67]

The relief of single, homeless men was another problem which concerned the city for the greater part of the depression decade. Before government-sponsored-and-operated camps were set up in 1932 to absorb the physically fit, single unemployed, civic authorities were responsible for their care. In the winter of 1930 such large numbers of homeless men had gathered in Saskatoon that it was decided to establish a relief camp at the Exhibition Grounds where board and sleeping accommodation could be provided.[68] The provincial government promised to pay two-thirds of the cost of relief provided in this way and in addition to furnish the camp with cooking utensils, stoves, and blankets. P. J. Philpotts, an ex-army officer, was made superintendent of the camp, and a local doctor was appointed to treat all the sick and to visit each day for parade inspection.[69]

From its opening the camp was a seedbed for discontent in Saskatoon. Even after November, 1932, when control of the camp passed to the provincial government,[70] there were constant complaints about conditions and agitation to hasten improvements.

Philpotts threatened to resign in April, 1932, because a band of radical agitators was preventing the maintenance of camp order and discipline, and co-operation from the Saskatoon police force was not forthcoming.[71] In February, 1933, the situation again became acute. A certain radical leader, appropriately called Sam Scarlett, was cited as the mainspring of unrest. He had apparently just been released from jail and was inciting the camp inmates to revolt. Posters urging "Slave Camp Workers" to wake up and organize, and cartoons depicting the Saskatchewan Relief Commission as a fat man pulling the balloons of greed, incompetence, ignorance, and prejudice were circulated. Discontent continued throughout March. An investigation by the Saskatchewan Relief Commission revealed that the radical element in the camp was well organized and in close contact with various groups of unemployed in the city of Saskatoon itself. In May, the inmates staged a demonstration when attempts were made to transfer fifty of them to the camp at Regina. One police officer died as a result of injuries suffered during the demonstration. It was decided to transfer the men remaining in the Saskatoon camp to a federal relief camp at Dundurn, and the Saskatoon camp was closed on June 30.[72] The city was thereby relieved of the headache of caring for large numbers of the physically fit, single unemployed.

There remained the problem of caring for the unfit persons in this category. Initially the city paid fifty cents per day for the board and room of such persons. In January, 1937, a request was made that this allowance be increased to sixty cents. Considerable dispute ensued as the provincial government refused to contribute eight percent of this total, since only fifty cents were allowed to the single unfit persons in Moose Jaw and Regina. Mayor R. M. Pinder pleaded the city's case for the increase by pointing out that the extra money paid helped to keep boardinghouse owners off relief, since recipients could afford to pay a little extra for their accommodation.[73] The government, therefore, agreed to the increase. Later in the year recipients asked that this money might be paid in cash rather than voucher form. The council granted this request,[74] and the relief of such persons caused little further trouble to Saskatoon administrators in the 1930's.

The problem of relieving families from other municipalities and transients became particularly acute in the second half of the 1930's. In some respects these were the most difficult problems with which Saskatoon relief officials had to deal. In June, 1935, the relief officer reported to the appeal board that the number of applications for relief from persons moving into the city from country points was increasing daily.[75] When such a person or family applied for relief, the relief officer referred the case to the provincial government so that it could determine where responsibility lay. While investigation was carried out, relief was administered at the expense of the government. If the enquiry revealed that the family was transient then relief was continued at the expense of the government. If another municipality was found to be responsible then negotiations began for the return of the family. Some municipalities, rather than having persons returned, preferred to relieve their indigents by reimbursing the city in which they were residing. Occasionally a family would refuse to return, in which case relief might be given at the expense of the government. Thus it was a possible, and indeed a frequent, occurrence for persons with residence qualifications in another municipality to be receiving relief in Saskatoon.

This situation was a source of perpetual annoyance to the civic officials. The reason for this was essentially financial. Outsiders were using the facilities of the city, their children were being educated there, and yet they were paying no taxes for these privileges. Moreover, such persons affected wage schedules detrimentally. The majority were prepared to accept employment at any rate. As a result local citizens were thrown out of work, wage schedules lowered, and the city's relief bill increased as bona fide residents lost their jobs. In July, 1936, the *Star*

*Phoenix* estimated that there were 600 families from rural points on the city's relief lists.[76] This figure seems exaggerated since in December of 1937 official records put the total at 44 families.[77]

Saskatoon was also faced with the problem of families moving into the city from rural points, maintaining themselves for the necessary twelve months and then applying for relief. In October, 1936, approximately thirty families of this kind applied for relief and Relief Officer Parker expressed his concern to Molloy: "This is a most serious situation, and more especially due to the fact it is fast approaching our winter season."[78] One particular case annoyed the relief officer. A certain family had applied for relief twelve months previously and been refused because of the lack of residence qualification. Somehow they managed to sustain themselves in the city for one year and reapplied. There was no alternative but to grant them relief.[79] Occasionally the rural municipality from which such people came was suspected of assisting them to go to Saskatoon. In December, 1937, Parker reported to the council in regard to two families who had apparently moved in from rural areas in order to establish themselves for relief. It was believed "in each case the rural municipalities in question not only encouraged but actually assisted the family to come into Saskatoon."[80]

It must be pointed out that the corollary of objecting to the relief of outsiders in Saskatoon was to require all indigent persons, who were the responsibility of the city, to be returned there for relief. This policy was rigorously followed. No exceptions were allowed. Occasionally this could result in hardship. A woman who had been in the Prince Albert sanatorium and whose parents lived in that city was informed on her recovery that she must return to Saskatoon for relief.[81] The harshness of this can be understood if the costs of relief and the numbers affected are considered. Relief officials were forced to keep strictly to policies because of the scale on which relief was required.

Direct relief costs in 1930 were exceptionally low. They increased sixty times in 1931, doubled in 1932 and doubled again between 1932 and 1934, which was the peak year of expenditure for the city. Costs decreased a little in 1935, and fell by almost one-half in 1936, with slight rises in 1937 and 1938, followed by a continuous and fairly swift decline. The reason for relief costs during the first half of the decade being more expensive to the city was that prior to December, 1936, Saskatoon paid a third of such expenditure. After that date the city financed only twenty percent. Consequently, the total cost of direct relief in 1934 and 1937 was almost the same, approximately $700,000.

However, even though civic contributions decreased in the later 1930's, the actual final cost of relief to Saskatoon remained high. This was due to the system adopted to finance relief: debenture issues on a large scale. Interest costs increased over four times between 1933 and

1940, and the burden of debt continued to trouble the city into the 1950's. Moreover, even though the city's share of actual direct relief decreased for 1935 onwards, it still had to pay total medical and adminstration expenses. These were substantial sums, approximately $30,000 dollars per year. Adminstration expenses alone in 1939 were almost twenty times the cost of direct relief in 1930.

Saskatoon experienced the same difficulties financing relief as Prince Albert. Provincial payments were continually in arrears. In December, 1937, the province owed the city $196,000.[82] A constant complaint was the amount of interest which the city had to pay in order to borrow money to finance the provincial and federal shares of relief, pending payment. In 1938 the council pointed out that it had cost the city $4,218.26 more for interest than it would have done if reimbursement had been made within two weeks of rendering Saskatoon's account.[83] Similarly in 1939 the council drew to the attention of the provincial government the fact that it had cost the city some $7,100 for bank interest on money borrowed in 1938 to finance the province's share of unemployment relief. The delay in payment, apart from the expense, embarrassed the city since it endangered its ability to secure further temporary bank advances.[84]

Throughout the 1930's the city council urged that the senior governments should assume larger shares of relief costs. In December, 1932, it suggested that the city's share be limited to a sum not exceeding ten percent of the total, which should include administration and hospital costs.[85] Similarly in 1936 the council reaffirmed this plea, although it suggested that a preferable state would be for the whole burden of unemployment relief to be removed entirely from the urban municipality.[86]

As the depression deepened the actual per capita cost increased as did the number of people on relief. During 1933 and 1934 the average cost per person per month increased by $.50, and it was estimated that it would increase by $1.70 in 1935. In December, 1930, 1,610 people were on relief or about 4.5 percent of the population. In 1931 the number on relief had increased to 2,500.[87] In 1932 this figured doubled.[88] In 1933 and 1934 about eighteen percent were receiving aid. No statistics are available for 1935 to 1937 but the numbers on relief probably remained about the same. In 1938 there was a decline, with an estimated fourteen percent on relief, and after this date the numbers continued to decline.

A study of urban municipalities suggests that the depression does not present a one-sided picture of dust, drought, and despair. While the economic depression and consequent unemployment brought misery, suffering, and humiliation to many, it also provided an environment in which charity and community spirit could operate. The work of local service clubs and generous individuals helped to make life for those on relief a more acceptable state.

The numbers in Saskatchewan on relief varied between ten percent and twenty-five percent in the urban areas. In Saskatoon between fifteen and eighteen percent were on relief, a figure perhaps not as high as might have been expected. The main problem for the urban centres was not so much the depth of depression as the duration. While unemployment was considerable, it was in the second half of the decade that suffering became most widespread and intense. The early thirties had exhausted municipal finances and administration. In some centres more difficulties were encountered in the second half of the decade in the form of complaints, political agitation, and transient invasions. Saskatoon, however faced its greatest problems in the first half of the decade, but after the institution of cash relief in 1934 most bona fide residents were satisfied. Rural dwellers seeking assistance and the lack of finances to cope with relief requirements were problems that affected all urban centres.

In all urban centres studied the need for relief was large enough to necessitate the creation of special committees or positions. The key figures in relief administration were the relief officer and his staff, since they came into daily contact with recipients and had to enforce the various aspects of relief policy. Although the relief officer was essentially the paid servant of the city or town, his attitude made a great difference to the way in which relief was administered. Relief officers inevitably were targets for criticism and abuse. In Saskatoon, the added effects of an unco-operative relief officer were apparent.

The war and increased prosperity reduced the number on relief rolls, but since there always are those in need, a number of changes arose out of the experience of the thirties. Relief procedures in Saskatoon and Prince Albert showed signs of being the most progressive since cash relief is the method favored by the Saskatchewan welfare department today. When the C.C.F. party formed the government in 1944, certain changes were made in the social services of the province. On November 2, 1944, the formation of a new department, the Department of Social Welfare, introduced a fresh approach to welfare problems. Social and economic security were recognized as the fundamental right of every human being. Welfare became a financial, consultative, and preventative service, not a matter of handing out money each week to the needy. Because such a program demanded long-range planning, an efficient province-wide administration was created with eight branch offices established in urban centres from which services could operate.

Direct relief turned into a social-aid program and became a joint municipal-provincial undertaking. The municipality was still in charge of relief administration and the residence laws were still operative.

257

However, there was more central control and organization than there had been in the 1930's. The attitude toward indigents was finally changing: "the Public assistance dollar has been one of the most important investments made in the Canadian way of life. It has enabled children to live in a large measure of normal life, with parents, home, church, school and recreation."[89] Welfare remained solely a municipal-provincial function until March, 1956, when an agreement was reached between the federal and provincial governments, by which the former was to pay forty-five percent of social aid and the municipality twenty-five percent. Further changes were introduced by the provincial Social Aid Act of 1959 by means of which the municipalities were reimbursed each month by the province for all social aid issued and were billed annually for a per capita share of province-wide costs. "This, in effect, did away with the residence requirement inherent in the age old concept that relief of the poor was a local responsibility."[90]

# Notes

## Big Bear

1 Peter Farb, *Man's Rise to Civilization As Shown By The Indians of North America...*, (New York, 1968) pp. 150-51.

2 See A. D. Fisher, "Culture Conflict on the Prairies: Indian and White," *Alberta Historical Review* (Summer, 1968) pp. 24-26, 29; and C. Wissler, "The Influence of the Horse in the Development of Plains Culture," *American Anthropologist* 16 (1914): 1-26.

3 For example R. G. Forbis, "The Old Woman's Buffalo Jump, Alberta," National Museum of Canada Bulletin No. 180 (1960); and D. J. Lehmer, "The Plains Bison Hunt — Prehistoric and Historic," *Plains Anthropologist* 8, No. 22 (1963).

4 Quoted in William T. Hornaday, "The Extermination of the Merican Bison, with a Sketch of its Discovery and Life History," *Smithsonian Report for 1887,* p. 527.

5 Robert M. Lowie, *Indians of the Plains,* (New York, 1963), p. 225.

5 Diamond Jenness, *Indians of Canada,* (Ottawa, 1932), pp. 316-317; and Alvin M. Josephy, *The Indian Heritage of America,* (New York, 1968), p. 70.

7 Ibid., pp. 49-50; and Frank G. Roe, *The North American Buffalo: A Critical Study of the Species in its Wild State,* (Toronto, 1951), p. 656.

8 *Canadian Sessional Papers* (C.S.P.), 1871, no. 23.

9 Public Archives of Canada (P.A.C.), C.O. 42/698, William Butler, *Report* on the North-West, March 10, 1871.

10 *Ibid.,* C.O. 42/715, Robertson Ross, *Report* on the North-West Provinces and Territories, December 10, 1872.

11 *Ibid.*

12 Quoted in W. G. Hardy, *From Sea Unto Sea,* (New York, 1960), p. 288; see also Paul Sharp, *Whoop-Up Country: The Canadian American West, 1865-1885,* (Minneapolis, 1955).

13 For details see George F. G. Stanley, *The Birth of Western Canada,* (Toronto 1936), pp. 199, 429-430.

14 *Ibid.,* p. 193.

15 G. F. G. Stanley, *Louis Riel,* (Toronto, 1963), p. 254.

16 *C.S.P.,* 1876, no. 9, Speech of Big Bear, Fort Carlton, October 23, 1875; and

259

Alexander Morris, *The Treaties of Canada with the Indians,* (Toronto, 1880), p. 174.

17  For Treaty Six (1876) see *Copy of Treaty Six Between Her Majesty the Queen and the Plain and Wood Cree Indians and Other Tribes of Indians at Fort Carlton, Fort Pitt and Battle River with Adhesions,* (Ottawa, 1964); and Canada: *Indian Treaties and Surrenders,* 1680 to 1890, vol. 2 (Ottawa, 1905), pp. 35-44.

18  W. B. Fraser, "Big Bear, Indian Patriot," *Alberta Historical Review,* Spring, 1966, p. 5.

19  Quoted in Paul Kane, *Wanderings of an Artist . . . ,* (Toronto, 1859), pp. 130-131.

20  Roe, *op. cit.,* p. 362; from *Palliser Journals,* pp. 54, 57, 84.

21  Quoted in Sir Cecil Denny, *The Law Marches West,* (Toronto, 1939), p. 27

22  Roe, *op. cit.,* p. 413; from Sam Steele, *Forty Years in Canada,* p. 87.

23  Roe, *op. cit.,* p. 401.

24  *Ibid.,* pp. 412-413.

25  *Ibid.,* p. 474.

26  Stanley, *Birth,* pp. 222-223; Stanley, *Riel,* p. 255.

27  Quoted in Roe, *op. cit.,* p. 358.

28  P.A.C., C.O. 42/757, Lorne to Beach, Sept. 4 and 29, 1879; and Dewdney to the Sup. Gen., Dec. 31, 1880 in C.S.P. VIII (1881), no. 14.

29  Hornaday, *loc. cit.,* p. 509.

30  Quoted in Stanley, *Birth,* p. 224.

31  Quoted from *Fort Benton Record,* Montana, May 7, 1880, in Stanley, *Riel,* p. 256.

32  See *Copy of Treaty Six, op. cit.,* pp. 14-15; Little Pine and Lucky Man Adhesions, Fort Walsh, July 2, 1879.

33  *Saskatchewan Herald,* March 24, 1879.

34  Stanley, *Riel,* p. 238.

35  Denny, *op. cit.,* pp. 127, 262ff.

36  C.S.P., 1882, no. 6, Dewdney to Sup. Gen., January 1, 1882.

37  *Canada: Indian Annuities,* 1882, pp. 55-56; P.A.C., *Record Group 10, Western (Black File) Series: Indian Affairs,* Indian Dept. file 29506-3; *Copy of Treaty Six, op. cit.,* p. 16; Big Bear Adhesion, Fort Walsh, Dec. 8, 1882.

38  Roe, *op. cit.,* p. 485.

39  *Ibid.,* p. 487.

40  Hornaday, *loc. cit.,* pp. 526-527; pp. 480-481.

41  Another minor cause of buffalo extermination was disease. In the upper North Saskatchewan foothills for example, a germ (Hemorrhagic Septicaemia), which flourishes in unclean areas, polluted the drinking places, and a number of buffalo died. See Roe *op. cit.,* Appendix J.

42  P.A.C., Black File, vol. 309, Memo of Indian Commissioner, Maple Creek, June 12, 1883.

43  *Indian Annuities* 1883, pp. 78-79; Big Bear's band paid at Fort Pitt, Oct. 2, 1883.

44  P.A.C., Black File, vol. 10042, Rae to Dewdney, Battleford, Nov. 10, 1883.

45  *Canada, House of Commons Debates,* 1885, p. 3143.

46  P.A.C., Black File, Ind. Dept. file 5307. Rae to Hayter Reed, Asst. Ind. Commissioner, Battleford, Jan. 17, 1883.

47  *C.S.P.,* 1885, no. 153, Crozier to Irvine, Battleford, June 25, 1884.

48  *Ibid;* Black File, vol. 309, Report of July 24, 1884.

49  See Stanley, *Birth,* pp. 285-288.

50  Quoted in *Ibid.,* p. 290. Supposed speech of Big Bear, Fort Carlton, July 31, 1884; and P.A.C., Black File, vol. 309, Rae to Dewdney, Prince Albert, July 29, 1884.

51  P.A.C. Black File, vol. 309, Dickens to officer commanding at Battleford, Fort Pitt, Jan. 12, 1885.

52  *Ibid.,* Report of Agent Bygr, Blackfoot Crossing, Feb. 25, 1885.

53  Quoted in William B. Cameron, *The War Trail of Big Bear,* (London, 1926), p. 48.

54  *Ibid.,* p. 72, 75,; Stanley, *Birth,* p. 339.

55  *Ibid.,* p. 75; and, Theresa Gowanlock, *Two Months in the Camp of Big Bear,* (Parkdale, 1885), p. 29.

56  Stanley, *Birth,* p. 341.

57  Cameron, *op. cit.,* pp. 111-112.

58  Quoted in Joseph Hicks, "With Hatten's Scouts in Pursuit of Big Bear," *Alberta Historical Review,* (Summer, 1970), p. 17.

59  For the Battle of Frenchman's Butte, May 28, 1885, see Stanley, *Birth,* p. 374; Cameron, *op. cit.,* pp. 189-193.

60  Cameron, *op. cit.,* p. 221.

61  Stanley, *Birth,* p. 379; *Indian Annuities 1885 and 1886,* pp. 277-281; pp. 251-255.

62  P.A.C., Black File, vol. 309, Williams to Dewdney, Battleford, Jan. 25, 1888.

## Colonization Companies in the 1880's

1   V. C. Fowke, *The National Policy and the Wheat Economy,* (Toronto: University of Toronto Press, 1957), p. 8.

2   The Mackenzie government had passed legislation in 1874 providing for the sale of public land at a reduced price to individuals willing to undertake the settlement of public lands. See the *Statutes of Canada,* 37 Vict., cap. 19, sec. 14.

3   Canada, Order in Council, Dec. 23, 1881, Ref. 39, 503.

4   *Canada, House of Commons Debates,* April 21, 1882.

5   *Canada, Sessional Papers,* 1883, no. 84.

6   Public Archives of Canada (P.A.C.), Department of the Interior, Dominion Lands Branch, no. 39658, H. I. Eberts to the Minister of the Interior, Dec. 31, 1881.

7   *Ibid.,* 42513, Messrs. Vahey and Wilkinson to the Minister of the Interior.

8   P.A.C., J. A. Macdonald Papers, vol. 312, Manning to J. A. Macdonald, Oct. 14, 1881.

9   *Ibid.,* vol. 261, W. B. Scarth to J. A. Macdonald, May 10, 1881.

10  P.A.C., Dominion Land Branch, 44447, Copy of the Agreement.

11  *Toronto Globe*, March 13, 1883.

12  *Ibid.*, March 30, 1882.

13  *Ibid.*, Feb. 22, 1882.

14  P.A.C., Dominion Lands Branch 41201, A. T. Drummond to the Minister of the Interior, Dec. 20, 1882.

15  Description by a Mounted Policeman named Donkin, quoted in B. Peel and E. Knowles, *The Saskatoon Story* (Saskatoon: M. East, 1952), p. 17.

16  *Toronto Globe*, Nov. 2, 1883, James Armstrong to the editor.

17  P.A.C. Dominion Lands Branch, 65600, R. Stephenson to W. Pearce, Nov. 14, 1883.

18  *Ibid.*, 93232, D. L. Macpherson to J. A. Macdonald, June 5, 1885.

19  Expecting to collect $10,000,000.00 through the sale of land to private enterprises, the government obtained only $756,507.02.

20  P.A.C., Dominion Lands Branch, 83083, vol. I, Thomas White to the Privy Council, June 22, 1886.

21  *Census of Canada*, 1891, p. 369; from a total of 25,515 people in 1881, the population of the North-West Territories increased to 66,699 in 1891.

22  *McPhillips Alphabetical and Business Directory of the District of Saskatchewan* (Qu'Appelle, N.W.T., 1888), p. 83.

23  *Toronto Globe*, March 29, 1884.

24  *The Prince Albert Times and Saskatchewan Review*, "Our Climate," Feb. 13, 1885, p. 2.

25  *Report of the Royal Commission on Dominion-Provincial Relations*, Book I (Ottawa, 1940), p. 53.

26  *The Winnipeg Daily Times*, Jan. 26, 1884.

27  W. L. Morton, *Manitoba, A History* (Toronto: University of Toronto, 2nd edition, 1967) p. 210.

28  *Ibid.*, p. 212.

29  *Canada, Sessional Papers*, 1885, no. 13, p. X.

30  *Ibid.*, no. 13, p. XI.

31  *Toronto Globe*, Dec. 27, 1881.

32  *Canada, Sessional Papers*, 1892, no. 13, p. XI.

33  P.A.C., Dominion Lands Branch, 41345, Memorial from J. Armstrong to the Minister of the Interior, Dec. 20, 1884.

34  A. S. Morton, *History of Prairie Settlement*, vol. II of C. Martin, *Dominion Lands Policy*, (Toronto: Macmillan, 1938), p. 279.

35  P.A.C., Dominion Lands Branch, 41345, J. Armstrong to the Minister of the Interior, Dec. 20, 1884.

36  *Ibid.*, 41202, vol. I, Petition from the Directors of the Montreal and Western Land Company to Governor-General Landsdowne, n.d.

## Edgar Dewdney and the Aftermath of the Rebellion

1  Archives of Saskatchewan, (A.S.), Macdonald Papers, Duplicates of the Dewdney, Macdonald correspondence held in the Public Archives of Canada, Ottawa, Letter, Dewdney to Macdonald, Aug. 7, 1885, p. 346.

2  Glenbow-Alberta Institute Archives, Calgary, Dewdney Papers, 1861-1926, vol. III, Aug. 17, 1885, p. 570.

3  A.S., Macdonald Papers, Reed to Dewdney, Aug. 31, 1885, p. 367.
4  Glenbow, Dewdney Papers, vol. III, Dewdney to Macdonald, April 12, 1886, p. 614.
5  North-West Territories, *Journals of the Council of the North-West Territories of Canada, 1877-1887.* (Hereafter cited as *J.C.N.W.T.*), Session of 1885, p. 61.
6  A.S., Macdonald Papers, Telegram, Dewdney to Macdonald, Nov. 16, 1885, p. 403.
7  *Ibid.*, Dewdney to Macdonald, Nov. 18, 1885, p. 409.
8  *Ibid.*, Telegram, Dewdney to Macdonald, Nov. 18, 1885, p. 404.
9  *Ibid.*, Dewdney to Macdonald, June 6, 1885, p. 318.
10 *Ibid.*, p. 317.
11 *Canada, Sessional Papers,* (hereafter cited as *C.S.P.),* 1880, no. 4, "Annual Report of the Department of Justice," Letter, June 20, 1885, p. 12.
12 Canada, Debates of the House of Commons, (hereafter cited as *D.H.C.),* 1886, March 8, Mr. Thompson (Antigonish), Minister of Justice, p. 61.
13 *Ibid.*
14 G.F.C. Stanley, *The Birth of Western Canada* (Toronto: University of Toronto Press, 1960), p. 378.
15 A.S., Macdonald Papers, Dewdney to Macdonald, Aug. 13, 1885, p. 350.
16 *Ibid.*, J. H. McElree to Dewdney, Aug. 11, 1885, p. 352.
17 *Ibid.*, Dewdney to Macdonald, Aug. 23, 1885, pp. 361-62.
18 *J.C.N.W.T.*, Session of 1885, p. 59.
19 *Prince Albert Times,* Feb. 12, 1886.
20 A.S., Macdonald Papers, Dewdney to Macdonald, June 19, 1885, pp. 276-77.
21 *Ibid.*, Reed to Dewdney, June 23, 1885, p. 287.
22 *Ibid.*, p. 298.
23 *Ibid.*, Father Lacombe to Dewdney, July 11, 1885, pp. 330-31.
24 *Ibid.*, Telegram, Dewdney to Macdonald, July 27, 1885, p. 340.
25 *D.H.C.*, July 16, 1885, p. 3433.
26 Dewdney Papers, vol. VI, Memo, Reed to Dewdney, July 20, 1885, pp. 1419-20.
27 *C.S.P.*, 1887, no. 6. "Annual Report of the Department of Indian Affairs," p. 106.
28 *Ibid.*, 1889, no. 16, "Annual Report of the Department of Indian Affairs," p. 124.
29 Glenbow, Dewdney Papers, vol. VI, Memo, Reed to Dewdney, July 20, 1885, p. 1416.
30 A.S., Macdonald Papers, Dewdney to Macdonald, Aug. 7, 1885, p. 348.
31 Glenbow, Dewdney Papers, vol. VI, Memo, Reed to Dewdney, July 20, 1885, p. 1420; *Ibid.*, vol. V, Reed to Dewdney, Aug. 29, 1885, p. 1239.
32 *C.S.P.*, 1886, no. 4, "Annual Report of the Department of Indian Affairs," p. 141.
33 *Ibid.*
34 *Ibid.*
35 Glenbow, Dewdney Papers, vol. V, Reed to Dewdney, Aug. 29, 1885, pp. 1232-33.

36  A.S., Macdonald Papers, Dewdney to Macdonald, Aug. 13, 1885, p. 351.
37  *Ibid.,* p. 350.
38  Glenbow, Dewdney Papers, vol. V, Reed to Dewdney, Aug. 29, 1885, p. 1235.
39  *C.S.P.,* 1886, no. 4, "Annual Report of the Department of Indian Affairs," p. xiv.
40  Glenbow, Dewdney Papers, vol. VI, Father Scollen to Dewdney, Jan. 5, 1886, p. 1739.
41  A.S., Macdonald Papers, Dewdney to Macdonald, Aug. 13, 1885, p. 350.
42  Sir C. E. Denny, *The Law Marches West* (London: J. M. Dent, 1939), p. 228.
43  A.S., Macdonald Papers, Dewdney to Macdonald, Sept. 25, 1885, p. 382.
44  *Ibid.,* Dewdney to Macdonald, Aug. 25, 1885, p. 361.
45  *Ibid.,* Sept. 25, 1885, p. 381.
46  Glenbow, Dewdney Papers, vol. III, Strange to Macdonald, Sept. 29, 1885, p. 574.
47  A.S., Macdonald Papers, Dewdney to Macdonald, June 23, 1885, p. 284.
48  *Ibid.,* Rae to Dewdney, June 15, 1885, pp. 285-86.
49  A. R. Turner, ed., "The Letters of P. G. Laurie," *Saskatchewan History* 14, no. 2, p. 51.
50  Norma Sluman, *Poundmaker* (Toronto: Ryerson Press, 1967), p. 278: *Fifty Years on the Saskatchewan,* (Battleford: Canadian North West Historical Society, 1929) pp. 158-59.
51  A.S., Macdonald Papers, Dewdney to Macdonald, June 23, 1885, p. 284.
52  *Ibid.,* Lacombe to Dewdney, July 11, 1885, pp. 330-32.
53  *Prince Albert Times,* Dec. 4, 1885.
54  A.S., Macdonald Papers, Telegram, Dewdney to Macdonald, July 7, 1885, p. 324; *Ibid.,* Dewdney to Macdonald, June 6, 1885, p. 267.
55  *Ibid.,* Telegram, Dewdney to Macdonald, May 20, 1885, p. 248.
56  *Ibid.,* Rae to Dewdney, June 15, 1885, pp. 285-86.
57  *Ibid.,* Macdonald to Dewdney, July 5, 1885, p. 323.
58  *Ibid.,* Telegram, Dewdney to Macdonald, July 7, 1885, p. 324.
59  *Ibid.,* June 28, 1885, p. 320.
60  *Ibid.,* July 15, 1885, p. 326.
61  *Ibid.,* Dewdney to Macdonald, July 16, 1885, p. 328.
62  *D.H.C.,* 1885, July 16, p. 3455.
63  A.S., Macdonald Papers, Dewdney to Macdonald, Aug. 7, 1885, p. 345.
64  *Ibid.,* Aug. 13, 1885, p. 353.
65  *Ibid.,* Aug. 25, 1885, p. 364.
66  Glenbow, Dewdney Papers, vol. VI, H. Langevin to Dewdney, Oct. 20, 1885, pp. 1432-33.
67  A.S., Macdonald Papers, Dewdney to Macdonald, Nov. 2, 1885, p. 389.
68  *Ibid.,* p. 390.
69  *Ibid.,* Nov. 6, 1885, p. 393.
70  *Ibid.*
71  Glenbow, Dewdney Papers, vol. VI, Report of James Anderson to Dewdney, Nov. 25, 1885, p. 1523.
72  *Ibid.,* Anderson to Dewdney, Nov. 29, 1885, p. 1525.

73  *Ibid.,* Dec. 3, 1885, p. 1528.
74  *Ibid.,* Dec. 8, 1885, p. 1529.
75  *Ibid.,* Dec. 16, 1885, p. 1535.
76  *Ibid.,* p. 1536.
77  *Prince Albert Times,* Dec. 25, 1885.
78  Glenbow, Dewdney Papers, vol. III, Dewdney to Macdonald, Dec. 29, 1885, p. 591.
79  *Ibid.,* vol. V, McKay to Dewdney, Jan. 8, 1886, p. 1261.
80  *Ibid.,* O. Richette to I. G. Baker & Co., Feb. 1, 1886, p. 1275.
81  *Ibid.,* pp. 1275, 1278.
82  *Ibid.,* vol. III, Dewdney to Macdonald, p. 606.
83  *Ibid.,* p. 607.
84  *Ibid.,* March 30, 1886, p. 611.
85  *D.H.C.,* May 4, 1886, p. 1075.
86  *Ibid.*
87  Glenbow, Dewdney Papers, vol. V, Dewdney to Macdonald, Jan. 26, 1886, p. 1266.
88  *Ibid.,* p. 1269.
89  *Prince Albert Times,* Feb. 12 and 26, 1886.
90  Glenbow, Dewdney Papers, vol. III. The reply to the telegram dated February 15, 1886, was on North-West Territory paper, but only the corrections were in Dewdney's handwriting, p. 599.
91  *Ibid.*
92  *D.H.C.,* 1886, May 13, p. 1257.
93  *Ibid.,* May 4, p. 1075.
94  *Ibid.,* May 13, p. 1258.
95  Glenbow, Dewdney Papers, vol. V, Reed to Dewdney, March 1, 1886, p. 1284.
96  *D.H.C.,* 1886, April 12, p. 684.
97  Glenbow, Dewdney Papers, vol. III, Dewdney to Macdonald, April 12, 1886, p. 613.
98  *C.S.P.,* 1887, no. 6, "Annual Report of the Department of Indian Affairs," p. 112.
99  Paul Sharp, *Whoop-Up Country* (Minneapolis: University of Minnesota Press, 1955), p. 128.
100 *C.S.P.* 1888, no. 15, "Annual Report of the Department of Indian Affairs," p. 188.
101 *Ibid.,* p. 197.

## The Bell Farm

1  *Regina Leader,* February 18, 1913, obituary of W. R. Bell.
2  *The Western World,* January, 1891, vol. I, p. 10.
3  *Regina Leader,* February 18, 1913.
4  Archives of Saskatchewan (AS), Department of the Interior, File no. 5617880.
5  *Ibid.*
6  Canada, Order-in-Council, No. 427, April 3, 1882.

7  *Ibid.*

8  *Ibid.*

9  Public Archives of Canada, (P.A.C.), R.G. 15, Bla, vol. 38. Copy of the agreement between the Qu'Appelle Valley Farming Company and the Canadian Pacific Railway, June 27, 1882.

10  A.S., *Department of the Interior*, File no. 5617880.

11  *Ibid.*, and By-Laws of the Company, published in 1882, which confirmed the allotment of 5,000 shares of stock to the twenty-four original subscribers and the allotment of 1,000 shares of paid-up stock "in payment in full for the services of William R. Bell and John Northwood, in purchasing the lands of said Company and in completing the organization thereof, . . . to be issued and delivered to the said parties in such amounts as they may in writing mutually agree upon and direct." (P.A.C., R.G. 15, Bla, vol. 38, By-Laws of the Qu'Appelle Valley Farming Company.)

12  A.S., Department of the Interior, File no. 5617880, President's Report, Qu'Appelle Valley Farming Company, 1883.

13  *Ibid.*

14  P.A.C., R.G. 15, Bla, vol. 38, President's Report, 1884.

15  A.S., Department of the Interior, File no. 5617880, J. Gordon to A. M. Burgess, June 13, 1883.

16  *Canada, Sessional Papers*, 1884, No. 12, pp. 11-12. Report of J. Gordon, Dominion Lands Agent, Regina, December 31, 1883.

17  Interview reprinted in *The Leader*, March 24, 1885.

18  *Regina Leader*, January 17, 1884.

19  *Ibid.*, February 21, 1884.

20  *Canada, Sessional Papers*, 1885, no. 13, pp. 13-14.

21  *Qu'Appelle Vidette*, October 16, 1884.

22  *Canada, Sessional Papers, 1886*, no. 8, p. 23.

23  A.S., Department of the Interior, File No. 5617880, Boyle to White, November 13, 1885.

24  *Qu'Appelle Vidette*, October 16, 1884.

25  Boyle to White, *op. cit.*

26  *Regina Leader*, January 17, 1883.

27  *Ibid.*, September 25, 1884.

28  Boyle to White, *op. cit.*

29  *Winnipeg Free Press*, October 25, 1902.

30  A.S., Department of the Interior, File. no. 5617880.

31  Canada, Order-in-Council, no. 350, March 2, 1885.

32  *Ibid.*

33  *Regina Leader*, March 24, 1885, Interview reprinted from the *Pall Mall Gazette.*

34  *Qu'Appelle Vidette*, March 5, 1885.

35  *Nor-West Farmer* (Winnipeg), vol. 4, no. 1, March, 1885; vol. 4, no. 3, May, 1885.

36  *Qu'Appelle Vidette*, April 1, 1886.

37  *Regina Leader*, May 18, 1886.

38  *Qu'Appelle Vidette*, August 5, 1886.

39 L. Murray, "St. John's College, Qu'Appelle, 1885-1894," *Saskatchewan History* (1958).

40 *Qu'Appelle Vidette,* January 2, 1885.

41 *Ibid.,* June 18, 1885.

42 *Canada, Sessional Papers,* 1886, no. 80, p. 22.

43 *Ibid.,* p. 26.

44 *Ibid.,* p. 28.

45 *Qu'Appelle Vidette,* February 4, 1886.

46 Boyle to White, *op. cit.*

47 The Qu'Appelle Farming Company may not have fulfilled its original agreement with the Canadian Pacific Railway Company, as the purchase price of $1.25 per acre was conditional on cultivating and cropping one-half the land within five years. (P.A.C., R.G. 15, Bla, Vol. 38.).

48 Saskatchewan Department of Agriculture, Lands Branch, Township General Register.

49 *Supreme Court (S.C.), N.W.T.,* no. 22, 1888.

50 *Qu'Appelle Vidette,* March 25, 1886.

51 *Canada, Sessional Papers,* 1887, no. 5, p. 25: Notice of Incorporation of Bell Farm Company Limited.

52 Regina Land Titles Office, Indenture registered August 18, 1886.

53 See, for example, Instrument 1725, deeding land from Qu'Appelle Valley Farming Company to Bell Farm Company "in consideration of $1.00," registered August 18, 1886, Regina Land Titles Office.

54 *S.C., N.W.T.,* no. 22, 1888: Sworn statement of Duncan McArthur, President, Commercial Bank of Manitoba, April 7, 1888.

55 Regina Land Titles Office, Indenture registered August 18, 1886.

56 Instrument 306, registered July 14, 1884, Regina Land Titles Office, confirms mortgage dated February 14, 1884, to Lord Elphinstone *et al.*

57 Regina Land Titles Office, Indenture registered August 18, 1886.

58 *Ibid.*

59 *Qu'Appelle Vidette,* December 12, 1885.

60 *Ibid.,* January 14, 1886.

61 *Ibid.,* February 11, 1886.

62 *Ibid.,* July 15, 1886.

63 *Ibid.,* April 14, 1887.

64 *Ibid.,* March 15, 1888.

65 For example, see *S.C., N.W.T.,* no. 22, 29-32, 37, 56-57, 71-79, and 127 of 1888.

66 *S.C., N.W.T.,* no. 22, 1888.

67 *S.C., N.W.T.,* no. 327, 1889. The liquidator was still winding up affairs of the company in 1902 (See *S.C., N.W.T.,* no. 327, 1902.)

68 *S.C., N.W.T.,* no. 92, 1888. Bell had still not recovered this sum in 1902 when he assigned the benefits of the judgement to a creditor (See *S.C., N.W.T.,* no. 327, 1902.)

69 *Regina Leader,* August 7, 1888.

70 *The Western World,* vol. 1, no. 1, January, 1891.

71 *Qu'Appelle Vidette,* June 6, 1889.

72 *Winnipeg Free Press,* October 25, 1902.

73 Certificate of Ownership to William Lewis Boyle, October 22, 1889, and to Canadian Co-operative Colonization Company, November 11, 1889, and Indenture between Bell Farming *[sic]* Company and William Lewis Boyle, registered in Regina Land Titles Office.

74 Application of Wm. R. Bell to register lands, filed May 30, 1890, and Certificates of Ownership to William Robert Bell and to the Canadian Co-operative Colonization Company, registered May 31, 1890, Regina Land Titles Office.

75 *Ibid.,* Transfer to Lord Brassey registered September 3, 1895.

76 *Ibid.,* Application of Wm. R. Bell.

77 See below, p. 59. Note that Bell acquired 320 acres of H.B.C. land, the south half of 26-18-13 W 2nd (See *S.C., N.W.T.,* no. 120, 1896) which would bring the confirmed acreage of his farm to 13,000 acres.

78 *Western World, op. cit.*

79 Cited in *Regina Leader,* July 30, 1889.

80 *Western World, op. cit.*

81 *Qu'Appelle Vidette,* September 14, 1893.

82 *Ibid.,* October 17, 1895.

83 *S.C., N.W.T.,* no. 71, 1896: Scottish American Investment Co., Ltd. vs. William Robert Bell, Statement of Claim.

84 *Ibid.,* Judgement.

85 *e.g.,* The Bank of Ottawa, in the amount of $547.04 *(S.C., N.W.T.,* no. 304 of 1896).

86 *Qu'Appelle Vidette,* May 28, 1896.

87 *Ibid.,* and also proprietor of Indian Head Hotel, cited in *The Leader,* April 2, 1896.

88 See *S.C., N.W.T.,* no. 304 of 1895 and no. 71 of 1896, Writs of Execution.

89 He was then, or later, a "large stockholder" in the Edmonton Coal Company *(The Leader,* February 18, 1913.)

90 At Brockville, Ontario in 1902, Sees *S.C., N.W.T.,* no. 327 of 1902.

91 T. Petty, *Echoes of the Qu'Appelle Lakes District,* p. 40.

## Yorkton During the Territorial Period, 1882-1905

1 A. Lalonde, "Settlement in the North-West Territories by Colonization Companies 1881-91" (unpublished Ph.D. Thesis, Laval University, 1969), pp. 85-87.

2 *Ibid.,* pp. 85-87, as cited from *The Mail,* February 2, 1882.

3 *Canada, Debates House of Commons,* April 21, 1882, p. 822.

4 *Ibid.,* April 21, 1882, p. 803.

5 *Yorkton Enterprise,* July 14, 1955.

6 Department of the Interior, Dominion Lands Branch, file no. 41345, Transcript of the Official Report on the York Farmers' Colonization Company, by R. Stephenson, Inspector of Colonization Companies, 1883.

7 *Ibid.*

8 Archives of Saskatchewan (A.S.), Department of Militia and Defense of the Dominion of Canada, Report upon the Suppression of the Rebellion in the North-West Territories and Matters in Connection therewith in 1885.

Appendix no. 2. Report on Organization of Company and Erection of Stockade at Yorkton, Major T. C. Watson to Major-General Middleton, January 20, 1886.

9  Lalonde, *op. cit.*, p. 203, as cited from the Department of the Interior, Dominion Lands Branch. File no. 83083, Memorial presented to the Minister of the Interior, December 23, 1884.

10  J. R. A. Pollard, "Railway and Settlement (1881-1891)," *Saskatchewan History* 1 (Summer 1948): 17.

11  A.S., [Z. M. Hamilton] "Colonization in Saskatchewan," Papers of the Saskatchewan Historical Society 68:54.

12  J. B. Hedges, *Federal Railway Land Subsidy Policy of Canada* (Cambridge, Mass.: Harvard University Press, 1934), p. 71.

13  A. S. Morton and C. Martin, *History of Prairie Settlement and 'Dominion Lands' Policy* (Toronto: Macmillan, 1938), pp. 284-286.

14  *Ibid.,* p. 302.

15  *Ibid.,* p. 303.

16  One source declares that the railway company encountered difficulties in construction. A more likely explanation, though, deals with the question of the location of the track which was to be laid. The land at the end of the steel would increase substantially in value. Possibly, the railway was reluctant to terminate their line on property that did not belong to them and, therefore, shifted the line four miles so that it would terminate on the railway's land.

17  A.S., Minute Book: Unincorporated Town and Village, 1894.

18  R. W. Murchie, *Agricultural Progress of the Prairie Frontier* vol. 5, (Toronto: Macmillan, 1936), pp. 51, 58.

19  Editorial, *Yorkton Enterprise,* July 26, 1901.

20  N. I. Gold, "American Migration to the Prairie Provinces of Canada 1890-1934" (unpublished D.Phil. thesis, University of California, 1933), pp. 131-132.

21  V. J. Kaye, *Early Ukrainian Settlements in Canada 1895-1900* (Toronto: University of Toronto Press, 1964), pp. 296-297, as cited from Public Archives of Canada, Department of the Interior, File no. 73855, Report *re* Galician and other colonies 1896-1901, Speers to Frank Pedley, Superintendent of Immigration, January 31, 1899.

22  S. Holt, *Terror in the Name of God* (Toronto: McClelland and Stewart, 1964), p. 35.

23  *Yorkton Enterprise,* July 6, 1933.

24  *Ibid.,* May 17, 1900.

25  *Regina Daily Standard,* August 4, 1906.


# The Harmony Industrial Association:
## A Pioneer Co-operative

1  For source materials for this article the author is indebted to the following: Mr. J. E. Paynter, Vancouver, British Columbia; Mr. R. W. Huston, Regina, Saskatchewan; and Mr. Harry J. Perrin, Spy Hill, Saskatchewan. The correspondence of these gentlemen with the author and with the provincial

archivist has been deposited in the Archives of Saskatchewan and is cited hereinafter as the J. E. Paynter Papers. The text of the constitution of the Harmony Industrial Association which is reprinted here is from the only known copy now in existence, in the possession of Mr. Perrin.

2   J. E. Paynter Papers.

3   *Ibid.*

4   *Prospectus of the Harmony Industrial Association (Co-operative System),* Birtle, Manitoba [1895], p. 19.

5   J. E. Paynter Papers.

6   See *Moosomin Spectator,* November 14, 1895.

7   The name appears to have been derived from the word "harmony" in the title of the association.

8   J. E. Paynter Papers.

9   61 Vict. Chap. 31, sect. 3, assented to June 13, 1898. See also discussion of the amendment in *House of Commons Debates,* 1898, cols. 5937-38.

10  See Report of the Deputy Minister of the Interior in *Canada Sessional Papers,* 1900, Paper No. 13, p. xvi.

11  The text printed here is taken from the copy owned by Mr. Harry J. Perrin of Spy Hill.


## From the Pampas to the Prairies:
The Welsh Migration of 1902

1   R. T. Jenkins, "The Development of Nationalism in Wales," *The Sociological Review* 27 (1935): 163.

2   See David Williams, *A History of Modern Wales* (London, 1950).

3   R. G. Owen, "Michael Daniel Jones," *The Dictionary of Welsh Biography Down to 1940* (London, 1959).

4   See R. Bryn Williams, *Gwladfa Patagonia, The Welsh Colony in Patagonia 1865-1965* (Cardiff, 1965), pp. 15ff.

5   See *London Times,* Sept. 8, 1856, p. 6.

6   Great Britain, *House of Commons Sessional Papers,* 1867, Vol. XLIX, Correspondence respecting the establishment of a Welsh Colony on the River Chubut, in Patagonia. See also Alun Davies, "Michael D. Jones a'r Wladfa," *Trafodion Cymdeithas Anrhydeddus y Cymmrodorion* 1966, part I, pp. 73-87. I am indebted to Mrs. D. G. Hughes, Edmonton, Alberta, for her translation of this article.

7   See Idris Jones, *Modern Welsh History: From 1485 to the Present Day* (London, 1960), p. 275; and David Williams, *op. cit.,* p. 275.

8   E. G. Bowen, "The Welsh Colony in Patagonia 1865-1885: A Study in Historical Geography," *Geographical Journal* 132 (1966): 16-31.

9   Public Records Office, London, Foreign Office records, F. O. 6/263, translation of an agreement between the Argentine Minister of the Interior and representatives of the colonization society.

10  R. Bryn Williams, *op. cit.,* p. 19.

11  Bowen, *op. cit.,* p. 24.

12  *Ibid.* See also interview with Mr. W. E. Davies, Regina, Sept. 1, 1970, in Archives of Saskatchewan, Regina, Sask.

13 Foreign Office records, F. O. 6/263, F. C. Ford to the Earl of Clarendon, April 22, 1866.

14 Great Britain, *House of Commons Sessional Papers,* 1867, Vol. XLIX, R. G. Watson to F. C. Ford, July 10, 1866.

15 R. Bryn Williams, *op. cit.,* p. 41.

16 Alun Davies, *op. cit.*

17 Foreign Office records, F. O. 4/496, W. A. C. Barrington to the Marquis of Lansdowne, April 25, 1901.

18 *Ibid.,* F. S. Clark to the Marquess of Lansdowne, Feb. 22, 1901.

19 H. E. Pritchard, *Through the Heart of Patagonia* (London, etc., revised ed., 1911), p. 37.

20 Public Archives of Canada, Department of Interior, Immigration Branch, File no. 214914, clipping. (These files cited hereinafter as Interior Files).

21 Foreign Office records, F. O. 6/496, Statement of F. Benbow Phillips and Llwyd Ap Iwan, London, Feb. 14, 1899. Ap Iwan was a son of Michael Daniel Jones.

22 *Ibid.,* undated memorandum of a law officer.

23 *Ibid.,* Report by E. Scott on the Welsh Colonies in Chubut, Dec. 15, 1901, p. 5.

24 *Canada, Sessional Papers,* 1893, Paper no. 13.

25 *C.S.P.,* 1898, Paper no. 13.

26 *C.S.P.,* 1899, no. 13.

27 The visitors' report is printed in *C.S.P.* 1901, Paper no. 25, part II, pp. 11-18. It was reprinted and widely distributed in Wales. See also Lewis H. Thomas, "Lloyd George's Visit to the North-West, 1899", *Saskatchewan History* 3, no. 1 (1950): 17-22.

28 W. L. Griffith to J. A. Smart, Interior File no. 34768.

29 Scott, *op. cit.* (See footnote 23).

30 *C.S.P.,* 1903, Paper no. 25. See also Interior File no. 34768, C.P.R. Passenger Traffic Manager to Deputy Minister of Interior, May 13, 1902.

31 Interior File no. 34768, J. Obed Smith to J. A. Smart, April 24, 1902 and April 29, 1902. See also Interior File no. 214914, Smith to F. Pedley, Superintendent of Immigration, July 5, 1902.

32 Interview with Mr. W. E. Davies, Regina, Sask.

33 Smith to Pedley, July 5, 1902, *loc. cit.*

34 *Manitoba Free Press,* Sept. 17, 1902.

35 Interview with Mr. W. E. Davies.

36 Report of the Commissioner of Immigration, Winnipeg, July 1, 1903, *C.S.P.,* 1904, Paper no. 25.

37 Archives of Saskatchewan, School District File no. 807, letter dated Feb. 15, 1904, to Commissioner of Education.

38 Interior File no. 34768, C. A. Magrath to Superintendent of Immigration, Sept. 25, 1901.

## Bannock, Beans, and Bacon:
An Investigation of Pioneer Diet

1 *Prince Albert Times,* January 31, 1883.

2   *Regina Leader,* March 15, 1883.
3   *Saskatchewan History* 1, no. 1, (1947), 6.
4   Mrs. L. M. Purdy, Balcarres, 1883.
5   Mrs. Mary A. Jordens, St. Hubert Mission, 1885.
6   Mrs. Howard Burdett, Golburn.
7   Mrs. Purdy's mother, mentioned earlier.

## Pioneer Church Life in Saskatchewan

*Places and dates used in the footnotes indicate the pioneer address and date of arrival in Saskatchewan of the person whose questionnaire is referred to.*

1   Mr. Louis Demay, St. Brieux, 1906.
2   Miss Clara Hermle, Leofeld, 1903; Mr. Arnold Dauk, Annaheim, 1904.
3   Mr. Hugo O. Bartel, Drake, 1906; Mr. J. L. Zacharias, Rosthern, 1894.
4   Mr. Sydney Chipperfield, Chickney, 1883; Mrs. Edith Stilborne, Pheasant Forks, 1883.
5   Mr. T. E. Allcock, Eastview, 1891.
6   Mr. W. A. Harrison, Meadow Bank, 1906.
7   Mr. William J. Scott, Milestone, 1903.
8   Mrs. William Taylor, Paynton, 1903.
9   Mrs. James Bews, Holbeck, 1906.
10   Mrs. J. L. Smith, Vossen, 1905.
11   Mrs. S. D. Manning, Kenaston, 1907.
12   Mr. Sidney S. May, Togo, 1913.
13   Mr. William A. Harrison, Meadow Bank, 1906.
14   Mr. A. G. Carter, Wadena, 1908.
15   Mrs. Peter McLellan, Clare, 1883.
16   Mrs. William Taylor, Paynton, 1903.
17   Mr. W. S. Rattray, Preeceville, 1887.
18   Mr. Victor C. McCurdy, Moosomin, 1883.
19   Mrs. T. C. Johns, Zelma, 1902.
20   Mrs. Thomas Goldsmith, Whitewood, 1884.
21   Mr. Arthur Wilson, Wiseton, 1904.
22   Mrs. W. S. de Balinhard, Yorkton, 1883.
23   Mrs. Marion Anderson, Moosomin, 1883.
24   Mrs. Joel Anderson, Willowbrook, 1902.
25   Mr. W. S. Rattray, Saltcoats, 1887.
26   Mr. Charles Davis, North Battleford, 1905.
27   Mrs. L. J. Gross, St. Boswells, 1910.
28   Mrs. A. B. Bjerke, Pelly, 1910.
29   Rev. C. B. Kerr, Redvers, 1903.
30   Mrs. John C. Knaus, McGuire, 1906.
31   Mrs. J. R. Aikenhead, Melfort, 1900.
32   Mrs. Peter McLellan, Clare, 1883.
33   Rev. William J. Scott, Milestone, 1906.
34   Mr. George Shepherd, Stalwart, 1908.
35   Mrs. H. J. Kenyon, Pheasant Forks, 1895.
36   Mr. Richard B. Lloyd, Notre Dame d'Auvergne, 1909.

37  Mr. Jacob Smith, Vossen, 1905.
38  Mr. Anton Riederer, Star City, 1901.
39  Mr. Louis Le Strat, St. Front, 1912.
40  Mr. Ole M. Anderson, Neewin, 1903.
41  Miss Gladys Saloway, Halcyonia, 1903.
42  Mr. D. H. Maginnes, MacKinnon (later Ermine), 1906.
43  Mrs. Fannie S. Dunlop, Wild Rose, 1902.
44  Mr. Charles Davis, North Battleford, 1905.
45  Mr. J. L. Zacharias, Rosthern, 1894.
46  Mr. E. E. Lundell, Earl Grey, 1906.
47  Mrs. Marion Anderson, Moosomin, 1883.
48  Mrs. Edna K. Adams, Drinkwater, 1907.
49  Miss Glayds Saloway, Halcyonia, 1903.
50  Mrs. Jean Hill, Carlea, 1911.
51  Mr. Robert Irving, Cumberland, 1904.
52  Mr. John Laidlaw, Grenfell, 1882.
53  Mr. L. V. Kelly, Rocanville, 1909.
54  Mr. Thos. J. Brownridge, Oakshela, 1889.
55  Mr. Robert Roycroft, Strasbourg, 1905.
56  C. A. Dawson and Eva R. Younge, *Pioneering in the Prairie Provinces* (Toronto: Macmillan, 1940) p. 233.
57  L. N. Tucker, *Western Canada* (London: Musson, 1908) p. 124.
58  Mrs. J. W. B. Archibald, Ashley, 1912; Mr. J. C. Wilson, Lashburn, 1904; Mr. F. J. Bigg, Meskanaw, 1893; Mr. William B. Spicer, Watson, 1905.
59  Mr. William Hodgson, Marshall, 1905.
60  Mr. Charles Davis, North Battleford, 1905.
61  Mrs. S. J. McFarlane, Star City, 1908.
62  Mrs. Andrew Doyle, Muenster, 1906; Mrs. John C. Knaus, McGuire, 1906.
63  Mrs. Hugh Cossar, Wishart, 1892.
64  Mr. William Kennedy, Fort Qu'Appelle, 1889.
65  Miss Harriet M. Stueck, Abernethy, 1886.
66  Mr. D. H. Maginnes, Ermine, 1906.
67  Mr. Louis Demay, St. Brieux, 1906.
68  Mrs. James Bews, Holbeck, 1906.
69  Mr. J. A. MacMurchy, Semans, 1905.
70  Mrs. Peter McLellan, Clare, 1883.
71  Mr. F. O. Langstaff, Wallace, 1892.
72  Mr. Arnold Dauk, Annaheim, 1904.
73  Mr. Louis Demay, St. Brieux, 1906.
74  Mr. J. L. Smith, Vossen, 1905.
75  Mrs. Elena Mackay, Kutawa, 1899.
76  Mrs. C. F. Sentance, Brombury, 1912.
77  Mr. E. O. Johnson, Sheho, 1907.
78  Mr. W. H. S. Gange, Red Deer Hill, 1894.
79  Mr. Godfrey Persson, Ohlen, 1892.
80  Mr. J. G. Mohl, Edenwold, 1908.
81  Mr. Charles Davis, North Battleford, 1905.

82  Mr. Louis Le Strat, St. Front, 1912.
83  Mr. J. L. Smith, Vossen, 1905.
84  Mrs. H. J. Seemann, Mazenod, 1910.
85  Mr. J. G. Mohl, Edenwold, 1908.
86  Mrs. H. C. Calverley, Waldeck, 1905.
87  Miss Charlotte Scoffham, Wapella, 1885.
88  Mrs. E. H. Olmstead, Moffat, 1885.
89  Mrs. J. Wilkie, Cottonwood, 1889.
90  Miss Lottie Meek, Blackwood, 1884.
91  Mrs. W. S. de Balinhard, Yorkton, 1883.
92  Mr. C. Evans Sargent, Gorefield, 1911.
93  Mr. F. J. Bigg, Meskanaw, 1893.
94  Mr. William B. Spicer, Watson, 1905.
95  Mr. Charles B. McMillan, Longlaketon, 1886.
96  Mrs. A. B. Bjerke, Pelly, 1910.
97  Mr. Lewis A. Hummason, Lockwood, 1906.
98  Mr. Elmer O. Johnson, Sheho, 1907.
99  Mrs. Wm. Taylor, Paynton, 1903.
100 Mr. L. V. Kelly, Rocanville, 1909.
101 Miss Lottie Meek, Blackwood, 1884.
102 Mrs. J. R. Aikenhead, Melfort, 1900.
103 Mrs. Arthur Jones, Senlack, 1910.
104 Mr. W. T. McMurdo, Lashburn, 1907.
105 Mrs. George Wilson, Rocanville, 1899.
106 Mr. A. D. Dixon, Maple Creek, 1883.
107 Mrs. E. H. Olmstead, Wolseley, 1885.
108 Mrs. D. A. Moorehouse, Wallard, 1911.
109 *Encyclopedia Canadiana* (Ottawa: Canadiana Company, 1958) vol. 10, p. 181.
110 Mr. J. B. Ewan, Alameda, 1894.
111 Mr. J. A. MacMurchy, Craven, 1905.
112 Mrs. T. C. Johns, Zelma, 1902.
113 Mr. H. G. Galloway, Estevan, 1892.
114 Mr. W. J. Boyle, Hawarden, 1909.
115 Mrs. Marion Anderson, Moosomin, 1883.
116 Mrs. Margaret Groshong, Mount Green, 1906.
117 Mr. Sidney Chipperfield, Chickney, 1883.
118 Mr. E. C. Watson, Wishart, 1903.
119 Mr. William Hodgson, Marshall, 1905.
120 Mrs. James Bews, Holbeck, 1906.
121 Mrs. A. B. Bjerke, Pelly, 1910.
122 Mrs. J. J. Meredith, Battleford, 1907.
123 Mr. C. Evans Sargent, Gorefield, 1911.
124 Mrs. William Taylor, Paynton, 1903.
125 Mr. Harvey Linnen, Francis, 1903.
126 Mrs. Hugh Cossar, Wishart, 1892.
127 Mr. Hugo Bartel, Drake, 1906.
128 Mr. D. H. Maginnes, Ermine, 1906.
129 Mrs. W. R. Groshong, Mount Green, 1906.

130  Mrs. Thos. Brownridge, Oakshela, 1889.
131  Miss Gladys Saloway, Halcyonia, 1903.
132  Mr. Sydney Chipperfield, Chickney, 1883.
133  Mr. Charles McMillan, Longlaketon, 1886.
134  Mrs. Richard Miles, Edenwold, 1886.
135  Mr. Jas. Barrie, Brightholm, 1906.
136  Mrs. Fannie S. Dunlop, Wild Rose, 1902.
137  Mr. Louis Demay, St. Brieux, 1906.
138  Mrs. William Taylor, Paynton, 1903.
139  Mrs. C. F. Sentance, Brombury, 1912.
140  Mr. Louis Le Strat, St. Front, 1912.
141  Mrs. S. J. McFarlane, Gronlid, 1908.

## The Constitution of Saskatchewan

1  Archives of Saskatchewan (A.S.), Scott Papers, Scott to Haultain, Dec. 24, 1904, p. 3760. This letter was written in reply to, and referred to, Haultain's invitation of Dec. 21, 1904.
2  *Regina Leader* Sept. 6, 1905.
3  Owing to the rapid rate of immigration into the new provinces, the acts provided for the taking of censuses every five years, between those ordinarily taken at ten-year intervals.
4  *Canada, House of Commons Debates*, 1905, p. 5680.
5  See Jean E. Murray, "The Provincial Capital Controversy in Saskatchewan," *Saskatchewan History* 5, no. 3, for an account of the dispute.
6  *Canadian Annual Review*, 1905, p. 114, quoting Senator Watson of Portage la Prairie in the *News* of May 2, 1905.
7  *Regina Leader*, Mar. 1, 1905.
8  Public Archives of Canada (P.A.C.), Laurier Papers, Sifton to Laurier, Jan. 22, 1905, pp. 93969-73.
9  *Ibid.*, Laurier to Sifton, Jan. 26, 1905, pp. 93974-6.
10  *Ibid.*, Sifton to Laurier, Feb. 1, 1905, pp. 94354-7.
11  *Canada, House of Commons Debates*, 1905, p. 3097.
12  Bolln vs. Nebraska (176 U.S., 83).
13  P.A.C., Laurier Papers, Sifton to Laurier, Jan. 22, 1905, pp. 93969-73.
14  *Ibid.*, Sifton to Laurier, June 19, 1905, pp. 94357-8.
15  *Ibid.*, McCarthy to Laurier, June 19, 1905, pp. 98721-2.
16  *Ibid.*, McCarthy to Fitzpatrick, May 23, 1905, pp. 97826-30; *Ibid.*, Laurier to McCarthy, June 21, 1905, p. 98723.
17  A.S., Scott Papers, Scott to Fitzpatrick, Mar. 25, 1905, p. 5632.
18  *Ibid.*, Scott to Laurier, May 26, 1905, p. 6049.
19  *Ibid.*, p. 6049.
20  P.A.C., Laurier Papers, Laurier to Creelman, May 27, 1905, p. 97948.
21  *Ibid.*, Shaughnessy to Laurier, May 29, 1905, pp. 97989-90.
22  A.S., Scott Papers, Scott to Laurier, May 26, 1905, p. 6051.
23  *Ibid.*, Scott to Cochran, Feb. 23, 1911, pp. 10429-32; Scott was relating the events in later years to Cochran.
24  *Ibid.*, Scott to Laurier, July 17, 1905, pp. 6064-5.

25  *Op. cit.*, Scott to Cochran.
26  *Ibid.*
27  P.A.C., Laurier Papers, Fitzpatrick to Laurier, June 14, 1905, p. 98563.
28  *Ibid.*, [Fitzpatrick] to Laurier, Mar. 28, 1905, p. 96104.
29  *Ibid.*, Scott to Laurier, Dec. 29, 1905, p. 104785; *ibid.*, Scott to Rutherford, Dec. 29, 1905, p. 104786.
30  *Ibid.*, Rutherford to Laurier, Jan. 10, 1906, pp. 105855-6.
31  *Ibid.*, Laurier to Scott, Jan. 4, 1906, p. 104801; *ibid.*, Jan. 16, 1906, p. 105857.
32  *Journals of the Province of Saskatchewan*, 1906, p. 86.
33  P.A.C., Willison Papers, Haultain to Willison, Aug. 5, 1906.
34  [1927] S.C.R. 365.

## The "Magic City on the Banks of the Saskatchewan":
The Saskatoon Real Estate Boom, 1910-1913

1   W. T. Easterbrook and H. G. J. Aitken, *Canadian Economic History* (Toronto, 1961), p. 477.
2   J. Clinkskill, "Reminiscences of a Pioneer in Saskatchewan," unpublished manuscript, Saskatoon, 1936, p. 27.
3   George Orwell, *Such, Such Were the Joys* (New York, 1953), p. 47.
4   Reported in the *Saskatoon Phoenix*, April 26, 1913.
5   Quoted in E. G. Drake, *Regina, The Queen City* (Toronto, 1955), p. 149.
6   Quoted in V. A. M. Kemp, *The Scarlet and Stetson: the Royal North West Mounted Police on the Prairies* (Toronto, 1964), p. 198.
7   B. Peel and E. Knowles, *The Saskatoon Story,* (Saskatoon, 1952), p. 70.
8   *Saskatoon Daily Star*, May 28, 1912.
9   Elbert Hubbard, *A Little Journey to Saskatoon,* (East Aurora, New York) 1913, p. 12.
10  See Peel and Knowles, *op. cit.*
11  City of Saskatoon, "Saskatoon Housing Report," 1961, p. 4.
12  Peel and Knowles, *op. cit.*, p. 73.
13  *Ibid.*, p. 77.
14  *Saturday Press*, Building and Development Supplement, November 16, 1912, p. 11.
15  A member of the Henry George Lecture Association visited Saskatoon in April, 1913, *Saskatoon Phoenix*, April 17, 1913.
16  Quoted in Wm. Pearce, *The Absurdity and Injustice of the Single Tax, as carried out in the Western Provinces of Canada* (Calgary, 1915), p. 1.
17  City of Saskatoon, "Special Report upon Assessment and Taxation," 1917, p. 9.
18  *Ibid.*, p. 4.
19  H. Mcl. Weir, City of Saskatoon Engineering Department, "Historical Treatise," unpublished manuscript, Saskatoon, 1963, pp. 18 and 30.
20  Henry Howard of the Investors Guardian, London, found that only 6 percent of the increase (from $40,000,000 to $60,000,000) in the net assessment valuation which occurred between 1912 and 1913 could be attributed to new building. The remainder of the advance was due to

increased site values. Henry Howard, Canada, *The Western Cities: their Borrowings and their Assets* (London: Investor's Guardian, 1914), p. 80.

21 City of Saskatoon, Annual Budget, 1921, p. 5.
22 Alan Gowans, *Looking at Architecture in Canada,* (Toronto, 1958), p. 167.
23 *Saturday Press, op. cit.,* p. 8.
24 *Saskatoon Daily Star,* May 16, 1913.
25 *Saskatoon Phoenix,* June 20, 1913.
26 Henry Howard, *op. cit.,* p. 85.
27 H. McI. Weir, *op. cit.,* p. 35.
28 City of Saskatoon, Annual Budget, 1920, p. 4.
29 S. L. Buckwood, "Land Policy in Saskatoon," *Habitat,* Jan.-Feb., 1962, pp. 2-5.
30 Elbert Hubbard, *op. cit.,* p. 14.

## The Elevator Issue, the Organized Farmers, and the Government, 1908-1911

1 Archives of Saskatchewan, Ministerial Papers of Hon. Walter Scott, esp. two files marked "Elevators," hereafter cited as Scott Papers. Scott was Premier of Saskatchewan from Sept. 5, 1905 to Oct. 20, 1916.
2 For a discussion of the problems which led the farmers to seek public ownership, an account of the issue in the three provinces, and a discussion of the elevator legislation which resulted, see V. C. Fowke, *The National Policy and the Wheat Economy* (Toronto: University of Toronto Press, 1957); and H. S. Patton, *Grain Growers' Co-operation in Western Canada* (Cambridge Mass.: Harvard University Press, 1928).
3 The matter had not yet been discussed in the Saskatchewan legislature; an opposition member had called for an inquiry in April, but it was decided that consideration should be suspended until after the Premiers' meeting. Scott made no public statement of his opinion of the Partridge Plan when the Premiers met—nor did he make one throughout the duration of the issue—but his correspondence indicates that his attitude was, at the least, one of skepticism. [A Manitoba farmer had written that the plan was "impracticable" and "paternalism carried to the extreme," and that its support by the farmers was doubtful. "I fancy that if the truth could be actually known," Scott commented, "it would be found that the opinion expressed is shared by a very large number of farmers, and it seems to me that the more carefully anybody studies the whole question, the more they will be driven towards the same opinion"] (See Scott Papers, Scott to Chevrier, May 6, 1908, p. 39767).
4 Patton, *op. cit.,* p. 83. A meeting of Grain Growers' in Saskatchewan in early February called the Premiers' reply "disingenuous" and expressed the hope that the campaign would be continued with "unabated vigour" *(The Canadian Annual Review of Public Affairs,* 1909, p. 535). The governments of Alberta and Manitoba actually petitioned for the necessary amendments to the B.N.A. Act; the Saskatchewan government did not. However, once the constitutional bogey was raised, Premier Scott was able to plead good intentions from its cover: he told the House that if the province could gain

the constitutional right to an elevator monopoly, "I would not hesitate for a moment about adopting the [Grain Growers'] scheme" *Regina Morning Leader,* Dec. 15, 1909, p. 3).

5  By Scott's account, "When we met the delegates here on 26th November they unanimously agreed to the suggestion that it would be unwise and unsafe for the Provinces to go into the elevator business except under monopoly conditions" (Scott Papers, Scott to Bryce, Feb. 20, 1909, p. 40210). The same assertion can be found in the *Speech from the Throne* to the second session of 1909.

6  *Ibid.,* Scott to Bryce, Dec. 8, 1909, p. 39876.

7  *Ibid.,* Scott to Roblin, Dec. 13, 1909, p. 40252.

8  The action of the Roblin government caught Scott by surprise. In the fall of 1909 the Manitoba Liberal Association had informed him of a "slight rumor" that the Manitoba government would adopt the Grain Growers' plan but he had attached little weight to it (see *ibid.,* Perry to Scott, Aug. 21, 1909, p. 40231). Roblin himself had betrayed no hint of his intentions in correspondence with Scott a few days before (*ibid.,* Roblin to Scott, Dec. 9, 1909, p. 40251). Scott's assessment was that the Manitoba Premier had been playing a waiting game. "I hardly know whether it was our action which forced Roblin's hand or whether we simply chanced by our action at that particular time to scrape in ahead of Roblin by a nose. The more I think of it the more inclined I am to the opinion that Roblin has played the game with regard to this question with exceeding astuteness during the past two years for the purpose of saving it until election time in Manitoba. Anyway we probably have no right to complain because his action in procuring the joint consideration put the subject into a position where it was no handicap to us in August of last year" (*ibid.,* Scott to F. H. V. Bulyea, Dec. 20, 1909, p. 39939). "August of last year" presumably refers to the Saskatchewan general election of 1908.

9  Not so the commissioner of agriculture, Hon. W. R. Motherwell, who, according to The *Leader,* declared his opposition to government operation of elevators during debate on the resolution (see edition of Dec. 15, 1909, p. 3).

10  Scott Papers, Scott to Roblin, Dec. 13, 1909, p. 40252.

11  He received a letter in November, 1909, suggesting that a solution to the elevator issue might be found in farmers' companies whose bonds might be guaranteed by the province, companies similar in principle to the co-operative creameries. Scott replied, "For some time past I have been thinking along pretty much the same line" (*ibid.,* Scott to Thomson, Nov. 23, 1909, p. 39881).

12  *See Regina Morning Leader,* Dec. 15, 1909, p. 3. The letter was from W. Hordern, Dundurn and is contained in Scott's correspondence (p. 39886).

13  Scott Papers, Scott to Bulyea, Dec. 29, 1909, p. 39938.

14  *Ibid.,* Scott to Frye, Dec. 29, 1909, p. 39932.

15  Scott initially considered a commission of five, composed of three farmers' representatives, a political economist, and an expert on elevator matters. The idea was abandoned when he was unable to find an elevator expert who was acceptable to both the government and the S.G.G.A. (see *ibid.,* Scott to Langley, Feb. 28, 1910, p. 40451).

16  *Ibid.,* Scott to Langley, Feb. 28, 1910, p. 40453. See also *Regina Morning Leader,* Feb. 8, 1911, p. 7.

17  To Langley must be credited the most ambitious statement of the Grain Growers' aims. He told the convention of 1910 that he "knew what they wanted. Their object was to cut the middle man clean out of the West. . . . " *(The Daily Standard,* Feb. 11, 1910). It left its author little room to hedge on drastic reform.

18  Scott Papers, Scott to Bulyea, Dec. 29, 1909, p. 39938.

19  It may or may not be significant that Scott had been told that Shortt was "not favorable to government owned elevators in any form" *(ibid.,* Aikin to Scott, Aug. 24, 1909, p. 40244). It is unlikely to be, for Shortt was, as noted, President Murray's first choice *(ibid.,* Murray to Scott, Jan. 6, 1910, p. 40395); and in any case, Scott's correspondence suggests that he was less interested in the political views of his political economist than in the latter's ability to command the confidence of the farmers.

20  *Ibid.,* Magill to Scott, Jan. 26, 1911, p. 40562. Magill took the trouble to outline his views to Scott when he discovered that inquiries were being made in Halifax which originated (he supposed, and Scott agreed) with the opposition party in Saskatchewan.

21  *Ibid.,* Magill to Scott, Jan. 16, 1911, p. 40558.

22  See S. M. Lipset, *Agrarian Socialism* (Berkeley and Los Angeles: University of California Press, 1950) pp. 25, 74.

23  *Report of the Elevator Commission of the Province of Saskatchewan,* (Regina: King's Printer, 1910).

24  Scott wrote to Magill when he heard the news: " . . . I want to say to you most heartily and sincerely that I never imagined it would be in the power of any person residing as far from Saskatchewan as is Nova Scotia to perform services for this Province of a kind to place me under such a debt of gratitude as you have done . . . . The simple truth is that you have saved us from the danger of being forced into a course pointing to dissatisfaction and possibly disaster. The unanimous recommendation from a Commission which we were asked by the Grain Growers to appoint and the personnel of which was officially approved by the Grain Growers' Executive places the Government in a comparatively safe position. Receipt of word that the Commission had unanimously agreed upon a Report removed a weight from my mind which was heavier than I have realized until it had gone" *(Scott Papers,* Scott to Magill, Oct. 28, 1910, pp. 40491-2). He later wrote that the Liberal members of the legislature "all join in the belief that the Report is simply a masterpiece . . . . " *(ibid.,* Scott to Magill, Jan. 30, 1911, p. 40564).

25  *Report of the Elevator Commission of the Province of Saskatchewan,* p. 96.

26  Scott Papers, Magill to Scott, undated but probably mid-October, 1910, p. 40490.

27  See *Report of the Elevator Commission of the Province of Saskatchewan,* esp. pp. 73-82.

28  *Ibid.,* Magill to Scott, Mar. 7, 1911, p. 40577. The reference presumably is to John Millar, a farmer of Indian Head who was chairman of the (Dominion) Royal Commission on the Grain Trade of Canada of 1906. The commission

incurred the disappointment of the organized farmers by turning down several proposals which they submitted. One was dominion ownership of terminal elevators.

29  *Loc. cit.*

30  *Ibid.,* Magill to Scott, undated but probably mid-October, 1910, pp. 40488-9; emphasis in original. Magill does not say what it was about the Manitoba system (not yet in operation) which so deterred Green; Green himself hints that it was the prices paid by the Manitoba government for elevators it took over (see *Regina Morning Leader,* Feb. 9, 1911, p. 6). Magill, in a letter, implied that the commission's main objection to the Manitoba system was its liability to the unwise financial practices commonly found, he said, among public utilities (see *Scott Papers,* Magill to Scott, Dec. 8, 1910, p. 40496; and cf. *Report of the Elevator Commission of the Province of Saskatchewan,* p. 39).

31  Scott Papers, Langley to Scott, Nov. 21, 1910, p. 40513.

32  *Regina Morning Leader,* Feb. 9, 1911, p. 6.

33  *Ibid.,* Dec. 15, 1909, p.7.

34  Scott Papers, Scott to Bryce, Dec. 8, 1909, p. 39876.

35  *Ibid.,* Scott to Aikin, Aug. 26, 1909, pp. 40245-6. E. A. Partridge, though not then president of the farmers' grain-dealing agency, was its most influential leader.

36  *Loc. cit.*

37  *Regina Morning Leader,* Mar. 8, 1911, p. 10. He was able to place E. N. Hopkins, then president of the S.G.G.A.; F. W. Green; A. G. Hawkes; and F. M. Gates among those present.

38  *Ibid.,* Mar. 8, 1911, p. 9.

39  *Loc. cit.*

40  Scott Papers, Scott to Bryce, Dec. 8, 1909, p. 39876. "With one year's intimate experience in the matter of aiding railways," he continued, "I begin to realize the position a Government would occupy in this Province were we directly constructing and managing railways and it is to be feared that in some respects an elevator system in the hands of a Government would be attended by similar dangers." The same fastidiousness was shown in the case of telephones, where it was once represented (by Langley) as an advantage of the existing program of farmer-owned systems over public ownership that "the government was relieved of the charge of discrimination . . . . " *(Regina Morning Leader,* Feb. 14, 1911, p. 5). That political advantage can accrue to a party which controls patronage is well known; not so well known, but of some importance, is that patronage also has its perils.

41  V. C. Fowke, *The National Policy and the Wheat Economy,* p. 143.

42  *Regina Morning Leader,* Aug. 3, 1910, p. 9.

43  It is worth noting, however, that Scott was prepared to see Dominion operation of terminal elevators. "No such dangers are involved in this proposal as would be the case as regards line elevators. In the terminals control has not so far succeeded in eliminating the defects of private operation. In fact if we had absolute security against manipulation in the terminals a good deal of the complaint against the line elevators would be removed" (Scott Papers, Scott to Bryce, Dec. 8, 1909, p. 39877). A week after

this letter was written the legislature passed a resolution calling for federal ownership and operation of the terminals. The resolution was proposed by Langley and accepted on behalf of the government by Mr. Motherwell, the commissioner of agriculture (see *Regina Morning Leader,* Dec. 15, 1909, p. 2). Motherwell's private views on the matter appear to have been quite different. "I might say . . . that in the estimation of practically everyone who is familiar with the trade the government control that was secured over these terminal elevators by the amendments to the Grain Act of last session of the Federal Parliament has given to the producers practically every safeguard and security in the way of control that government ownership would give" (Archives of Saskatchewan, Ministerial Papers of Hon. W. R. Motherwell, "Grain Elevators;" Motherwell to William Martin, M.P., Jan. 27, 1909).

44  *Regina Morning Leader,* Mar. 8, 1911, p. 10.

45  *Ibid.,* Feb. 9, 1911, p. 5. The *Leader* concurred in an editorial: "It was not . . . because of any particularly firm adherence to the principle of government ownership of all utilities that led the Grain Growers to declare for the application of that principle to grain elevators, but rather a profound belief that only in government ownership could be found that relief, and redress of their wrongs, which they demanded" *(ibid.,* Feb. 20, 1911, p. 4).

46  The suspense contributed to an embarrassing tactical error on the part of the opposition party. The Provincial Rights (later Conservative) party had declared itself in support of public ownership before the appointment of the commission; thenceforth it remained uncommitted until the day the Grain Growers' convention debated the commission's report. The opposition leader, F. W. G. Haultain, rose to address the legislature as the farmers neared a decision and, evidently believing that they would reject the report, he spoke against it and renewed his party's advocacy of public ownership. Soon afterwards the Grain Growers voted to accept the report.

Scott took delight in the opposition's mistake. "Now when I tell you," he wrote Magill, "that Haultain has jockeyed himself into a position of direct hostility to our scheme,—into a position necessitating the presenting of the square issue to the people whenever our next elections are held,—a position in which he will stand for abolishing our scheme if he is elected and for thereafter immediately providing Government elevators,—I am sure you will comprehend what I mean when I state that your work has put the boot on the other foot. We are now in clover or on velvet and it is Haultain who is enjoying the sensation of political shivers" (Scott Papers, Scott to Magill, Feb. 23, 1911, p. 40566). He later had some amusement in the legislature at Haultain's expense. "And what is his prescription? His only patent nostrum—his whole stock-in-trade,—the only remedy he has in his political medical chest,—the bottle he wants to rub on for every known ill to which the body politic is heir,—the great and only Haultain's Harmless Healer for Helpless People, Public Ownership and Operation" *Regina Morning Leader,* Mar. 8, 1911, p. 9).

47  And at the one following. It was debated at the convention of 1911 and resulted in a deadlock: 92 delegates voted to continue the mutual system and 92 to institute public development of rural service *(Regina Daily Standard,* Feb. 10, 1911, p. 3). The government amended the terms of the mutual

program in the session of 1912-13 and public ownership of telephones ceased to be an issue. For a discussion of the government's handling of the telephone issue, see D. S. Spafford "Telephone Service in Saskatchewan," unpublished Master's thesis, University of Saskatchewan, 1961.

48  *Regina Daily Standard,* Feb. 13, 1911, p. 1.
49  See W. A. Mackintosh, *Agricultural Co-operation in Western Canada,* Kingston, Queen's University, 1924, p. 34, for a brief summary of Partridge's views. Mackintosh states that co-operation was, for Partridge, "not an alternative but a stepping stone to government ownership."

## The French-Canadians and the Language Question, 1918

1   Archives of Saskatchewan (A.S.), *Scott Papers,* The Town of Vonda Appeal from Court of Revision, Sept. 15, 1911, pp. 35193-194.
2   *Revised Statutes of Saskatchewan,* 1909, chap. 100, sec. 45, sub-sec. 2.
3   A.S., Scott Papers, Scott to MacKinnon, Jan. 2, 1913, pp. 35274-275.
4   *Statutes of Saskatchewan,* 1912-13, chap. 35, sec. 3.
5   A.S., Scott Papers, MacKinnon to Scott, Dec. 30, 1912, pp. 35271-273.
6   *Ibid.,* Scott to MacKinnon, Jan. 2, 1913, pp. 35274-275.
7   *Ibid.,* MacKinnon to Scott, Jan. 19, 1913, pp. 35299-309.
8   *Regina Daily Province,* May 25, 1914.
9   This provision did not apply to the primary course in French permitted under chap. 23, sec. 177, sub-sec. 1, *Statutes of Saskatchewan,* 1915.
10  *Regina Evening Province and Standard* [hereafter cited as *Evening Province*], May 26, 1915.
11  *Ibid.,* May 26, 1915.
12  *Ibid.,* June 3, 1915.
13  *Ibid.,* Dec. 27, 1915.
14  *Ibid.,* Jan. 20, 1916.
15  "Report of Proceedings, Meeting of Delegation of Grand Orange Lodge of Saskatchewan and Government on Jan. 20, 1916," reproduced in G. M. Weir, *Evolution of the Separate School Law in the Prairie Provinces* (n.p.,n.d.), Appendix II, pp. 126-42.
16  *Grain Growers' Guide,* Feb. 23, 1916.
17  *Regina Morning Leader,* March 3, 1916.
18  *Ibid.,* March 11, 1916.
19  *Ibid.,* June 12, 1917; *Regina Daily Post,* June 16, 1917.
20  A.S., Turgeon Papers, General Files, 1909-21, Kitchener L.O.L. No. 2671, Prince Albert.
21  *Regina Daily Post,* Feb. 13, 1918.
22  *Ibid.*
23  *Grain Growers' Guide,* Feb. 20, 1918.
24  *Regina Daily Post,* Feb. 16, 1920.
25  *Saskatoon Phoenix,* Feb. 2, 1918.
26  *Regina Morning Leader,* Feb. 20, 1918.
27  *Le Patriote de l'Ouest* [hereafter cited as *Patriote*], 30 jan. 1918. At the 1917 S.S.T.A. convention, non-English trustees narrowly tabled a resolution

requesting the Department of Education to institute a uniform system of English-language readers to replace the existing *Alexandra Readers, Canadian Catholic Readers, Bi-Lingual Series of Readers,* and *Eclectic Series of German Readers.*

28 *Saskatoon Phoenix, Daily Post, Daily Star,* Feb. 15, 1918.
29 W. Calderwood, "The Rise and Fall of the Ku Klux Klan in Saskatchewan," (unpublished M.A. thesis, University of Saskatchewan, Regina, 1968), p. 181.
30 *Regina Daily Post,* Feb. 25, 1918.
31 *Ibid.,* Feb. 21, 1918.
32 *Ibid.,* Feb. 22, 1918.
33 *Ibid.*
34 *Patriote,* 27 fév. 1918.
35 *Regina Morning Leader,* Feb. 22, 1918.
36 A.S., Martin Papers, J. F. Bryant to Martin, March 26, 1918, pp. 17670-671.
37 A.S., Papers of *l'Association Catholique Franco-Canadienne de la Saskatchewan* [hereafter cited as A.C.F.C. Papers], File 44A, J. McCarthy to J. M. Reynaud, Feb. 27, 1918.
38 *Regina Daily Post,* March 27, 1918.
39 *Saskatoon Phoenix,* Feb. 22, 1918.
40 *Patriote,* 27 fév. 1918.
41 *Ibid.,* 11 déc. 1918.
42 A.C.F.C. Papers, File 34A, *Appel aux Commissaires d'Ecole,* n.d.
43 A.S., Turgeon Papers, General Files, R. Denis to Turgeon, 6 mai 1918.
44 *Ibid.,* Turgeon to Denis, 13 mai 1918.
45 *Regina Daily Post,* March 8, 1918.
46 *Ibid.,* March 7, 1918.
47 *Regina Morning Leader,* June 17, 1918; A.S., Turgeon Papers, General Files, Secretary of Synod to Turgeon, Aug. 20, 1918.
48 *Saskatoon Daily Star,* Sept. 14, 1918.
49 A.S., Martin Papers, 53 Ed., *passim.*
50 A.S., Department of Education, 3, D. P. McColl: Memorandum for Mr. Martin *re* Foreign languages in schools, Jan. 2, 1918.
51 *Ibid.,* R. F. Blacklock: Memorandum for Mr. McColl *re* Foreign languages in schools, Jan. 3, 1918.
52 *Ibid.,* 12(a), Schools Teaching Foreign Languages in 1918.
53 A.S., Martin Papers, Memorandum: Suggested Amendments to Section 177 of the School Act, Aug. 12, 1918, p. 17681.
54 A.C.F.C. Papers, File 63A, A. F. Auclair to Denis, 27 sept. 1918.
55 *Patriote,* 11 déc. 1918.
56 A.S., Scott Papers, W. R. Motherwell to Scott, Dec. 13, 1918, p. 78108.
57 *Ibid.,* Scott to Sir W. Laurier, Dec. 27, 1918, p. 78164.
58 *Ibid.,* Motherwell to Martin, Dec. 10, 1918, p. 78123.
59 *Ibid.,* Turgeon to Scott, Dec. 18, 1918, p. 78147.
60 *Ibid.,* Motherwell to Scott, Dec. 13, 1918, p. 78109-110.
61 *Ibid.,* Motherwell to Laurier, Dec. 14, 1918, (Confidential), pp. 78131-132.
62 *Ibid.,* Turgeon to Scott, Dec. 12, 1918, p. 78103.

63    A.S., Turgeon Papers, G.F., O.-E. Mathieu to Turgeon, 17 déc. 1918.
64    A.S., Scott Papers, Turgeon to Scott, Dec. 18, 1918, pp. 78145-148.
65    A.C.F.C. Papers, File 63A, Auclair to Denis, 27 sept. 1918.
66    *Patriote,* 7 juillet 1920.
67    *Ibid.,* 25 déc. 1918.
68    *Regina Daily Post,* Dec. 18, 1918; *Statutes of Saskatchewan* 1918-19, chap. 48.
69    *Regina Daily Post, Saskatoon Daily Star,* Dec. 18, 1918.
70    *Regina Daily Post,* Dec. 18, 1918.
71    *Regina Daily Star,* Dec. 19, 1918.
72    *Patriote,* 25 déc. 1918.
73    A.C.F.C. Papers, File 63A, Auclair to Denis, 27 sept. 1918.
74    *Patriote,* 25 déc. 1918.
75    *Regina Post,* Dec. 19, 1918.
76    *The Language Question before the Legislative Assembly of Saskatchewan, Addresses by Hon. W. M. Martin, Hon. W. R. Motherwell, Hon. S. J. Latta, Hon. C. A. Dunning,* (Prince Albert: Le Patriote de l'Ouest, 1919.)
77    A.S., Martin Papers, Official Hansard, pp. 18549-558.
78    *Ibid.,* pp. 18655-659.
79    *Ibid.,* pp. 18684-692.
80    *Patriote,* 25 déc. 1918.
81    Although the term "primary course" had never been given a precise definition prior to 1918, the Department of Education considered grades one and two as a "reasonable interpretation." A.S., Turgeon Papers, General Files, A. Ball to J. Gagnon, Feb. 8, 1915. The primary course in the French language was abolished by Premier J. T. M. Anderson's Saskatchewan Co-operative government on March 9, 1931.
82    A.S., Motherwell Papers, Education, Laurier to Motherwell, Dec. 21, 1918.

## C. A. Dunning and the Challenge of the Progressives, 1922-1925

1    W. L. Morton, *The Progressive Party in Canada* (Toronto: University of Toronto Press, 1950), p. 110.
2    F. W. Anderson, "Some Political Aspects of the Grain Growers' Movement (1915-1935) With Particular Reference to Saskatchewan," (unpublished Master's thesis, University of Saskatchewan, 1949), pp. 62-63, 66-67.
3    *Regina Morning Leader,* October 1, 1921; December 2, 1921.
4    *Ibid.,* December 6, 1921.
5    *The Canadian Annual Review of Public Affairs* (C.A.R.), 1922, pp. 798-799.
6    Public Archives of Canada (P.A.C.), Dafoe Papers, John W. Dafoe to Sir Clifford Sifton, December 31, 1921.
7    *Regina Morning Leader,* April 5, 1922.
8    *Grain Growers' Guide,* April 26, 1922.
9    *Saskatoon Daily Star,* April 10, 1922; April 15, 1922.
10    Archives of Saskatchewan (A.S.), Dunning Papers, C. A. Dunning to G. F. Chipman, April 12, 1922.
11    *Ibid.,* J. B. Musselman to C. A. Dunning, June 9, 1922.

12 *Ibid.*, C. A. Dunning to Hon. T. H. Johnson, April 8, 1922.
13 Douglas Library, Queen's University, Kingston (hereafter cited as Douglas Library), Dunning Papers, C. A. Dunning to Hon. Walter Scott, July 17, 1922.
14 *Ibid.*
15 *Regina Morning Leader,* June 15, 1922.
16 *Directory of Saskatchewan Ministries, Members of the Legislative Assemblies and Elections, 1905-1953* (hereafter cited as *Directory of Sask. Ministries).* Saskatchewan Archives Board, 1954, p. 85.
17 Douglas Library, Dunning Papers, C. A. Dunning to Hon. Walter Scott, July 17, 1922.
18 *C.A.R.,* 1923, p. 713.
19 Douglas Library, Dunning Papers, W. R. Motherwell to C. A. Dunning, March 19, 1923.
20 *Ibid.*, C. A. Dunning to W. R. Motherwell, March 24, 1923.
21 *Directory of Members of Parliament and Federal Elections for the Northwest Territories and Saskatchewan, 1887-1966,* Saskatchewan Archives Board, 1967, p. 38.
22 *Grain Growers' Guide,* April 18, 1923.
23 *Ibid.*, May 9, 1923. The newspaper based its claim on the report by two Progressive M.P.'s, R. A. Hoey and A. J. Lewis, who had been present when, it was alleged, Gardiner had made his controversial announcement.
24 *Regina Morning Leader,* October 13, 1923.
25 *Ibid.*, October 6, 1923.
26 *Ibid.*, October 19, 1923.
27 *Directory of Sask. Ministries,* p. 95.
28 Indeed John W. Dafoe observed, "The Dunning Government has quite recovered its position in the province and could, I think, quite safely appeal to the people; (P.A.C., Dafoe Papers, John W. Dafoe to Sir Clifford Sifton, February 13, 1924.)
29 *Grain Growers' Guide,* January 30, 1924.
30 Douglas Library, Dunning Papers, C. A. Dunning to Philip Duff, January 19, 1924.
31 *C.A.R.,* 1924-25, p. 409.
32 *Regina Morning Leader,* March 8, 1924.
33 *Ibid.*, September 29, 1924.
34 *Directory of Sask. Ministries,* p. 123.
35 *Ibid.*, p. 78.
36 *C.A.R.,* 1921, pp. 793, 809.
37 *Regina Morning Leader,* March 26, 1924.
38 P.A.C., Dafoe Papers, Clifford Sifton to J. W. Dafoe, January 28, 1925.
39 *Budget Speech delivered by Hon. C. A. Dunning, Provincial Treasurer of Saskatchewan, in the Legislative Assembly, January 9, 1925* (Regina: King's Printer, 1925), pp. 14-17.
40 *Regina Morning Leader,* February 18, 1925; March 5, 1925; March 21, 1925.
41 *Ibid.*, May 11, 1925. In the two northernmost ridings, Ile à la Crosse and Cumberland, the election was deferred until July 21, 1925. *(Directory of Sask. Ministries,* p. 40.)

42 *Ibid.,* May 11, 1925.

43 *Ibid.,* May 14, 1925.

44 *Directory of Sask. Ministries,* pp. 74-124.

45 The lack of a strong opposition press also made it extremely difficult to follow the Conservative and Progressive campaigns, since few if any of their meetings were covered by the Liberal newspapers.

46 *Regina Morning Leader,* May 30, 1925.

47 *Ibid.,* May 13, 1925; May 14, 1925; June 2, 1925.

48 *Ibid.,* May 14, 1925.

49 *Ibid.,* May 21, 1925; June 2, 1925.

50 *Directory of Sask. Ministries,* pp. 40-41. The two deferred elections in Ile à la Crosse and Cumberland also went Liberal, making the Liberal strength 52 in a legislature of 63 seats. *(C.A.R.,* 1925-26, p. 468.) In the 1921 general election, by way of comparison, the Liberals had won 46 seats, the Independents 7, and the Conservatives 3. *(Directory of Sask. Ministries,* pp. 38-39.)

51 For a more detailed study of Liberal party organization during these years see Escott M. Reid, "The Saskatchewan Liberal Machine Before 1929," *Canadian Journal of Economics and Political Science* 2, no. 1, pp. 27-40.

## The Saskatchewan Farmer-Labor Party, 1932-1934:
How Radical Was It At Its Origin?

1 Several authors interpret the early years of the Farmer-Labor party and the C.C.F. in this manner. See, for example, S.M. Lipset, *Agrarian Socialism,* Anchor Books (Garden City, New York: Doubleday and Company, Inc. 1968), chap. 6; and John W. Bennett and Cynthia Krueger, "Agrarian Pragmatism and Radical Politics," in Lipset, *Agrarian Socialism,* pp. 357-360, for an application of this interpretation at the provincial level. For a similar view in regard to the national C.C.F. see Walter Young, *The Anatomy of a Party: The National C.C.F. 1932-1961* (Toronto: University of Toronto Press, 1969) chap. 6; and Leo Zakuta, *A Protest Movement Becalmed* (Toronto: University of Toronto Press, 1964), pp. 35-38.

2 The party was founded at a joint convention of the United Farmers of Canada (Saskatchewan Section) and the Independent Labor party. The U.F.C. voted to enter politics in February, 1931 at its annual convention and political organization began in some constituencies as early as July. From the beginning it was assumed that political action would involve some type of co-operation with labor. In October a province-wide Independent Labor party was formed at a convention in Regina. M. J. Coldwell was selected leader, and co-operation with the United Farmers' political movement was approved. Thus the stage was set for the formal launching of the Farmer-Labor party the following summer.

3 *Regina Leader Post,* May 23, 1930, p. 23.

4 Archives of Saskatchewan (A.S.), U.F.C. Papers, Minutes and Reports of the 1931 U.F.C. Convention, p. 211.

5 *Ibid.,* p. 200.

6 *Regina Leader-Post,* October 26, 1931, p. 2.

7   A.S., C.C.F. Papers, Minutes of Political Directive Board Meeting, September 24, 1932, p. 9.

8   *Ibid.*

9   *Ibid.*, p. 10.

10  Young, *National C.C.F.*, p. 40.

11  See, for example Lipset, *Agrarian Socialism*, pp. 108-110.

12  A.S., U.F.C. Papers, Minutes and Reports of the 1931 Convention, p. 160.

13  Lloyd was an active left-winger within the U.F.C. In the late 1920's he was among those who bitterly criticized the leadership of the farmers' movement for not being radical enough. See A.S., Edwards Papers, George Edwards to W. J. Brummett, August 22, 1927.

14  A.S., U.F.C. Papers, Minutes and Reports of the 1931 U.F.C. Convention, p. 161.

15  Like Lloyd, Mills was active in the Farmers' Unity League in the early 1930's. See Mills, *Stout Hearts Stand Tall* (Vancouver: Evergreen Press, 1971), p. 196.

16  A.S., U.F.C. Papers, Minutes and Reports of the 1931 U.F.C. Convention, p. 161.

17  *Ibid.*

18  *Ibid.*, p. 170. What is also significant is that Johnson cannot simply be dismissed as a right wing spokesman within the U.F.C. He was a strong supporter of George Williams, U.F.C. president from 1929-31 and one who always was considered to be on the left of the farmers' movement.

19  A.S., U.F.C. Papers, Minutes and Reports of the 1931 U.F.C. Convention, p. 198.

20  *Ibid.*, p. 200.

21  *Ibid.*, p. 209.

22  See Leo Courville, "The Saskatchewan Progressives" (unpublished M.A. thesis, University of Saskatchewan, Regina), pp. 208-210, and Hoffman "The Saskatchewan Provincial Election of 1934," chap. 4.

23  A.S., U.F.C. Papers, Minutes and Reports of the 1931 U.F.C. Convention, p. 208.

24  *Ibid.*, p. 201.

25  *Ibid.*, p. 209. McNamee was a well-known farm radical. In 1933 he ran as a United Front candidate in a federal by-election in Mackenzie constituency, against a candidate nominated by the C.C.F.

26  A.S., U.F.C. Papers, Minutes and Reports of the 1931 U.F.C. Convention, pp. 209-210.

27  Young, *National C.C.F.*, p. 40.

28  A.S., C.C.F. Papers, Minutes of Political Directive Board Meeting, September 24, 1932, p. 9.

29  *Western Producer*, the leading farm paper in the province advocated an inflated currency throughout the early 1930's. See, for example, *Western Producer*, June 21, 1934, p. 6. Mackenzie King, the national Liberal leader was shocked to find the popularity of inflation among western Liberals. See H. B. Neatby, *William Lyon Mackenzie King 1924-1932 The Lonely Heights* (Toronto: University of Toronto Press, 1963), p. 396.

30  Letter to *Western Producer* March 8, 1934, p. 17.

31  A.S., Violet McNaughton Papers, File No. E70, Socialistic Groups, 1931-1942, McNaughton to George Williams, November 9, 1932.
32  A.S., C.C.F. Papers, F. Gable to George Williams, March 2, 1933, p. 29276.
33  *Ibid.*, E. M. Graham to Frank Eliason, January 28, 1933, p. 24588.
34  *Ibid.*, Eliason to E. M. Graham, February 14, 1934, p. 24592.
35  *Ibid.*, Eliason to W. Olsen, February 19, 1934, p. 25063.
36  *Regina Leader-Post*, January 17, 1933, p. 8.
37  A.S., C.C.F. Paper, Subject Files, 1931-1952, *What is this Socialism*, 1932, p. 29006.
38  *Ibid.*, p. 29008.
39  W. G. Godfrey, "The 1933 Convention of the Co-operative Commonwealth Federation" (unpublished M.A. thesis, University of Waterloo, 1965), pp. 43-45. Angus MacInnis, then a labor delegate from British Columbia, objected to the Saskatchewan delegates' interpretation of socialism. He argued: "If the farmer wants a co-operative commonwealth in which everything is socialized but himself, then he better have a commonwealth of his own." *Ibid.*, p. 42.
40  *Leader-Post*, August 5, 1933, p. 8.
41  *Ibid.*, July 7, 1933, p. 12.
42  *Ibid.*, January 10, 1934, p. 8. The selection of Coldwell as Farmer-Labor leader was itself an indicator of the moderate nature of the party. A veteran of the Progressive movement, he was looked upon as less radical than the other serious contender for the leadership, George Williams. Shortly after Coldwell was picked as leader, he was depicted by the *Leader-Post* as: "a thoughtful student of affairs, solid, steady, a keen debater, modest and capable . . . ." *Ibid.*, September 12, 1932, p. 3.
43  A.S., C.C.F. Paper, Williams to Frank Eliason, March 13, 1933, pp. 12069-12070.
44  *Ibid.*, Eliason to George Williams, March 16, 1933, p. 12071.
45  *Ibid.*
46  *Saskatoon Star-Phoenix*, December 11, 1930, p. 3.
47  *Ibid.*, December 10, 1930, p. 3.
48  *Furrow, (Saskatoon)*, February, 1931, p. 1.
49  *Saskatoon Star-Phoenix*, December 12, 1930, p. 1.
50  *Saskatoon Furrow*, February, 1931, p. 1.
51  *Western Producer*, December 18, 1930, p. 2.
52  A.S., C.C.F. Papers, D. Disberry to Frank Eliason, January 7, 1932, pp. 12958-12960.
53  *Ibid.*, Also see Ivan Avakumovic, "The Communist Party of Canada and the Prairie Farmer: The Inter-War Years" Western Perspectives 1, (Toronto: Holt, Rinehart and Winston, 1974).
54  A.S., C.C.F. Papers, D. Disberry to Frank Eliason, January 7, 1932, p. 12959.
55  *Ibid.*, p. 12960.
56  *Furrow, (Saskatoon)*, November, 1930, p. 2.
57  *Ibid.*, March 1932, p. 1.
58  *Ibid.*, January 15, 1933, p. 2.

59  *Ibid.*, August, 1932, p. 4.

60  *Ibid.*, April, 1934, p. 3.

61  *Western Producer,* August 20, 1931, p. 7.

62  *Furrow, (Saskatoon),* August, 1932, p. 2.

63  *Ibid.*, December 15, 1932, p. 2.

64  *Ibid.*, January 15, 1932, p. 2.

65  Eliason's attitude toward the League was comparable to that taken by Woodsworth, Coldwell, and David Lewis toward the Communists at the national level throughout the 1930's. See Young, *National C.C.F.,* pp. 255-284. Eliason was one of the *Furrow's* favorite targets. See *Furrow,* January 15, 1933, p. 2 for an editorial entitled "Mr. Eliason Shows His Hand."

66  *Western Producer,* December 15, 1932, p. 5.

67  A.S., U.F.C. Papers, Miscellaneous Correspondence File, Eliason to J. F. Hogg, April 4, 1935.

68  A.S., C.C.F. Papers, Eliason to George Williams, October 28, 1932, p. 12001.

69  *Ibid.*

70  *Ibid.*, Eliason to Members of the Farmer-Labor Constituency Committee in the Elrose Provincial Constituency, October 26, 1932, pp. 12958-12961.

71  *Ibid.*, Eliason to M. J. Coldwell, October 26, 1932, p. 3110.

72  *Ibid.*, Eliason to H. Greenwood, January 11, 1933, p. 24612.

73  Young, *National C.C.F.,* p. 255.

74  Later during the 1930's the C.C.F. ran into similar problems in a few other parts of the province. See Peter Sinclair, "The Saskatchewan C.C.F. and the Communist Party in the 1930's," *Saskatchewan History* 26, no. 1 (Winter, 1973), pp. 1-10.

75  A.S., C.C.F. Papers, Williams to Frank Eliason, September n.d., 1932, p. 12002.

76  Bennett and Krueger, "Agrarian Pragmatism and Radical Politics," p. 357.

77  Mr. Douglas made this remark in an unpublished address delivered March 24, 1973 at the Social Gospel Conference held at the University of Saskatchewan, Regina Campus.

## Relief Administration in Saskatoon During the Depression

1  *Report of the Rowell-Sirois Commission on Dominion-Provincial Relations* (hereafter R.S. Commission) vol. 1, p. 150, table 50.

2  *Ibid.*, p. 164, table 58.

3  *Submission by the Government of Saskatchewan to the Rowell-Sirois Commission,* vol. 1, pp. 47-48.

4  *Ibid.*, p. 55.

5  Archives of Saskatchewan, (A.S.) Department of Municipal Affairs, Bureau of Labour and Public Welfare, (L.P.W.), roll 38, file 41.

6  R.S. Commission, vol. 1, p. 172.

7  James H. Gray, *The Winter Years* (Toronto, 1966), p. 14.

8  Archives of Saskatchewan, F. Eliason Papers, Biography of a Swedish Emmigrant *[sic]*, p. 51.

9 L.P.W., roll 30, file 3, circular 58, T. M. Molloy to the Towns and Villages, September 28, 1934.
10 Saskatoon Council Minutes, July 18, 1932.
11 *Ibid.,* Bylaw No. 2277, October 3, 1932.
12 Civic Relief Board Minutes, October 12, 1932.
13 *Ibid.,* November 14, 1932.
14 *Ibid.,* February 27, 1933.
15 *Saskatoon Star-Phoenix,* March 16, 1933.
16 Saskatoon Council Minutes, October 17, 1933.
17 Saskatoon Council Minutes, Bylaw No. 2396, June 5, 1934.
18 L.P.W., roll 38, file 41, Molloy to F. Eliason, May 27, 1935.
19 Relief Appeal Board Minutes, June 21, 1937, reply to request of the Central Association of Unemployed and Welfare Associations of June 14, 1937.
20 L.P.W., roll 38, file 41.
21 Saskatoon Council Minutes, June 18, 1932. It was the official policy of the city not to give relief to persons who had been married for less than one year.
22 A.S., Saskatchewan Relief Commission, roll A, file 4, T. Bunting, Investigation for the Saskatchewan Relief Commission, report on relief conditions in Saskatoon, March 13, 1933.
23 Saskatoon Council Minutes, December 8, 1930.
24 Civic Relief Board Minutes, June 1, 1933.
25 *Saskatoon Star-Phoenix,* June 2, 1933.
26 L.P.W., roll 37, file 41, J. W. Estey to P. M. Parker, January 7, 1936.
27 *Ibid.,* Mr. D. to Premier W. Patterson, March 23, 1935.
28 *Ibid.,* Molloy to Leslie, April 1, 1936.
29 L.P.W., roll 38, file 41, P. J. Boeckler to Dawson, October 21, 1937.
30 *Ibid.,* Parker to Molloy, December 10, 1936.
31 *Ibid.,* Parker to Molloy, April 8, 1936.
32 *Ibid.,* Parker to Dawson, August 12, 1938.
33 Saskatoon Council Minutes, June 16, 1930.
34 *Ibid.,* June 23, 1930.
35 *Ibid.,* November 9, 1931.
36 *Ibid.,* December 19, 1932.
37 *Ibid.,* July 3, 1939.
38 *Ibid.,* August 14, 1939.
39 *Ibid.,* November 16, 1933.
40 L.P.W., roll 38, file 41.
41 *Ibid.,* Saskatoon's reply to L.P.W. circular letter 151, February 17, 1936.
42 L.P.W., roll 37, file 41, Molloy to Mr. E., January 29, 1936.
43 Saskatoon Council Minutes, June 8, 1931.
44 *Ibid.,* April 11, 1932.
45 *Ibid.,* November 9, 1931.
46 *Ibid.,* November 10, 1931.
47 *Ibid.,* May 19, 1932.
48 *Ibid.,* May 19, 1932.
49 *Ibid.,* June 6, 1932.
50 *Ibid.,* August 15, 1932.

51 *Saskatoon Star-Phoenix,* March 7, 1933, comment of M. Jorgenson.

52 *Ibid.,* January 30, 1934.

53 Civic Relief Board Minutes, December 21, 1932.

54 A.S., Saskatchewan Relief Commission, roll A, file 3, Wylie to Anderson, March 11, 1933.

55 *Ibid.,* roll A, file 3.

56 *Ibid.,* Bunting to the Saskatchewan Relief Commission, March 14, 1933.

57 Civic Relief Board Minutes, September 21, 1933.

58 *Saskatoon Star-Phoenix,* September 24, 1934.

59 Saskatoon Council Minutes, February 4, 1935.

60 L.P.W., roll 38, file 41.

61 *Saskatoon Star Phoenix,* March 30, 1936.

62 Saskatoon Council Minutes, July 6, 1931.

63 *Ibid.,* October 13, 1931.

64 *Saskatoon Star-Phoenix,* November 15, 1932.

65 Saskatoon Council Minutes, June 20, 1938.

66 L.P.W. roll 38, file 40, City Clerk M. C. Tomlinson to Minister of Municipal Affairs Parker, March 1, 1939.

67 Saskatoon Council Minutes, April 24, 1939.

68 *Ibid.,* December 8, 1930, 570 men had registered with the relief department.

69 *Ibid.,* December 8, 1932.

70 *Ibid.,* November 7, 1932.

71 A.S., Saskatchewan Relief Commission, roll A, file 2, Saskatoon Relief Camp.

72 *Ibid.*

73 L.P.W., roll 38, file 41, Pinder to Molloy, January 19, 1937.

74 Saskatoon Council Minutes, November 15, 1937.

75 Relief Appeal Board Minutes, June 7, 1935.

76 *Saskatoon Star-Phoenix,* July 9, 1936.

77 L.P.W., roll 38, file 41.

78 *Ibid.,* Parker to Molloy, October 29, 1936.

79 *Ibid.*

80 Saskatoon Council Minutes, December 6, 1937.

81 L.P.W., roll 38, file 41.

82 *Ibid.*

83 Saskatoon Council Minutes, May 8, 1933.

84 *Ibid.,* February 27, 1939.

85 *Ibid.,* December 9, 1932.

86 L.P.W., roll 37, file 41.

87 Saskatoon Council Minutes, 1931.

88 L.P.W., roll 30, file 3.

89 *Annual Report of the Department of Social Welfare,* 1948-1949, p. 47.

90 *Social Welfare in Saskatchewan,* Department of Social Welfare, 1960, p. 19.

# Index